THE
IMPLIED READER

Patterns of Communication in Prose Fiction
from Bunyan to Beckett

By WOLFGANG ISER

THE JOHNS HOPKINS UNIVERSITY PRESS
BALTIMORE AND LONDON

The Johns Hopkins University Press
701 West 40th Street
Baltimore, Maryland 21211
The Johns Hopkins Press Ltd., London

Originally published 1974
Second printing, 1975
Johns Hopkins Paperbacks edition, 1978
Fourth printing, 1987

This book was originally published as
*DER IMPLIZITE LESER: Kommunikationsformen des
Romans von Bunyan bis Beckett*
(Munich: Wilhelm Fink, 1972).

Library of Congress Cataloging-in-Publication Data

Iser, Wolfgang.
    The implied reader.

    Translation of Der implizite Leser.
    Includes bibliographical references.
    1. Fiction—History and criticism. I. Title
PN3491.I813   809.3'3   73-20075
ISBN 0-8018-2150-9 (paperback)

FOR LORE

CONTENTS

vii

CONTENTS

ACKNOWLEDGMENTS

T his English version of my collection of essays, *Der implizite Leser* (Munich, 1972), could never have been written without the indefatigable assistance of David Henry Wilson, who enabled me to give an English shape to a German book. My thanks are also due to Professor J. Hillis Miller, Yale University, for his part in initiating this project, and to J. G. Goellner, Associate Director of The Johns Hopkins University Press, for making the process of publication so pleasant and painless.

The following essays have already been published in English and are reprinted here—the first with substantial additions—by permission of the editors concerned: "The Generic Control of the Aesthetic Response: An Examination of Smollett's *Humphry Clinker*," *Southern Humanities Review* 3 (1969): 243-57. "The Reading Process: A Phenomenological Approach," *New Literary History* 3 (1972): 279-99. "The Role of the Reader in Fielding's *Joseph Andrews* and *Tom Jones*," in *English Studies Today, Fifth Series*. Papers read at the Eighth Conference of the International Association of University Professors of English, held at Istanbul 1971, ed. Sencer Tonguc. Istanbul (1973): 289-325.

INTRODUCTION

The history of the novel as a 'genre' began in the eighteenth century, at a time when people had become preoccupied with their own everyday lives. Like no other art form before it, the novel was concerned directly with social and historical norms that applied to a particular environment, and so it established an immediate link with the empirical reality familiar to its readers. While other literary forms induced the reader to contemplate the exemplariness they embodied, the novel confronted him with problems arising from his own surroundings, at the same time holding out various potential solutions which the reader himself had, at least partially, to formulate. What was presented in the novel led to a specific effect: namely, to involve the reader in the world of the novel and so help him to understand it—and ultimately his own world—more clearly.

The present collection of essays is an attempt to lay the foundations for a theory of literary effects and responses based on the novel, since this is the genre in which reader involvement coincides with meaning production. Such a theory, if it is to carry any weight at all, must have its foundations in actual texts, for all too often literary critics tend to produce their theories on the basis of an esthetics that is predominantly abstract, derived from and conditioned by philosophy rather than by lit-

erature—with the regrettable result that they reduce texts to the proportions of their theories, instead of adapting their theories to fit in with
the texts. Thus between texts and theories there has arisen a broad
stretch of no-man's-land, and it should now be the task of literary her-
meneutics to map the topography of this region. In these essays I have
approached this no-man's-land and tried to gain access to it without going so far as to map it, for this would require a properly formulated and
specific theory of literary effect, such as I hope to develop at some future date. In setting out the basic material for this theory, I have not
sought to shape the essays into a distilled history of the novel, but have
dipped into the history at those points where it seems to me that something new and significant took place. It is true that this may in turn give
rise to a sort of history, but this will not record the succession of characteristics developing within the genre so much as the succession of activities which the novel, from Bunyan to Beckett, has demanded of its readers.

Though the novel deals with social and historical norms, this does not
mean that it simply reproduces contemporary values. The mere fact that
not all norms can possibly be included in the novel shows that there
must have been a process of selection, and this in turn, as we shall see, is
liable to be less in accordance with contemporary values than in opposition to them. Norms are social regulations, and when they are transposed into the novel they are automatically deprived of their pragmatic
nature. They are set in a new context which changes their function, insofar as they no longer act as social regulations but as the subject of a discussion which, more often than not, ends in a questioning rather than a
confirmation of their validity. This is frequently brought about by the
varying degrees of negation with which the norms are set up in their fictional context—a negation which impels the reader to seek a positive
counterbalance elsewhere than in the world immediately familiar to
him. The challenge implicit in the negation is, of course, offered first
and foremost to those whose familiar world is made up of the norms
that have been negated. These, the readers of the novel, are then forced
to take an active part in the composition of the novel's meaning, which
revolves round a basic divergence from the familiar.

This active participation is fundamental to the novel; the title of the
present collection sums it up with the term 'implied reader'. This term
incorporates both the prestructuring of the potential meaning by the
text, and the reader's actualization of this potential through the reading
process. It refers to the active nature of this process—which will vary
historically from one age to another—and not to a typology of possible
readers.

xii

Linking all these essays is one dominant, and it seems to me, central
theme: discovery. The reader discovers the meaning of the text, taking
negation as his starting-point; he discovers a new reality through a fiction which, at least in part, is different from the world he himself is used
to; and he discovers the deficiencies inherent in prevalent norms and in
his own restricted behavior. Let me repeat, however, that the essays in
this collection are concerned only with the historically changing contents
of this discovery and do not attempt to make a specific theory out of it.

Nevertheless, it is worth pointing out that discovery is one form of esthetic pleasure, for it offers the reader two distinct possibilities: first, to
free himself—even if only temporarily—from what he is and to escape
from the restrictions of his own social life; second, actively to exercise
his faculties—generally the emotional and the cognitive. No one, so far
as I know, has ever written a history of discovery as an esthetic pleasure,
but if one were to do so—as I have tried to show in these essays—one
would have to regard discovery as a kind of esthetic blank that is filled
in differently in accordance with the nature both of individuals and of
historical periods.

This fact emerges clearly in the evolution of the novel from Bunyan
to Beckett. At the end of the seventeenth century, discovery was a process offering reassurances as regards the *certitudo salutis,* thus relieving the
distress caused by the Calvinist doctrine of predestination. In the eighteenth century men were concerned with discovering that which the prevailing philosophy of empiricism was unable to determine: namely, what
human nature consists of, how moral conduct can be developed from it,
and how one can actually grasp reality itself—which, like the problem of
moral conduct, had become more and more elusive in the light of the
empiricists' rejection of all a priori knowledge. In the nineteenth century
the attention of the 'discoverers' was turned to subjectivity—first to
its social role and then to its overall structure. In the one case, discovery meant a critical opposition to conventions; in the other, an attack
on the prevailing myth of the self-sufficiency of the individual, and finally—building the transition to modern times—a fundamental questioning of identity itself.

While the eighteenth-century novel reader was cast by the author in a
specific role, so that he could be guided—directly, or indirectly, through
affirmation or through negation—toward a conception of human nature
and of reality, in the nineteenth century the reader was not told what
part he was to play. Instead, he had to discover the fact that society had
imposed a part on him, the object being for him eventually to take up a
critical attitude toward this imposition. For him to perform this func-

tion, i.e., to accept the role of critic, it was essential that the novel refrain from explicitly telling him what to do, for criticism must at least appear to be spontaneous if it is to have any value for the critic himself. In order for this complex process to be put into operation, the author had to use a variety of cunning stratagems to nudge the reader unknowingly into making the 'right' discoveries.

The process has become even more complex in the twentieth-century novel, for here the discovery concerns the functioning of our own faculties of perception. The reader is meant to become aware of the nature of these faculties, of his own tendency to link things together in consistent patterns, and indeed of the whole thought process that constitutes his relations with the world outside himself. This means that the novel no longer confines itself to telling a story or to establishing its own patterns, for now it also deliberately reveals the component parts of its own narrative techniques, separating the material to be presented from the forms that serve its presentation in order to provoke the reader into establishing for himself the connections between perception and thought. But then the reader realizes how far short of the mark are his attempts at consistency-building, since he has had to ignore so much of the potential content of the text in order to formulate his restricted interpretation. In this way, the reader is forced to discover the hitherto unconscious expectations that underlie all his perceptions, and also the whole process of consistency-building as a prerequisite for understanding. In this way he may then be given the chance of discovering himself, both in and through his constant involvement in 'home-made' illusions and fictions.

All the essays presented here tend to revolve to a greater or lesser extent around this theme. They were, however, written at different times and for different occasions, and although they have all been thoroughly revised in preparation for this collected edition, they are bound at times to retain traces of their originally independent existence. This is true particularly of a section of the essay on Ivy Compton-Burnett, which was directly relevant to the essay on subjectivity and so has been included there too. For this esthetically disturbing, but in the circumstances essential re-use of material, I crave the reader's indulgence, and hope that he will nevertheless experience through this collection an increasing insight into the fascinating process of reading and reacting.

THE IMPLIED READER

1

BUNYAN'S *PILGRIM'S PROGRESS:*
The Doctrine of Predestination and the
Shaping of the Novel

I

J ohn Bunyan's religious and sociological importance has long
been a subject of great interest to literary critics. Herbert
Schöffler,[1] for instance, used the findings of Ernst Troeltsch[2]
and Max Weber[3] to show the links between sociology and literature that
were apparent in the works of Bunyan and in other writings of the dissent. In his study of the social origins of writers during the early period
of the Enlightenment, Schöffler also pinpointed the conditions that gave
rise to the particular form of literature produced at that time. The most
interesting feature of his study deals with the lower-class, Puritan origi-
nators of a new literary genre: the novel. As Schöffler's main concern
was with the sociological problem of how fiction actually came into being in a Calvinist environment that was on principle hostile to literature
as devil's work, he gave little or no consideration to the special form of
this new genre and to the processes that shaped it. It is enough for
Schöffler to maintain: "It is clear that *Pilgrim's Progress* takes its place
in the great line of historical, narrative edifying literature" which, "how-

---

[1] Herbert Schöffler, *Protestantismus und Literatur* (Leipzig, 1922).
[2] Ernst Troeltsch, *Gesammelte Schriften,* I (Tübingen, 1912).
[3] Max Weber, *Gesammelte Aufsätze zur Religionssoziologie,* I (Tübingen, 1920).

ever, is clearly continued in the allegorical and fictitious."[4] He uses a similar argument to explain the origins of Defoe's *Robinson Crusoe:* this, the first novel of the dissent, grew out of Defoe's moral writings—especially the *Family Instructor,* which "lies directly before the beginning of Defoe's assiduous work in the field of the novel, and clearly shows the way in which forms of the novel developed out of the moral vade mecum."[5] According to Schöffler, the difference between Bunyan and Defoe lies simply in the progressive weakening of the old Calvinist orthodoxy. Puritan conduct-books led ultimately to exemplary fiction, and Defoe's literary fiction arose from moral and religious exemplarity. And so for Schöffler the link between truth and fiction is a genetic problem that can be solved in terms of secularization. "It was a significant though coincidental development that *Robinson* was published during the very same weeks as the inner collapse of the old Calvinist dissent became finally obvious; and it was equally significant for the development of the mind that the first novel by a religious, lower-class citizen was written at the same time when the Enlightenment was relaxing all religious rigorism and exerting its most powerful effect on the English middle classes."[6]

Important though Schöffler's findings may be for our understanding of the sociological development of the novel, they completely ignore one very fundamental question: What exactly *is* a novel? Schöffler sees it as a secularized book of devotion, and for him secularization is identical with the Enlightenment. This, however, is no definition, if only for the fact that books of devotion—principally conduct-books—already contained features which, if they were not exactly fictional, were at least stylized and arose from the desire to convey the Calvinist doctrine of predestined salvation, together with the anguish of the individual soul, in such a way that the reader could actually be edified. And so it might be said that fiction descended from the idea of predestination rather than from secularization, for as "concord-fiction"[7] it had to counterbalance the fears that predestination aroused in the Puritan sects. Schöffler says that Bunyan represented "a starting-point for everything that was created by the dissent and Puritanism of the 18th century,"[8] but he does not explain in what way this was so.

The question of Bunyan's status is given an equally limited answer

---

[4] Schöffler, *Protestantismus*, p. 154.
[5] Ibid., p. 156.
[6] Ibid., pp. 165 f. Schöffler is referring to the conference at Salters' Hall in 1719.
[7] This term is used by Frank Kermode, *The Sense of an Ending. Studies in the Theory of Fiction* (New York, 1967), pp. 63 f.
[8] Schöffler, *Protestantismus*, p. 154.

by Tillyard in his comprehensive work on the English epic.[9] Tillyard takes no account of Schöffler's arguments, and his book in fact tends to head in a completely different direction. While Schöffler considers *Pilgrim's Progress* to be an anticipation of eighteenth-century developments, Tillyard reverses it back into the tradition of the epic and identifies Bunyan as a Puritan epic writer.

Tillyard and Schöffler in fact mark two extreme positions as regards an evaluation of *Pilgrim's Progress*. Schöffler sees Bunyan as a precursor of the novel, because the first novelists of the eighteenth century also sprang from the dissent; Tillyard sees him as a Puritan epic writer, because his work is concerned principally with presenting the "numinous."[10] The following analysis of *Pilgrim's Progress* uses these two extremes as its starting-point; we shall try to gauge the part played by each and to elucidate the situation that gave rise to this landmark in literary history.

II

Ever since Coleridge, critics have been fully aware of the strange interrelation of epic and novel that constitutes the basic structure of *Pilgrim's Progress*. Mere allegory is surpassed through the sheer aliveness of the characters, and it is this that gives the work its appeal. Talon, in his thorough and basic study of Bunyan, says: ". . . ils [i.e., the characters] ont trop de chair et de sang pour être allégoriques, mais ils donnent à l'oeuvre cette vie et cette clarté qu'on y loue traditionnellement."[11] This fact alone speaks against the solely epic view of the work: the epic deliberately set out to idealize the past, and to do so it had to establish a certain distance[12] between itself and its reader's present. Distance was an integral feature. But the more alive characters are the smaller is this distance, and if characters seem genuinely to be made of flesh and blood, then their presence is immediate and not remote. And immediacy is a basic feature of the novel, not of the epic.

The apology with which Bunyan introduces his book sums up the subject matter as follows:

This Book it chalketh out before thine eyes
The man that seeks the everlasting Prize;

---

[9] E. M. W. Tillyard, *The English Epic and Its Background* (London, 1954).
[10] Ibid., p. 386.
[11] H. Talon, *John Bunyan: L'Homme et l'Oeuvre* (Paris, 1948), p. 252; see also E. A. Baker, *The History of the English Novel*, III (London, 1929), p. 57.
[12] The structure of epic distance has been systematically described by H. R. Jauss, *Zeit und Erinnerung in Marcel Prousts 'A la Recherche du Temps Perdu'* (Heidelberg, 1955), following B. Groethuysen; see esp. chap. 1.

3

It shews you whence he comes, whither he goes,
What he leaves undone, also what he does;
It also shews you how he runs and runs,
Till he unto the Gate of Glory comes.[13]

Man's quest for salvation forms the all-embracing background for the events, which are to find their culmination only in the future. Here again the work differs from the epic in that the latter presented ideal, normative conduct as something that took place in a remote past and therefore represented a goal already attained. The only epic element in this subject matter is the paradigmatic search for salvation, which loomed large in all human activities.[14] Tillyard himself drew attention to the fact that *Pilgrim's Progress* diverges from the medieval pattern of the pilgrimage, as shown in Deguileville's work (translated by Lydgate) *Le Pèlerinage de la Vie Humaine:* ". . . for Deguileville the pilgrimage is only partly the affair of the lonely soul, being largely the passage through the prescribed stages of an education in holiness by means of concrete religious acts."[15] And so the first 10,000 verses contain instructions for the pilgrim before he starts off on his journey.[16] Set against Deguileville's medieval allegory, Bunyan's work strikingly accentuates the importance of the individual soul, giving it precedence over means of grace, the institution, and the hierarchy. This obvious change of emphasis was conditioned by the Calvinist doctrine of predestination.[17]

This doctrine makes the goal of the pilgrimage—the attainment of the *certitudo salutis*—into something objectively unattainable. It excludes any active participation in the acquisition of grace. And so for Bunyan there could be no gradual education to holiness, such as there was for Deguileville, for man was either chosen or damned. If he wanted to go forth and search for salvation, he would have to behave differently from the pilgrim who, by fulfilling certain set tasks, could rest assured of finding grace. While the goal for the medieval pilgrim was a gradual "education in holiness," that of the Puritan pilgrim was the urgent question of finding out whether he had been allotted to the sheep or the goats. And so instead of beginning with a list of detailed instructions, Bunyan's

---

[13] John Bunyan, *The Pilgrim's Progress* (Everyman's Library) (London, no date), p. 6.

[14] One consequence of the Norman Conquest was the fact that it took a long time for a native English form of the epic to come into being. In contrast to the traditional epic, the English epic of the late Middle Ages and the Renaissance is typified by a lack of any historical restrictions. The English epic, as regards its form, stands on the borderline between the classical epic and the allegory.

[15] Tillyard, *The English Epic*, p. 393.

[16] See C. S. Lewis, *The Allegory of Love* (London, 1953), p. 268.

[17] See also Tillyard, *The English Epic*, p. 393.

4

allegory starts off with the picture of a pilgrim in anguish and despair through the awareness of his own sinfulness.

As the Puritan believed that he was already saved or damned, his only escape from total passivity was to hunt for signs of his hoped-for salvation. And so the absence of any *certitudo salutis* led him to pay closer attention both to himself and to the world around him. The more signs he found the greater seemed his chances of salvation,[18] but even then his certainty had inevitably to remain subjective, which meant that doubt must persist right through to the end of his life—as is the case with Christian in *Pilgrim's Progress*.[19] He could only continue to look for more and more signs in his own soul and in empirical reality, thus paradoxically bringing about a revaluation of what the Calvinist doctrine had dismissed as worthless and irredeemable.[20] This search was of considerable significance for literature. "Interposed between dogmatic predestination and human inadequacy there is a mediating level of literary fiction, which promises security, orientation, and a cure for religious despair. The withholding of grace and the absolute transcendency of God give rise to the demand for a fictive, more humane cosmos of epic events."[21]

Any literary representation of the exemplary road to salvation therefore has to lay particular emphasis on the human side of the characters involved, and this means a departure from the symbolic presentation of the epic. If a gradual *certitudo salutis* can only be gauged by what happens in man's inner being, the stock figures of epic and allegory will no longer suffice, for as Lukács has pointed out, the epic character has no inner being: "for there is no exterior, no otherness for the soul. Whilst this goes off on its adventures and comes through them all unscathed, it remains unacquainted with the real torment of the search and the real danger of the find: such a soul never puts itself at risk; it is not yet aware that it can lose itself, and never thinks of having to search for itself."[22] And so the moment the soul develops an awareness of the torment of

[18] See G. Thiel, *Bunyans Stellung innerhalb der religiösen Strömungen seiner Zeit* (Sprache und Kultur der germanischen und romanischen Völker. A. Anglistische Reihe, VII) (Breslau, 1931), pp. 136 ff. In this otherwise well-informed study, Thiel does, however, overlook the vital fact that the *certitudo salutis* can only be subjective; see p. 142.

[19] See Bunyan, *Pilgrim's Progress*, pp. 156 f.

[20] The consequences for the history of economics have been shown in detail by Max Weber and R. H. Tawney, *Religion and the Rise of Capitalism* (London, 1926). See also H. Bock, "Typen bürgerlich-puritanischer Lebenshaltung in England im 17. und 18. Jahrhundert," *Anglia* 65 (1941): 153 ff.

[21] Gerd Birkner, *Heilsgewissheit und Literatur. Metapher, Allegorie und Autobiographie im Puritanismus* (Theorie und Geschichte der Literatur und der schönen Künste, 18) (Munich, 1972), p. 102.

[22] Georg von Lukács, "Die Theorie des Romans," *Zeitschrift für Ästhetik und Allgemeine Kunstwissenschaft* 11 (1916): 226 f.

the search and the possibility of losing itself, the universality of the epic is destroyed. Once characters begin to fear for their own salvation, their humanity becomes a subject for scrutiny, and thus runs counter to any representative function, because instead of embodying salvation they adopt an attitude toward it. Thus the characters develop a striking polarity: on the one hand, they remain drawn to the goal that dominates their whole existence—salvation; on the other, their humanity, their inner world, is bound to be accentuated in order to bring out their subjective mitigation of the theocratic Calvinist doctrine. So long as the goal of salvation is binding events together, the perspective is that of the epic, for the rigid framework permits only one center of orientation; but once the characters become preoccupied with their subjective inner world, they cease to act as mouthpieces for a specific dogma and leave the realm of the epic. It is precisely those "normal human feelings,"[23] which Tillyard appears to regard as one of Bunyan's epic features, that bring *Pilgrim's Progress* out of the epic plane and onto the level of the novel.

The polarity which we have been discussing is already indicated in the prologue. Here Bunyan actually appeals to those human feelings his book is to be concerned with. After first dealing with the paradigmatic nature of all the events that are to take place along the road to salvation, the apology continues:

This Book will make a Traveller of thee,
If by its Counsel thou wilt ruled be;
It will direct thee to the Holy Land,
If thou wilt its directions understand: . . . .
This Book is writ in such a Dialect
As may the minds of listless men affect:
It seems a novelty, and yet contains
Nothing but sound and honest Gospel strains.
Would'st thou divert thyself from Melancholy?
Would'st thou be pleasant, yet be far from folly?
Would'st thou read Riddles, and their Explanation?
Or else be drowned in thy Contemplation?
Dost though love picking meat? Or would'st thou see
A man i'th'Clouds, and hear him speak to thee?
Would'st thou be in a Dream, and yet not sleep?
Or would'st thou in a moment laugh and weep?
Wouldest thou lose thyself, and catch no harm,
And find thyself again without a charm?

[23] Tillyard, *The English Epic*, p. 386.

6

Would'st read thyself, and read thou know'st not what,
And yet know whether thou art blest or not,
By reading the same lines? O then come hither,
And lay my Book, thy Head and Heart together.[24]

The book is meant to appeal to each individual reader, whatever his disposition, and its aim is to lead the believer to recognize himself. Thus the idea of salvation is treated predominantly as a means of illuminating human reality and not as an end in itself. And so the gradual acquisition of *certitudo salutis* puts a subjective slant on the objective events. It is in fact the ultimate uncertainty of salvation that leads to closer and closer inspection of the self, for it is only through his own transformation that the believer can detect the signs he is looking for. As the idea of salvation is intangible, he can only observe its reflections and refractions in the spectrum of human conduct. The literary presentation of such observation is therefore bound to lay emphasis on the human side of the story, which continually undermines the epic or allegorical side. In *Pilgrim's Progress*, the various levels of presentation all reveal the workings of this process.[25]

III

One very striking element of *Pilgrim's Progress* is the varied narrative technique. The book is set as a dream vision, but for long sections this fact is virtually expunged by the force and immediacy of the dialogue. This shift in balance opens up two different perspectives of the events presented.

The dream vision is an old stratagem of the allegory, but it is doubtful whether Bunyan deliberately wanted to fit in with the rhetorical tradition. In the *Apology* he emphasizes that the Bible alone can justify his 'literary' venture,[26] and so if he does make use of rhetorical techniques, it is in order to serve his own particular ends and not to cultivate a literary tradition. The dream device enables him to create a vision of the exemplary road to salvation, but in *Pilgrim's Progress* this is not the traditional vision, allowing access to the world beyond; instead it gives us access to total knowledge of this world only. The narrator is able to see the whole of the road—unlike the pilgrim, who can see only what lies

---

[24] Bunyan, *Pilgrim's Progress*, pp. 6 f.

[25] R. Sharrock, *John Bunyan* (London, 1954), pp. 73 f., rightly emphasizes the uniformity of the first part of *Pilgrim's Progress:* "The First Part of *The Pilgrim's Progress* is a complete and self-sufficient narrative; it has no need of a sequel to make plain either its religious meaning or its unity of atmosphere."

[26] See Bunyan, *Pilgrim's Progress*, pp. 4 and 6.

immediately before him. However, the pilgrim's view is presented just as directly as the narrator's, so that we see all events from two quite different perspectives. When the narrator is giving his account the action is linear; events and characters are relevant only insofar as they bring out the exemplariness of the road to salvation; in their confrontation with the different vices—in Vanity Fair especially—Christian and Faithful simply embody virtues, and their characters are totally absorbed by their allegorical function. But these allegorical actions reported by the narrator are frequently interrupted and sometimes even obliterated by the dialogue of the characters, and then the all-seeing narrator gives way to the human beings caught up in the situation he has been describing; his only function then is simply to link together the situations and conversations, without offering any omniscient interpretation. In these passages the characters come alive, and we share their doubts and uncertainties as the hazards of the journey become even greater. The dream narrator knows that the pilgrim will win through, but the pilgrim himself does not know this and can only call upon his own reserves of strength and resolution to lead him forward. As Christian himself says on the way: "If I can get to the Celestial City, I am sure to be in safety there. I must venture: To go back is nothing but death; to go forward is fear of death, and life everlasting beyond it. I will yet go forward."[27] For Christian, safety is a future promise, but he can never be sure that the promise will be fulfilled—hence the uncertainty that characterizes his view of the road, as opposed to the total knowledge of the dream narrator who describes that road to us.

This contrast in perspectives is evident even in isolated details of the narrative. When, for instance, Christian approaches the Palace Beautiful, at first he has no idea what this place actually is. He sees lions at the entrance and is frightened and despondent. And so we see the palace through the eyes of the pilgrim. But then at once the dream narrator changes the perspective by remarking: "The Lions were chained, but he saw not the chains."[28] The effect of this change on the reader is that instead of sharing in Christian's fears as if they were his own he can stand outside them again and view them more as an expression of the general human condition. He is no longer exclusively caught up in Christian's experiences, but is given the chance to assess the latter's situation and his reactions to it. The same applies to the temptations offered by Worldly Wiseman. Christian has no idea whose hands he has fallen into—for

[27] Ibid., p. 45.
[28] Ibid., p. 47.

8

him the tempter appears to be nothing if not a thorough gentleman—but the narrator has already told the reader all about him. Christian has to learn by experience who this "gentleman" really is.[29] And so again, the reader has been given extra information which puts him in a superior position and enables him to recognize and evaluate the trials and tribulations along the road to salvation.

And so the narrative technique alternates between omniscient narration and dialogue, and the increasing preponderance of dialogue is an indication of the increasing importance of subjectivity within an objective context. But the reader is never allowed to be totally absorbed in the immediacy of the characters' reactions; he is constantly reminded or made aware of the overall situation, so that he can attain a more balanced judgment of human conduct generally and, ultimately, of his own in particular. This change of perspective is an integral feature of the edification provided by *Pilgrim's Progress,* and it also brings about a dramatic switch of tensions: although the reader knows right from the start that the pilgrim will arrive safely in the Promised Land, the dialogue is so direct and alive that this knowledge at times fades right out of the reckoning; at others, he is aware of the end result, and so his interest lies not in whether the pilgrim will arrive, but in what the pilgrim has to do in order to get there. This latter form of tension is epic, since the outcome of the adventures is already known. But at those times when the reader loses sight of the end result and shares in the pilgrim's uncertainty as to whether he will arrive or not we have a different form of tension. "And so in the tension of the 'whether at all' there is contained a time element in the form of a conception of the future, in which the accent lies on the obscurity and opaqueness of everything future."[30] The future along the road to salvation is always present in the dialogues as an either/or that can never be resolved through preestablished ideals but only by the course of time. This tension is characteristic of the novel.

We can now see clearly the two poles between which the action takes its course: at the one extreme we have the objective, exemplary road to salvation, described directly by the dream narrator; at the other, we have the increasing, subjective certitude of salvation, developed during the dialogues. Salvation is an a priori precondition for all events in the book; certitude must be gained a posteriori. Man's destiny—the search for salvation—is clear from the beginning; the certainty of finding—the fulfill-

[29] Ibid., pp. 23 f.

[30] C. Lugowski, *Die Form der Individualität im Roman* (Neue Forschung, 14) (Berlin, 1932), p. 42.

ment of this destiny—is identical with death. The objective goal can only
be reached through subjective "self-experience,"[31] and this process is
communicated to the reader by the alternation between dream vision
and dialogue and the respective tensions arising from this alternation.

For the most part, *Pilgrim's Progress* is written in prose, but at various
specific points the language changes to verse. It is unlikely that Bunyan's
intention was merely to conform to the old form of the 'prosimetrum',
for he only makes use of rhetorical means to serve his own particular
strategic ends. The verse passages are generally very short, and so they
act rather as interruptions to the otherwise prevailing prose. If we are
to understand the significance of the verse, it might be advisable first to
take a closer look at the prose.

As we have seen, it is in the dialogue that certainty is sought after;
here the speaker endeavors to ascertain his own situation and to open
the eyes of his partner to the signs of increasing knowledge of salvation.
Inevitably then the language takes on an argumentative character, for experiences have to be weighed and the significant elements singled out.
The argumentation demands a discriminating use of language, not only
in order to increase its effectiveness but also to incorporate all the given
factors that make up the pilgrim's experiences. It is only by bringing
out all the apparent trivia and contingencies of individual situations that
the speaker can enhance his partners' awareness of their own positions.
As virtually all the characters are passing along the road to salvation,
they do not need to inform each other of the necessity of the journey.
But in order for them to know where they stand on this allegorical road,
they need a constant analysis of what they are and of the empirical situation they are in. Many of the dialogues therefore take the course almost
of a trial, and the discussion—typified by a profusion of causal particles—
gives rise to knowledge, though this need not always have a positive value, as we can see from the discussion between Christian and Worldly
Wiseman. "Only prose can embody with equal power the tribulation and
the triumph, the conflict and the coronation, the search and the sancti-
fication; only its unlimited flexibility and its rhythmless linkage can capture with equal force fetters and freedom, the given weight and the
fought-for lightness of the world that is now immanently radiant with
the discovered sense."[32]

---

[31] This term is taken from E. Harding, *Selbsterfahrung* (Zürich, 1957) (German translation),
but is not used in the psychological context which this book discusses.

[32] Lukács, "Theorie des Romans," p. 247.

10

The prose dialogues of *Pilgrim's Progress* unfold the characters' fluctuations of mind and efforts to conquer their own uncertainty. They give rise to the whole picture of the pilgrim's empirical situation, and they reflect the Puritan reader's own inner conflicts. And it is precisely because the nuances of the prose unfold the empirical conditions surrounding the pilgrim that the verse passages take on such a special significance, for they offer something of which the Puritan reader could never be sure.

Many of the incidents in *Pilgrim's Progress* are rounded off with a few verses, which, as it were, sum up the conflict that has just taken place. After Christian has recognized his error in following Worldly Wiseman, the verse starts: "When Christians unto Carnal Men give ear."[33] The verse abstracts from the concrete instance in order to offer all Christians general criteria of conduct arising out of the individual error. This is another edifying element of the book, for here the Puritan reader is shown how to overcome the doubts and temptations which the prose dialogue enabled him to experience virtually as his own. But if the end result given by the verse is to be unambiguous and universal, it must separate itself from the single situation from which it arose, and so frequently the subject of the verses is no longer the individual pilgrim, but pilgrims in general.[34] If the name of the particular character *is* retained, however, the message takes on an increased degree of exemplariness, as shown for instance with Faithful's conduct in Vanity Fair.[35] The need to explain Faithful's significance once more in verse is an indication of the extent to which his behavior was orientated by ideas which sprang from his character as a human being, rather than from his ideality as a personification. The scaling down of characters to their exemplary values is a predominant feature of most of the verses.[36] But this very fact gives extra significance to those verses that are spoken by the pilgrim himself. Undoubtedly their edifying effect is all the more striking. After Christian has been given a scroll which symbolizes for him the first unmistakable sign of a gradual certitude, he reaches Hill Difficulty. As he comes to climb the hill, the narrative breaks off into verse:

This Hill, though high, I covet to ascend;
The difficulty will not me offend;
For I perceive the way to life lies here:
Come, pluck up, Heart, let's neither faint nor fear:

[33] Bunyan, *Pilgrim's Progress*, p. 24.
[34] Ibid., pp. 44, 75, 134, passim.
[35] Ibid., pp. 94 and 99.
[36] Ibid., pp. 148, passim.

> Better, though difficult, the right way to go,
> Than wrong, though easy, where the end is woe.[37]

These lines lay emphasis on Christian's firm resolve to continue his quest. As he has just received the first sign of grace, he is no longer put off by the difficulty of the way, but he talks of the effort required to conquer his own typically human weakness and fear, which might otherwise make him take the wrong way. The fact that Christian speaks these verses himself draws attention to his ability to extract the right conclusions from his own situation. And in this he satisfies a basic requirement of Puritan edification.

The function of the verse, then, is to pinpoint the general significance of particular events. While the prose unfolds the *personificatio* of the characters, the verse extracts the *significatio*. So long as events and reactions are the subject of the narrative, the language remains prose, but when the abstract, edifying idea behind these events is to be placed in the forefront, prose gives way to verse.

The distinctions we have observed in the language and the narrative perspectives apply also to the characters themselves. Basically there are two separate groups of characters in *Pilgrim's Progress:* the one purely functional, the other extending beyond mere function. Such characters as Evangelist, Pliable, and Obstinate only appear on the scene at set moments in the story and then disappear again. Evangelist, for instance, always comes when Christian is in need of heavenly guidance.[38] Once this has been given, he withdraws. Pliable and Obstinate have similarly fixed functions: they allegorize Christian's situation at his departure and embody the conflict that arises within him. Obstinate *is* Christian, insofar as he seems determined to take the road to salvation at all costs; Pliable *is* Christian in that he remains completely open to all the suggestions of those that want to divert him from his quest. But once Christian is actually on the way, Obstinate and Pliable disappear—they have played their part and fade from the scene.[39] They are only functional, representing an abstract idea in a situational context, and so they cannot be developed as characters in their own right. In this respect they correspond to the pattern of the epic and the allegory.

The second group of characters, however, is not purely functional. The principal member of this group is, of course, Christian himself, but

[37] Ibid., p. 43.
[38] Ibid., pp. 12 f. and 22.
[39] Lugowski, *Form der Individualität,* p. 99.

he is also accompanied for much of the way by Hopeful and Faithful, who are far more than just embodiments of a single idea. In them the reader has to recognize the reflection of his own doubts as well as his own hopes, and for this purpose it is essential that they should at times fall out of their allegorical character, for if they were to behave as ideal pilgrims, the link with the Puritan reader would be broken and the work would lose much of its edifying effect. The importance of these characters is indicated technically by a sort of narrative close-up, in marked contrast to the paucity of description with which the functional figures are presented. This is particularly true of Christian. Right at the beginning we are offered a thoroughly detailed picture of him. He reads, weeps, trembles, and finally gives vent to a cry of despair. In torment he rushes home from work, and then at first tries to hide his agony in order that his wife and children should not notice his suffering. But he cannot remain silent for long, as his anguish steadily increases. Finally he tells them what is troubling him. They are all amazed and think "that some frenzy distemper had got into his head."[40] As night approaches, they hope his health may improve with sleep, and so they hurry him off to bed. But Christian sighs and weeps right through the night, and next morning everything seems even more hopeless to him than it did the previous day. Now people begin to mock him, then they remonstrate with him, and finally they ignore him, in the belief that this will cure him. But Christian retires to his room, not knowing what has happened to him, and then prays and feels sorry for himself. After this he goes out to the fields again, reads, and prays, in the hope that this may calm the inner storm.[41] This description of the initial situation in *Pilgrim's Progress* offers a series of concrete details. Christian is observed much more closely than the other characters, and the vividness of his portrayal is in obvious contrast to their comparative anonymity: Christian is not shown to us as an exemplary pilgrim, but as a man plunged into the despondency that in fact is the first sign of grace.[42] This opens up a particular perspective which continues right through to the end of the book. When Christian reaches the River of Death and sees the towers of the Celestial City beyond, in spite of the many signs of salvation he has received he once more gives way to black despair. Again the human side of the pilgrim takes over in the form of care, fear, and hopelessness. It is because of this emphasis on the human side that Christian is not surrounded at the beginning by allegorical figures that might interpret his conduct; in-

---

[40] Bunyan, *Pilgrim's Progress*, p. 12.
[41] Ibid., pp. 11 f.
[42] See also A. West, *The Mountain in the Sunlight* (London, 1958), p. 28.

13

stead he is shown with his wife and children—"Children of my bowels"[43]
—who indicate the human situation in which the quest for grace can only
appear as a disturbance. For the family, this preoccupation with an obscure salvation is explicable only as a form of madness.

There is another important side to the opening scene of the book. Although he is in anguish, Christian is by no means resolved to set out on
the quest for salvation; on the contrary, he would like to be rid of this
oppressive feeling, which takes on the image of a burden he has to bear.[44]
He is far from being the ideal pilgrim joyfully preparing for his journey;
instead he is shown as a man whose one concern is to be relieved of his
suffering. And this is why on the way he is subjected to so many different temptations, for he has to learn that he can only obtain the relief he
longs for when he has left behind those weaknesses that determine his
character as a human being. The very theme of the pilgrim's way is that
Christian has to become aware of the paradoxical fact that the desire for
relief, which arises out of his humanity, is only to be fulfilled by overcoming that same humanity. The pilgrim himself, as a man, is the actual
source of the temptations—whether they be to lead him astray, or to
make him doubt his incipient certitude, because nothing in this world
can ever be truly certain. This is why, at the Palace Beautiful, Christian
acknowledges the fact that humanity is an annoyance to the man set on
salvation.[45]

The two groups of characters then reveal the same two perspectives
we have already observed in relation to narrative techniques and use of
prose and verse. If the characters are purely functional, then it is the abstract idea of salvation that is uppermost; when the characters cease to
be mere personifications, emphasis is thrown on human conduct and
motivation. The two planes are complementary, in that the *certitudo
salutis* can only be subjective, with the pilgrim extracting the signs from
his own individual human experiences.

IV

The alternation of perspectives and the mixture of 'human' and 'functional' characters have certain far-reaching effects on the allegorical mode
of presentation in *Pilgrim's Progress*. As from Prudentius's *Psychomachia*
onward, the allegory, as *bellum intestinum,* possessed certain specific

---

[43] Bunyan, *Pilgrim's Progress,* p. 11.
[44] Ibid., p. 23.
[45] Ibid., pp. 51 f.

structural characteristics,[46] and these remained consistent right through to the Renaissance. The vices and virtues struggling for the soul did not personify any psychological qualities, but put the soul in the context of an overriding reality.[47] Consequently the soul was only the object of the allegorical presentation, while the superior truth was the subject. This is why the soul—still regarded by Prudentius as corresponding typologically to the Church—and the allegorical self in medieval court allegories were both presented more or less as abstractions. "An allegorical being, however human may be the form given to it, can never take on the individuality of a Greek god or a saint or any other real subject: because in order for it to correspond to the abstraction of its meaning, it must hollow out all subjectivity so that any fixed individuality disappears completely."[48] This idea is prevalent both in *Anticlaudianus* and in the *Roman de la Rose*. The 'homo perfectus' and the 'amant' remain abstract figures, and are only real within the limits of a nonsubjective world. The allegory—as Walter F. Otto put it so succinctly—represents "not a personification, but in actual fact a depersonification."[49]

Despite these impersonal elements of the allegory, we must not overlook the vital interaction that takes place between the abstract ideas and the concrete situations they are transposed into. The character in the allegory is not the subject matter, but neither is the theological or moral canon. "As a literary form, it [i.e., the allegory] effects a *concordia discors*. Its achievement lies in combining what discursive thought can only conceive of as separate. It links the significance of the general with the situational present of the concrete."[50] This link results from the basic feature of the allegorical mode of presentation, which is a "noun with a fixed, general, abstract connotation fitted into a particular situation in the text,"[51] thus bringing about the paradoxical idea of "a contextual merging of the mutually exclusive linguistic poles of abstraction and sit-

[46] Re the conception of the allegory in the ancient tradition and the renewed discussion of the difference between allegory and symbol, see H. R. Jauss, "Form und Auffassung der Allegorie in der Tradition der *Psychomachia,*" in *Medium Aevum Vivum* (Festschrift für Walther Bulst) (Heidelberg, 1960), pp. 179 ff.

[47] See also H. E. Greene, "The Allegory as employed by Spenser, Bunyan, and Swift," *PMLA* 4 (1888/89): 145 ff., though his definitions are much too formalistic. The distinction he tries to draw between symbol and allegory is not convincing. On the same problem, see W. Benjamin, *Schriften,* I (Frankfurt, 1955), p. 283. Re the conception of the allegory in the eighteenth century, see B. H. Bronson, "Personification Reconsidered," *ELH* 14 (1947): 163 ff.

[48] G. W. F. Hegel, *Ästhetik,* ed. F. Bassenge (Berlin, 1955), p. 393.

[49] Quoted from *Germanisch-Romanische Monatsschrift* 39 (1958): 314.

[50] Birkner, *Heilsgewissheit und Literatur,* p. 115; for this aspect of the allegory I am indebted to Birkner's work.

[51] H. Engels, "*Piers Plowman*—Eine Untersuchung der Textstruktur mit einer Einleitung zur mittelalterlichen Allegorie," Dissertation, Cologne, 1968, p. 38.

uation."[52] It is no doubt this structure of interaction that explains the fascination which allegory has had down through the ages as a mode of presentation. But this same structure is also an important key to historical insight, for the framework of interaction shown by the "contextual merging of . . . abstraction and situation" has been filled with a variety of pictures, depending on the historical function it has had to serve.

Historically, the 'situation' became increasingly important within this structure, and in Bunyan's allegory—against the background of predestination—it is unmistakably in the forefront. This shift in the balance of the structure brings about a far-reaching change in the conception of the allegorical figures. In *Pilgrim's Progress* there are three distinct types of figures, and the interaction between them brings out the originality with which Bunyan manipulated abstract ideas in the context of a situation. There are personified virtues and vices, personified qualities, and the central figure of the pilgrim himself, who steps out of the allegorical framework at various turning-points in his life. The fact that the virtues and vices do not fight with Christian all at the same time arises out of the journey metaphor. Simultaneity here gives way to a succession of stages, in accordance with the Stoic convention. But in fact the virtues—Good-Will, Charity, Piety, Prudence, etc.—do *not* fight with the pilgrim at all; nor do the vices, from Worldly Wiseman to Ignorance. Only once is the pilgrim ever involved in a fight, and that is with Apollyon who, as the Devil, embodies the absolute opposite to the quest for salvation. Like Evangelist, he represents the spiritual level of the Scriptures, in the form of a symbol. Apollyon and Evangelist mark the two spiritual poles of the salvation process and as such transcend the allegorical pattern.

The individual relationships between virtues and vices and Christian himself are established by discussions. The virtues and vices are constantly appealing to him, thereby presupposing that there is a side of Christian's character on which they can work. And so the object of the dialogue is persuasion, which means that the allegorical figure must have an inner self that is open to persuasion. It is through this inner self that the character outstrips the allegory, and the pilgrim takes on a sort of double role.

This is made clear by the second group of figures which—like Faithful and Hopeful—represent personified qualities and are of greater importance than the others by virtue of the fact that they are Christian's closest companions along the road to salvation. The change of emphasis in the allegorical pattern of interaction is clear from the very names—Faith-

[52] Ibid., p. 44.

ful and Hopeful, not Faith and Hope. Christian is no longer the object but the subject of the action, with his inner qualities—set as they are on salvation—being personified as his companions. When Christian leaves the Palace Beautiful, he learns from the watchman that Faithful is also on the road. Christian remarks: "I know him; he is my Townsman, my near Neighbour, he comes from the place where I was born."[53] This quality of faith is already inherent in Christian, but it only takes on a real form after he has gone through the torments of the awareness of sin and has begun to view these as signs of future grace. But before Christian can actually join up with Faithful, he has to fight Apollyon and go through the Valley of the Shadow of Death in order to test the certainty of the faith now developing. Finally, in Vanity Fair, this faith gives testimony of its unshakableness through the death that Faithful is ready to suffer. And so it is only after this vital confirmation that Hopeful comes on the scene as the new companion, whose support Christian needs right up to his death. If the sequence of Faithful/Hopeful is principally an indication of the uncertainty of the Puritans' road to salvation, nevertheless it also shows how a readiness to believe can turn into hopeful perseverance. And so the allegorical schema is less an illustration of the Calvinist doctrine of predestination than an attempt to take the sting out of this doctrine by concentrating on the possibilities of experience open to the believer. The fact that Faithful and Hopeful become the pilgrim's companions gives precedence to the human situation. This must in any case be predominant within the schema of allegorical interaction, if only because the idea of predestination presented as an allegory would inevitably lead from a need for faith to black despair. Here the virtues and vices do not struggle exclusively for the soul, as they did in the medieval allegory; instead, it is the soul itself, filled with its own resolve, that yearns for the Celestial City. As the longing cannot incorporate its own fulfillment, the allegorical sense is conveyed by adjectives. The numinous is allegorized by nouns when it is concerned with the human soul; the self is allegorized by adjectives when the only impulsion is a longing for the transcendental world beyond.

So long as the allegory personifies abstractions, naturally all individuality is bound to be excluded; the *significatio* dominates, and its concrete representation is limited to its single function. However, when it is human qualities that are being allegorized, the allegorical figure does not have to be confined to the feature it represents, for it does not personify any theological or moral canon, but relates the inner self to a particular goal. And

---

[53] Bunyan, *Pilgrim's Progress*, p. 57.

so personified qualities contain an inherent duality, such as we see in Faithful and Hopeful. Although Faithful represents man's pious resolve, he departs from this 'character' whenever he confesses to features that are not connected with this function—for instance, when he admits to occasionally giving way to lusts of the flesh[54] (which can scarcely be regarded as essential to the personification of faith). At such moments, the personification takes on individual features which even begin to compete with the abstract function, incorporating human frailties into the allegorical *significatio*.[55] The same applies to Hopeful, who confesses his past enjoyment of "Rioting, Revelling, Drinking, Swearing, Lying, Uncleanness, Sabbath-breaking, and what not."[56] These characters do not merely personify the pilgrim's readiness to believe and to hope, but they show that this readiness can only come from the conquest of human weakness. And in this way they depart from the traditional schema of the allegory and approach that of the novel, in that they first have to work out for themselves the meaning of their own destiny. In the medieval allegory, this meaning was given a priori, but Bunyan's work is for much of the time concerned with overcoming weakness precisely by the character's finding out this meaning for himself. In this respect we find literary fiction trying to accomplish that which the Calvinist dogma had excluded, and it is little wonder that *Pilgrim's Progress* was read as a book of devotion, for it filled a psychic gap that had been created by the doctrine of predestination.

In the character of the pilgrim himself, the guidelines for edification are given concrete form. If, with Faithful and Hopeful, the allegorical function still outweighs the human aspect, the same cannot be said of Christian. Faithful and Hopeful take on their human characteristics through their occasional departures from their allegorical function, but they never develop this contrast themselves, whereas Christian reflects on everything that happens to him in a number of highly individual monologues.[57] The very form of the monologue presupposes an inner self as addressee, and it transcends the allegorical structure of the work insofar as Christian's inner voices are no longer allegorized. C. S. Lewis has pointed out that with the medieval allegory, the moment a character starts 'thinking' about a certain conflict, the different sides are at once

[54] Ibid., p. 70.
[55] See, amongst others, Talon, *John Bunyan*, pp. 232 f.
[56] Bunyan, *Pilgrim's Progress*, p. 137.
[57] Ibid., pp. 45 f., passim.

translated into allegorical figures.[58] Christian, however, does his own thinking; he forms a relationship with himself and does not need a superimposed reality to gain a clear vision of his own situation. Instead, he looks for motives and reasons that can eventually enable him to correct himself, and this preoccupation with himself mirrors the radical isolation of man as brought about by the doctrine of predestination. As has already been pointed out, the Calvinist pilgrim could do nothing to ensure his own salvation, but could only search for signs. And so the lack of any certitude meant that the pilgrim's one and only source of information about his ultimate destiny was himself. This was why the monologues in the *Pilgrim's Progress* were of particular interest to Puritan readers, for Christian's search for reassurance offered them a guideline as to how they should examine themselves.

The pilgrim's monologues are already a departure from the traditional schema of the allegory; through them he becomes what Forster called a "flat character,"[59] but this is only one departure from tradition: another lies in the frequent repetition of particular events. After Christian has been led astray by Worldly Wiseman and made to believe that the road to salvation is the wrong one for him to take, Evangelist comes on the scene. Through a series of questions, Evangelist compels Christian to repeat his meeting with Worldly Wiseman and to see it in a completely different light. Christian is then able to reassess his own conduct, to recognize his mistakes, and to understand the consequences which he had not been aware of when he was directly involved in the events.[60] Similar situations recur during other phases of his pilgrimage. For instance, when he reaches the Wicket-gate and meets the watchman, Good-Will,[61] the latter questions him in an almost Socratic manner, compelling him to relive various experiences he has already been through. As a result, Christian is able to gain insight into these events and to find his own way toward clearing up his own confusion and correcting his own mistakes. He is not punished for having strayed from the path of salvation; instead he is induced by the functional and allegorical figures to think over his situation. When, in the Palace Beautiful—one of the most important stages of his journey—he is again forced to relive past events, his insight is so developed that he recognizes his own human nature as the greatest obstacle along the path to salvation. Prudence asks him: "Do you not

---

[58] See Lewis, *Allegory of Love*, p. 30.

[59] See E. M. Forster, *Aspects of the Novel* (Pocket Edition) (London, 1958), pp. 43 ff.

[60] See Bunyan, *Pilgrim's Progress*, pp. 23 ff.

[61] R. Sharrock, "Spiritual Autobiography in *The Pilgrim's Progress*," *RES* 24 (1948): 114, interprets the "Wicket-gate" as the entrance to the community of the faithful.

yet bear away with you some of the things that then you were conversant withal?" Christian replies: "Yes, but greatly against my will; especially my inward and carnal cogitations; with which all my countrymen, as well as myself, were delighted; but now all those things are my grief; and might I but choose mine own things, I would choose never to think of those things more; but when I would be doing of that which is best, that which is worst is with me."[62]

The pilgrim has obviously come a long way since his despairing cry of "What shall I do?"[63] at the beginning of the book. He realizes now that human weakness stands in the way of the longed-for certitude, but through his own reflections he can gradually overcome this weakness. The actions arising from his self-correction lead to experiences which enhance this insight and take him in a direction that promises a greater degree of certainty and consolation.

The experiences gained during the early part of the book—up to the Palace Beautiful episode—are often invoked again during subsequent episodes. At the beginning Christian was constantly being made more aware of himself by the various allegorical figures, but he now proceeds to use his insight, in accordance with the idea of the Puritan mission, in order to enhance the self-awareness of his fellow pilgrims. When he meets Faithful, he begins to explore the latter's life history, for he wants to spur him on to the same insight that he achieved through his encounter with the vices and virtues. Faithful has naturally already recognized many of his own human errors, and so Christian does not need to induce him to self-correction, in the manner of Evangelist, Good-Will, or Prudence. But Christian's questions still have an important influence on Faithful, who is sometimes rather too ready to believe and, for instance, unexpectedly falls victim to the glib speeches of Talkative, until he is enjoined to be more vigilant by Christian, who has seen through this chatterbox straight away.[64]

Christian's experiences have an even greater effect in his relations with Hopeful. The vital event here is the discussion they have when crossing the Enchanted Ground.[65] The subject of this discussion is the *certitudo salutis*. Christian asks Hopeful the customary question how the expectation of salvation formed itself within him. This makes Hopeful think about himself, and he learns to distinguish between the true and false signs. The content of this dialogue is virtually a psychological exposé of

[62] Bunyan, *Pilgrim's Progress*, p. 51.
[63] Ibid., p. 11.
[64] Ibid., pp. 79 f.
[65] Ibid., pp. 136 ff.

the salvation process, for it revolves continually around the subject of how the *certitudo salutis* awakens in man: "Why, what was it that brought your sins to mind again? . . . And how did you do then? . . . And did you think yourself well then?" [66] Hopeful feels himself compelled to confront his expectations of salvation with his own human disposition, because only such a conscious confrontation can bring about the necessary degree of security for a proper evaluation of the signs. The process that the allegorical figures set in motion during Christian's period of development is now begun by Christian himself for Hopeful. Thus Christian's experiences are confirmed, and we know that in the context of Calvinist orthodoxy such a confirmation marked an important stage in the devotional account of incipient certitude. Through correcting his own mistakes, Christian gradually takes on the role of guide; it is he that is now the 'presbyter.' The extent to which experience qualifies him for this role is apparent from something Hopeful says. When Christian asks him the vital question about the origins of his expectations, Hopeful replies: "Nay, do you answer that question yourself, for you are the older man." [67] Greater experience is the basic criterion in evaluating expectations of grace, although in the light of the doctrine of predestination these must always remain basically subjective and approximate. But experience only takes place when preconceptions are called in question by a process of self-examination. Christian tries to inspire this insight in others, in order to prevent them from blocking the road to salvation through the prevailing uncertainty of their expectations. The vital importance of reflection is stressed by Christian during his encounter with Ignorance: "There is none righteous, there is none that doeth good. . . . The imagination of man's heart is evil from his youth. Now then, when we think thus of ourselves, having sense thereof, then are our thoughts good ones, because according to the Word of God." [68]

Ignorance—to whom this admonition is addressed—had exalted the feelings of the heart to the position of highest authority, and so had lost the ability to distinguish between certitude and illusion. He embodies pure subjectivity, believing he can do without experience because he regards the voice of the heart, like the law, as an adequate guide for his own conduct. But a blind faith in one's own heart, or in the precepts of the law, means relinquishing the possibility of conscious acquaintance with one's own situation, for such an insight can only come about through experience; it is experience that reconciles the pilgrim's human

[66] Ibid., p. 138.
[67] Ibid., p. 149.
[68] Ibid., p. 145.

distress with the idea of salvation, relieving the unbearable tensions of the soul and leading eventually to increasing certitude. Christian has learned this lesson, and subsequently corrects in others the naive belief that the promptings of the heart can offer an infallible guide. From the pilgrim's self-inspection there arise a series of experiences as he sallies forth into the world and puts his own body and soul in jeopardy in order to triumph over himself. This series of experiences foreshadows the history of the hero which forms the basic pattern of the eighteenth-century novel.[69]

The significance of experience is clearly brought out during one of the key episodes of the whole story. Christian tells Hopeful the tale of Little-Faith, who on the road to salvation was attacked and robbed by three bandits, Faint-Heart, Mistrust, and Guilt.[70] After a brief description of what happened, there comes a long dialogue between Christian and Hopeful, and in the course of this Christian corrects the false conclusions which Hopeful draws from the conduct of Little-Faith. Hopeful's viewpoint is theologically relevant and understandable, for he remarks that after the robbery Little-Faith clearly lacked the courage to go along the road he knew to be the right one. One would have expected Christian to accept this judgment, for it fits in with the demands any pilgrim had constantly to make of himself in the face of the hardships he was bound to encounter on the way. But Christian's extremely revealing reply is unmistakably a reproach.[71] For him any abstract argument that is not based on concrete experience is a source of irritation, and he proceeds to justify Little-Faith's reaction by referring to just such experience:

> As for a great heart, Little-faith had none; and I perceive by thee, my Brother, hadst thou been the man concerned, thou art but for a brush, and then to yield. And verily since this is the height of thy stomach, now they [i.e., the robbers] are at a distance from us, should they appear to thee as they did to him, they might put thee to second thoughts. But consider again . . . I myself have been engaged as this Little-faith was, and I found it a terrible thing . . . I was clothed with Armour of proof. Ay, and yet though I was so harnessed, I found it hard work to quit myself like a man: no man can tell what in that Combat attends us, but he that hath been in the Battle himself.[72]

[69] See also W. F. Schirmer, *Antike, Renaissance und Puritanismus* (Munich, 1924), pp. 209 f., and W. Kayser, "Die Anfänge des modernen Romans im 18. Jahrhundert und seine heutige Krise," *Deutsche Vierteljahrsschrift für Literaturwissenschaft und Geistesgeschichte* 28 (1954): 434.

[70] Bunyan, *Pilgrim's Progress*, p. 125.

[71] Ibid., p. 128.

[72] Ibid., pp. 129 f.

Only someone who has been in a similar situation is qualified to judge Little-Faith, for only through a similar experience can one feel the degree of anguish that torments the pilgrim on his journey. If this anguish were merely measured by the abstract demands of religious creeds, it would inevitably turn into despair. But the presentation of the exemplary pilgrimage is meant to *cure* the faithful of their despair. This is why Christian defends Little-Faith's despondent reaction, for this is something that all pilgrims have to face at one time or another. However, once it has been faced, the question is how much one is able to learn and benefit from one's anguish. Christian himself is no longer afraid, but it is only *after* one has passed through such fears that one can assess their true significance.

Here, then, we are shown the meaning and importance of experience. The *certitudo salutis* does not arise out of the one-sided guidance of theological commandments, and this is why Christian corrects Hopeful, who can only think in theological terms and therefore overlooks the spontaneity of human reactions in moments of danger. Neither the promptings of the heart nor the precepts of religious dogma are adequate guides for the pilgrim on his journey: the former will make him lose his way in self-justification and the latter in despair. The fact that Christian went through the same despondency as Little-Faith and yet still took his place in the scheme of salvation, because he was able to transform his distress into beneficial knowledge, is what constitutes the instructional basis of *Pilgrim's Progress*. The members of Calvinist sects discovered themselves in Christian—not only in their weak humanity but also through the promise that by self-examination they could overcome their weakness and so attain an increasing degree of certitude. As far as the composition of *Pilgrim's Progress* is concerned, the episode of Little-Faith occupies a special position in that it is the only story in the whole book that is told by one of the characters for the purpose of demonstration. It has the nature of an exemplary narrative[73] concerned not with different stages along the road to salvation, or with the theological demands arising out of these, but simply and solely with human motivation. It throws emphasis on typically human behavior which offers a different view of events than that demanded—or even allowed—by the abstract idea of salvation. This is why there is very little of the allegory about this episode, particularly in the vital second part. Hopeful cannot really understand Little-Faith's

---

[73] Re the form of the exemplary narrative, see Lugowski, *Form der Individualität,* pp. 139 ff.

behavior, because from the standpoint of salvation it seems inconsistent; but for Christian this inconsistency is removed through his own experience in a similar situation.

Experience then is the force that mediates between the human character and its hidden destiny. The withholding of certitude activates the human potential, the manifestations of which orientate the character toward the goal he is striving after. Consequently the focal point of attention is no longer the goal, i.e., salvation, but the means of attainment, i.e., self-examination through experience. This process is fraught with difficulties, because each experience can only call forth subjective and, therefore, unreliable reactions. In order to mitigate the ensuing dangers, the pilgrim must undergo and observe more experiences through which he may accumulate a degree of insight into himself and thereby into his goal. There thus evolves a history of the pilgrim in which the attainment of the objective virtually coincides with the activation of his own human potential through experience. And so in *Pilgrim's Progress* the theological withholding of certitude stimulates human self-assertion, the development of which foreshadows the pattern of the eighteenth-century novel.

V

"Wherever there prevails a mood of intense piety, and wherever life beyond is regarded as the true one, and life here as merely transitory, this life is experienced and shaped as a migration."[74] This is the starting-point of *Pilgrim's Progress*. But the journey is not treated by Bunyan just from one point of view, for there are temporary reconciliations as well as lasting conflicts in Christian's encounters with the world. The pilgrimage in fact begins *before* the journey, in the sense that there are certain as yet incomprehensible signs of salvation which lead to the progressive isolation of the pilgrim before he even knows that he is going on a journey. In Christian's case, this is when he experiences the familiar world as something repugnant. He leaves his family and his birthplace, because he feels "the Powers and Terrors of what is yet unseen."[75] The decision to seek salvation involves cutting all ties with the familiar world, and this in turn means isolation. As Talon has pointed out, it is only after he has taken this decision that the pilgrim is given the name Christian.[76] Through his inner distress, the pilgrim has freed himself from the anonymity of the City of Destruction, and so he becomes a person in his

[74] E. Dabcovich, "Syntaktische Eigentümlichkeiten der Fioretti," in *Syntactica und Stilistica* (Festschrift für Ernst Gamillscheg) (Tübingen, 1957), p. 100.
[75] Bunyan, *Pilgrim's Progress*, p. 15.
[76] See Talon, *John Bunyan*, pp. 165 f.

own right. But these sacrifices gain him nothing positive. When Pliable asks Christian " . . . but, my good Companion, do you know the way to this desired place?", Christian can only answer: "I am directed by a man, whose name is Evangelist, to speed me to a little Gate that is before us, where we shall receive instruction about the way."[77] There is a striking contrast between the radical decision to leave the familiar world and the unknown mystery of the road now opening up before Christian. And so at first most of his actions have a negative quality, because there is no concrete promise as yet to fill the gap of the repugnant world he has rejected. His motivation is not the prospect of future bliss, but a desire to escape from the distressing present. All he does know is that this radical devaluation of his past life can lead him closer to the expectation of something as yet concealed from him. Thus his journey becomes a probing search, which occasionally leads him astray, because the goal remains uncertain and because his only guidelines are his objections to the familiar world and to the weaknesses of human nature.

Christian's sharp conflict with the world—which marks the beginning of the salvation process—is developed thematically in the course of the various adventures that follow. Time and again he is exposed to the dangers and temptations of this world, and it needs all his physical and mental strength to overcome them. But in contrast there are also episodes in which the conflict fades away. Palace Beautiful,[78] Plain Ease,[79] The River of the Water of Life,[80] The Delectable Mountains,[81] and the Country of Beulah[82]—these are all points along the journey at which the pilgrim feels a fairy tale harmony with his surroundings. At such times there is a sense of paradisal security, and the pilgrim has a foretaste of the bliss which is at most a vague inspiration for him during the conflicts of his other adventures. The surprising aspect of these episodes is that they are direct descendants of medieval secular romances, finding their way into this exemplary conduct-book[83] despite the Puritan abhorrence of literature. Both the name and the various features of the Palace Beautiful are a direct reference back to romances of chivalry, to whose enchantments, as Schirmer has stressed, the Puritans were not altogether unsusceptible

---

[77] Bunyan, *Pilgrim's Progress*, p. 15.
[78] Ibid., pp. 47 ff.
[79] Ibid., p. 107.
[80] Ibid., p. 111.
[81] Ibid., pp. 119 ff.
[82] Ibid., pp. 153 f.
[83] See Schirmer, *Antike, Renaissance und Puritanismus*, p. 209 f. and Sharrock, "Spiritual Autobiography," pp. 102 ff., who looks at *Pilgrim's Progress* entirely from the standpoint of the conduct-book.

in their childhood years.[84] The castle by the wayside, the lovely ladies, the Round Table, and the display of treasures are all component parts of vulgarized court romances.[85] These basic features, however, undergo a definite transformation in Bunyan, for they are set in a different frame of reference. Thus the Palace is changed into the Church,[86] and the ladies into cardinal virtues, while the discussion at the table concerns salvation, and the sight of the treasures provides inner reassurance; romantic wrappings are filled with Christian contents. The same applies to the other places where the pilgrim feels tempted to linger awhile. At such moments we find the trappings of the *locus amoenus* mixed with those of the *hortus conclusus,* and they convey an unmistakable atmosphere of Paradise.

The repertoire of motifs from medieval romances is called upon whenever the fundamental conflict between man and world is to be temporarily relieved. With the disappearance of this opposition, the world seems ideal and idyllic, its transfiguration bringing about a surprising harmony between man and reality. But as the orthodox Puritan believed that man's situation was characterized by the conflict and not by the harmony, this inner bliss could only be illustrated through a repertoire from outside the Puritan tradition. The very fact that Bunyan used such a repertoire shows the extent to which the Calvinists abandoned their radical contempt for the world when it had to serve as the setting for an unmistakable manifestation of grace. Although the pilgrim sets forth in the hope of ensuring salvation through overcoming the contemptible world, this very world miraculously changes into a nascent paradise the moment he feels his expectations might come true. "Just as entrance into the sacral precincts means for the believer participation in the hierophany, so the literary fiction of the enclosure offers the possibility of an illusory integration of the self into the totality of salvation. . . . The form of the Romance, which reconciles extremities . . . , offers a literary matrix in which the inner world of the believer and the transcendent world of salvation—which Calvinism had completely separated—can once more be reconciled to one another."[87] The fictionally presented certainty of fulfillment of the yearnings shared by all Puritans was a vital feature of the process of edification, because it offered the imaginary achievement of what was excluded by the doctrine of predestination. The pat-

---

[84] Schirmer, *Antike, Renaissance und Puritanismus,* p. 200.

[85] See H. Golder, "Bunyan and Spenser," *PMLA* 45 (1930): 216, who also discusses the difficult problem of sources.

[86] See Talon, *John Bunyan,* p. 173.

[87] Birkner, *Heilsgewissheit und Literatur,* pp. 109 and 150.

tern of the romance, with its sequence of fight–pathos–fulfillment,[88] corresponded to typical expectations insofar as the genuine anguish of faith was shown, as it were, in the mirror of its possible relief. The fact that the inner struggles and conflicts dominate the pilgrim's journey is representative of the situation of all believers. But only through reflections of and on such a situation can the preconditions be brought about whereby the fairy tale glow surrounding all the places of blissful security can take on the form of a real promise. Thus it is the doubts and despair of the pilgrim that make credible the certitude of fulfillment presented in the schema of the romance.

Of course the havens of security are only sketched in very briefly, for they mark end-points or transitions in the series of past and future ordeals. Indeed this very sparsity indicates on Bunyan's part an acute psychological sense for the effectiveness of the edifying process he had set in motion. A glimpse is far more inspiring than overexposure. It is also worth pointing out that his use of the romance sequence of fight–pathos –fulfillment shows how the same schema can be used for different purposes at different times. This is true not only of medieval court literature as compared with Bunyan's work but also of that same literature compared with the early novel, which during the eighteenth century was to use this same schema in a quite unforeseeable manner.

If the pattern of the romance smacks of triviality through its removal or fulfillment of fears and longings, this affirmative outcome in a Puritan context has a definite historical significance, which considerably outweighs the triviality. For here the affirmation is an indication of how great must have been the distress and despair of the ordinary believer, since his negative situation could only be compensated by fiction. As far as the history of the novel is concerned, this affirmative tendency has undergone a gradual but irrevocable reversal, until now, with the modern novel, we have a high potential of negation in fiction that seeks to break up all the fixed structures of expectation and conduct in the reader.

VI

The epic and allegory of the Middle Ages were firmly based on what Lukács called "God-given security";[89] Bunyan's *Pilgrim's Progress* arises out of the total withdrawal of such security. This vital loss gives human existence an unexpected significance, because only through self-observation was it possible to attain any degree of assurance. Thus the transcendent nature of salvation increases the value of man himself in a manner

[88] Ibid., p. 152.
[89] Lukács, "Theorie des Romans," p. 394.

27

that counterbalances the devaluation brought about by the doctrine of predestination. This is why in *Pilgrim's Progress* so much emphasis is laid on human situations. In this way, individuality increasingly becomes an end in itself, "because it finds in itself that which is essential to it and which makes its life an authentic life—not as the given basis of life, but as something to be searched for."[90] Christian's story is one of an increasing self-awareness, and in this respect it is indisputably a novel, or at least a novel in-the-making. Self-awareness requires experience, and this is what Christian gains in his confrontation with the world. In the novel, experience is the keynote of the action, whereas in the epic and allegory everything was subsidiary to the idea. In *Pilgrim's Progress* the increasing importance of experience is an indication of the fact that this was the only way to get over the consequences of the doctrine of predestination. In a 'God-forsaken' world, it offers the one chance of human self-understanding. Through it, the self and the world can be reconciled in a new way, but since there can be no paradigmatic, universally applicable reconciliation, literary fiction can only offer situational answers to each of the historical problems that need to be solved. The history of these problems and answers constitutes the history of the novel.

Bunyan was faced with the paradoxical task of adapting the conductbook—which for all its systematic orientation remained essentially private—in such a way that he could ensure the general applicability of individual certitude necessary for edification. The conduct-books were first and foremost 'statements of account', which were edifying to the extent that they showed the possibility of attaining certitude of election here and now. But this depended on the absolute truth of the experiences recorded, and the private nature of these was more of a hindrance than a help to the process of edification. And so gradually fabricated stories, which could generalize distress and certitude, provided the most appealing form of edification. One would have assumed that the fictionalization would devalue the trustworthiness of the certitude, but this was clearly not the case, as can be seen from the history of responses to *Pilgrim's Progress.* Obviously, the fictional humanizing of theological rigorism must have fulfilled an elementary historical need, since the Calvinists' strict distinctions between truth and fiction were allowed to fade into the background. And from this historical observation, we might draw a conclusion that will apply to all forms of fiction, from *Pilgrim's Progress* right through to the experimental works of today: namely, that literature counterbalances the deficiencies produced by prevailing philosophies.

[90] Ibid., pp. 260 f.

2

THE ROLE OF THE READER
IN FIELDING'S *JOSEPH ANDREWS*
AND *TOM JONES*

I

A new province of writing":[1] this is what Fielding called his novels. In what way new? Innovations as such in literature are very difficult to perceive; it is only when they are set against a familiar background that we can get some idea of their novelty. Once the new is distinguished from the old, there arises a certain tension, because we have lost the security of the familiar without knowing for sure the precise nature of the innovation. For what is new comes into being through changes in the reader's mind—the casting aside of old assumptions and preconceptions. It is difficult for Fielding as an author to define these changes, since he is concerned with presenting the new and not with merely changing the old.

For innovation itself to be a subject in a novel, the author needs direct cooperation from the person who is to perceive that innovation—namely, the reader. This is why it is hardly surprising that Fielding's novels, and those of the eighteenth century in general, are so full of direct addresses to the reader, which certainly have a rhetorical function, though this is by no means their only function. John Preston's book *The Created Self* is the first full-length study of these apostrophies, which he interprets in

---

[1] Henry Fielding, *Tom Jones* (Everyman's Library) (London, 1957), II, 1: 39.

terms of rhetoric only: "I make no attempt to provide a 'rhetoric of reading', though no doubt this would be worth doing. Rather I trust that the rhetorical principles in question will provide a unifying point of view for these four novels (i.e. *Moll Flanders, Clarissa, Tom Jones,* and *Tristram Shandy*), and yet not seem unduly arbitrary or restrictive. And I should be glad to feel that such an approach might prompt other more radical enquiries into the nature of the reader's role in fiction."[2]

This recommendation for a more radical enquiry can be taken as a starting-point for our discussion. The role which the Fielding novel assigns to its readers is not confined to a willingness to be persuaded. In the act of reading, we are to undergo a kind of transformation, such as W. Booth has described in connection with fiction in general: "The author creates, in short, an image of himself and another image of his reader; he makes his reader, as he makes his second self, and the most successful reading is one in which the created selves, author and reader, can find complete agreement."[3] But this transformation of the reader into the image created by the author does not take place through rhetoric alone. The reader has to be stimulated into certain activities, which may be guided by rhetorical signposts, but which lead to a process that is not merely rhetorical. Rhetoric, if it is to be successful, needs a clearly formulated purpose, but the "new province of writing" that Fielding is trying to open up to his readers is in the nature of a promise, and it can only rouse the expectations necessary for its efficacy if it is not set out in words. The reader must be made to feel for himself the new meaning of the novel. To do this he must actively participate in bringing out the meaning and this participation is an essential precondition for communication between the author and the reader. Rhetoric, then, may be a guiding influence to help the reader produce the meaning of the text, but his participation is something that goes far beyond the scope of this influence. Northrop Frye has referred to an attack on Jakob Böhme which aptly describes the conditions leading to the reader's act of production: "It has been said of Boehme that his books are like a picnic to which the author brings the words and the reader the meaning. The remark may have been intended as a sneer at Boehme, but it is an exact description of all works of literary art without exception."[4]

[2] John Preston, *The Created Self. The Reader's Role in Eighteenth-Century Fiction* (London, 1970), p. 3.

[3] Wayne C. Booth, *The Rhetoric of Fiction* (Chicago, [4]1963), p. 138.

[4] Northrop Frye, *Fearful Symmetry. A Study of William Blake* (Princeton, [3]1967), pp. 427 f.

Eighteenth-century novelists were deeply conscious of this interplay with the reader. Richardson once wrote—admittedly in a letter, and not in the novel itself—that the story must leave something for the reader to do.[5] Laurence Sterne, in *Tristram Shandy,* describes this vital process with the same unmistakable clarity with which he disclosed the principles of fiction as practiced in the novel during the first half of the eighteenth century. He writes in II, 11: "no author, who understands the just boundaries of decorum and good-breeding, would presume to think all: The truest respect which you can pay to the reader's understanding, is to halve this matter amicably, and leave him something to imagine, in his turn, as well as yourself. For my own part, I am eternally paying him compliments of this kind, and do all that lies in my power to keep his imagination as busy as my own."[6] The participation of the reader could not be stimulated if everything were laid out in front of him. This means that the formulated text must shade off, through allusions and suggestions, into a text that is unformulated though nonetheless intended. Only in this way can the reader's imagination be given the scope it needs; the written text furnishes it with indications which enable it to conjure up what the text does not reveal.

Fielding, too, often speaks of the offer of participation that must be made to the reader, if he is to learn to fulfill the promise of the novel. There is a clear reference to this in *Tom Jones:*

> Bestir thyself therefore on this occasion; for, though we will always lend thee proper assistance in difficult places, as we do not, like some others, expect thee to use the arts of divination to discover our meaning, yet we shall not indulge thy laziness where nothing but thy own attention is required; for thou art highly mistaken if thou dost imagine that we intended, when we began this great work, to leave thy sagacity nothing to do; or that, without sometimes exercising this talent, thou wilt be able to travel through our pages with any pleasure or profit to thyself.[7]

This typical appeal to the reader's "sagacity" aims at arousing a sense of discernment. This is to be regarded as a pleasure, because in this way the reader will be able to test his own faculties. It also promises to be profitable, because the need for discernment stimulates a process of learning in the course of which one's own sense of judgment may come under scrutiny. Here we have a clear outline of the role of the reader, which is ful-

---

[5] Cf. Samuel Richardson, *Selected Letters,* ed. J. Carroll (Oxford, 1964), p. 296.
[6] Laurence Sterne, *Tristram Shandy* (Everyman's Library) (London, 1956), II, 11: 79.
[7] *Tom Jones,* XI, 9: 95.

filled through the continual instigation of attitudes and reflections on those attitudes. As the reader is maneuvered into this position, his reactions—which are, so to speak, prestructured by the written text—bring out the meaning of the novel; it might be truer to say that the meaning of the novel only materializes in these reactions, since it does not exist per se.

II

This rough outline of the reader's role is something we can elaborate on. in more detail with reference to *Joseph Andrews* and *Tom Jones,* so that we can see more clearly the nature of the activity required of the reader as he produces the meaning of the novel. In the very first sentence of *Joseph Andrews,* the author mentions the fact that the "mere English reader"[8] will certainly have different conceptions and also different expectations regarding the reading that lies ahead of him. For his reading habits are conditioned by epics, tragedies, and comedies, the underlying principles of which are called to mind so that the enterprise of our own author can be separated from them. Certainly the association of this novel with the hallowed forms of traditional literature was intended by Fielding, primarily, to raise the status of his tale in prose; but just as clear is the intention underlying his description of his work as a "comic epic poem in prose."[9] By listing his deviations from the classical models, he is drawing attention to the unique features of his enterprise. And so the "classical reader"[10] will find pleasure in the "parodies or burlesque imitations"[11] precisely because they conjure up the very 'genre' which they set out to transform.

This process can be linked with what Gombrich terms in esthetics 'schema and correction'.[12] Fielding calls to mind a whole repertoire of familiar literary 'genres', so that these allusions will arouse particular expectations from which his novel then proceeds to diverge. These subsequent divergences are the first step toward innovation.

In the preface, Fielding specifies the differences between his novel and classical predecessors, but these informative indications gradually disappear as the reader begins to fall in with the book. In the first of the initial essays of the novel, again he makes use of a familiar repertoire.

---

[8] Henry Fielding, *Joseph Andrews* (Everyman's Library) (London, 1948), Author's Preface: xxvii.
[9] Ibid.
[10] Ibid., p. xxviii.
[11] Ibid.
[12] Cf. E. H. Gombrich, *Art and Illusion* (London, [2]1962), p. 99.

But here the starting-point is contemporary rather than ancient literature. It is true that he alludes to classical and medieval Lives,[13] but his
main concern here is with Colley Cibber's *Autobiography* and Richardson's *Pamela,* which both fit in perfectly with Fielding's intentions, since
they each present a life-story.[14] But here it is no longer a question of
Fielding showing the differences between his work and the models alluded to. Instead they are shown to be exemplary in a way that Fielding pretends he wants to emulate with his *Joseph Andrews*[15]—and this
regardless of the fact that one biography is fictitious and the other real,
though it is ironically pointed out that there is much fiction in the real
one, and in the fictitious much that presumes to be exemplary for real
life.

If the beginning of the introduction emphasized the divergences from
the established repertoire, now the stress is laid on the similarities, so that
the reader is left to discover the differences for himself—though these
always remain clearly visible thanks to the ever-present irony.[16] *Joseph
Andrews* is not to be read, then, as a glorification of the hero—in the
mould of the Cibber *Autobiography*—or as a moral vade mecum for
worldly success, like Richardson's novel. Here, too, schemata are corrected, though the correction is never formulated. As a result there appears a gap between the familiar repertoire in the novel and one's own
observation of it.

These gaps heighten our awareness, and their effectiveness lies in the
fact that they conceal something of vital importance. As we have seen,
the reader is forced to discover for himself the divergences from the
established repertoire, and at first sight this seems simple enough. The
ironic style is sufficient to show us that the text means the opposite of
what it says; but the situation becomes rather more complicated when
we ask, "What will the opposite of Richardson's *Pamela* and Colley Cibber's *Autobiography* look like?" The answer to this is far from obvious,
and so the ironic allusions can no longer be regarded as a mere reversal
of the written statement.

By negating the familiar, the irony indicates that now something is to
be communicated of which hitherto there has been no proper conception. Our attention is drawn to the difficulty of deducing the exemplary
from the private. Consequently, this negating irony drives us to seek the
proper conception beyond the confines of the familiar models; and in

[13] Cf. *Joseph Andrews,* I, 1: 1.
[14] Cf. ibid., p. 2.
[15] Ibid.
[16] Ibid.

this way, the nonfulfillment of those expectations aroused by the presence of the familiar, becomes the spur that pricks our imagination into action.

The repertoire of the familiar in *Joseph Andrews* is not confined to established literary patterns; it also incorporates various norms that were generally accepted in Fielding's day. The transplanting of these norms into the novel results in their transformation, for here they are presented in a different light from that in which they appeared at the time within the "collective consciousness"[17] we call society. This esthetic arrangement of social norms has certain consequences for the reader which can best be illustrated through the character of Abraham Adams, the real hero of the novel. The list of virtues that Fielding unfolds contains nearly all the qualities that would make up the perfect man. And yet it is his very possession of all these qualities that makes Adams totally incapable of dealing with this world, as Fielding actually points out.[18] The list of virtues is not seen from a Christian or a Platonic stand-point now, but from a worldly one, and from this totally different perspective the virtues appear to lose all their validity; they seem to belong to the past, for they are no longer capable of inspiring sensible conduct in the present. The question now arises as to whether this means that amoral conduct is best suited to this world. Or does it mean that we have to find a compromise relationship between norm and world? If this were so, surely any such compromise would be an intolerable strain, since the two factors—contemporary norms and worldly demands—would forever be tugging us in opposite directions. Virtues cannot be contemplated separately from the world, and the world cannot be viewed without the background of virtue. Is the conflict to be resolved? If so, how, and why? The answers are not given us. They are the gaps in the text. They give the reader the motivation and the opportunity to bring the two poles meaningfully together for himself.

Here, then, we have our first insight into the nature of the reader's active participation, as mobilized by the novel. The repertoire of the familiar—whether it be literary tradition, contemporary 'Weltanschauung', or social reality—forms the background of the novel. The familiar is reproduced in the text, but in its reproduction it seems different, for its component parts have been altered, its frame of reference has changed, its validity has, to a degree, been negated. But if the starting-point of the novel is a set of negations, then the reader is impelled to counterbalance

---

[17] In this essay, 'norm' is understood in the sense in which Jan Mukařovský, *Kapitel aus der Ästhetik* (edition suhrkamp) (Frankfurt, 1970), pp. 43 ff., has defined it.

[18] Cf. *Joseph Andrews*, I, 3: 5.

these negations by seeking their positive potential, the alternate fulfillment of which we shall henceforth call the realization of the text.

Fielding's preoccupation with this aspect of the reader's role can be
traced from the remarks in the preface right through the initial essays in
the novel. After drawing distinctions between his own novel and traditional writings, he continues: "Having thus distinguished Joseph Andrews
from the productions of romance writers on the one hand and burlesque
writers on the other, and given some few very short hints (for I intended
no more) of this species of writing, which I have affirmed to be hitherto
unattempted in our language; I shall leave to my good-natured reader to
apply my piece to my observations."[19] The reader, then, must apply the
author's remarks to his novel, but the text will not tell him how to do
this. The application will coincide largely with the realization. In the
preface, however, Fielding does outline the sphere in which this application is to take place, for he promises that the reader will have revealed
to him the sources of the ridiculous which, he says, spring from the discovery of affectation and hypocrisy.[20] The intention of the novel, then,
is not the presentation of affectation and hypocrisy, but the uncovering
of their ridiculousness, which always occurs with the penetration of
those false appearances that mask all social vices.
However, a discovery of this nature does not end with the unmasking
of vice. Fielding simply says that the veil will fall from the ridiculous,
without saying that this absurdity might carry with it some indication
as to the proper way to conduct oneself. So far the reaction of the reader will signify no more than a feeling of superiority, and the question
arises as to what lies behind this superiority evinced by our laughter. At
best it is an awareness of the potential presence of what proper conduct
should be, although we cannot discount the possibility that our superiority is also based on a misunderstanding. The reader, therefore, must not
only see through the original false appearances; he must also set out
even more intensively to discover the preconditions for model conduct,
to make sure that this superiority, obtained through the unmasking of
absurd vices, does not in its turn become a false appearance. In this
process, ridicule performs a very different function from its function in
the literature of the past: it ceases to stigmatize the lower classes and
instead stimulates the reader's mind into trying to formulate the poten-

[19] Ibid., Author's Preface, p. xxxii.
[20] Cf. ibid., pp. xxx f.

tial morality contained in the unmasking. In order to set such a mental process into operation, the intention of the novel cannot be the subject of narration, for it is only by reconstructing for himself the unformulated part of the text—in this case, the correct mode of conduct—that the reader can experience this intention as a reality.

How this reality is constituted is indicated about half-way through *Joseph Andrews* in Fielding's final theoretical essay (III, 1). He would like to feel that the novel is a kind of mirror, in which the reader can see himself, as it were, through the characters he has been laughing at in apparent superiority. It is his purpose "not to expose one pitiful wretch to the small and contemptible circle of his acquaintance; but to hold the glass to thousands in their closets, that they may contemplate their deformity, and endeavour to reduce it, and thus by suffering private mortification may avoid public shame."[21]

If looking in the glass gives the reader the opportunity for self-correction, then the role assigned to him is clear. In taking this opportunity, he is bound to encounter sides of himself that he had not known about or—worse still—had not wanted to know about; only then can he see that the correct mode of conduct first involves shaking off the familiar. However, it is obvious that correct conduct as such is only a potential thing, which will come into being in as many different ways as there are situations. Fielding makes his characters react almost mechanically and invariably, following the straight and narrow path of their own habits, and in this way the reader is called upon to replace the motivation presented by a motivation that will remove the imbalance of the characters' conduct.

The text, however, leaves out this corrective motivation, although it is not difficult to find. These omissions are repaired by the reader's own imagination. As the text invites him to imagine for himself what would be the right reaction to the given situation, he is bound to make the necessary adjustments consciously, and this process must in turn make him conscious of himself, of his own conduct, and of the customs and prejudices that condition it. This new awareness, Fielding hopes, will make the reader suddenly see himself as he really is, and so the role that he is to play in uncovering the hidden reality of the text will lead ultimately to his uncovering and correcting the hidden reality of himself.

III

If this intention is to be realized, the process of change cannot be left

---

[21] Ibid., III, 1: 144.

entirely to the subjective discretion of the reader—he must, rather, be gently guided by indications in the text, though he must never have the feeling that the author wants to lead him by the nose. If he responds as the author wants him to, then he will play the part assigned to him, and in order to elicit the correct response, the author has certain strategems at his disposal. One of them we have already seen in connection with the repertoire of the familiar—namely, negation. Expectations aroused in the reader by allusions to the things he knows or thinks he knows are frustrated; through this negation, we know that the standards and models alluded to are somehow to be transcended, though no longer on their own terms. These now appear to be, as it were, things of the past; what follows cannot be stated, but has to be realized. Thus negation can be seen as the inducement to realization—which is the reader's production of the meaning of the text. It initiates the act of imagination by which the reader makes the virtual actual, proceeding from the now obsolete norms of the past right through to the 'configurative' meaning of the newly formed present. This is why we often have the impression when reading that we are experiencing the story as an event in our own lives.

In order for such an experience to be possible, the distance between the story and the reader must at times be made to disappear, so that the privileged spectator can be made into an actor. A typical technique used for this purpose is to be seen right at the beginning of the novel, when Joseph has to resist the advances of Lady Booby and her maid. Lady Booby leads on her footman, whom she has got to sit on her bed, with all kinds of enticements, until the innocent Joseph finally recoils, calling loudly upon his virtue. Instead of describing the horror of his Potiphar, Fielding, at the height of this crisis, continues:

> You have heard, reader, poets talk of the statue of Surprise; you have heard likewise, or else you have heard very little, how Surprise made one of the sons of Croesus speak, though he was dumb. You have seen the faces, in the eighteen-penny gallery, when, through the trap-door, to soft or no music, Mr. Bridgewater, Mr. William Mills, or some other of ghostly appearance, hath ascended, with a face all pale with powder, and a shirt all bloody with ribbons;—but from none of these, nor from Phidias or Praxiteles, if they should return to life—no, not from the inimitable pencil of my friend Hogarth, could you receive such an idea of surprise as would have entered in at your eyes had they beheld the Lady Booby when those last words issued out from the lips of Joseph.

"Your virtue!" said the lady, recovering after a silence of two minutes; "I shall never survive it!"[22]
As the narrative does not offer a description of Lady Booby's reaction, the reader is left to provide the description, using the directions offered him. Thus the reader must, so to speak, enter Lady Booby's bedroom and visualize her surprise for himself.

The directions contained in this passage are revealing in several ways. They direct attention to certain social differences between potential readers of the novel. As in the preface, Fielding differentiates between the "mere English reader" and the "classical reader." The one can gear his imagination to the hair-raising shock tactics of well-known contemporary actors; the other can bring the scene to life through classical associations. But such passages also show that Fielding was not only concerned with catering for a varied public; he was also at pains to transcend the social or educational limitations of the individual, as his novel was to reveal human dispositions that were independent of all social strata.

This differentiation between possible types of reader also motivates the variety of directions enabling the reader to imagine Lady Booby's surprise. These directions consist of a whole series of "schematised views,"[23] which present the same event from changing standpoints. There are so many of these views that the means of presentation seems to bypass the thing presented—or in this case, not presented—Lady Booby's surprise. In fact it is the very gap between the "schematised views" and their object that enables the reader to understand the indescribability of that object, thus indicating that he must now picture for himself what the given pictures are incapable of conveying.

The nondescription of Lady Booby's surprise, and the insistence on its inconceivability, create a gap in the text. The narrative breaks off, so that the reader has room to enter into it. The "schematised views" then guide his imagination, but in order that they should not be felt as restrictions, there follows the confession of their inadequacy. Thus the reader's imagination is left free to paint in the scene. But instead of a concrete picture, the reader's imagination is far more likely to create simply the impression of a living event, and indeed this animation can only come about because it is not restricted to a concrete picture. This is why the character suddenly comes to life in the reader—he is creating instead of merely observing. And so the deliberate gaps in the narrative are the

[22] Ibid., I, 8: 20.
[23] For the specific connotation of this term cf. Roman Ingarden, *Das literarische Kunstwerk* (Tübingen, [2]1960), pp. 270 ff.

means by which the reader is enabled to bring both scenes and characters to life.

This process is not set in motion without careful forethought. In this connection there are two observations that are worth making. If the "schematised views" of Lady Booby's reaction are all going to fall short of their target, the question arises as to whether such very precise indications are in fact totally irrelevant to the steering of the reader's imagination. Classical references are interwoven with contemporary, the former creating an effect of pathos, the latter of comedy, if not of farce. The mixture of pathos and comedy tears apart the false appearance with which Lady Booby tried to conceal her lasciviousness. The result is an opportunity for discovery, and the more the reader brings to life himself, the greater the discovery.

Our second observation is along the same lines. Before the scene with Lady Booby, Fielding placed another similar scene, in which Joseph was confronted by the passions of Slipslop. As in the Booby affair, the reader is given a few directions as to how he is to picture these 'attacks'.[24] Between these two scenes, Fielding says: "We hope, therefore, a judicious reader will give himself some pains to observe, what we have so greatly laboured to describe, the different operations of this passion of love in the gentle and cultivated mind of the Lady Booby, from those which it effected in the less polished and coarser disposition of Mrs. Slipslop."[25] Fielding seems to suggest that the effects of love vary according to social standing. And so we are led to anticipate that the scene with Lady Booby will show how the passion of an aristocrat differs from that of a maidservant. The more directly the reader can participate in the removal of such distinctions, the more effective will be this shattering of false expectations. Ideally, then, the reader should take over production of the whole scene, so that the process of animation will lead up to an enhanced awareness of all the implications. The technique mobilizes the reader's imagination, not only in order to bring the narrative itself to life but also—and even more essentially—to sharpen his sense of discernment.

In *Joseph Andrews,* Fielding makes various observations about the reader's role as producer. In the second theoretical essay, for example, he says that reading his book is like a journey, during which the occasion-

---

[24] Cf. *Joseph Andrews,* I, 6: 14.
[25] Ibid., I, 7: 15.

al reflections of the author are to be regarded as resting places which will give the reader the chance to think back over what has happened so far. As these chapters interrupt the narrative, Fielding quite logically calls them "vacant pages."[26] Now these "vacant pages" are themselves large-scale versions of vacancies that occur right through the text, for instance in the Lady Booby scene. And just as the reader is to 'reflect' during these "vacant pages," so too must he reflect during all the other vacancies or gaps in the text. The gaps, indeed, are those very points at which the reader can enter into the text, forming his own connections and conceptions and so creating the configurative meaning of what he is reading. Thanks to the "vacant pages," he can reflect, and through reflection create the motivation through which he can experience the text as a reality. He forms what we might call the 'gestalt' of the text, and it is worth noting that this, too, is indicated by Fielding in *Joseph Andrews*.

When, toward the end of the novel, Adams holds in his arms the son whom he had presumed to be drowned, his overwhelming joy causes him to forget the virtues of moderation and self-control that he has always preached, regardless of what was going on around him; but Fielding intervenes on his hero's behalf: "No, reader; he felt the ebullition, the overflowings of a full, honest, open heart, towards the person who had conferred a real obligation, and of which, if thou canst not conceive an idea within, I will not vainly endeavour to assist thee."[27] The reader is shown the event and the outer appearance, but he is invited, almost exhorted, to penetrate behind that appearance, and finally to thrust it aside altogether, by conceiving the idea *within*. This is an almost direct statement of the role of the reader in this novel. From the given material he must construct his own conception of the reality and hence of the meaning of the text.

This process can perhaps be seen most clearly in the character of Parson Adams and his contacts with the outside world. The vitality of his character is derived largely from the surprises he offers the reader. Even his name, Abraham Adams, suggests conflicting elements in him.[28] The unshakable faith of the biblical Abraham applies to all the parson's convictions, and yet at times these are thwarted by the Adam in him. These

---

[26] Ibid., II, 1: 60.
[27] Ibid., IV, 8: 249.
[28] Cf. Ian Watt, "The Naming of Characters in Defoe, Richardson and Fielding," *RES* 25 (1949): 335, who has given such an illuminating account of the component parts forming the name of Richardson's Pamela Andrews, but who does not seem to avail himself of his insight when he comes to dealing with names in *Joseph Andrews*.

contrasting schemata encroach on each other, and one sometimes represses the other, so that the character cannot be regarded either as Abraham or as Adam; it seems, indeed, as if the character keeps freeing itself from its apparent characteristics. Through the conflict of schemata, the character takes on a definite individuality,[29] at times approaching caricature, and always full of potential surprises for the reader. Caricature depends for its effect on distortion, but distortion in turn depends for its effect on our conception of what is normal. Otherwise, how should we know something was being distorted? In the case of Parson Adams, the unshakable faith of Abraham is blended with the human weakness of Adam—Adam's pragmatic difficulties with Abraham's abstract resolution. These features are emphasized to the point of caricature, but it is for us to decide what the 'normal picture' should look like. At the same time, it is the very oddness of the picture presented that surprises us, and this unexpectedness stimulates those reactions that bring the character to life.

This bringing to life, however, is not an end in itself. It has the function of involving the reader in an action, the meaning of which he must discover for himself. The character is not aware of the conflicting schemata within himself, and the results of this ignorance are apparent right through the novel. Parson Adams, not knowing what he is, takes part in a variety of confrontations with the world, always reacting quite spontaneously, and nearly always reacting inappropriately. The reader, though, is 'in the picture'; not only is he aware of Adams's polarity but also, thanks to the author's numerous directions, he is aware of how inadequately Adams applies his ideal qualities in dealing with the world. Now what does the reader do with this knowledge? The episodes in the novel often become a test for the reader's own capabilities. He sees the world through the eyes of the hero, and the hero through the eyes of a pragmatic world. The result is conflicting views, linked only by their completely negative nature. From Adams's point of view, the worldly conduct of people seems underhand, selfish, and sordid; in the eyes of the world, Adams is ingenuous, narrow-minded, and naive. These two perspectives are completely dominant, and there is no indication whatsoever as to how people really *should* behave. This total absence of balance is intensified by the fact that the characters themselves remain quite unaware of the shamelessness of their so-called worldly wisdom or, in the case of Adams, the impracticality of his idealism.

---

[29] For a detailed discussion ot this problem in the medium of painting cf. Gombrich, *Art and Illusion*, pp. 279 ff., esp. pp. 302 f.

And so the narrative itself has distinctly negative features, although one cannot go so far as to say that the text actually proclaims the sordidness of the world or the stupidity of virtue. The overprecision with which the two negative poles have been presented inevitably adumbrates the positive features that are not formulated in the text. The form, then, of this unwritten text, becomes apparent to the reader as he reads, and so he begins to uncover what we might call the virtual dimension of the text. Virtual, as it is not described in the text; a dimension, insofar as it balances even if it cannot reconcile the two conflicting, mutually negating poles. The virtual dimension is brought about through our forming the 'gestalt' of the text; here we establish consistency between contrasting positions; this is the configurative meaning of the text, where the unformulated becomes concrete; and finally this is the point at which the text becomes an experience for the reader.

At first sight, the configurative meaning may appear simple enough to find: the polarity shows all too clearly the inadequacy of Adams's virtuous conduct and the baseness of worldly behavior. Adams should learn to adapt himself better to the world, and worldly people should realize the depravity of their vices. The reader sees the faults of both sides. However, on closer analysis, this apparent simplicity and symmetry will be seen to be misleading—a fact which enables our virtual dimension to take on a far more complex reality. The fact that Adams's steadfast virtue prevents him from adapting himself to the situations that arise, does not mean that the virtual balance would be found in continual adaptation to circumstances. For those characters who do adapt themselves to each new situation unmask their own worldly corruption.[30] And so although a balancing of the two poles will take place in the virtual dimension, this will not be in the sense of reconciling steadfastness with inconstancy, cunning with virtue; it will be a convergence at a point somewhere between or even above the two poles. It is possible simply because the reader has that which both poles lack and, in equal measure, need: insight into themselves. The acquisition of this insight is the aim that Fielding pursues, and the process of bringing characters and scenes to life is the means to this end.

As the reading process coincides with the establishment of the virtual dimension of the text, the impression might arise that the reader's balancing of the poles will gradually endow him with a degree of superiority over the characters. In the matter of overall observation, he *is* super-

---

[30] Cf. Irvin Ehrenpreis, "Fielding's Use of Fiction. The Autonomy of Joseph Andrews" in *Twelve Original Essays on Great English Novels*, ed. Charles Shapiro (Detroit, 1960), p. 23.

ior, but in another sense the superiority must be shown to be illusory or else the novel could not work as a glass reflecting the reader's own weaknesses—as Fielding intends it to do. Furthermore, it would be impossible to gain the right kind of insight, since this can only come about through awareness of one's own inadequacy and not in an affirmation of one's own superiority. And so the strategy of the novelist must be such that the reader, in bringing about the virtual dimension, is actually entangled in what he has produced. Only in this way does the reading process become something alive and dramatic, and this is vital since its meaning is not to be illustrated by the characters, but is to take place within the reader.

For this purpose, the author must employ stratagems of various types, with a view to involving the reader on as many levels as possible. First, the reader must be given this feeling of superiority, and so the author takes care to supply him with knowledge that is unavailable to the characters. This privileged position is necessary because if the reader is to play the part intended for him, then for the duration of his reading he must be, so to speak, taken out of himself. The easiest way to entice him into opening himself up is to give him a grandstand view of all the proceedings. This is achieved by a simple stratagem: putting Adams in a variety of situations that he cannot see through. For instance, even at the end, when he meets Peter Pounce, Lady Booby's steward, we read: "Peter was a hypocrite, a sort of people whom Mr. Adams never saw through."[31] The very character who is possessed of the highest degree of integrity is devoid of the faculty emphasized in Fielding's preface as the intention of the novel: seeing through hypocrisy.

This defect in Adams runs through all the episodes of the novel in so unmistakable a fashion that the reader inevitably begins to look down on this, the novel's ambassador of morality. He feels that he has a far better grasp of Adams's situation than the parson himself, confined as he is within the limitations of his own steadfast convictions; the reader's feeling of superiority begins to grow. But his recognition of the unsuitability of Adams's mode of conduct has two sides, for it puts the reader in the position of the worldly wise, thrusting him closer to those characters to whom Adams seems ridiculous. In condemning Adams's lack of pragmatic sense, the reader unexpectedly finds himself on the side of those very people whose pretensions he should be seeing through and who can hardly represent the proper perspective from which he is to judge Adams.

[31] *Joseph Andrews*, III, 12: 212.

And so the reader's insight becomes distinctly ambivalent. He cannot identify himself with the viewpoint of the worldly wise, for that would mean abandoning the insight he had gained in the unmasking of their hypocrisy. But when throughout a whole series of situations he finds himself sharing their views, which nevertheless he cannot allow to be his guide, then he is left in a state of suspense; his superiority becomes an embarrassment. The problems thus aroused are necessary to entangle him in the configurative meaning he is producing; only when this happens, can the effect of the novel really begin to work on the reader.

If Adams's conduct often strikes the reader as naive, such an impression naturally shows Adams in a negative light, and the question arises as to whether the reader is in a position to nullify this negative impression. The reason for what we regard as Adams's impracticality lies, after all, in his moral steadfastness; and this is what the reader comes up against in all those situations that reveal the impracticality. Is moral steadfastness to be regarded, then, as a condition for doing the wrong thing? Or does the reader now discover how small a part morality plays in the formation and application of his insight, even though he thinks he knows opportunism cannot be the criterion, either? At such moments he lacks orientation, which is something Adams has, without any self-doubts; he begins to fall from his position of superiority, and the configurative meaning of the novel becomes altogether richer. For now the moral conflict—of which the characters are generally relieved, thanks largely to the intervention of providence—takes place in the reader himself.

The conflict can only be resolved by the realization of the virtual morality. This has already been prestructured by the strategems of the text insofar as the reader's acquired insight separates him from the society of the worldly wise and also shows him that his supposed superiority over Adams can only be based on a lack of moral steadfastness within himself. This is how the reader becomes trapped by his superiority. If he feels superior to the worldly wise, because he can see through them, then when he turns his attention to Adams, he is obliged to see through himself, because in the various situations he reacted differently from Adams. And if he wants to see through Adams, in order to maintain his superiority, then he is obliged to share the views of those whom he is continually unmasking. The worldly wise are lacking in morality, the moralist in self-awareness, and these two negative poles carry with them a virtual ideality against which the reader must measure himself; this ideality is the configurative meaning of the text, the product of the reader's own insight, creating standards below which he must not fall. This process, whereby the reader formulates the unwritten text, requires active participation on his part, and thus the formulated meaning becomes a direct product and a direct experience of the reader.

"A Book is a machine to think with."[32] So said I. A. Richards, and it seems that *Joseph Andrews* is one of the first novels of the eighteenth century to which this description can be well and truly applied. We can see clearly from the role of the reader, as we have observed it, that the novel is no longer confined to the presentation of exemplary models, à la Richardson, inviting emulation; instead the text offers itself as an instrument by means of which the reader can make a number of discoveries for himself that will lead him to a reliable sense of orientation. A theme in *Joseph Andrews* that lends support to this conception of the novel is that of the relationship between book and world.

There are a number of situations in which Adams thinks he can settle the controversies and supply the urgently needed elucidations by referring to books—especially to Homer[33] and Aeschylus. For him, books and the world are the same thing; he still clings to the time-honored view that the world is a book, and so the meaning of the world must be present in a book. For Adams it goes without saying that literature, as an imitation of Nature, is a great storehouse of good conduct,[34] so that the actual deeds of men can only be measured against this criterion and are naturally always found wanting. This explicit affirmation of the value of literature involves implicitly imprisoning oneself in a fabric of phantasy and delusion. This in turn prevents one from making a correct assessment of empirical situations, since these are generally far too complex to be dealt with in accordance with one set formula. Very few issues are so cut-and-dried that they can be settled by reference to fictional example, and so Fielding's hero becomes quite absurd whenever he tries to supply a literary reduction of some empirical problem and believes that he has thus found the solution.

Occasionally, however, Adams seems to depart spontaneously from his models, for instance in the scene when he throws his beloved Aeschylus into the fire. In a different context, Mark Spilka says of this scene: "Here Adams has literally stripped off an affectation while revealing his natural goodness—the book is a symbol, that is, of his pedantry, of his excessive reliance upon literature as a guide to life, and this is what is

---

[32] I. A. Richards, *Principles of Literary Criticism* (London, 1960, [1]1924), p. 1.
[33] Cf. *Joseph Andrews*, II, 17: 138 ff.
[34] Cf. ibid., II, 9: 100, and II, 2: 151 f.

tossed aside during the emergency. Later on, when the book is fished out of the fire, it has been reduced to its simple sheepskin covering— which is Fielding's way of reminding us that the contents of the book are superficial, at least in the face of harsh experience."[35] This spontaneous gesture is a manifestation of the incongruity of book and world, which Adams is not yet conscious of, even though he occasionally acts accordingly. The reader, however, is aware that the old equation of book and world has been negated and that the book has taken on a new function. Instead of representing the whole world, the novel illustrates points of access to the world; to do this it must offer the reader a kind of lens by means of which he will learn to see the world clearly and be able to adapt himself to it. Since the world is far greater in scope than the book can ever be, the book can no longer offer panacea-like models, but must open up representative approaches to which the reader must adjust for himself. This is the didactic basis of Fielding's novel, made necessary by the empiric variety of the world. The right mode of conduct can be extracted from the novel through the interplay of attitudes and discoveries; it is not presented explicitly. And so the meaning of the novel is no longer an independent, objective reality; it is something that has to be formulated by the reader. In the past, when book and world were regarded as identical, the book formulated its own exemplary meaning, which the reader had only to contemplate; but now that the reader has to produce the meaning for himself, the novel discloses its attitudes through degrees of negation, thwarting the reader's expectations and stimulating him to reflection which in turn creates a counterbalance to the negativity of the text. Out of this whole process emerges the meaning of the novel. Historically speaking, perhaps one of the most important differences between Richardson and Fielding lies in the fact that with *Pamela* the meaning is clearly formulated; in *Joseph Andrews* the meaning is clearly waiting to be formulated.

IV

Since it is the reader who produces the configurative meaning of the novel, certain controls are essential to prevent his subjectivity from playing too dominant a part. This is the function of the author-reader dialogue, the extent of which in Fielding varies in proportion to the increased complexity of the narrative. This is certainly the case in *Tom Jones*. This

[35] Mark Spilka, "Comic Resolution in Fielding's Joseph Andrews" in *Fielding. A Collection of Critical Essays* (Twentieth Century Views), ed. Ronald Paulson (Englewood Cliffs, 1962), p. 63.

imaginary dialogue refrains from prescribing norms of judgment for the reader, but it continually gives him guidelines as to how he is to view the proceedings. The reader is offered a framework for his realization of the text, and this is not confined merely to the initial essays, but is often in the form of directives right in the middle of the action. This system of control might be called the explicit guidance of the reader; its function is to allow the implicit guidance to take its full effect. The complexity of *Tom Jones* arises from its subject matter, the presentation of human nature, of which the unmasking of affectation and hypocrisy—the theme of *Joseph Andrews*—embodies only one aspect; instead of seeing through, it is a matter now of recognizing. The difference is pinpointed by John Preston's description of the plot: "The plot of *Tom Jones,* then, may be best understood in terms of the way it is read. Its structure is the structure of successive responses to the novel. It exists in the reader's attention rather than in the written sequences. This means that its effect is epistemological rather than moral. It helps us to see how we acquire our knowledge of human experience; it is a clarification of the processes of understanding."[36] This clarification is synchronic with insight into human nature, and the question we are concerned with is how the reader can be made to bring it about.

We shall confine ourselves to the development of the principle underlying the reader's role in *Tom Jones.* Our attention will be turned mainly to the way in which the complexity arising from a presentation of human nature can be preserved, although at the same time it must inevitably be simplified by the stratagems which the author uses in order to convey it.

In this context, the imaginary dialogue with the reader offers much that is revealing. When Fielding explains the reason for his many theoretical essays, he defines a basic principle that gives shape to the whole novel:

And here we shall of necessity be led to open a new vein of knowledge, which if it hath been discovered, hath not, to our remembrance, been wrought on by any antient or modern writer. This vein is no other than that of contrast, which runs through all the works of the creation, and may probably have a large share in constituting in us the idea of all beauty, as well natural as artificial: for what demonstrates the beauty and excellence of anything but its reverse? Thus the beauty of day, and that of summer, is set off by the horrors of night and winter. And, I

---

[36] Preston, *The Created Self,* p. 114.

believe, if it was possible for a man to have seen only the two former, he would have a very imperfect idea of their beauty.[37]

The importance Fielding attaches to this principle of contrast can be seen from his claim that he is the first to have written about it. Even if this is merely taken to be a rather bold piece of self-advertisement, at least it indicates clearly to the reader that this principle will provide him with a key to the narrative. And perhaps ultimately there may be grounds for regarding Fielding's claim as at least plausible.

The principle of contrasts sheds a significant light on the role intended for the reader of *Tom Jones*. If a phenomenon can only be properly conveyed with the aid of its contrast, this means that the reader must provide the link between the two, so that he is very much drawn into the imaginative process necessary to evoke the phenomenon. The contrast that Fielding calls the "reverse" implies that an idea, a norm, or an event can only take on its full shape in the reader if it is accompanied more or less simultaneously by its negative form. This will bring out what is concealed if one sees the phenomenon only in isolation, and so the negative form, through its contradictory character, helps to reveal the true content of the phenomenon by outlining all that is missing from it. In the resultant interaction between the positive and the negative, there comes into being a whole dynamic process—not in the text itself, for this only sets up the two sides of the contrast, but in the imagination of the reader, which is to produce a picture of the phenomenon. This picture does not coincide with either of the two contrasting sides; its position is rather in the space between them,[38] where it forms what is not given in the text—namely, an explicit conception of the phenomenon concerned. And so the negative form has two functions: it establishes a contrast, and through the resulting differences brings about an essential condition for the understanding of the phenomenon. Fielding rightly considered this process to be a "new vein of knowledge."

However, the principle of contrasts is not only vital to understanding. It also constitutes an important stratagem for guiding the reader and ensuring that the text will be understood in the way the author intended it to be. Pairs of contrasts give rise to a relatively clear view of the object, and so the author can control the formation of this view through the relation of the contrasts. This will also sharpen the reader's sense of dis-

---

[37] *Tom Jones,* V, 1: 153.

[38] For a more detailed analysis of the function of 'gaps' in literary texts cf. Wolfgang Iser, "Indeterminacy and the Reader's Response in Prose Fiction," in *Aspects of Narrative* (English Institute Essays), ed. J. Hillis Miller (New York, 1971), pp. 1–45.

cernment and will lead to closer if not more reflective reading. For as one reads, one is forced to make many comparisons which concern not only the difference between the phenomenon and its negative form but also the images that have been formed and retained in one's memory by the balancing of previous contrasts, and that now form a background for the image that is to come into being at this particular moment. This process reveals the virtual dimension of the novel,[39] which is produced by means of contrasts and at the same time prestructured by them to the extent that they enable the reader to realize (in the sense of make real) the intention of the work.

The contrasts in *Tom Jones* are far from being uniform; they are sufficiently varied to conjure up an equally varied image of human nature in the reader's imagination. But one thing must be kept in mind: the principle of contrast is primarily a strategem used in the novel, and it is not a definition of human nature itself, which for all its contrastive variety does have a virtual point of convergence. The idea of the "reverse" can be observed at all different levels of the novel: most obviously on the level of the story, and most diffusely in the interplay of the characters.

Human nature, says Fielding at the start of the novel, will be set against contrasting backgrounds: ". . . we shall represent human nature at first to the keen appetite of our reader, in that more plain and simple manner in which it is found in the country, and shall hereafter hash and ragoo it with all the high French and Italian seasoning of affectation and vice which courts and cities afford. By these means, we doubt not but our reader may be rendered desirous to read on for ever."[40] Revealing human nature through a fabric of social contrasts can have two implications. First, there is the reference to a socially differentiated public that has varying degrees of familiarity with the opposed poles of town and country. Here, as in *Joseph Andrews,* we see Fielding trying to gauge the disposition of his readers by means of class orientation and then to transcend it through the representation of human nature. For in the course of the novel, this will always seem to vary according to the background, so that only the technique of contrast can bring to light the hidden sides that inevitably stimulate the reader into trying to discover the identity of human nature. This is why, according to Fielding, the reader will want to read on forever. Second, this method of revealing human nature im-

---

[39] For the specific connotation of this term cf. ibid., pp. 23 ff.
[40] *Tom Jones,* I, 1: 3.

plies a schema that will determine the structure of the contrasts within the story.[41] If human nature appears first against a background of country life, then the reader will perceive a number of aspects which will be concealed or even completely suppressed when human nature is 'transferred', so to speak, to the town. However, the reader does have a built-in guide at his disposal, and this enables him to perceive human nature against its new town background, and so gain a sharper insight into those circumstances that have caused a distortion in the picture he had already formed of human nature. Thus he will not only discover the potential goodness in the apparently corrupt nature of man, as evinced by the hero; he will also understand the conditions responsible for this reversal of the image.

In order to make sure that the reader is sufficiently activated, certain sections of the story are specially reinforced. A typical example is the intercalated tale of the Man of the Hill, whose character was originally akin to that of the hero, but who has been turned by bitter experience into a whole-hearted misanthropist who can believe in nothing but the badness of human nature.[42] This story within a story is in the Cervantes tradition and has the same function as in *Don Quixote:* it transforms the intention of the main action into its very opposite, in order to give the reader a clear view of what he is supposed to see. When the Man of the Hill reduces human nature to incurable corruption, at that very moment the hero realizes its "utmost diversity":[43] The greater the contrasts, the greater the reader's obligation to form his own judgment. The extremity of the contrast demands a change in the two poles, which disappear in a general view of human nature, since the reduction to a single quality (or defect) is as emphatically negated as the uncontrolled diversity. If this intercalated story of the Man of the Hill is tedious—as many readers find—the reason lies in the fact that the contrast is too clear-cut. The conclusion suggested to the reader is predetermined, and leaves practically no room for him to maneuver.

This is not so with those contrasts where the poles are not pulled apart, but telescoped together. There are a large number of examples—mainly toward the end of the novel—the most striking being where the hero is in danger of final and complete ruination through the rendezvous

---

[41] This point was also stressed by R. S. Crane, "The Concept of Plot and the Plot of 'Tom Jones'," in *Critics and Criticism 'Ancient and Modern,'* ed. R. S. Crane (Chicago, 1952), p. 632, who maintained that the various contrasts and their possible resolutions give rise to "a pervasively comic form" of the plot of *Tom Jones.*

[42] Cf. *Tom Jones,* VIII, 15: 386.

[43] Ibid.

with Lady Bellaston. But before Tom follows up the ominous invitation, a chapter is inserted[44] which brings him together with the highwayman whose life he once saved. Thus the reader sees the one almost inexcusable lapse of the hero against the background of his goodness, which remains unshakable even in situations of the utmost peril. The effect of these contrasts is telescopic in the sense that we are made aware of human corruptibility, but this awareness is tempered by the reassuring reminder of Tom's inherent goodness. The emphasis at this point on human weakness is necessary to counterbalance our otherwise total sympathy for the hero, which would obscure the very human tendency to be led astray by the seamier side of life. For the presentation of human nature would be incomplete if it were reduced to perfect conformity with an ideal moral code.

And so the reader is not merely told a story; instead he has constantly to observe and deduce. Fielding remarks right at the beginning that he has not spread his story out to its fullest extent, but has confined it to significant events so that the reader can use the ensuing pauses for reflection: ". . . that by these means we prevent him [i.e., the reader] from throwing away his time, in reading without either pleasure or emolument, we give him, at all such seasons, an opportunity of employing that wonderful sagacity, of which he is master, by filling up these vacant spaces of time with his own conjectures."[45]

The vacant spaces in the text, here as in *Joseph Andrews,* are offered to the reader as pauses in which to reflect. They give him the chance to enter into the proceedings in such a way that he can construct their meaning. How necessary this is can be seen from the interaction of the characters. Two indications given to the reader, both pointing in the same direction, show him the difficulty with which he is to be confronted. In one of the initial essays on the socially variegated dispositions of his readers, from whom in the last analysis his judgments derive, Fielding observes: ". . . life most exactly resembles the stage, since it is often the same person who represents the villain and the heroe."[46] In a different context this statement occurs in a different form: "For though the facts themselves may appear, yet so different will be the motives, circumstances, and consequences, when a man tells his own story, and when his enemy tells it, that we scarce can recognize the facts to be one

---

[44] Cf. ibid., XIII, 10: 192 ff.
[45] Ibid., III, 1: 71.
[46] Ibid., VII, 1: 254.

and the same."[47] If this is so, then the sagacity that Fielding steadfastly attributes to his readers is not to be exercised on the mere facts or on the contradictory words and actions of the persons concerned; it is to penetrate behind these. With this act of penetration, the reader himself produces a reversal, for the inconsistency he experiences summons up those memories which are contradicted by the surprising facts and unexpected actions. Now a balancing operation is set in motion, and this aims at finding a point of convergence that will provide a motivation for the surprises and contradictions. This process is of considerable importance to the relationship of reader to hero. The more the reader discovers of the hidden motives, the greater will be his sympathy for the hero, which is vital for the single reason that in him human nature is shown in action. The consequence of this for the reader, in his role as observer, is that he thereby learns to distinguish between motive and action.[48]

This sense of discernment is enhanced by the rich repertoire of contemporary norms incorporated into the novel and presented as the respective guiding principles of the most important characters. In general, these principles are set out as more or less explicit contrasts. This applies to Allworthy (benevolence) in relation to Squire Western (ruling passion), and to the two pedagogues, Square (the eternal fitness of things) and Thwackum (the human mind [as] a sink of iniquity), in their relations to each other and, individually, to Allworthy. There are also other facets of this novel that are set out in contrasts: for instance, love, in the sequence of Sophia (the ideality of natural inclinations), Molly Seagrim (temptation), and Lady Bellaston (depravity). There are other contrasting relations along the same lines, but these are frequently only the background to set off the hero. Thus we have the contrasting relationship between Tom and Blifil: the latter follows the norms of his instructors and gets corrupted; the former goes against them, and becomes all the more human.

The much praised complexity of the novel arises first and foremost from the fact that the hero is placed against the very variegated backgrounds of a whole repertoire of norms. The resultant situations generally reveal a discrepancy: the reader realizes that the conduct of the hero cannot be subsumed under the norms, while the norms shrink to a re-

---

[47] Ibid., VIII, 5: 333.

[48] Fielding emphasized this idea in Tom Jones, III, 1: 72, by stating explicitly: "Now, in the conjectures here proposed, some of the most excellent faculties of the mind may be employed to much advantage, since it is a more useful capacity to be able to foretel the actions of men, in any circumstance, from their characters, than to judge of their characters from their actions. The former, I own, requires the greater penetration; but may be accomplished by true sagacity with no less certainty than the latter."

strictive definition of human nature. This is already an interpretation, for in the text such 'syntheses' are presented only very rarely. How does this interpretation come about? The discrepancies demand to be smoothed out, for clearly the reader cannot look through the contrasting perspectives of norm and hero simultaneously—instead he will switch from one to the other. If the norm is to be made the theme then he will adopt the standpoint of the hero, and vice versa. An abandoned theme does not disappear completely, but becomes a virtual position enabling us to comprehend the theme. This textual structure guides the attention of the reader, and indeed often conveys the impression to him that in changing levels he is operating the perspectives himself. When the hero violates the given norms—which happens with extraordinary frequency—the resultant situation is open to two possible interpretations: either the norm appears to be an excessive simplification of human nature—in which case the hero constitutes the virtual level of observation—or the violation shows what is lacking in human nature—and then it is the norm that acts as the virtual standpoint.

This stratagem has certain consequences for the way in which human nature is presented to the reader. With those characters that represent a norm—especially Allworthy, Squire Western, Square, and Thwackum—human nature contracts into a single principle, which inevitably puts a negative slant on all things that are not in agreement with that principle. This is true even of Allworthy,[49] whose allegorical name indicates a moral integrity which, however, through its one-sidedness frequently blocks his vision and even his judgment. Thus the apparently negative aspects of human nature fight back, as it were, against the principle itself and cast doubts upon it in proportion to its limitations. In this way the negation of other possibilities by the norm in question gives rise to a virtual diversification of human nature, which takes on a definite form to the extent that the norm is revealed as a restriction on human nature. Negation here shows those "imperative and exhortatory" characteristics that Kenneth Burke has ascribed to it,[50] for it directs the reader's attention to the virtual diversity of human nature that is excluded by the norm.

Now if we are to be given a view of human nature that is to run counter to the prevailing norms, then this view cannot itself have a normative character. If it did, then it would suffer from the same limitations as are exposed by the implicit negation of the norms. Fielding cannot simply

---

[49] Cf. Michael Irwin, *Henry Fielding. The Tentative Realist* (Oxford, 1967), pp. 137 f. and the conclusion he draws from what might be considered an inconsistency in the portrayal of Allworthy.

[50] Kenneth Burke, *Language as Symbolic Action* (Berkeley and Los Angeles, 1966), p. 423.

offer up a particular value as a cast-iron representation of human nature, because such a positive reification would be as unacceptable a reduction as that of the negated norms. It is true that Fielding does postulate a value—that of good-nature—but this can only be presented by way of certain refractions. In relation to the norms, the hero's good heart appears more like something corrupt, since it can only show itself by violation of the norms.[51] And then again this goodness is refracted by the diverse circumstances in which the hero lands himself. Empirical situations influence the form in which this value can actually be manifested. Because of the limitations inherent in these situations, it is not the value itself which emerges so much as distortions of it, so that an adequate picture of its virtual 'gestalt' can only be put together by means of a large number of distorted manifestations.

This whole process is a vital strategem for the way in which human nature is presented in *Tom Jones*. The norms embodied in the minor characters act as a restriction which unfolds a whole series of negated possibilities almost like a fan; as far as the hero is concerned, both norms and empirical circumstances act as restrictions, unfolding his good-nature again in a fan of distorted manifestations. And so we have two distinct sets of negative presentations of human nature, and it is up to the reader to release the positive that is inherent in these negatives.

As Fielding so frequently reminds us, this realization of human nature requires our own sagacity. This means that we must penetrate the outer appearances of situations and perspectives, and get through to their motivations; by uncovering the immanent motive, we can assess and correct the situation, and through the resultant judgment show that human nature is characterized by its independence of, and superiority to any given situation. What the hero has yet to learn—"prudence" and "circumspection"[52]—is what Fielding makes the subject of the exercise he is giving to the reader's sagacity. This exercise combines the esthetic with the didactic intention of the novel: the esthetic pleasure lies in the opportunity for the reader to discover things for himself; the didactic profit lies in his availing himself of this opportunity, which is not intended by the author as an end in itself, but is to serve as training for the reader's sense of discernment.

It is scarcely surprising that at certain critical moments Fielding casts his readers in the role of advocate: ". . . as I am convinced most of my

---

[51] So ". . . it was the universal opinion of all Mr Allworthy's family that he (i.e., Tom Jones) was certainly born to be hanged" (*Tom Jones*, III, 2: 73).
[52] Cf. *Tom Jones*, III, 7: 92, and XVIII, Chapter the Last: 427.

readers will be much abler advocates for poor Jones"[53]—the reader being, as it were, in opposition to the two pedagogues, who with their faulty judgments continually censure Tom's conduct. The recurrent use of such legal images[54] underlines the aim of the novel—to induce the reader to make balanced judgments. For only then will it be possible for the many facets of human nature offered in *Tom Jones* to be integrated into a properly proportioned model of it. The diversity which comes about through the negation of prevailing norms can no longer be conveyed in terms of those norms. And so the reader must form his judgment from one case to the next, for it is only through a whole chain of such judgments that he can form a conception of this diversity. The presentation of the appearance of human nature by means of different situations demands that the reader should think in terms of situations, and this reflects an historical trend of the eighteenth century—namely, the revaluation of empirical reality as against the universal claims of normative systems.

The role of the reader as incorporated in the novel must be seen as something potential and not actual. His reactions are not set out for him, but he is simply offered a frame of possible decisions, and when he has made his choice, then he will fill in the picture accordingly. There is scope for a great number of individual pictures, as is evident from the history of the reception of Fielding's novels.[55] Fielding was to a certain extent aware that, despite the directions given in the author-reader dialogue and the implications of the role assigned to the reader, the scope for realization could not be rigidly controlled. He speaks occasionally of the skepticism of the reader,[56] which will hinder the development of some of his intentions. He was also convinced that his novel offered the reader views which the latter was bound to find in conflict with his own experience:

> For though every good author will confine himself within the bounds of probability, it is by no means necessary that his characters, or his incidents, should be trite, common, or vulgar; such as happen in every

---

[53] Ibid., III, 9: 95.

[54] These images become very conspicuous when Fielding deals with the moral function of conscience which is cast into the role of "the Lord High Chancellor" who "judges, acquits, and condemns according to merit and justice" (*Tom Jones*, IV, 6: 118).

[55] Cf. F. T. Blanchard, *Fielding the Novelist. A Study in Historical Criticism* (New Haven, 1926) and Heinz Ronte, *Richardson und Fielding. Geschichte ihres Ruhms* (Kölner Anglistische Arbeiten 25) (Leipzig, 1935).

[56] *Tom Jones*, VIII, 1: 317.

street, or in every house, or which may be met with in the home articles of a newspaper. Nor must he be inhibited from showing many
persons and things, which may possibly have never fallen within the
knowledge of great part of his readers. If the writer strictly observes
the rules above-mentioned, he hath discharged his part; and is then in-
titled to some faith from his reader, who is indeed guilty of critical
infidelity if he disbelieves him.[57]

Whenever this "critical infidelity" occurs in the reception of the novel,
then the work is reduced to the level of its individual reader's disposition;
but the reader's role—despite the necessity for making selections—is meant
to open him up to the workings of the text, so that he will leave behind
his individual disposition for the duration of his reading. In this way, and
in this way only, he will gain a positive and active insight into human nature. The fact that throughout their long history Fielding's novels have
aroused so many different reactions and have yet survived is proof enough
of the diversity of human nature and of Fielding's genius in conveying it.

[57] Ibid., p. 321. Preston, *The Created Self,* p. 198, has remarked on Fielding's idea of the
reader: "Thus the reader, who only matters to Fielding in so far as he *is* a reader, is being defined
by what the book will demand of him."

3

THE GENERIC CONTROL OF THE
ESTHETIC RESPONSE:
An Examination of Smollett's *Humphry Clinker*

I

Although a novel addresses itself to a reader, literary criticism has been mainly concerned with the author's point of view, paying little attention to how the reader might be affected. If one changed this predominant perspective a text would have to be studied according to the influence it exercises over the reader. Such an approach would concern itself less with the actual subjects portrayed than with the means of communication by which the reader is brought into contact with the reality represented by the author. In other words, this observation is concerned primarily with the form of a work, insofar as one defines form basically as a means of communication or as a negotiation of insight. Kenneth Burke has introduced into the critical discussion of form the terms "semantic" and "poetic meaning." He defines "semantic meaning" with the statement that "the semantic ideal would attempt to get a description by the elimination of attitude." "Poetic meaning," on the other hand, is intended to awaken specific attitudes in the reader by what Burke calls the "strategy of communication."[1] It is worth not-

---

[1] Kenneth Burke, *The Philosophy of Literary Form* (New York [Vintage Book], 1967), pp. 109 f. and 128.

ing that he equates the term "poetic" with the effect a text has upon the reader.

It is certainly not easy to define this poetic meaning, but one might perhaps suggest that it lies in the communication of new experiences hitherto unknown to the reader. In support of this contention, we could quote Henry James, who wrote in 1883: "The success of a work of art . . . may be measured by the degree to which it produces a certain illusion; that illusion makes it appear to us for the time that we have lived another life—that we have had a miraculous enlargement of experience."[2] If one examines a text from the standpoint of what reactions it might arouse in the reader, it must be admitted that there are as yet very few reliable criteria for such a study. One could of course analyze the rhetoric contained in a text, since the interplay of rhetorical devices has the function of persuading and so manipulating the reader. In his book *The Rhetoric of Fiction,* Wayne Booth developed certain classifications for the rhetoric of prose. They show that the reader can be influenced by applying various devices: disclosure, partial disclosure, concealment, direction of intention, evocation of suspense, introduction of the unexpected—these are all means of stimulating a specific reaction in the reader. If one follows that line, works of art should be analyzed less from the point of view of representation than from that of suggestion. The text should be understood as a combination of forms and signs designed to guide the imagination of the reader.

The effectiveness of a text does not depend solely on rhetoric, however. The critic must also take into consideration the reader's expectations. Through his past experiences, the educated reader expects specific things from prose and poetry; but many works of art play about with those expectations formed by particular periods of literature in the past. The expectations can be shattered, altered, surpassed, or deceived, so that the reader is confronted with something unexpected which necessitates a readjustment. If this does happen, the reader gains what Henry James called an "enlargement of experience." However, texts do not necessarily have to be based on expectations formed by the literature of the past. They can themselves awaken false expectations, alternately bringing about surprise and frustration, and this in turn gives rise to an esthetic experience consisting of a continuous interplay between 'deductive' and 'inductive' operations which the reader must carry out for himself. In this way, the experience communicated through the work of art becomes real to the reader. For whenever his expectations are not ful-

[2] *Theory of Fiction: Henry James,* ed. with an Introduction by James E. Miller, Jr. (Lincoln, Nebraska, 1972), p. 93.

filled, the reader's mental faculties are at once directed toward an attempt to comprehend the new situation with which he is confronted. Furthermore, it is common literary experience that a text has different effects at different times. Certainly the inconstancy of our own ideas may be largely responsible for this change, but at the same time the text itself must contain the conditions by which it can take on a different appearance at different times.[3] The various effects produced by the great works of art, from Homer down to the present age, are a sufficient evidence for this. An analysis of expectations thus enables the critic to appreciate the many-sidedness of meaning contained in a text. Finally, the study of the effectiveness of a text also sheds light on the problem of mixed 'genres', for the overlapping of different forms makes it possible to communicate the unknown through the known, which brings about the expansion of our experience. As a result of this, an analysis of effects is bound to take into consideration the historical dimension of literature, which has been at times unduly neglected by those who tried to direct our intentions to a thorough analysis of literary form.

II

The following examination of Smollett's last novel, *Humphry Clinker,* is just an attempt at studying the esthetic response brought about by a new combination of significant forms which had been developed in eighteenth-century prose fiction. Smollett's *Humphry Clinker* indicates a conspicuous change in the eighteenth century of that form of narrative prose which had found its first visible outlines a good fifty years before in Defoe's *Robinson Crusoe,* written in 1719. But the passing of this tradition of the novel, created by Defoe and culminating in Richardson and Fielding, should not be misconstrued as an exhaustion of all its possibilities; in fact the traditional forms of the novel, developed during the eighteenth century, undergo a definite transformation in Smollett's last work, in which we can find both an adherence to tradition and a departure in new directions. Erwin Wolff described *Humphry Clinker* "as a bridge-head which, after some two decades full of epigons and imitators, leads to new developments."[4] There is also to be taken into account that only a few years before the publication of *Humphry Clinker,* the first Gothic novel, Wal-

[3] For a more detailed discussion see Wolfgang Iser, "Indeterminacy and the Reader's Response in Prose Fiction," in *Aspects of Narrative* (English Institute Essays 1971), ed. J. Hillis Miller (New York, 1971), pp. 1–45.
[4] Erwin Wolff, *Der englische Roman im 18. Jahrhundert* (Kleine Vandenhoeck-Reihe 195–197) (Göttingen, 1964), p. 122.

pole's *The Castle of Otranto,* had appeared in 1764. With his introduction of the miraculous, Walpole intended to surpass the traditional novel.
In his preface to the second edition he says:

> It was an attempt to blend the two kinds of Romance, the ancient and
> the modern. In the former, all was imagination and improbability; in
> the latter, nature is always intended to be, and sometimes has been,
> copied with success. Invention has not been wanting; but the great re-
> sources of fancy have been dammed up by a strict adherence to com-
> mon life. But if, in the latter species, Nature has cramped imagination,
> she did but take her revenge, having been totally excluded from old
> romances. The actions, sentiments, and conversations, of the heroes
> and heroines of ancient days, were as unnatural as the machines em-
> ployed to put them in motion.[5]

In view of this statement, *Humphry Clinker* is well worth our attention;
for, like Walpole, Smollett attempted a blend of his own by using the
forms of the epistolary novel, the book of travels, and the picaresque
novel—all of which were greatly favored in the eighteenth century. Thus
we can say that *Humphry Clinker* marks the point of intersection in the
development of narrative prose. The interplay of the traditional forms
in this novel is an indication that Smollett was concerned with meeting
the most diverse expectations of his public. Yet the various novel forms
combined in *Humphry Clinker* do begin to influence one another, thereby changing the traditional expectations of the eighteenth-century reader.

In discussing these various forms, first of all we should perhaps examine them separately. *Humphry Clinker* consists of eighty-two letters,
divided up among five correspondents. Two-thirds of the letters are written by Matthew Bramble, head of a Welsh family, and his nephew Jerry
Melford, who has just come down from Oxford. Eleven letters are from
Jerry's sister Lydia, six from Bramble's sister Tabitha, and ten from the
maid Winifred Jenkins. The letters are addressed to various people, but
the replies are not included in the novel. This one-sided correspondence
sets *Humphry Clinker* apart from those novels based on an exchange of
letters, as exemplified, most strikingly, in Richardson's *Clarissa Harlowe.*
The Bramble family is on tour, and their letters give an account of their
impressions of the various events that occur during the journey from
Wales to Bath, London, and Scotland. In this way the epistolary novel
and the travel book are combined in a single form so that Maynadier, in
his introduction to *Humphry Clinker,* could assert that: "There is no

---

[5] Horace Walpole, *The Castle of Otranto and the Mysterious Mother,* ed. Montague Summers
(London, 1924), pp. 13 f.

doubt, then, that *Humphry Clinker* is a novel in the shape of a book of travels, or travels in the shape of a novel, whichever way you choose to put it."[6] We must remember, though, that this smooth interweaving of the two forms of presentation was not standard practice in the eighteenth century. Defoe's *Journal of the Plague Year* had introduced the travel book in the form of letters written by only one correspondent—usually the author—and thus affording only his point of view.[7] Besides, the only epistolary characteristics in this type of travel literature were the mode of address, the conclusion, and the occasional use of the first person singular. Smollett himself wrote his *Travels through France and Italy* in 1764/65 as a series of letters, but these are "almost void of the intimate remarks which one expects in personal correspondence."[8] L. Martz has shown that Smollett's *Travels* are often nothing but compilations—"In fact, it may well be said that without the preceding thirteen years of compilation, Smollett's *Travels* would never have appeared."[9] Here, as elsewhere in travel literature, the epistolary form is imposed on the collected material without ever taking on a genuine character of its own.

Humphry Clinker is different not only from this kind of travel book but also from the epistolary novel developed by Richardson. Richardson's novels grew out of a background of puritanical literature and dealt with the spiritual life of the characters. The letter form offered itself as a means whereby Richardson could capture the introspection he sought to portray. In the preface to *Clarissa Harlowe* he wrote the following about his characters: ". . . it will be found, in the progress of the Work, that they very often make such reflections upon each other, and each upon himself and his own actions, as reasonable beings must make, who disbelieve not a Future State of Rewards and Punishments, and who one day propose to reform."[10] The letter form facilitates this self-examination insofar as it externalizes inner emotions. Richardson continues in his preface to *Clarissa Harlowe:* "All the Letters are written while the hearts of the writers must be supposed to be wholly engaged in their subjects (The events at the time generally dubious): So that they abound

[6] H. G. Maynadier, "Introduction," *The Expedition of Humphry Clinker.* Tobias Smollett, *The Works*, ed. H. G. Maynadier (New York, 1902), XI and XII: x.

[7] See Natascha Würzbach, "Die Struktur des Briefromans und seine Entstehung in England," Dissertation, Munich, 1964, pp. 40 f.

[8] Louis L. Martz, *The Later Career of Tobias Smollett* (Yale Studies in English, 97) (New Haven, 1942), p. 71.

[9] Ibid., p. 88; see also Osbert Sitwell, "Introduction," Tobias Smollett, *Travels through France and Italy* (Chiltern Library) (London, 1949), pp. v ff.

[10] Samuel Richardson, *The Novels* (The Shakespeare Head Edition) (Oxford, 1930–31). *Clarissa or, The History of a Young Lady Comprehending the most Important Concerns of Private Life,* I: xii. (All quotations from Richardson's novels are taken from this edition.)

not only with critical Situations, but with what may be called instantaneous Descriptions and Reflections (proper to be brought home to the breast of the youthful Reader)."[11] This writing "to the Moment,"[12] as Richardson put it in his preface to *Sir Charles Grandison*, brings about an extraordinary close relationship between the events and the character's reactions. The letter-writer never manages to stand away from the events or from himself, thus lending a personal immediacy to the situations he is in, a fact which is moreover indicated by the use of the present tense.[13] In this way, the self-examination is presented as if it were a real event. Richardson claimed that his form of presentation was not only a "novelty"[14] but also "a Story designed to represent real Life."[15] The intention of this story was to point out to his reader the principle of self-knowledge on which he was to base his life. This self-examination inevitably calls for an increasing variety of every-day situations, as can be seen from the ever broadening scope of Richardson's novels after *Pamela*, but there always remains a moral code as the fixed yardstick by which the growing multiplicity of human actions is to be measured.

If *Humphry Clinker* is considered against this background, only the form of observation that we find in the different correspondents can be equated with that developed by Richardson. The individual personality of the letter-writer is present in everything he records. However, in Smollett the observations are no longer concerned with self-analysis, but with the changing situations that occur during the journey through town and country. For Richardson, the letter form was a means of self-revelation[16] to be achieved through a variety of situations, and it was on this central theme of self-discovery that the events of the epistolary novel were hinged. For Smollett, this central theme loses its importance. Richardson attached importance to the individual situation of his heroines only insofar as it led them to self-analysis and all the consequences resulting from it, but Smollett takes the situation itself as a theme. Richardson's presentation of reality served mainly to portray the moral attitude of his heroines, while Smollett's is not concerned with this function, and precisely on this account his presentation becomes all the more complex

---

[11] Ibid., p. xiv.

[12] Samuel Richardson, *The History of Sir Charles Grandison*, I: ix.

[13] Concerning the function of the present tense in narrative literature, see Harald Weinrich, *Tempus. Besprochene und erzählte Welt* (Stuttgart, 1964), pp. 44 ff.

[14] Richardson, *Clarissa*, VII: 325.

[15] Ibid., p. 328.

[16] See also F. G. Black, *The Epistolary Novel in the Late Eighteenth Century* (Eugene, Oregon, 1940), and Bertil Romberg, *Studies in the Narrative Technique of the First-Person Novel* (Stockholm, 1962), pp. 220 ff.

and subtle, since it is seen through the filter, as it were, of individual observation. Consequently, Bramble's and Melford's letters are no longer characterized by a certain motivation, as Richardson demanded with his presentation of "the fair Writer's most secret Thoughts" and "undisguised Inclinations."[17] Bramble and Melford often jump from one subject or observation to another, for neither of them is concerned with pondering over his moral situation—they both want to reproduce the world around them.

This even applies to those sections where the letter-writers speak of their own emotions. Bramble tells Dr. Lewis—the addressee of his letters—how, quite unexpectedly, he met a number of old friends whom he had not seen for forty years or more. He revels in the possibilities of friendship and draws a vivid picture of the jolly company of his friends. But he does not forget to include the concrete details of this unexpected reunion. When he introduces himself to one of his friends, he tells us: "The moment I told him who I was, he exclaimed, 'Ha! Matt, my old fellow-cruiser, still afloat!' and, starting up, hugged me in his arms. His transport, however, boded me no good; for, in saluting me, he thrust the spring of his spectacles into my eye, and, at the same time, set his wooden stump upon my gouty toe; an attack that made me shed tears in sad earnest."[18] The overflow of feelings is suffused with the prosaic description of the unexpected pain in eye and toe; then suddenly the pain again turns to laughter, and finally the initial joy of the reunion passes and they each recall the trials and tribulations of the years gone by. Bramble only reports what happened, and there is no moralizing stylization in this account of a potentially very emotional situation. Pain and joy, sadness and sorrow are the elements he combines in this single situation, and the frequent changes of emotions show that even when the letter is dealing with the personal feelings of the writer it is still meant to be nothing but a transcription of his observations. The writer is concerned with what is happening around him, and he depicts the events as they appear to him.

The difference, then, between the letter form developed by Richardson and that used by Smollett is plain to see. In *Humphry Clinker,* introspection with subsequent moral examination is no longer the focal point of events. Instead, the letter form becomes the medium for an intensified observation of the outside world, as the complexity of changing situations is no longer visualized from the standpoint of a single inter-

---

[17] Samuel Richardson, *Pamela or, Virtue Rewarded,* I: iii.
[18] *Humphry Clinker,* I: 82.

pretation. The very fact that Smollett's characters do not look at the outside world from the single vantage point of a moral standard, makes the reality of that world all the richer. This may well be at the expense of the coordination Richardson achieved through the moral orientation of his work, but, as we shall see later, Smollett accomplished this in another form. And so we can say that Smollett took over the letter form which had been perfected in *Clarissa Harlowe,* removed its moral significance and made it into a perspective for the observation of man and his environment.

This observation is extended by the travel book form, which unfolds a detailed picture of all the different localities visited by the Bramble family. The full title of the novel is *The Expedition of Humphry Clinker;* the travel book and the epistolary forms are its component parts, and their superimposition one on the other results in each of them undergoing a certain change. The description of the journey in *Humphry Clinker* is markedly different from that which Smollett himself had given in his voluminous *Compendium of Voyages,*[19] at which we shall look for a moment. This compendium makes use of all the travel literature available at the time to impart the most detailed information on *Customs, Manners, Religion, Government, Commerce, and Natural History of most Nations in the Known World*[20]—as we learn from the subtitle of the work. The collection and communication of information is the guiding purpose of the book. This is true not only of Smollett's *Compendium* but also of travel literature in general. Narrative passages are of secondary importance and at most serve to form a kind of connection between the events reported.[21] "This neglect of individual experiences is manifested consistently throughout such voyages as those of Rogers, Gemelli, Baldaeus, and Nieuhoff, in which the traveller himself is not a great figure, whereas his historical observations are of prime significance. . . . Preference for description over adventure is particularly obvious in cruising voyages."[22]

---

[19] Cf. Martz, *Tobias Smollett,* pp. 23 ff.
[20] For details see ibid., p. 44.
[21] This even applies to Defoe's use of travel literature in his novels. A. W. Secord, *Studies in the Narrative Method of Defoe* (New York, 1963), p. 111, believes this actually to be the guiding principle of composition for *Robinson Crusoe:* " 'Robinson Crusoe,' finally, is not so much a fictitious autobiography (as Professor Cross suggests) as it is a fictitious book of travel, the courses and geographical matters of which are based upon more or less authentic relations, but the details of which are largely invented by Defoe from suggestions contained in these relations. Defoe shifts the emphasis from matters of interest only to seamen to others which are of more general human concern, and from mere incident to characterization."
[22] Martz, *Tobias Smollett,* pp. 44 f.

From this material, which itself contains very little personal experience, Smollett makes a further selection, preferring whatever is of informative value to the presentation of individual impressions.[23] In doing so, however, Smollett is only giving further emphasis to the tendencies that always underlay travel literature. Martz characterizes this *Compendium* as an attempt at a massive synthesis: "To meet the trend of the times, with its increasing insistence on classification and synthesis, these scattered facts must now be marshalled into order. . . . Thus in the segregation of narrative and descriptive details the process of systematization takes another step forward."[24]

In *Humphry Clinker,* this form of travel book is not retained. There is a good deal of information about individual localities, but the communication of such information is no longer an end in itself. This fact becomes obvious when the same place is presented to us from two or even more than two separate points of view. A clear illustration of this is provided by the different impressions of Ranelagh, the famous London pleasure resort, conveyed by Bramble and Lydia in their letters. Bramble writes:

> The diversions of the times are not ill suited to the genius of this incongruous monster, called the public. Give it noise, confusion, glare, and glitter, it has no idea of elegance and propriety. What are the amusements at Ranelagh? One half of the company are following one another's tails, in an eternal circle, like so many blind asses in an olive mill, where they can neither discourse, distinguish, nor be distinguished; while the other half are drinking hot water, under the denomination of tea, till nine or ten o'clock at night, to keep them awake for the rest of the evening. As for the orchestra, the vocal music especially, it is well for the performers that they cannot be heard distinctly.[25]

Lydia describes the same place as follows:

> Ranelagh looks like the enchanted palace of a genius, adorned with the most exquisite performances of painting, carving, and gilding, enlightened with a thousand golden lamps, that emulate the noonday sun; crowded with the great, the rich, the gay, the happy, and the fair; glittering with cloth of gold and silver, lace, embroidery, and precious stones. While these exulting sons and daughters of felicity tread this round of pleasure, or regale in different parties, and separate lodges, with fine imperial tea and other delicious refreshments,

[23] See ibid., pp. 45 ff.
[24] Ibid., pp. 48 and 50.
[25] *Humphry Clinker,* I: 134.

65

their ears are entertained with the most ravishing delights of music, both instrumental and vocal. There I heard the famous Tenducci, a thing from Italy—it looks for all the world like a man, though they say it is not. The voice, to be sure, is neither man's nor woman's; but it is more melodious than either; and it warbled so divinely, that, while I listened I really thought myself in paradise.[26]

The breaking up of identical realities according to different points of view forms a basic element of the whole novel and brings about a substantial change in the motivation that lay behind the travel book. Even where the epistolary form had been imposed on the travel book form— as in Smollett's *Travels through France and Italy*—the accounts had remained authoritative because they were given by one traveler only.[27] The possibility of differing impressions, however, is contrary to the purpose of the travel book: namely, to convey information about unknown places. In the two examples we quoted above there is no longer any question of conveying information about the famous London pleasure resort; the divergent impressions simply draw attention to the extent to which the same thing can look different to different people. And so Smollett's presentation of the journey is not concerned primarily with the things that are experienced, but with the way in which they are experienced. Thus the events reported take on a double meaning: first, they reveal the subjectivity that colors the perception of the individual, as we see in the reactions of Bramble and Lydia to Ranelagh; and second, they rouse a greater interest in the various possibilities of perception that are opened up to the reader's imagination. What one person sees, another will miss; yet both seem to experience something that is characteristic of the situation. Here the revelation is no longer one of factual information, but is concerned with the abundance of viewpoints contained even in the most trivial of situations, which will still have as many sides as there are observers. In the traditional travel book, the description of a locality helped to build up a complete factual picture of the relevant place or region, but in Smollett's novel the accounts of towns and scenes are relieved of this function. If they are to be presented for their own sakes,

[26] Ibid., p. 139. Lydia can't help remarking, in the very same letter, that her uncle seems to have a different view of the very same locality: "People of experience and infirmity, my dear Letty, see with very different eyes from those that such as you and I make use of" (p. 141).

[27] A. D. McKillop, *The Early Masters of English Fiction* (Lawrence, Kansas, [2]1962), p. 172, has drawn attention to the consequences of that technique: "The travel episode becomes brief and specifically localized; the style becomes more simple and precise. At the same time, it should be noted, compilation as such cannot center or color the story. How interesting after all are the details from guidebooks which Smollett gathers in the 'Travels'? There is a gap between mere appropriation of material and the expression of an individual's attitude or humor."

they must be sufficiently interesting in their own right, and so they have to be considered from all angles; this in turn means that the reader must use his own imagination to bring about a coordination of the different aspects of reality. By dispensing with the compilation of knowledge as the central theme of the travel book, Smollett facilitates a more vivid presentation of the towns and regions included in the journey. At the same time the individual episodes contribute greatly toward the delineation of the characters, whose own personalities condition their vision and so effect the splitting up of individual realities and events into their various aspects.

In addition to the form we have been discussing, *Humphry Clinker* also shows at least the rudiments of a third form—the picaresque novel. Critics are generally agreed that there are few traces of the picaresque in Smollett's later work,[28] but we should not ignore those traces which are to be found. Smollett's early novels are largely under the influence of Le Sage. In his preface to *Roderick Random,* he describes the intention of his satire: "The same method has been practised by other Spanish and French authors, and by none more successfully than by Monsieur Le Sage, who, in his Adventures of Gil Blas, has described the knavery and foibles of life, with infinite humour and sagacity. The following sheets I have modelled on his plan, taking the liberty, however, to differ from him in the execution, where I thought his particular situations were uncommon, extravagant, or peculiar to the country in which the scene is laid."[29] Shortly after the publication of *Roderick Random* in 1748, Smollett translated *Gil Blas.* Although the chief forms of presentation used in *Humphry Clinker* are the travel book and the epistolary novel, neither the hero nor some of the adventures of the Bramble family can come under the heading of these genres.

It would indeed be difficult to decide whether the various events of the journey should come under the heading of travel book or picaresque novel. Even if we might feel that the more elaborate narrative episodes— such as the naked Bramble's rescue from the sea by Clinker, who pulls his master painfully by the ear to get him out of the water, though in fact Bramble is in no danger whatever[30]—belong rather to the episodical

---

[28] See, among others, Wolff, *Der englische Roman,* p. 120; Martz, *Tobias Smollett,* p. 88 and Alexandre Lawrence, "L'Influence de Lesage sur Smollett," *Revue de Littérature Comparée* 12 (1932): 533–45.

[29] Tobias Smollett, *The Adventures of Roderick Random,* I: xxxii.

[30] See *Humphry Clinker,* II: 7 ff.

structure of the picaresque novel than to the travel book, these passages have the same function for the novel as the description of Ranelagh and other topographical sections: to mirror the different reactions of different individuals, in exactly the same way that we see in their observations of Bath, London, and Scotland. And yet the juxtaposition of adventures with topographical descriptions shows us that the traces remaining from the picaresque novel now have a different function to perform.

The succession of adventures which in the picaresque novel were linked together mainly by chance associations gave the narrative a realistic nature. Nevertheless, in this kind of novel—up to and including Smollett's *Roderick Random*—the many situations were never offered purely for themselves, but formed the basis for parody and satire.[31] The picaresque novel under its guise of realism was always presented in a certain light so as to satirize the times. In *Humphry Clinker*, however, the few adventures scattered through the book have lost this satirical function, and thus direct attention to the episodes themselves. Just as with the topographical descriptions, the episodes have to be broken down into various perspectives to show that they, too, are experienced by individual characters, and that their real significance is only to be seen in the variations of different people's viewpoints. In this respect the picaro, whose first-person account had combined the most heterogeneous exploits into the unity of the picaresque novel, now has lost his prime function.

In *Humphry Clinker* the picaro is still the hero of the title, but he is a mere shadow of himself: he does not write a single letter and is presented only in the subjective visions of different people; he is a ragamuffin picked up on the way, employed as a servant, and exposed to the whims and fancies of the Bramble family. His introduction into the story may be seen as an indication of his function: before Melford actually names the hero in a letter, Humphry Clinker is portrayed in a situation that is scarcely happy for him in the eyes of Bramble and Tabitha, who are, respectively, amazed and deeply shocked by his somewhat scanty attire.[32] This double perspective, occasionally supplemented by further points of view, is maintained almost to the end of the novel. Moreover, the relations between individual members of the family and Clinker are characterized by strange inconsistencies, and the family is never quite unani-

---

[31] For a more detailed discussion of this particular aspect see Jurij Striedter's introductory remarks to his book *Der Schelmenroman in Russland* (Berlin, 1961), p. 7 ff., and H. R. Jauss, "Ursprung und Bedeutung der Ich-Form im *Lazarillo de Tormes*," *Romanistisches Jahrbuch* 8 (1957): 290 ff.
[32] See *Humphry Clinker*, I: 121 ff.

mous in its judgment of Clinker. When eventually we do find unanimity, the end of the novel is in sight.

Smollett did not call his novel 'The Expedition of Matthew Bramble'—which would have corresponded to the actual course of events in the book; neither does his titular hero fulfill the functions of a picaro. Clinker does resemble the picaro in his behavior, but he is in no way the cunning rascal that looks at the world from the standpoint of the outsider and joins all the merry tales together in his account.[33] In the traditional picaresque novel, the picaro had the function of drawing a satirical picture of the world through the story of his life, but in Smollett this function is replaced by another. Instead of presenting his hero as looking back over his life, Clinker becomes real to us only insofar as he is seen by the other characters in the novel. Thus he inevitably loses that superiority which the cunning picaro always kept in the face of all adversity; in Smollett's novel he is not even given the chance to express his own point of view, as he appears only in the views given of him by other people. Since Clinker never speaks for himself, he seems more helpless than all the others, but this only throws into relief the manner in which they behave toward him. Thus we see how inconsistent human relationships really are, and how strongly they are influenced by chance occurrences and trivialities. The reader cannot help being struck by the differently motivated views through which Clinker is seen, and the passiveness of the hero will arouse his sympathy.

III

We now can formulate a provisional conclusion from the remarks so far. In its structure, *Humphry Clinker* contains three forms of novel which are interwoven almost without a visible join. Only if one examines the historical conditions and the subject matter of *Humphry Clinker* does the combination become apparent. It is this interweaving of the three forms—if one may include the travel book as a form of novel—and the discarding of their original basic functions which constitutes the originality of *Humphry Clinker*. Smollett takes over from Richardson the complex letter form with several correspondents, but leaves out the self-examination leading to moral analysis which had been the central theme of the epistolary novel in the first half of the eighteenth century. He also takes over the travel book form as giving a panoramic view of a

---

[33] See F. W. Chandler, *The Literature of Roguery* (London, 1907), I: 5.

number of localities, but he no longer interprets this as a compendium of topographical information. Finally, he joins on the picaresque novel, but removes the satirical intention of the picaro's adventures. All three forms on their own are characterized by the fact that they each give empirical reality a certain meaning. The epistolary novel of the Richardson school is only concerned with the every-day world insofar as it provides a means of testing the moral strength of the characters. The travel book demands an abundance of empirical details because they alone can bring about the necessary information. The picaresque novel has need of the empirical world so that it can set it up for satirical examination. In all these forms empirical reality is limited by each specific intention. But Smollett brings them all together in his novel, removes the basic intention of each form, and so releases reality from its former restrictions. As a result, the reality presented by Smollett does not appear without order, but at the same time it does not serve to establish a preconceived meaning. The combination of the three forms transforms them into channels of perception through which reality is to be seen. Observation of the empirical world is only possible if this world can be classified, and the forms of letter, travel book, and picaresque novel perform precisely this function when their task is reduced to that of describing and classifying.

At the same time this combination of forms leads to an increased breadth and vividness: the letter presents reality through intimate observation, the travel book displays a panorama of ever-changing pictures, and the traces remaining of the picaresque novel reflect the complexity of human relationships through contrasts and varying viewpoints. This combination, however, is not meant merely to do away with the basic principle in each form, but it is to exploit to the utmost the possibilities of vivid, concrete presentation inherent in those forms. This redirection is necessary if empirical reality is no longer to serve as a guide to a preconceived truth, but is to be examined in its own right. Indeed, we can say that the more forms of observation are combined in the study of empirical reality, the greater will seem its variety of aspects. The nineteenth-century novel was developed along these lines. In any case, Smollett's technique shows that there is no short cut to the presentation of reality. If one wishes to get as accurate a vision of empirical reality as possible, the methods of perception must be freed from all preconceptions. In this respect, Smollett's novel shows the spirit of Scottish empiricism.[34]

---

[34] See M. A. Goldberg, *Smollett and the Scottish School. Studies in Eighteenth Century*

The arrangement of the three forms coordinates empirical reality for the reader's imagination, since it is only through them that the varieties of perception can be made concrete. Through the letter form, the reader is confronted directly with the characters, and since none of the addressees writes in return, the reader must take their place. The events are not coordinated for him; he himself must combine the pieces of information he finds in the various letters. This relationship is in accordance with the threefold purpose of the novel: the overall structure of the novel gives a shape to empirical reality, then this reality is split up among the varying viewpoints of the characters, and, finally, the multiplicity of concrete—but limited—aspects must 'coalesce' in the reader's imagination, to use a term from eighteenth-century associational psychology.[35] The variety of addressees and the fact that Smollett does not print their attitude to the Bramble family's letters helps to stimulate the reader's imagination. If the recipients of the letters were to reply, as in Richardson's *Clarissa Harlowe,* they would surely express their own views on the events, and the reader's reaction would be limited to judging them. Here, however, the reader must take the place of the recipients, and in the novel these are construed as people varying in temperament, so that a large number of different attitudes toward the whole correspondence are suggested to the reader. His knowledge surpasses that of the individual characters, and since the author has, to a large extent, withdrawn himself from the action and no longer comments on it, the reader himself becomes the agent that must combine all the different elements. He can put himself in the place of each addressee, and simply because of his greater knowledge he can understand the letters of each correspondent not only as a source of information but also as a revelation of character. In several of the letters this device is stated explicitly. When Melford has drawn, as he often does, a character sketch of one of the people in his uncle's circle, he ends by saying: "Having given you this sketch of Squire Paunceford, I need not make any comment on his character, but leave it at the mercy of your own reflection."[36] In order not only to promote but also to direct the reflection on the part of the reader, the individual characters had to be composed in such a manner as to bring the blending of the three forms of novel to full fruition.

Thought (Albuquerque, 1959), who interprets Smollett's novels in terms of the common-sense school which tried to balance and to reconcile contradictions and contrasts prevailing in eighteenth-century thought.

[35] The importance of associational psychology for eighteenth-century esthetics has been stressed by W. J. Bate, *From Classic to Romantic. Premises of Taste in Eighteenth Century England* (Harper Torchbooks) (New York, 1961), pp. 118 ff.

[36] *Humphry Clinker,* I: 105.

IV

One∙of Matthew Bramble's letters contains the revealing sentence: "With respect to the characters of mankind, my curiosity is quite satisfied; I have done with the science of men, and must now endeavour to amuse myself with the novelty of *things.*"[37] This denotes the sacrifice of a basic theme in the novel of the eighteenth century, which had been given its almost classical definition a good twenty years before the publication of *Humphry Clinker* in the preface to Fielding's *Tom Jones:* "The provision, then, which we have here made is no other than *Human Nature.* Nor do I fear that my sensible reader, though most luxurious in his taste, will start, cavil, or be offended, because I have named but one article . . . nor can the learned reader be ignorant, that in human nature, though here collected under one general name, is such prodigious variety, that a cook will have sooner gone through all the several species of animal and vegetable food in the world, than an author will be able to exhaust so extensive a subject."[38]

For Smollett's main character, as indeed for all the other characters in *Humphry Clinker,* this subject has been exhausted, since they are no longer meant to exemplify the variety of human nature; instead, their main concern is the world around them. This shift of interest implies that no plot can develop any longer from the interplay of the characters; occasional traces of it only serve to motivate the end of the novel. Smollett even stresses this tendency by an additional device, for when the various couples are finally married off, he slightly ridicules the symbolic value of the denouement.[39] Marriage no longer stands for the climax of human relationships, but is simply a means for tying up all the loose ends.[40] This is made quite obvious by the fact that Melford cloaks his feelings about these events in a metaphor taken from the theater: "The fatal knots are now tied. The comedy is near a close, and the curtain is ready to drop; but the latter scenes of this act I shall recapitulate in order."[41] The relations between the characters are but comedy, whereas the function of their real lives consists in giving a subjective view of the world they experience. Therefore, they do not embody any longer an abstract ideal—as Richardson's heroines do—but are shown as having individual traits

---

[37] Ibid., p. 162.
[38] Henry Fielding, *The Works,* ed. E. Gosse (Westminster and New York, 1898), III: 4 f.
[39] See *Humphry Clinker,* II: 259 ff.
[40] This technique became a convention and was still observed well into the nineteenth century. See Walter Scott, *Waverley* (The Nelson Classics) (Edinburgh, no date), pp. 540 ff.
[41] *Humphry Clinker,* II: 259.

which enable them to coordinate the contingency of the empirical world. The "novelty of things"—to quote Bramble again—becomes visible only when seen through individual peculiarities. How is this brought about?

The main characters in *Humphry Clinker* are conceived as humors. Bramble, Lismahago, and Tabitha are repeatedly characterized as such.[42] However varied may have been the status of the humor in the seventeenth and early eighteenth-century literature,[43] it underwent a spectacular rise in the course of the eighteenth century.

The two outstanding qualities of the eighteenth-century humor had already been named by Congreve: "Humour is from Nature" and "shews us as we are."[44] Further features are: "A singular and unavoidable manner of doing, or saying any thing, Peculiar and Natural to one Man only; by which his Speech and Actions are distinguished from those of other Men."[45] Man's nature finds its expression in the uniqueness of the humor. As a result, even the most eccentric features of the humor can be understood, since they have their origin in 'Nature' and thus are part of the community that embraces all men. This ambivalence of the humor, which consists in its representation of both the unique and the general, is pointed out in almost every discussion on this phenomenon. It is expressly stated and summarized by Corbyn Morris in his important essay dealing with comedy in the eighteenth century. He says: "humour is nature unembellished."[46] This means that humor can be defined neither as an ideal conception of man nor as a product of his habits and manners. Humor represents nothing but itself as originating from nature. "The humorists," as Stuart Tave had remarked in his book on *The Amiable Humorist*, "have an individuality as detailed and strikingly vivid as their creators can fashion. Their claim to universal significance rests less and less, in the later eighteenth century, on their being representatives of a species, manner types, and more on their uniqueness. The smallest details of their existence are recorded because it is there that reality resides. It is the 'little occurrences of life,' the 'nonsensical *minutiae*,' Sterne said, that best exhibit the truth of character."[47]

---

[42] See ibid., pp. 7 and 159. Smollett's conception of the humors has been outlined by W. B. Piper, "The Large Diffused Picture of Life in Smollett's Early Novels," *Studies in Philology* 60 (1963): 45 ff., and Herbert Read, *Reason and Romanticism. Essays in Literary Criticism* (New York, 1963), pp. 198 ff.

[43] See Stuart M. Tave, *The Amiable Humorist. A Study in the Comic Theory and Criticism of the 18th and Early 19th Centuries* (Chicago, 1960).

[44] William Congreve, *The Works*, ed. Montague Summers (London, 1923), III: 163.

[45] Ibid., p. 165.

[46] Quoted by Tave, *The Amiable Humorist*, p. 119.

[47] Ibid., p. 167.

Here, in Tave's definition of the humor, we find the rudiments of Smollett's characters. The reduction of humor to uniqueness entails observation of reality as absolutely necessary for the individual character. Thus character and reality are dependent on each other. The character is delineated through the manner in which he observes reality, while the contingency of reality can obtain coherence only through individual perception. Thus the delineation of the character and his unique observation of the world are interrelated for the purpose of forming the reality of the novel. *Humphry Clinker* leaves no doubt whatsoever that the reality of the novel consists in the varying interrelation between the humor and the world around him; the humor is no longer punished by the world for his eccentricity, and the world is no longer regarded as an arena in which the character has to prove his moral strength. Instead, character and reality are shown in their mutual reflection. This presentation aims at a delineation of the character through his individual perception and at an illustration of topographical localities through the form in which they are observed. Thus, humor and reality lose the function of expressing a meaning beyond themselves, as was the case in the traditional eighteenth-century novel. In *Humphry Clinker,* therefore, the character is presented in his formal uniqueness, while the world offers itself as an abundance of subtly varied topographical and sometimes historical details. These elements form the reality of the novel, with the character being defined through the medium of a contingent world, and the world acquiring consistency through the medium of observation. In their mutual reflection, world and character are transformed and come to life in the reader's imagination.

In this respect Smollett's novel conforms to a basic principle established by Lord Kames, in his *Elements of Criticism,* concerning the enjoyment of literature: "A third rule or observation is, That where the subject is intended for entertainment solely, not for instruction, a thing ought to be described as it appears, not as it is in reality."[48] For the sake of this enjoyment, the 'appearance' of the world needs to be distinguished from the 'reality', and the idiosyncrasies of the humor provide the ideal starting-point for this distinction.

For example, when Bramble describes York Cathedral, he complains not only about the unsuitable architecture of the edifice but also about the cold and the musty air inside the church. In his view, such buildings have been erected almost exclusively "for the benefit of the medical

---

[48] Henry Home of Kames, *Elements of Criticism* (Edinburgh, [9]1817), II: 290. When Bramble arrives in Edinburgh, where Lord Kames lived, he writes to Dr. Lewis: "Edinburgh is a hot-bed of genius." *Humphry Clinker,* II: 84.

faculty."[49] Now Bramble suffers from gout and rheumatism, and his pains make it necessary for him to go to Bath and so motivate his whole journey. It is for this reason that he has had to give up the country life he loves so much, and consequently all his impressions are prejudiced by this affection, which again influences his mode of perception. He sees the cathedral in accordance with the individual quirks of his own temperament. And, indeed, how else could he see it? In this way empirical reality is presented in an unaccumstomed light; the idiosyncrasies of the humor reveal unexpected facets of the outside world, so that the very eccentricity of the character discovers new ways of experiencing reality.

We might say that the humor, through his extreme reactions, increases the possibilities of perception; it paves new ways of seeing things, while others are completely ignored. The characters themselves know comparatively little of the effects of their humor, but the reader of the novel does, because he has read all the letters and is fully aware of the correspondent's limitations. In nearly every letter, some situation is depicted at one particular moment, which entails its reduction to one single viewpoint. Generally, the following letters correct this viewpoint inasmuch as they supplement or question it—at the price of other one-sided and eccentric viewpoints, as must be added.

For the reader, the succession of letters brings about a telescoping of situations in which—paradoxically enough—the characters reveal themselves and their surroundings through the very fact that they see everything from their own limited point of view. Consequently, the task of coordination is handed over to the reader, for he alone has all the information at his disposal. The one-sidedness of these viewpoints gives a sharp outline to the world that is described, whereas their blending results in its modification. It is this interrelation that forms lively images in the mind of the reader and enables him to be transported into the individual character and his experience of reality. In this respect, the ideas developed by Lord Kames just ten years before the publication of Smollett's novel, in an important section entitled "Narration and Description" in his *Elements of Criticism,* sound almost like a commentary on *Humphry Clinker:*

> In narration as well as in description, objects ought to be painted so accurately as to form in the mind of the reader distinct and lively images. . . . The force of language consists in raising complete images; which have the effect to transport the reader as by magic into the very place of the important action, and to convert him as it were

[49] *Humphry Clinker,* II: 2.

into a spectator, beholding every thing that passes. . . . Writers of genius, sensible that the eye is the best avenue to the heart, represent every thing as passing in our sight; and, from readers or hearers, transform us as it were into spectators: a skilful writer conceals himself, and presents his personages: in a word, every thing becomes dramatic as much as possible.[50]

This transformation of the reader into a spectator is achieved in *Humphry Clinker* by the interaction of the different forms; with its combination of three kinds of novel, its interplay between character and world, and its telescoping of different perspectives of observation in the sequence of letters, *Humphry Clinker* presents "distinct and lively images" of man and his surroundings. The less ideally man and the world around him are conceived, the more complex must be the forms and their interplay in the novel, so that the interdependence of character and reality can be transported into the reader's imagination.

The combination of forms leads to a new imaginative unity, the esthetic quality of which consists in its integral ambivalence. *Humphry Clinker* can neither be read exclusively as a presentation of human character, nor as a description of topographical and historical realities of the eighteenth century. The characters in this novel only become clear through the way in which they see reality, whereas reality is mirrored in their reflections. This means that character and reality are presented as complementary, each taking shape through the other, and neither meant to propagate any set principle.

How can their relation be defined? The answer lies in the humoristic conception of the situations. Although reality in *Humphry Clinker* is

---

[50] Kames, *Elements*, II: 291 f. and 312. E. L. Tuveson, *The Imagination as a Means of Grace. Locke and the Aesthetics of Romanticism* (Berkeley and Los Angeles, 1960), p. 153, has remarked that *Elements* "was to be the textbook of aesthetic theory for some time."
Concerning this particular technique employed by Smollett, Sir Walter Scott made an illuminating observation: "It is, however, chiefly in his profusion, which amounts almost to prodigality, that we recognise the superior richness of Smollett's fancy. He never shows the least desire to make the most either of a character, or a situation, or an adventure, but throws them together with a carelessness which argues unlimited confidence in his own powers. Fielding pauses to explain the principles of his art, and to congratulate himself and his readers on the felicity with which he constructs his narrative, or makes his characters evolve themselves in its progress. These appeals to the reader's judgment, admirable as they are, have sometimes the fault of being diffuse, and always the great disadvantage, that they remind us we are perusing a work of fiction; and that the beings with whom we have been conversant during the perusal, are but a set of evanescent phantoms, conjured up by a magician for our amusement. Smollett seldom holds communication with his readers in his own person. He manages his delightful puppet-show without thrusting his head beyond the curtain, like Gines de Passamont, to explain what he is doing; and hence, besides that our attention to the story remains unbroken, we are sure that the author, fully confident in the abundance of his materials, has no occasion to eke them out with extrinsic matter." Sir Walter Scott, *The Miscellaneous Prose Works* (Paris, 1837), III: 94 f.

presented through the mirror of subjectivity, the interrelation between world and character is not regarded as contradictory. Each character is —as we know—confined to his humor, and it is this very confinement that preconditions his perception and knowledge. Consequently, the reality he experiences is bound to be limited. At the same time, however, every expression of character is conditioned by the world, upon which he himself has but little influence. This state of affairs is particularly evident in those parts of the novel where the characters wish to act morally. Clinker's well-meant spontaneous decision, for instance, to save his master who is in no danger whatsoever, entails painful consequences for poor Bramble. At all events, he becomes the laughingstock of all those watching, as he is dragged by the ear out of the sea, a naked object of derision.[51] Thus the original benevolent motive is frustrated by the various circumstances which are beyond Clinker's control. And in the same way in which the motives are obscured when they are to be put into action, empirical reality can never be totally revealed by the character's perception. There is more to the character than he himself can reveal, and there is more to reality than its limitations can show. For the reader of the novel, this impression gradually grows through the accumulation of situations which bring to light the blind spots and hidden motives of the individual characters.

This insight is not without repercussions on the situations described. Precisely because the mode of narration does unfold the hidden aspects to the reader's imagination, many of the unquestioned and one-sided judgments, pronounced in the various letters, take on an element of the grotesque. The continuum of situations pointing to the author's presence forms a most striking contrast to each of the letters, which against this background bring to light what has been left in the dark. The projection of those observations to the continuum of situations turns out to be the basis of the comic element in *Humphry Clinker,* since the correspondence as a whole opens the reader's eyes to the ambivalence of each letter. In this way the letters contain both what is to be seen and what is concealed, so that the series of letters as a whole eliminates the contrast between the infinite complexity of life and the inevitably limited manner of its presentation.

V

The sense of comedy in the novel implies that the events described do not represent reality, but suggest it. Reality in *Humphry Clinker* is a

[51] *Humphry Clinker,* II: 7 ff.

complex interplay of novel forms, characters, and situations. It suggests various possibilities of combination without giving them a final shape, so that this task is left to the reader's imagination. This transition from representing reality to suggesting it shows that the world in *Humphry Clinker* is no longer meant to depict a set principle, but that through the interplay of forms and elements, the possibilities of human experience are to be suggested to the reader. The complex technique of the novel serves this purpose, and it is certainly no coincidence that *Humphry Clinker* and *Tristram Shandy,* which mark the end of the traditional eighteenth-century novel, should both induce the reader, through the form of composition, to take a fuller part in the coordination of events.

The shift of interest from representation to suggestion has an historical parallel in the discussion on esthetics at the end of the eighteenth century, and the blending of forms in *Humphry Clinker* reminds one of the mode of observation described in the associational psychology of the eighteenth century. Bate once characterized it as follows: "The associative capacity, interrelating as it does all functions and faculties of thought, is also aware of whatever added character its object assumes from any relationships or analogies it may have with other specific phenomena: it comprehends, in other words, that pertinent arrangement, interconnection, or mutual influence of various particulars which, in the aesthetic realm, comprises fitness, design, pattern, or, in the larger sense, form."[52] Such a form fulfills its function only if it sets the imagination working and guides it in a certain direction, without limiting it too much, so that the impulses suggested can take on an individual form of their own,[53] for only then can this suggested reality actually materialize.

This very process is described by Dugald Stewart in his analysis of the imagination in *Elements of the Philosophy of the Human Mind.* This work, published in 1792, forms the culminating point of the traditional theory of the imagination in the eighteenth century.[54] Stewart belonged

---

[52] Bate, *From Classic to Romantic,* p. 122.

[53] This process is very similar to the one described by Hume: "Among a thousand different opinions which different men may entertain of the same subject, there is one, and but one, that is just and true; and the only difficulty is to fix and ascertain it. On the contrary, a thousand different sentiments, excited by the same object, are all right: Because no sentiment represents what is really in the object. It only marks a certain conformity or relation between the object and the organs or faculties of the mind; and if that conformity did not really exist, the sentiment could never possibly have being. Beauty is no quality in things themselves: It exists merely in the mind which contemplates them; and each mind perceives a different beauty." David Hume, *The Philosophical Works,* ed. T. H. Green and T. H. Grose (London, 1882), III: 268.

[54] See Tuveson, *The Imagination as a Means of Grace,* p. 180 and M. H. Abrams, *The Mirror and the Lamp* (Norton Library) (New York, 1958), p. 161.

to the Scottish common sense school, of which there are many traces in Smollett's work.[55] In the *Elements* we read:

When the history or the landscape Painter indulges his genius, in forming new combinations of his own, he vies with the Poet in the noblest exertion of the poetical art: and he avails himself of his professional skill, as the Poet avails himself of language, only to convey the ideas in his mind. To deceive the eye by accurate representations of particular forms, is no longer his aim; but, by the touches of an expressive pencil, to speak to the imaginations of others. Imitation, therefore, is not the end which he proposes to himself, but the means which he employs in order to accomplish it: nay, if the imitation be carried so far as to preclude all exercise of the spectator's imagination, it will disappoint, in a great measure, the purpose of the artist. In Poetry, and in every other species of composition, in which one person attempts, by means of language, to present to the mind of another, the objects of his own imagination; this power is necessary, though not in the same degree, to the author and to the reader. When we peruse a description, we naturally feel a disposition to form, in our own minds, a dictinct picture of what is described; and in proportion to the attention and interest which the subject excites, the picture becomes steady and determinate. It is scarcely possible for us to hear much of a particular town, without forming some notion of its figure and size and situation; and in reading history and poetry, I believe it seldom happens, that we do not annex imaginary appearances to the names of our favourite characters. It is, at the same time, almost certain, that the imaginations of no two men coincide upon such occasions; and, therefore, though both may be pleased, the agreeable impressions which they feel, may be widely different from each other, according as the pictures by which they are produced are more or less happily imagined.[56]

The "new combinations" stressed by Stewart promote the reader's

---

[55] See Goldberg, *Smollett and the Scottish School,* pp. 1 ff.

[56] Dugald Stewart, *Elements of the Philosophy of the Human Mind* (London, [5]1814), I: 492 f. Stewart was also well acquainted with Lord Kames's *Elements* and was full of praise for Kames's achievement: "The active and adventurous spirit of Lord Kames, here, as in many other instances, led the way to his countrymen (i.e., the Scottish philosophers and critics); and, due allowances being made for the novelty and magnitude of his undertaking, with a success far greater than could have been reasonably anticipated. The *Elements of Criticism,* considered as the first systematical attempt to investigate the metaphysical principles of the fine arts, possesses, in spite of its numerous defects both in point of taste and of philosophy, infinite merits, and will ever be regarded as a literary wonder by those who know how small a portion of his time it was possible for the author to allot to the composition of it, amidst the imperious and multifarious duties of a most active and useful life." Dugald Stewart, *Collected Works,* ed. Sir William Hamilton (Edinburgh, 1877), I: 463.

participation, which is true of Smollett's novel in the sense that the various forms anticipate specific expectations on the part of the reader. Letter, travel book, picaresque novel and humors are the elements of the eighteenth-century novel which form the link with what the reader is accustomed to. Their interplay makes him see these familiar forms in a new combination, thus opening his eyes to new possibilities of human experience. In this respect, *Humphry Clinker* preconditions the pattern of communication brought to perfection in the nineteenth-century realistic novel, with the difference, however, that the forms combined by Smollett imply more of their original contents than we find in the nineteenth-century novel, which, instead, develops a more elaborate technique of narration. This development can be exemplified by the increasing refinement of technique as a means of influencing the reader's imagination. The actual differences, however, between Smollett and the nineteenth-century realistic novel do not affect their relation. The pattern of communication in *Humphry Clinker,* with its anticipation of the reader's expectations through the use of certain forms for the purpose of creating—by their interplay—a multiple perspective of reality, is to be found again in the realistic novel of the nineteenth century.

This fact reveals an important esthetic implication which is contained but not actually brought to the fore in the pattern we have described. In concluding, we shall cast a brief glance at this implication. We have seen that for various reasons the forms are combined more or less without a join; a flaw in this join, therefore, indicates a failure in the attempt at combination rather than any deliberate intention. One can, however, imagine a case in which the forms are deliberately made to clash with one another. In this case there will be a radical change in the intention underlying the conception of the novel, for the clash of forms must destroy one of the prime intentions of the realistic novel: the illusion of reality. Instead of evoking a manifold picture of reality, this clash of forms will create a semantic reality of its own, which can be tackled by the reader only through interpretation. This, however, is a problem that concerns the modern novel, and is, so to speak, another story.

4

FICTION—THE FILTER
OF HISTORY:
A Study of Sir Walter Scott's *Waverley*

I

I n the "General Preface" to the *Waverley Novels,* Scott reflects on
his own situation as narrator. He tries to clarify his intentions,
which—unlike those of earlier novelists—are no longer concerned
with expounding moral norms. Instead, he takes as his guide his own personal development, as he seeks to explain the curious innovation of history as the subject of fiction. His starting-point, he says, is as follows: "I
had nourished the ambitious desire of composing a tale of chivalry, which
was to be in the style of the Castle of Otranto, with plenty of Border
characters and supernatural incident."[1]

This 'ambition' links Scott to a form of novel that had arisen specifically out of reactions against the morally orientated novels of the eighteenth
century. The Gothic novel restored to the genre the element of the mysterious and the uncanny which the moral novels of the eighteenth century
had tried hard to eliminate. Fielding had taken care to make his own
position clear as regards the principles underlying his novels: "I would
by no means be thought to comprehend those persons of surprising genius,
the authors of immense romances, or the modern novel and Atalantis
writers; who, without any assistance from nature or history, record per-

---

[1] Sir Walter Scott, *Waverley* (The Nelson Classics) (Edinburgh, no date), p. xiii.

sons who never were, or will be, and facts which never did, nor possibly can, happen; whose heroes are of their own creation, and their brains the chaos whence all their materials are selected."[2] Here he was clearly excluding all elements of the 'unnatural' from his presentation of human nature. But the Gothic novel of the eighteenth century was built around the fantastic and the supernatural, the purpose of which Horace Walpole outlined in the preface to the second edition of the *Castle of Otranto:*

> Desirous of leaving the powers of fancy at liberty to expatiate through the boundless realms of invention, and thence of creating more interesting situations, he [i.e., the author] wished to conduct the mortal agents in his drama according to the rules of probability; in short, to make them think, speak, and act, as it might be supposed mere men and women would do in extraordinary positions. He had observed, that, in all inspired writings, the personages under the dispensation of miracles, and witnesses to the most stupendous phenomena, never lose sight of their human character.[3]

Walpole is at pains to show that he introduces the supernatural in order to create situations that will call forth new and unexpected reactions from his characters. This increase in interesting situations and the resultant diversification of human conduct arose out of the desire to reconcile the old form of the novel with the new.[4] Walpole points out that in the old novel "imagination" was predominant, but the action or plot proved to be improbable. In the new novel, on the other hand, though there is no lack of "Invention," the primary claims of nature mean a restriction of "imagination." Now Walpole wishes to break this "strict adherence to common life," and to introduce the extraordinary in order to extend what he regards as the hitherto limited sphere of action in the novel. This, he feels, is the only way to disclose forms of human conduct that

---

[2] Henry Fielding, *Joseph Andrews* (Everyman's Library) (London, 1948), p. 143.

[3] Horace Walpole, *The Castle of Otranto and the Mysterious Mother* (Constable's Edition), ed. Montague Summers (London, 1924), p. 14.

[4] See ibid., pp. 13 f. Concerning the difference, see also Clara Reeve, *The Progress of Romance,* ed. Esther M. McGill (New York, 1930), p. 111: "The Romance is an heroic fable, which treats of fabulous persons and things.—The Novel is a picture of real life and manners, and of the times in which it is written. The Romance in lofty and elevated language, describes what never happened nor is likely to happen.—The Novel gives a familiar relation of such things, as pass every day before our eyes, such as may happen to our friend, or to ourselves; and the perfection of it, is to represent every scene, in so easy and natural a manner, and to make them appear so probable, as to deceive us into a persuasion (at least while we are reading) that all is real, until we are affected by the joys or distresses, of the persons in the story, as if they were our own." See also John Colin Dunlop, *History of Prose Fiction,* ed. Henry Wilson (London, 1898), I: 1.

had been excluded by the moral novels of the eighteenth century. His declared aim is to make the extraordinary seem probable.[5]

It was this intention that made the Gothic novel interesting for Scott; the link between his "Border characters" and "supernatural incident" corresponds to the technique with which Walpole strove after a diversification and extension of human reactions. The many "supernatural incidents" were also meant by Scott to derestrict the natural, and he intended to show the consequences of this derestriction in a world of historically verifiable characters. However, Scott confesses that this intention soon took a turn in a different direction,[6] for in his increasing preoccupation with the folklore and history of Scotland, he found the historical supplanting the supernatural. And this immediately ensured a greater degree of probability for the variety of human reactions than Walpole had been able to achieve. History stood as guarantor for all the quirks and peculiarities of human conduct; and history also opened the way to an even greater variety of situations than the supernatural could create. And so Scott's original attachment to the Gothic novel prepared the way for his new subject matter: the representation of historical reality.

Walpole's Gothic novel had broken with the principle of *imitatio naturae*[7] and through the introduction of the fantastic had brought about an artificial extension of the possibilities for presenting human conduct. As Scott's starting-point was this same Gothic novel, we can hardly expect him to adhere to classical poetics in presenting history. Nevertheless, he was faced with the massive problem of how he could actually mould historical reality in the form of diverse modes of individual human conduct. To start with, he considered his own personal experience of the publication of an historical novel. He had himself arranged publication of Joseph Strutt's posthumous novel *Queen-Hoo-Hall,* but this had proved a failure.[8] Scott attributed the failure to the fact that the wealth of historical detail in *Queen-Hoo-Hall* could only appeal to the antiquarian. He concluded that historical information and situations could only be taken as subject matter for a novel if it was possible for them to be translated into terms that were relevant for the reader. In the preface to *Ivanhoe,* Scott again refers to *Queen-Hoo-Hall;* he describes the quality which that

---

[5] See Walpole, *The Castle of Otranto,* p. 14.
[6] See Scott, *Waverley,* p. xiii; see also Sir Herbert Grierson, *History and the Novel: Sir Walter Scott Lectures 1940–1948* (Edinburgh, 1950), p. 37.
[7] See Walpole, *The Castle of Otranto,* pp. 13 f.
[8] See Scott, *Waverley,* pp. xvi f.

work lacked and which he considered to be a basic principle for his own novel:

> It is necessary, for exciting interest of any kind, that the subject assumed should be, as it were, translated into the manners, as well as the language, of the age we live in . . . The late ingenious Mr. Strutt, in his romance of Queen-Hoo-Hall, acted upon another principle; and in distinguishing between what was ancient and modern, forgot, as it appears to me, that extensive neutral ground, the large proportion, that is, of manners and sentiments which are common to us and to our ancestors.[9]

It is on this "neutral ground" that the links must be forged between the reader and historical reality. The technique of communication is thus of fundamental importance in this type of novel, and we shall now try to analyze how the technique is made to operate in *Waverley.*

The direction of Scott's style, as outlined in the "General Preface" to the *Waverley Novels,* is given a revealing, concrete form right at the beginning of *Waverley, Or, 'Tis Sixty Years Since.* Scott deliberately chose this title because it points to the intended process of animating history and making it real in the reader's mind. The title outlines the interrelationship between the main character and historical reality, and in order to make his intentions quite clear, Scott runs through a few more variants of the title. "Had I, for example, announced in my frontispiece, 'Waverley, a Tale of Other Days,' must not every novel-reader have anticipated a castle scarce less than that of Udolpho?"[10] Such a title would have blurred the historical outline, for the indeterminacy of the period would have made the past seem like a fantasy without any connection with the present. *Waverley* would then have been a Gothic novel, leaving unlimited scope for the invention of fantastic situations. Clearly then, for Scott the past can only take on historical reality if it is linked with the present, for the world portrayed in the Gothic novel remains unhistorical precisely because it lacks this link. The title that he did choose brings together the character and the period, and this tells us a good deal about the function of Waverley himself.

He is to mediate between the historical events of 1745 and the present day, and so embodies the "neutral ground" on which historical reality is to be translated into terms conceivable for the contemporary reader.

---

[9] Sir Walter Scott, *Ivanhoe,* ed. Andrew Lang (London, 1901), pp. xlvii f.
[10] Scott, *Waverley,* p. 10.

This function of transforming a given reality makes him very different from, for instance, the Fielding hero. The latter's exemplary course of life was the focal point of interest, and this was orientated by the realization of moral principles. Waverley, however, does not dictate the course of events—he is dependent on the given reality that he is to bring to life.

This fact is confirmed by another title variant: "Or if I had rather chosen to call my work a 'Sentimental Tale,' would it not have been a sufficient presage of a heroine with a profusion of auburn hair, and a harp, the soft solace of her solitary hours, which she fortunately finds always the means of transporting from castle to cottage, although she herself be sometimes obliged to jump out of a two-pair-of-stairs window, and is more than once bewildered on her journey, alone and on foot, without any guide but a blowzy peasant girl, whose jargon she can hardly understand?"[11] With this allusion, Scott separates his own intentions from those of the sentimental novel which, in the second half of the eighteenth century, had as its subject the passions and sufferings of the 'enlightened' hero. In a sentimental novel, reality would have been reduced to the trials and tribulations of a wounded heart. Reality would have been determined by the sufferings of tearful characters and would have taken on an abstract connotation to the extent that it could only be presented as a round of knavery alternating with beautiful dreams. Such an overvaluation of the sentiments would make the reality presented most improbable, and Scott would be transplanting the implicit heroine of his title into a kind of fairy-tale atmosphere. Furthermore, if the main character were to be given too much importance in relation to the events, he would disturb the balance so vital to Scott's intentions and so satisfactorily established by the actual title of the novel.

Finally, Scott asks what expectations the reader would have formed if the title had promised an account of contemporary conditions: "Or again, if my Waverley had been entitled 'A Tale of the Times,' wouldst thou not, gentle reader, have demanded from me a dashing sketch of the fashionable world?"[12]

The presentation of contemporary reality would raise two problems for Scott. First he would have to work out a principle of selection in order to pinpoint the representative elements of contemporary events. But he sees himself as in no position to establish such a principle, as he cannot choose between foreground interests and the desire for sensations. Second, he would be obliged to act merely as a reporter of current

[11] Ibid., pp. 10 f.
[12] Ibid., p. 11.

events, so that the figure of the hero would become an increasing embarrassment as far as the structure of the novel was concerned. For a reporter is expected to give many details about many people, and since he himself thus acts as the mediator, Waverley's function would become superfluous. And so for Scott, the present day was no subject matter for a novel, and in this respect he was quite different from his great successors in France, who tended more and more to set their novels in the present.

These reflections on possible titles are a clear indication that Scott was not aiming exclusively at a description of the past, or an illustration of the present, or the life-story of a hero. So long as these three elements remain separate, they are irrelevant for Scott, for it is only through their interaction that the novel attains its subject matter. The historical past must be brought to life to avoid the label of the Gothic novel; interest in the fate of the hero must be kept down so that the historical novel will not be taken for a sentimental novel; and finally, the present can only be a point of reference and not a subject of portrayal, or else the novel would 'sink to the level of mere reporting.' Bringing the past to life requires the presence of the main character, for he—the passive hero[13]—represents the thoughts and feelings of the contemporary reader; in this way, historical reality is transformed for the reader to experience for himself.

II

What does Scott mean by historical reality?

> I beg pardon, once and for all, of those readers who take up novels merely for amusement, for plaguing them so long with old-fashioned politics, and Whig and Tory, and Hanoverians and Jacobites. The truth is, I cannot promise them that this story shall be intelligible, not to say probable, without it. My plan requires that I should explain the motives on which its action proceeded; and these motives necessarily arose from the feelings, prejudices, and parties of the times. I do not invite my fair readers . . . into a flying chariot drawn by hippogriffs, or moved by enchantment. Mine is a humble English postchaise, drawn upon four wheels, and keeping his Majesty's highway. Such as dislike the vehicle may leave it at the next halt, and wait for the conveyance of Prince Hussein's tapestry, or Malek the Weaver's flying sentry-box.[14]

Scott feels that what may seem like a lot of tedious historical details are

---

[13] See Georg Lukács, *Der historische Roman* (Berlin, 1955), p. 31. A closer analysis of Lukács's is not possible here if the subject under discussion is to be adhered to.
[14] Scott, *Waverley*, pp. 43 f.

in fact essential if one is to discern the human motives underlying and formulating historical reality. The individual impulses that drive men to act are, in their turn, answers to existing historical situations. Historical reality then, for Scott, is a network of interactions arising out of situation and response. Such situations are concrete manifestations of human motives, and each motive is conditioned by and, in turn, conditions the particular circumstances surrounding a sequence of events. In this feature of historical reality, Scott comes closest to the intention which had germinated out of his original model, Walpole's *Castle of Otranto*. However, there now arise so many individual possibilities of reaction that an account of them all might become tedious. And yet Scott considers such a display to be the basic driving force behind his novel,[15] for it is only in this way that he can attain the necessary degree of verisimilitude.

Thus the presentation of individual human conduct and of the events arising out of that conduct is endowed with verisimilitude by history and no longer depends on a set of preestablished norms, as was the case in the eighteenth-century novel. Verisimilitude is not guaranteed by personal experience, as with Defoe and Richardson; nor does it arise out of the norms of human conduct that Fielding deduced from the temporary aberrations of his heroes and the complicated machinations of the 'reality' around them; nor is it linked with what Fielding called "experience"[16] —the trying and testing of potentially existing virtues. If the verisimilitude of events and reactions is vouched for by history alone, then it cannot be interpreted either as an adumbration of truth,[17] or as an esthetic effect.

This in-built verisimilitude testifies to the originality of Scott's conception of reality, for this no longer serves to illustrate moral norms but, instead, is taken as an end in itself. It can only be successfully disclosed through the 'wandering viewpoint' of the reader, which Scott depicts with the metaphor of the post chaise.[18] This indicates the problems attending comprehension and perception of historical reality—a continual change of viewpoint is necessary, because it is no longer possible to find a single, ideal position that will command a total panorama. Thus Scott warns his readers that they will have to be patient, or else wait for an Oriental magic carpet to enable them to get a total view of reality. If reality is only to be uncovered by means of a long and difficult journey, then obviously it is no longer going to be the clear-cut setting for some

---

[15] Ibid., p. 44, in a footnote Scott again emphasizes this fact.

[16] See Henry Fielding, *Tom Jones* (Everyman's Library) II (London, 1909), XIII, 1: 158.

[17] For a thorough discussion regarding this question, see H. Blumenberg, *Paradigmen zu einer Metaphorologie* (Bonn, 1960), pp. 88 ff.

[18] The metaphor of the post-chaise can also be found, incidentally, in a similar context in Fielding's *Tom Jones*, which Stendhal greatly admired (see *Tom Jones*, XI, 9: 91 ff.).

underlying, philosophical system. Scott's images of the post chaise and the magic carpet show the basic difference between a reality that is a subject in itself, and a reality that is only the testing ground for a philosophical idea.

While Scott disguises his methods of presentation in metaphors, our task is to find out precisely how the new subject matter of reality is translated and transplanted into the mind of the reader. Our starting-point is that interrelationship between human motivation and historical situation from which Scott derives the network of interactions that constitute his 'reality'. For this network to be communicated to the reader, he needs a hero whose individuality will be played down rather than emphasized, for the character must never take precedence over the events. Thus even the name 'Waverley' hints at the hero's function, since he is to take no decisive part himself, but is, rather, to reflect historical situations and the conduct of genuine historical figures.[19]

III

Both in the introduction and the epilogue to *Waverley*, Scott emphasizes the fact that the troubles of the civil war, as described in his novel, are gathered mainly "from the narrative of intelligent eye-witnesses."[20] While Scott the narrator uses eye-witnesses to link the events of 1745 to the present, the same process is repeated in the action of the novel. Waverley is made aware of the impending decline of Scotland by the accounts of people he meets.[21] The first time he realizes the difference between past and present is in the meeting with the Baron of Bradwardine. This Lowland nobleman still recalls the days when traditional customs governed life in the Scottish villages. He himself tries to adhere to these old traditions, but this only makes him seem odd;[22] his narrative, however, authenticates the reality of the past world he describes. The political present has so distorted the relics of Scottish village life, that now only eye-witnesses can describe how things used to be, and details of old folklore can only be brought to life for Waverley by the words of the Baron.

This fanning out of history into sections of the past, depending on the age and standpoint of the eye-witness, is the dominant principle of pre-

[19] See also Stewart Gordon, "Waverley and the 'Unified Design,' " *ELH* 18 (1951): 111.

[20] Scott, *Waverley*, pp. 554 f.; see also pp. lxxiv, 123 f. footnote, 570; also references to a similar guarantee of events in *Heart of Midlothian*, made by Dorothy Van Ghent, *The English Novel. Form and Function* (New York, 1961), p. 115.

[21] See Scott, *Waverley*, pp. 96, 98 ff., 117, 121, 128 f., 146 ff., 149, and 172.

[22] See especially ibid., pp. 109 ff.

sentation in *Waverley*. It is repeated when Waverley himself comes into contact with the archaic-seeming Highland clans. Here, though, the technique undergoes a subtle refinement which might be described as the telescoping of different sections of reality, as offered by the eye-witnesses. The more peculiar and archaic past reality becomes, the more complicated is the process of its resuscitation. Waverley first learns from Rose Bradwardine all about the age-old relations between the Highland clans and the people of the Lowlands.[23] The impression arising from this is then elaborated on through the account given by the bodyguard of the Highland chief whom Waverley meets after leaving the Baron's estate.[24] The conversation with Fergus Mac-Ivor reveals another aspect of clan life,[25] and this, in turn, is extended by Flora Mac-Ivor's descriptions in an unforeseeable direction.[26] Thus from several points of view, comprising several different social levels, we are presented with historical rituals and rhythms of life within a single clan. This eradicates the one-sidedness of the single eye-witness account, and the picture of this clan's history thus becomes fuller and fuller, though at the same time we realize that these sections do not constitute the whole picture, which will in fact be extended and diversified with every new viewpoint. This additional potential adds more fuel to the reader's imagination, where the various sections of reality merge into a vivid mosaic. And so historical reality is shown as a chequered variegation of the past, according to the standpoints in time and space of the different eye-witnesses. The sections are presented in no special order of importance, and indeed this lack of specific orientation and of any overriding conception of reality is what endows the eye-witness presentation with its own special quality. Scott himself says that his intention is simply to preserve the past from oblivion,[27] and it is precisely this multiplicity of viewpoints that enables him to fulfill his intention. The minor characters in the novel ensure that historical ways of life are continually communicated to the present, and thus a reality is saved that would otherwise have perished with the passing of time. This process depends on the presence of Waverley, who acts as the link between the reader and the past. As for the story, it is no longer concerned with a single event enclosed within a particular period of time; instead, the novel shows how situations of the civil war be-

---

[23] Ibid., pp. 118 ff.
[24] Ibid., pp. 146 ff. and 149.
[25] Ibid., pp. 160 ff.
[26] Ibid., pp. 172 ff.
[27] Ibid., p. 554; see also David Daiches, "Scott's Redgauntlet," in *From Jane Austen to Joseph Conrad. Essays collected in memory of James T. Hillhouse*, ed. R. C. Rathburn and M. Steinman, Jr. (Minneapolis, 1958), p. 46.

gin to reach out into an ever expanding past, revealing more and more aspects and more and more surprises.

Historical reality, then, is a cohesively patterned phenomenon that has to be communicated; its relative homogeneity is brought about by the fact that the authenticity is guaranteed each time by an eye-witness, who does not allow the past to disintegrate into a pile of amorphous facts, but instead reports on his own world, which seems to him to be a complete and unquestionable one. Thus although each section of reality is permeated by the reactions of the particular character, it is these reactions that make the past credible, that give the events narrated a sort of spontaneous order, and that provide the reader with personal access to an otherwise alien reality. Similarly, when he is describing the events of the war itself and the period leading up to it, Scott again takes care to authenticate his account with eye-witness reports.[28] This care shows that Scott's view of history coincides neither with the Hegelian idea of a continual process, nor with the mere accumulation of facts. Scott had learned his lesson from the failure of *Queen-Hoo-Hall,* yet did not impose any idealistic construction on history. His eye-witnesses bring to life only their own particular section of the fading past, so that each account clearly presents only one aspect of reality and never the whole. If the individual sections do sometimes overlap, this simply serves to make one aware that reality can only be presented through a continual expansion of what we know.

The eye-witness accounts ensure that only those aspects of reality are captured that have actually been in existence. But by revealing Scotland's past through a variety of different characters, Scott also draws attention to the inevitable individualization of reality, for each aspect carries with it the limitations of its reporter, and is clearly only a part of a far greater whole. Reality is something that is constantly individualized and diversified. And so each particular section of the narrative restricts the reality presented, and at the same time points to the open-endedness of its own presentation. And thus we perceive, at one and the same time, the self-containment of historical events and the unceasing movement and changeability of historical processes.

Scott defined historical reality as an interaction of human motivation and historical situations.[29] In order to understand this idea more fully,

---

[28] See Scott, *Waverley,* pp. 554 f., 570, and lxxiv.
[29] Ibid., p. 44

we shall look at two specific examples. At the beginning of the novel, the close relationship between character and reality is outlined in the person of Richard Waverley, the father of the 'hero'. As the second son of a noble family, Richard Waverley feels that he is underprivileged, for he believes that the title is really due to him and not to his elder brother.[30] It is therefore quite natural for him to join the new party of the House of Hanover and to abandon his family's traditional loyalty to the Stuarts.[31] The Tory, then, becomes a Whig and begins to take an active part in political affairs at the start of the civil war. The interweaving of motivation and historical reality—the structural principle behind Scott's characters—is strikingly reflected in Richard Waverley. His firm political views in fact arise out of the personal disadvantage of his birth, which Richard hopes to counteract through a political career. He involves himself in matters which, as regards their political goals, are of no concern to him. Hence Scott's talk of the "mixed motives"[32] underlying Richard's decisions and the political opportunism which in various ways endangers his own family.[33] He takes an active part in the troubles of the civil war, and yet has no genuine political conviction, since his attitude stems from a personal problem connected with the historical reality of primogeniture. If Richard Waverley had been out to do away with primogeniture, then his political fight would at least have had a political motive, but his motive is merely to cover up the damage done to his self-esteem, by actively contributing to the political formation of the present. However, the personal motives are in fact diverted until they are almost unrecognizable, and finally he himself can no longer tell what gave rise to his actions, the consequences of which become his sole preoccupation.[34] The reality which is shaped by people arises from origins that can no longer be kept check on. Again, though, it must be stressed that the network of motives that give rise to historical reality is not to be interpreted as a platform for a priori ideas. If reality arises out of subjective reactions to historical conditions, then clearly there must be as many sides to reality as there are subjective reactions. Since these subjective impulses can lead to any number of possible consequences, reality takes on an element of opacity very far from the clear-cut orientation of the traditional novel. And, indeed, the reality shaped by the characters in this novel is often radically different from that connected with their original motives,

[30] Ibid., pp. 14 f.
[31] Ibid., pp. 15 f.
[32] Ibid., p. 14.
[33] Ibid., p. 469.
[34] Ibid., pp. 201 ff.

which represented their original reaction to the given reality confronting them.

The Baron of Bradwardine is another case in point. He sides with the Stuarts, fights in the army of the Pretender, loses all his possessions, exposes his daughter to the greatest danger, and is finally forced himself to live as an outlaw.[35] He is committed perhaps to a greater extent than any other character in the book, and one is bound to suppose that all his actions are governed by his loyalty and his conviction of the divine right of the Stuarts. And yet we learn that this total devotion arises out of his desire to be allowed to take off the King's shoes after the battle— "which was the feudal service by which he held the barony of Bradwardine."[36] This eccentricity, revealing the impenetrability of human motivation, shapes political reality, and this contributes to the imponderability of history.

All the most important minor characters are based on this principle. There is always a strange contrast between the factual reality of political events and the motives of the people involved in them. The imaginations of the characters are inspired by historical facts: Richard Waverley by primogeniture, the Baron of Bradwardine by a ceremony. And so it is a concrete historical circumstance that sets off the subjective impulses of these people, but the consequences of their reactions show in what unexpected directions an historical situation can lead once it has sown its seed in the human mind. It is this mirroring of events through their surprising consequences that first enables Scott to produce an illusion of historical reality. For the reality conceived in the novel is fictitious—it is not a chronicle of the civil war. The fiction is based on the reflections and reactions of the individual characters, whose subjective transformation of historical situations gives rise to the reality of the novel. This reality, being historical, inevitably precludes any superimposed symbolic dénouement. This is why the reactions of the characters to given situations are so erratic and would, in different times and under different circumstances, themselves be quite different—as Scott states explicitly of the most important of the minor characters, Fergus Mac-Ivor.[37] The vast potential scope of reaction bears witness to the constant individualization and consequent dynamic diversification of history. The facts are true, but they are made probable by means of fiction, and it is only this fiction that enables Scott to produce the illusion of historical reality. In the epilogue to *Waverley,* he himself comments on this form of illusion:

[35] Ibid., pp. 488 ff.
[36] Ibid., p. 110; see also pp. 374 f. and 377 f.
[37] Ibid., pp. 154 f.

". . . for the purpose of preserving some idea of the ancient manners of which I have witnessed the almost total extinction, I have embodied in imaginary scenes, and ascribed to fictitious characters, a part of the incidents which I then received from those who were actors in them. Indeed, the most romantic parts of this narrative are precisely those which have a foundation in fact."[38] In transforming eye-witness accounts of historical facts into a fiction, Scott ensures that the highly romantic-seeming situations retain their basis of fact, for they would seem incredible were it not for the fictitious characters that authenticate them.

This apparent paradox is what underlies the special illusion of historical reality. If the past is to be made tangible in all its individualized ramifications, it must seem to be consistent. But historical consistency can only be a fiction, as otherwise the past would be artificially structured by nonhistorical categories. A fictitious consistency enables the singularities of history to be related to one another, and this is why Scott transplanted his authenticated reality into fictitious figures and imaginary situations. On the other hand, if an individual historical fact is given in isolation, its effect will be romantic, because stripped of any fictitious connections it will seem as if it can only have been invented. Truth, as they say, is stranger than fiction—and in this case, fiction prevents the truth from seeming too strange. But if this fictitious consistency ensures that the past will be comprehensible, it is only natural that the contingent elements of the past should begin to take on a fantastic character—and this Scott attempts to play down by constant reference to real historical events. He had learned from the *Queen-Hoo-Hall* affair that the mass of historical facts needed consistency if it was to be brought to life, and so the fictitious consistency is what guarantees the truth-to-life of the historical reality presented. This would seem to imply, in fact, that if history is to be linked to the present, its presentation is bound to fall back on esthetic means.

IV

We must now take a closer look at the function of the hero, Waverley himself. Our discussion of the various possible titles has already drawn attention to the functional connection between the past, the 'passive hero' and the present. Waverley has the task of bringing a differentiated past into the present. At the beginning of the novel, Scott ponders on the name of his hero. He wants to free him from all associations with traditional heroes: "I have, therefore, like a maiden knight with his white

[38] Ibid., p. 554.

shield, assumed for my hero, WAVERLEY, an uncontaminated name, bearing with its sound little of good or evil, excepting what the reader shall hereafter be pleased to affix to it."[39] With this neutrality, Waverley, being uncommitted, is clearly to represent the world of the reader; he is in fact the viewing-glass through which the reader may observe the events that are to form his experience of historical reality. Like the reader, Waverley has no immediate connection with the ancient Scotland that he is to discover. His initial feeling of unfamiliarity with and secret embarrassment at Scottish customs—which is only to be conquered through his gradual understanding of them[40]—automatically establishes a link between his own and the reader's reactions. Scott observed that distance allowed only an unclear perception, but this in its turn began to act as something magic and attractive.[41] Waverley's comprehension is inextricably bound up with his imagination. Scott gives repeated descriptions of the process which leads from the imagination to an understanding of the world. In his youth, for instance, Waverley heard many tales of the past: "From such legends our hero would steal away to indulge the fancies they excited. In the corner of the large and sombre library . . . he would exercise for hours that internal sorcery by which past or imaginary events are presented in action, as it were, to the eye of the muser."[42] Through "internal sorcery" Waverley brings past events to life by transforming them into actions. Here we have one important function of the imagination: by investing and reenacting traditional or legendary facts with imaginary human actions and reactions, it can resuscitate the past. Here Scott is simply indicating the way in which the process can take place.

He gives further indications when, for the first time, Waverley makes contact with an unfamiliar world through his meeting with the Baron of Bradwardine: "But although Edward and he differed *toto coelo,* as the Baron would have said, upon this subject, yet they met upon history as on a neutral ground, in which each claimed an interest. The Baron, indeed, only cumbered his memory with matters of fact; the cold, dry, hard outlines which history delineates. Edward, on the contrary, loved to fill up and round the sketch with the colouring of a warm and vivid imagination, which gives light and life to the actors and speakers in the drama of past ages."[43]

[39] Ibid., pp. 9 f.
[40] See also Alexander Welsh, *The Hero of the Waverley Novels* (Yale Studies in English, 154) (New Haven, 1963), p. 51.
[41] Scott, *Waverley,* p. 235.
[42] Ibid., p. 32.
[43] Ibid., p. 98.

According to the definition given by Scott in the preface to *Ivanhoe,* history as "neutral ground" comprises both the factual uniqueness of an event and the feelings and reactions of people toward this event. Historical facts do not disclose the motives of the "actors and speakers," and this is why Waverley tries to reenact in his imagination the conditions that gave rise to or arose out of a particular event. Thus the context of historical situations becomes vivid again, after being, as it were, squeezed out by the passage of time. The imagination fills the framework of historical fact with the picture of dramatic human confrontations, and it is this which makes historical reality genuinely interesting. Events are freed from their fixed abode in the past, and are brought back to life with the attendant diversification that characterizes all real events.

Scott speaks of the "drama of past ages," and it is Waverley's imagination that animates the "actors and speakers." Scott began his *Essay on the Drama* with the following definition: "A DRAMA (we adopt Dr. Johnson's definition, with some little extension) is a poem of fictitious composition in dialogue, in which the action is not related but represented. A disposition to this fascinating amusement, considered in its rudest state, seems to be inherent in human nature."[44] The active imagination, then, is an integral part of human nature, which does not relate but reenacts what happened in the "drama of past ages." In this way, the time gap between past and present is bridged, and history loses the apparently clear-cut dimensions it had assumed through the passage of time. The imagination releases all the circumstances that cannot be perceived in the mere historical fact, and it brings to life all the conditions that led to the formation of historical reality. Imagination and reality interact upon one another, so that in the reality of the novel, neither history nor imagination can assume a completely dominant role. The imagination establishes what Collingwood called the "emotional charge"—the response to the "sensum" of a given situation.[45]

There are moments when Waverley experiences an exciting convergence of reality and imagination:

> Waverley could not help starting at a story which bore so much resemblance to one of his own day-dreams. Here was a girl scarce seventeen, the gentlest of her sex, both in temper and appearance, who had witnessed with her own eyes such a scene as he had used to conjure up in his imagination, as only occurring in ancient times, and spoke of it coolly, as one very likely to recur. . . . It seemed like a

---

[44] Sir Walter Scott, *The Miscellaneous Prose Works* (Edinburgh, 1878), II: 575.
[45] See R. G. Collingwood, *The Principles of Art* (Oxford, 1938), pp. 162 f.

dream to Waverley that these deeds of violence should be familiar to men's minds, and currently talked of, as falling within the common order of things and happening daily in the immediate vicinity, without his having crossed the seas, and while he was yet in the otherwise well-ordered island of Great Britain.[46]

At this moment, imagination and reality, past and present seem to have become interchangeable for Waverley, for a scene conjured up by his imagination does not, in fact, belong to some distant age but is happening here and now. This surprising coincidence of imagination and reality is confirmed by the eye-witness, and so historical reality is restored to the present by the imagination, while the imagination fulfills itself by bringing history to life. Waverley is so excited by this interaction because his imagination has always been fired by those elements of the past that seem to have vanished into obscurity.[47] The imagination must create a path to the apparently inaccessible, and historical reality is ideal material for it, insofar as past human conflicts are not totally wrapped in mystery. The imagination can achieve comprehension through animation, and this represents a perfectly valid category of historical comprehension.[48] The imagination endows the individual events of the past with a consistency that is quite different from any philosophical pattern-forming. It is disciplined by the concreteness of events, while the unconfinable fluidity of events attains consistency without being restricted to any single, ultimate purpose. Thus reality and imagination become virtually inseparable, and this in turn implies that history can best be captured by esthetic means. In *Waverley*, Scott has set history free from its chains of fact; he uses the imagination of his hero to communicate the live reality behind the facts. Scott took care to particularize this function of the imagination by contrasting his own hero with that of Cervantes: "My intention is not to follow the steps of that inimitable author, in describing such total perversion of intellect as misconstrues the objects actually presented to the senses, but that more common aberration from sound judgment which apprehends occurrences indeed in their reality, but communicates to them a tincture of its own romantic tone and colouring."[49]

Scott's hero is aware of the gap between his imagination and reality. He cannot produce a purely imaginary world, if only because his imag-

---

[46] Scott, *Waverley*, pp. 121 and 123.

[47] See, for instance, ibid., pp. 133 and 112.

[48] See Heinrich Rickert, *Kulturwissenschaft und Naturwissenschaft* (Tübingen, [3]1915), pp. 79 f.

[49] Scott, *Waverley*, p. 35.

ination depends on reality for its importance. At the same time, though, whatever is communicated by the hero is bound to be colored by his own personality. However, Waverley is a 'passive hero', representing the sentiments of the reader himself, and so the coloring he gives to the reality he communicates will in fact be a vital aid in establishing contact with the reader. It is the very imperfection of the hero that guarantees his esthetic effectiveness.

Though Waverley differs from Don Quixote in that, despite his imaginativeness, he does not construct an imaginary world, nevertheless he is exposed to the danger of getting lost in his imagination: ". . . a thousand circumstances of fatal self-indulgence have made me the creature rather of imagination than reason."[50] The imagination tends to be perilous when it develops into a vehicle for the hero's wish-fulfillments. At such moments it becomes obvious that the imagination can only perform its proper function when it is directly related to a given reality. This observation is confirmed by the blotting-out of "romantic spirit" and "exalted imagination" when the hero is temporarily involved in war emergencies and is thus totally preoccupied with saving his own skin.[51] Once he is forced to concentrate completely on getting out of such situations, imagination fades right away, for it is not an instrument to dictate forms of action. Only when the hero is free from the immediate pressures of distressing situations will his imagination fulfill the purpose of reenacting historical reality.

As we have seen already, this process involves a change in the hitherto conventional conception of the novel-hero. He can no longer be the focal point of interest. The ideal intentions which still permeate even Waverley's life[52] are gradually squeezed out by his new function. His imagination is not allowed to dwell upon any one single event, for such a preference would imply an evaluation of reality. Indeed, the communication of historical reality through the imagination leads almost to a loss of identity in Waverley, for he must be open to all situations but must identify with none. Only in this way can his imagination create a

---

[50] Ibid., p. 214.

[51] See ibid., p. 296.

[52] The recent monograph by Welsh is concerned with this form of presentation: "The argument of the book is a simple one. The passive hero has always seemed to me the most extraordinary and significant feature of the Waverley Novels. I set out to account for this hero's inactivity from a study of the text of the novels. The result of the inquiry is a thematic study centering on the relations of property, anxiety, and honor, and supported by excursions into the history of ideas" (pp. vii f.). For a different conception of the passive hero, see Walter Bagehot, *The Works*, ed. Mrs. Russel Barrington (London, 1915), III: 67; Gerhard Buck, *In Fortsetzung Bagehots. Die Waverley Romane Sir Walter Scotts* (Britannica, 13), p. 3; David Daiches, *Literary Essays* (Edinburgh, 1956), p. 89; and Donald Davie, *The Heyday of Sir Walter Scott* (London, 1961), p. 30.

trustworthy experience out of the contingencies of historical reality.

The potential limitlessness of this whole process makes how to end the novel a problem. While the hero's function is to bring past reality to life, history itself does not come to any end—as Scott's subtitle indicates—and so the novel can only come to a stop if the main figure once more steps into the foreground. But this would mean a total change of emphasis as regards the subject matter of the novel, with Waverley taking precedence over events and history supplying only the trappings for the hero's development. Scott deals with this problem by adopting an ironic style in depicting his hero at the end. The reader is bound to be interested in Waverley's personal situation after the civil war, but Scott dampens down this interest by constantly interrupting his description of Waverley whenever he is on the verge of tying up the various ends of the action.[53] He merely indicates how things reached this particular point, and then adds apologetically that he does not want to overtax the reader's patience. Thus he tends more and more to gloss over the personal details of Waverley's life, and when finally he comes to the obligatory marriage—in the tradition of the eighteenth-century novel— he makes the following ironic observation: "But before entering upon a subject of proverbial delay, I must remind my reader of the progress of a stone rolled down hill by an idle truant boy . . . it moves at first slowly, avoiding by inflection every obstacle of the least importance . . . but when the story draws near its close, we hurry over the circumstances, however important, which your imagination must have forestalled, and leave you to suppose those things, which it would be abusing your patience to relate at length."[54] Scott simply leaves it to the reader to imagine and paint in the details of the conventional ending, for to describe the obvious and expected would be again to overtax the reader's patience. This ironic treatment of convention shows that Scott certainly did not want the end of his novel to be interpreted as the visible self-fulfillment of the hero. And so Scott uses irony and omission to preserve the integrity of his intentions: to push his hero discreetly into the background, and to leave historical reality—as conjured up with the aid of that hero—properly situated in the foreground.

V

There remains finally the question of how Scott manages technically to communicate the picture of an individualized historical past. A full dis-

---

[53] See Scott, *Waverley*, pp. 497 and 517.
[54] Ibid., p. 539.

cussion of this technique would require a separate essay, and we must restrict ourselves here to just a few basic observations. When, as narrator, Scott wishes to produce a vivid idea of specific persons or events, he splits them up into a variety of aspects, and as we view the characters and the situations from different perspectives, so the pictures gradually become fuller, and the potential expands. This process emerges, for instance, in the portrayal of Gilfillan when he meets Waverley in Major Melville's house. First the narrator offers a detailed description of Gilfillan; then Waverley supplements this with another, quite unexpected view, which vividly intensifies the impressions given by the narrator: ". . . Waverley was irresistibly impressed with the idea that he beheld a leader of the Roundheads of yore, in conference with one of Marlborough's captains."[55]

This is typical of Scott's technique of presentation. By fanning out the character into a series of perspectives, Scott creates a heightened awareness of the *potential* character. The way is laid open for the imagination to penetrate the diversification and to bind the various aspects together in a unified picture, as we can see from Waverley's reaction when he meets Gilfillan. It is the imagination that gives consistency to the narrator's apparently disordered presentation, and it is this consistency that raises the description to the level of vivid perception. There are many instances of this technique in *Waverley,* and it is used to describe situations as well as characters. The exodus of the Highland clans from Edinburgh is one example.[56] The narrator sets out his series of observations, and these are then drawn together through Waverley's reactions, which bring the whole event to life in the reader's imagination.

This very technique is what gave rise to Stendhal's objections to the historical novel. The danger attendant on such detailed historical descriptions is that they may become boring, because Scott's historical 'tableau' and the communicative reactions of the hero do not leave the reader with enough free play to get himself personally involved: the reactions and the historical facts are presented by the author or his minor characters in such a clear-cut manner that the reader is bound to become too passive. Scott's French successors kept reality and reaction apart, so that the world to be deduced from the behavior of their characters took on a suggestive note very different from Scott's technique of intermediary communication.[57]

---

[55] Ibid., p. 281.
[56] Ibid., pp. 348 ff.
[57] Concerning Scott's reception in England, see John Henry Raleigh, "What Scott Meant to the Victorians," *Victorian Studies* 7 (1963): 7 ff.

Furthermore we cannot equate Scott's 'perspectivism' with that of the modern novel since Flaubert and Henry James. Scott's splitting of his subject matter into perspectives always serves the specific aim of communicating historical events. While the modern novel seeks to create its subject through a profusion of perspectives, Scott's subject is already present and is divided up purely for the sake of achieving an enhanced vividness. At the same time, Scott's aims separate him from his predecessors, such as Fielding, in that he is no longer committed to the principle of *imitatio naturae*. The priniciple of *imitatio historiae* demands only that history be made vivid in the present; this involves translating factual reality into "fictitious characters" and "imaginary scenes," because only in this way can historical diffuseness be overcome and presented coherently for subjective comprehension and experience. Fiction, however, is a phenomenon of form; traditionally it had always served art in completing what in nature appeared to be incomplete. With history for its subject matter, the novel now had to cope with the problem of presenting a fixed reality without making it seem complete, since historical reality is continuous and indeterminable. It might be said that Scott's greatness lies in his ability to create the illusion of historical reality without confining that reality to the illusion he created.

5

THE READER AS A COMPONENT
PART OF THE REALISTIC NOVEL:
Esthetic Effects in Thackeray's *Vanity Fair*

I

Y ou must have your eyes forever on your Reader. That alone constitutes . . . Technique!"[1] Ford Madox Ford's exhortation to
the novelist draws attention to one of the few basic rules that
have governed the novel throughout its relatively short history. This
awareness as a prerequisite for steering the reader has always exerted a
fundamental influence on the form of the narrative. From the start the
novel as a 'genre' was virtually free from traditional constraints and so
the novelists of the eighteenth century considered themselves not merely as the creators of their works but also as the law-makers.[2] The events
they devise also set out the standards regarded as necessary for judging
the events; this is shown clearly by Defoe and Richardson in their pref-
aces and commentaries, and especially by Fielding in the innumerable
essays with which he permeates his narrative. Such interventions are
meant to indicate how the author wants his text to be understood, and

---

[1] Ford Madox Ford, "Techniques," *The Southern Review* I (1935): 35. The dots are part of
the original text and are used by Ford to accentuate "Technique."
[2] See Henry Fielding, *Joseph Andrews* (Everyman's Library) (London, 1948), "Author's
Preface": xxxii; and *Tom Jones* (Everyman's Library) (London, 1962), II, 1: 39; also Samuel
Richardson, *Clarissa, or The History of a Young Woman Comprehending the most Important
Concerns of Private Life* (The Shakespeare Head Edition) (Oxford, 1930–31), VII: 325.

also to make the reader more deeply aware of those events for the judgment of which his own imagination has to be mobilized. With the author manipulating the reader's attitude, the narrator becomes his own commentator and is not afraid to break into the world he is describing in order to provide his own explanations. That this is a deliberate process is demonstrated by a sentence from Fielding's *Tom Jones:* "And this, as I could not prevail on any of my actors to speak, I myself was obliged to declare."[3]

And so the novel as a form in the eighteenth century is shaped by the dialogue that the author wishes to conduct with his reader. This simulated relationship gives the reader the impression that he and the author are partners in discovering the reality of human experience. In this reader-oriented presentation of the world, one can see an historical reflection of the period when the possibility of a priori knowledge was refuted, leaving fiction as the only means of supplying the insight into human nature denied by empirical philosophy.

The author-reader relationship, which was thus developed by the eighteenth-century novel, has remained a constant feature of narrative prose and is still in evidence even when the author seems to have disappeared and the reader is deliberately excluded from comprehension. While Fielding offers this reassurance to his readers: "I am, indeed, set over them for their own good only, and was created for their use, and not they for mine,"[4] Joyce, at the other end of the scale drops only the ironic information that the author has withdrawn behind his work, "paring his fingernails."[5] The reader of modern novels is deprived of the assistance which the eighteenth-century writer had given him in a variety of devices ranging from earnest exhortation to satire and irony. Instead, he is expected to strive for himself to unravel the mysteries of a sometimes strikingly obscure composition. This development reflects the transformation of the very idea of literature, which seems to have ceased to be a means of relaxation and even luxury, making demands now on the capacity of understanding because the world presented seems to have no bearing on what the reader is familiar with. This change did not happen suddenly. The stages of transition are clearly discernible in the nineteenth century, and one of them is virtually a half-way point in the development: the so-called 'realistic' novel. An outstanding example of

[3] Fielding, *Tom Jones,* III, 7: 93.
[4] Ibid., II, 1: 39.
[5] James Joyce, *A Portrait of the Artist as a Young Man* (London, 1966), p. 219. The full sentence reads: "The artist, like the God of creation, remains within or behind or beyond or above his handiwork, invisible, refined out of existence, indifferent, paring his fingernails."

this is Thackeray's *Vanity Fair*. Here, the author-reader relationship is as different from the eighteenth-century 'dialogue' as it is from the twentieth-century demand that the reader find for himself the key to a many-sided puzzle. In Thackeray, the reader does have to make his own discoveries, but the author provides him with unmistakable clues to guide him in his search.

The first stage in our discussion must be to modify the term 'author'. We should distinguish, as Wayne Booth does in his *Rhetoric of Fiction*, between the man who writes the book (author), the man whose attitudes shape the book (implied author), and the man who communicates directly with the reader (narrator): "The 'implied author' chooses, consciously or unconsciously, what we read; . . . he is the sum of his own choices. . . . This implied author is always distinct from the 'real man' —whatever we may take him to be—who creates a superior version of himself, a 'second self', as he creates his work."[6] The narrator, of course, is not always to be identified with the implied author. In the novels of the nineteenth century it happens again and again that the narrator moves even further and further away from the implied author by virtue of being an actual character in the story itself. Traces of this kind of narrator are already apparent in Dickens's novels, and in Thackeray's *Vanity Fair* he is a complete character in his own right. It is almost as if the implied author, who devised the story, has to bow to the narrator, who has a deeper insight into all the situations. What the implied author describes is interpreted by the narrator to a degree far beyond what one might normally deduce from the events. One is bound to ask the purpose of this clear though sometimes complex separation between narration and commentary, especially in a 'realistic' novel which is supposed to represent reality as it is. The justification lies in the fact that even a realistic novel cannot encompass total reality. As Arnold Bennett once remarked: "You can't put the whole of a character into a book."[7] If the limitations of the novel are such that one cannot reveal a complete character, it is even more impossible to try to transcribe complete reality. And so even a novel that is called realistic can present no more than particular aspects of a given reality, although the selection must remain implicit in order to cloak the author's ideology.

[6] Wayne C. Booth, *The Rhetoric of Fiction* (Chicago, 1961), pp. 74 f. and 151. Kathleen Tillotson, *The Tale and the Teller* (London, 1959), p. 22, points out that Dowden, in 1877, had already differentiated between the author as an historical person and the author as narrator. He calls the narrator of George Eliot's novel "that second self who writes her books."

[7] Quoted by Miriam Allott, *Novelists on the Novel* (Columbia Paperback) (New York, 1966), p. 290; see also Hans Blumenberg, "Wirklichkeitsbegriff und Möglichkeit des Romans," in *Nachahmung und Illusion* (Poetik und Hermeneutik, I), ed. H. R. Jauss (Munich, 1964), pp. 21 f.

II

Thackeray's *Vanity Fair* is also governed by this principle, which is clearly reflected by the different titles of the original version and the final one. The first, consisting of eight chapters, was called "Pen and Pencil Sketches of English Society," indicating that the reality described was meant primarily as a reproduction of social situations; the final version, "Vanity Fair," is concerned less with depicting social situations than with offering a judgment of them. This quality is commented on by Thackeray himself in a letter written a few years after the publication of *Vanity Fair:* ". . . the Art of Novels *is* . . . to convey as strongly as possible the sentiment of reality—in a tragedy or a poem or a lofty drama you aim at producing different emotions; the figures moving, and their words sounding, heroically."[8] "Sentiment of reality" implies that the novel does not represent reality itself, but aims rather at producing an idea of how reality can be experienced. Thus *Vanity Fair* not only offers a panorama of contemporary reality but also reveals the way in which the abundance of details has been organized, so that the reader can participate in the organization of events and thus gain the "sentiment of reality." This is the reason why the novel continues to be effective even today, though the social conditions it describes are only of historical interest. If the past has been kept alive, this is primarily due to the structural pattern through which the events are conveyed to the reader: the effect is gained by the interplay between the implied author who arranges the events, and the narrator who comments on them. The reader can only gain real access to the social reality presented by the implied author, when he follows the adjustments of perspective made by the narrator in viewing the events described. In order to ensure that the reader participates in the way desired, the narrator is set up as a kind of authority between him and the events, conveying the impression that understanding can only be achieved through this medium. In the course of the action, the narrator takes on various guises in order to appear as a fully developed character and in order to control the distance from which the reader has to view the scenes unfolded before him.

At the start of the novel, the narrator introduces himself as "Manager

---

[8] William Makepeace Thackeray, *The Letters and Private Papers,* ed. Gordon N. Ray (London, 1945), II: 772 f. For an historical discussion on the relationship between commentary and story, see Geoffrey Tillotson, *Thackeray the Novelist* (University Paperbacks) (London, 1963), pp. 209 ff.

of the Performance,"[9] and gives an outline of what the audience is to expect. The ideal visitor to 'Vanity Fair' is described as a "man with a reflective turn of mind";[10] this is an advance indication of what the reader has to accomplish, if he is to realize the meaning of the proceedings. But at the same time, the Manager promises that he has something for everyone: "Some people consider Fairs immoral altogether, and eschew such, with their servants and families: very likely they are right. But persons who think otherwise, and are of a lazy, or a benevolent, or a sarcastic mood, may perhaps like to step in for half an hour, and look at the performances. There are scenes of all sorts: some dreadful combats, some grand and lofty horse-riding, some scenes of high life, and some of very middling indeed; some love-making for the sentimental, and some light comic business."[11] In this way the Manager tries to entice all different types of visitors to enter his Fair—bearing in mind the fact that such a visit will also have its after-effects. When the reader has been following the narrator for quite some time, he is informed: "This, dear friends and companions, is my amiable object—to walk with you through the Fair, to examine the shops and the shows there; and that we should all come home after the flare, and the noise, and the gaiety, and be perfectly miserable in private."[12] But the reader will only feel miserable after walking through the Fair if, unexpectedly, he has come upon himself in some of the situations, thereby having his attention drawn to his own behavior, which has shone out at him from the mirror of possibilities. The narrator is only pretending to help the reader—in reality he is goading him. His reliability is already reduced by the fact that he is continually donning new masks: at one moment he is an observer[13] of the Fair, like the reader; then he is suddenly blessed with extraordinary knowledge, though he can explain ironically that "novelists have the privilege of knowing everything";[14] and then, toward the end, he announces that the

[9] William Makepeace Thackeray, *Vanity Fair*, I (The Centenary Biographical Edition), ed. Lady Ritchie (London, 1910), p. liii.

[10] Ibid., p. liv.

[11] Ibid., for the irony of the author's commentary, see Ulrich Broich, "Die Bedeutung der Ironie für das Prosawerk W. M. Thackerays unter besonderer Berücksichtigung von 'Vanity Fair'," Dissertation, Bonn, 1958, p. 78.

[12] Thackeray, *Vanity Fair*, I: 225.

[13] This comes out strikingly in his remark at the end of the novel: "Ah! *Vanitas Vanitatum!* which of us is happy in this world?" Thackeray, *Vanity Fair*, II: 431; there are also less striking instances, when the author pretends that he does not quite know what is happening in the minds of his characters; *Vanity Fair*, I: 236.

[14] Ibid., p. 29.

whole story was not his own at all,[15] but that he overheard it in a conversation.[16] At the beginning of the novel the narrator is presented as Manager of the Performance, and at the end he presents himself as the reporter of a story which fell into his hands purely by chance. The further away he stands from the social reality depicted, the clearer is the outline of the part he is meant to play. But the reader can only view the social panorama in the constantly shifting perspectives which are opened up for him by this Protean narrator. Although he cannot help following the views and interpretations of the narrator, it is essential for him to understand the motivations behind this constant changing of viewpoints, because only the discovery of the motivations can lead to the comprehension of what is intended. Thus the narrator regulates the distance between reader and events, and in doing so brings about the esthetic effect of the story. The reader is given only as much information as will keep him oriented and interested, but the narrator deliberately leaves open the inferences that are to be drawn from this information. Consequently, empty spaces are bound to occur, spurring the reader's imagination to detect the assumption which might have motivated the narrator's attitude. In this way, we get involved because we react to the viewpoints advanced by the narrator. If the narrator is an independent character, clearly separated from the inventor of the story, the tale of the social aspirations of the two girls Becky and Amelia takes on a greater degree of objectivity, and indeed one gains the impression that this social reality is not a mere narration but actually exists. The narrator can then be regarded as a sort of mediator between the reader and the events, with the implication that it is only through him that the social reality can be rendered communicable in the first place.

III

The narrator's strategy can be seen even more clearly in his relations with the characters in the novel and with the reader's expectations. *Vanity Fair* has as the subtitle, *A Novel without a Hero,* which indicates that the characters are not regarded as representing an ideal, exemplary form of human conduct, as established by the conventions of the eighteenth-century novel. Instead, the reader's interest is divided between two figures who, despite the contrast in their behavior, can under no circum-

[15] See Thackeray, *Vanity Fair*, II: 344. This is the first definite statement that the author "the present writer of a history of which every word is true" makes the personal acquaintance of important characters in his novel at the ducal Court of Pumpernickel.

[16] Ibid., p. 404. John Loofbourow, *Thackeray and the Form of Fiction* (Princeton, 1964), p. 88, suggests: "In *Vanity Fair*, the Commentator is a dimension of dissent."

stances be regarded as complementary or even corrective. For Becky, no price is too high for the fulfillment of her social ambitions; her friend Amelia is simple and sentimental. And so right at the beginning we are told:

> As she is not a heroine, there is no need to describe her person; indeed I am afraid that her nose was rather short than otherwise, and her cheeks a great deal too round and red for a heroine; but her face blushed with rosy health, and her lips with the freshest of smiles, and she had a pair of eyes which sparkled with the brightest and honestest good-humour, except indeed when they filled with tears, and that was a great deal too often; for the silly thing would cry over a dead canary-bird; or over a mouse, that the cat haply had seized upon; or over the end of a novel, were it ever so stupid.[17]

The details of such a description serve only to trivialize those features that were so important in the hero or heroine of the traditional novel. These details give the impression that something significant is being said about the person described, but the succession of clichés, from the round red cheeks and sparkling eyes to the soft-hearted sentimentality, achieve their purpose precisely by depriving the character of its representative nature. But if Amelia is deprived of traditional representative qualities and is not to be regarded as the positive counterpart to the unscrupulous, sophisticated Becky, then the novel denies the reader a basic focal point of orientation. He is prevented from sympathizing with the hero—a process which till now had always provided the nineteenth-century reader with his most important means of access to the events described—as typified by the reaction of a reviewer to Charlotte Brontë's *Jane Eyre:* "We took up *Jane Eyre* one winter's evening, somewhat piqued at the extravagant commendations we had heard, and sternly resolved to be as critical as Croker. But as we read on we forgot both commendations and criticism, identified ourselves with Jane in all her troubles, and finally married Mr. Rochester about four in the morning."[18] In contrast, *Vanity Fair* seems bent on breaking any such direct contact with the characters, and indeed the narrator frequently goes out of his way to prevent the reader from putting himself in their place.

This occurs predominantly through the narrator's comments on the particular patterns of behavior developed by Amelia and Becky in critical situations. He reveals the motives behind their utterances, interpolat-

---

[17] Thackeray, *Vanity Fair,* I: 6.
[18] Quoted by Kathleen Tillotson, *Novels of the Eighteen-Forties* (Oxford Paperbacks, 15) (Oxford, 1961), pp. 19 f.

ing consequences of which they themselves are not aware, so that these occasions serve to uncover the imbalance of the characters.[19] Often the behavior of the characters is interpreted far beyond the scope of the reactions shown and in the light of knowledge which at best could only have been revealed by the future.[20] In this way the reader is continually placed at a distance from the characters. As Michel Butor once pointed out, in a different context: "If the reader is put in the place of the hero, he must also be put in the hero's immediate present; he cannot know what the hero does not know, and things must appear to him just as they appear to the hero."[21] In *Vanity Fair*, however, the characters are illuminated by a knowledge to which they themselves have no access. They are constantly kept down below the intellectual level of the narrator, whose views offer the reader a far greater stimulus to identification than do the characters themselves. This detachment from the characters is part of the narrator's avowed intention: ". . . as we bring our characters forward, I will ask leave, as a man and a brother, not only to introduce them, but occasionally to step down from the platform, and talk about them: if they are good and kindly, to love them and shake them by the hand; if they are silly, to laugh at them confidentially in the reader's sleeve: if they are wicked and heartless, to abuse them in the strongest terms which politeness admits of."[22] The characters in this novel are completely hedged in by such judgments, and the reader sees all their actions only when they have been refracted by the narrator's own critical evaluations. The immensity of his presence makes it impossible for the reader to live their lives with them, as did the reviewer we have quoted, during his reading of *Jane Eyre*. The actual gap between the characters' actions and the narrator's comments stimulates the reader into forming judgments of his own—thereby bridging the gaps—and gradually adopting the position of critic himself.

It is mainly this intention that shapes the composition of the characters, and there are two dominant techniques to be observed. The first part of the novel reproduces letters which Becky and Amelia write to each other. The letter makes it possible to reveal the most intimate thoughts and feelings to such a degree that the reader can learn from the correspondents themselves just who they are and what makes them 'tick'. A

---

[19] See Thackeray, *Vanity Fair*, I: 67, 94 f., 108 f., 146, 210 ff., 214, passim.
[20] Ibid., pp. 20, 26 f., 32, 37 f., 291, 296 f.; II: 188, passim.
[21] Michel Butor, *Repertoire*, transl. H. Scheffel (Munich, 1965), II: 98.
[22] Thackeray, *Vanity Fair*, I: 95 f.

typical example is Becky's long letter telling Amelia all about her new surroundings at the Crawley family's country seat. Becky's impressions end with the spontaneous self-revelation: "I am determined to make myself agreeable."[23] Fitting in with present circumstances remains her guiding principle throughout her quest for social advancement. Such a wish is so totally in keeping with her own character that the maneuvers necessary for its fulfillment constitute for Becky the natural way to behave. Thus we see that in society, self-seeking hypocrisy has become second nature to man. In the letters, however, Becky's self-esteem remains so constant that she is clearly quite unaware of her two-facedness. The obvious naiveté of such self-portraits is bound to provoke the reader into critical reaction, and the heading of the chapter that reproduces Becky's letter is already pointing in this direction, for the unmistakably ironic title is: "Arcadian Simplicity."[24] Thus the self-revelation of the letter actually justifies the narrator for not taking the character as it is, but setting it at a critical distance so that it can be seen through. Elsewhere we read: "Perhaps in Vanity Fair there are no better satires than letters."[25] But the intention of the satire is for the reader himself to uncover, for the narrator never offers him more than ironic clues. The narrator's keen concern to give the impression that he never commits himself to ultimate clarity reveals itself at those times when he accidentally reaches an 'understanding' with his reader, but then remembers that such an exchange of experiences goes beyond the limits of his narrative: ". . . but we are wandering out of the domain of the story."[26]

The second technique designed to rouse the critical faculties of the reader is revealed in Amelia's almost obsessive habit of "building numberless castles in the air . . . which Amelia adorned with all sorts of flower-gardens, rustic walks, country churches, Sunday schools, and the like."[27] This day-dreaming is typical of Amelia,[28] who devises these beautiful visions as an escape from the narrow confines of her social existence. Her whole outlook is governed by expectations that generally arise out of chance events in her life and are therefore as subject to fortuitous change as the social situations she gets into. The dependence of these often very sentimental day-dreams on the circumstances of the moment shows not only the fickleness of her behavior but also the disorientated nature of her desires, the fulfillment of which is inevitably frustrated by

---

[23] Ibid., p. 120.
[24] Ibid., pp. 112 ff.
[25] Ibid., p. 227.
[26] Ibid., II: 31.
[27] Ibid., I: 146.
[28] Ibid., pp. 37, 39 f., 145, 317 f.; II: 39 f., 277 f., 390, 401, 408, and 423 f.

the apparently superior forces of her environment. The projection of hopes which cannot be realized leads to an attitude which is as characteristic of Amelia as it is of Becky, who for different motives also covers up what she really is, in order to gain the social position she hankers after.[29] Despite the difference in their motives, both Amelia's and Becky's lives are largely governed by illusions, which are shown up for what they are by the fact that whenever they are partially realized, we see how very trivial the aspirations really were.[30] The characters themselves, however, lack this awareness, and this is hardly surprising, as their ambitions or longings are often roused by chance occurrences which are not of sufficient lasting importance to give the characters a true sense of direction. Becky certainly has greater drive in her quest for social advancement, and one would therefore expect a greater degree of continuity in her conduct; but this very ambition requires that she should adapt her conduct to the various demands made by the different strata of society; and this fact in turn shows how malleable and therefore illusory are the conventions of social life. What is presented in Becky's life as continuity should not be confused with the aspirations of the eighteenth-century hero, who went forth in order to find out the truth about himself; here it is the expression of the many-sided sham which is the very attribute of social reality.

When the narrator introduces his characters at the beginning of the novel, he says of Becky: "The famous little Becky Puppet has been pronounced to be uncommonly flexible in the joints, and lively on the wire."[31] As the characters cannot free themselves from their illusions, it is only to be expected that they should take them for unquestionable reality. The reader is made aware of this fact by the attitude of the narrator, who has not only seen through his 'puppets', but also lets them act on a level of consciousness far below his own. This almost overwhelming superiority of the narrator over his characters also puts the reader in a privileged position, though with the unspoken but ever-present condition that he should draw his own conclusions from the extra knowledge imparted to him by the narrator. There is even an allegory of the reader's task at one point in the novel, when Becky is basking in the splendor of a grand social evening:

The man who brought her refreshment and stood behind her chair, had talked her character over with the large gentleman in motley-

29 Ibid., II: 151 f., 209, passim.
30 Ibid., p. 188.
31 Ibid., I: lv. On Becky the puppet, see H. A. Talon, *Two Essays on Thackeray* (Dijon, no date), pp. 7 f.

coloured clothes at his side. Bon Dieu! it is awful, that servants' inqui-
sition! You see a woman in a great party in a splendid saloon, surrounded by faithful admirers, distributing sparkling glances, dressed to
perfection, curled, rouged, smiling and happy:—Discovery walks re-
spectfully up to her, in the shape of a huge powdered man with large
calves and a tray of ices—with Calumny (which is as fatal as truth) behind him, in the shape of the hulking fellow carrying the wafer-biscuits,
Madam, your secret will be talked over by those men at their club at
the public-house to-night. . . . Some people ought to have mutes for
servants in Vanity Fair—mutes who could not write. If you are guilty,
tremble. That fellow behind your chair may be a Janissary with a bow-
string in his plush breeches pocket. If you are not guilty, have a care
of appearances: which are as ruinous as guilt.[32]

This little scene contains a change of standpoints typical of the way in
which the reader's observations are conditioned throughout this novel.
The servants are suddenly transformed into allegorical figures with the
function of uncovering what lies hidden beneath the façades of their
masters. But the discovery will only turn into calumny from the standpoint of the person affected. The narrator compares the destructive effect of calumny with that of truth and advises his readers to employ
mutes, or better still illiterate mutes, as servants, in order to protect themselves against discovery. Then he brings the reader's view even more sharply into focus, finally leaving him to himself with an indissoluble ambiguity: if he feels guilty, because he is pretending to be something he is not,
then he must fear those around him as if they were an army of Janis-
saries. If he has nothing to hide, then the social circle merely demands
of him to keep up appearances; but since this is just as ruinous as deliberate hypocrisy, it follows that life in society imposes roles on all concerned, reducing human behavior to the level of play-acting. All the
characters in the novel are caught up in this play, as is expressly shown
by the narrator's own stage metaphor at the beginning and at the end.
The key word for the reader is 'discover', and the narrator continually
prods him along the road to discovery, laying a trail of clues for him to
follow. The process reveals not only the extent to which Becky and
Amelia take their illusions for reality but also—even more strikingly—the
extent to which reality itself is illusory, since it is built on the simulated
relationships between people. The reader will not fail to notice the gulf
between 'illusion' and 'reality', and in realizing it, he is experiencing the
esthetic effect of the novel: Thackeray did not set out to create the con-

---

[32] Thackeray, *Vanity Fair*, II: 112.

ventional illusion that involved the reader in the world of the novel as if it were reality; instead, his narrator constantly interrupts the story precisely in order to prevent such an illusion from coming into being. The reader is deliberately stopped from identifying himself with the characters. And as the aim is to prevent him from taking part in the events, he is allowed to be absorbed only to a certain degree and is then jerked back again, so that he is impelled to criticize from the outside. Thus the story of the two girls serves to get the reader involved, while the meaning of the story can only be arrived at by way of the additional manipulations of perspective carried out by the narrator.

This 'split-level' technique conveys a far stronger impression of reality than does the illusion which claims that the world of the novel corresponds to the whole world. For now the reader himself has to discover the true situation, which becomes clearer and clearer to him as he gets to know the characters in their fetters of illusion. In this way, he himself takes an active part in the animation of all the characters' actions, for they seem real to him because he is constantly under obligation to work out all that is wrong with their behavior. In order that his participation should not be allowed to slacken, the individual characters are fitted out with different types and degrees of delusion, and there are even some, like Dobbin, whose actions and feelings might mislead one into taking them for positive counterparts to all the other characters. Such a false assumption is certainly perceived, even if not intended, by the narrator, who toward the end of the novel addresses the reader as follows: "This woman [i.e., Amelia] had a way of tyrannising over Major Dobbin (for the weakest of all people will domineer over somebody), and she ordered him about, and patted him, and made him fetch and carry just as if he was a great Newfoundland dog. . . . This history has been written to very little purpose if the reader has not perceived that the Major was a spooney."[33] What might have seemed like noble-mindedness was in fact the behavior of a nincompoop, and if the reader has only just realized it, then he has not been particularly successful in the process of 'discovering'.

The esthetic effect of *Vanity Fair* depends on activating the reader's critical faculties so that he may recognize the social reality of the novel as a confusing array of sham attitudes, and experience the exposure of this sham as the true reality. Instead of being expressly stated, the cri-

[33] Ibid., p. 399. Re the character of Dobbin, see Talon, *Two Essays,* p. 31; re the name, see J. A. Falconer, "Balzac and Thackeray," *English Studies* 26 (1944/45): 131.

teria for such judgments have to be inferred. They are the blanks which the reader is supposed to fill in, thus bringing his own criticism to bear. In other words, it is his own criticism that constitutes the reality of the book. The novel, then, is not to be viewed as the mere reflection of a social reality, for its true form will only be revealed when the world it presents has, like all images, been refracted and converted by the mind of the reader. *Vanity Fair* aims not at presenting social reality, but at presenting the way in which such reality can be experienced. "To convey as strongly as possible the sentiment of reality" is Thackeray's description of this process, which he regarded as the function of the novel. If the sense of the narrative can only be completed through the cooperation of the reader (which is allowed for in the text), then the borderline between fiction and reality becomes increasingly hazy, for the reader can scarcely regard his own participation as fictional. He is bound to look on his reactions as something real, and at no time is this conviction disputed. But since his reactions are real, he will lose the feeling that he is judging a world that is only fictional. Indeed, his own judgments will enhance the impression he has that this world is a reality.

How very concerned Thackeray was to confront the reader with a reality he himself considered to be real is clear from the passage already quoted, in which the narrator tells the reader that his object is to walk with him through the Fair and leave him "perfectly miserable" afterward. Thackeray reiterates this intention in a letter written in 1848: "my object . . . is to indicate, in cheerful terms, that we are for the most part an abominably foolish and selfish people . . . all eager after vanities . . . I want to leave everybody dissatisfied and unhappy at the end of the story—we ought all to be with our own and all other stories."[34] For this insight to take root in the reader, the fictional world must be made to seem real to him. Since, in addition, the reader is intended to be a critic of this world, the esthetic appeal of the novel lies in the fact that it gives him the opportunity to step back and take a detached look at that which he had regarded as normal human conduct. This detachment, however, is not to be equated with the edification which the moral novel offered to its readers. Leaving the reader perfectly miserable after his reading indicates that such a novel is not going to offer him pictures of another world that will make him forget the sordid nature of this one; the reader is forced, rather, to exercise his own critical faculties in order to relieve his distress by uncovering potential alternatives arising

---

[34] Thackeray, *The Letters and Private Papers,* II: 423.

out of the world he has read about. "A man with a reflective turn of mind" is therefore the ideal reader for this novel. W. J. Harvey has re-marked, in a different context:

A novel . . . can allow for a much fuller expression of this sensed penumbra of unrealized possibilities, of all the what-might-have-beens of our lives. It is because of this that the novel permits a much great-er liberty of such speculation on the part of the reader than does the play. Such speculation frequently becomes, as it does in real life, part of the substantial reality of the identity of any character. The charac-ter moves in the full depth of his conditional freedom; he is what he is but he might have been otherwise. Indeed the novel does not merely *allow* for this liberty of speculation; sometimes it *encourages* it to the extent that our sense of conditional freedom in this aspect becomes one of the ordering structural principles of the entire work.[35]

IV

The aspect of the novel which we have discussed so far is the narrator's continual endeavor to stimulate the reader's mind through extensive commentaries on the actions of the characters. This indirect form of guidance is supplemented by a number of remarks relating directly to the expectations and supposed habits of the novel-reader. If the fulfill-ment of the novel demands a heightened faculty of judgment, it is only natural that the narrator should also compel the reader—at times quite openly—to reflect on his own situation, for without doing so he will be incapable of judging the actions of the characters in the novel. For this process to be effective, the possible reader must be visualized as playing a particular role with particular characteristics, which may vary accord-ing to circumstances. And so just as the author divides himself up into the narrator of the story and the commentator on the events in the story, the reader is also stylized to a certain degree, being given attributes which he may either accept or reject. Whatever happens he will be forced to react to those ready-made qualities ascribed to him. In this manner the double role of the author has a parallel in that of the reader, as W. Booth has pointed out in a discussion on the narrator:

. . . the same distinction must be made between myself as reader and the very often different self who goes about paying bills, repairing leaky faucets, and failing in generosity and wisdom. It is only as I read that I become the self whose beliefs must coincide with the au-thor's. Regardless of my real beliefs and practices, I must subordinate

[35] W. J. Harvey, *Character and the Novel* (London, 1965), p. 147.

my mind and heart to the book if I am to enjoy it to the full. The author creates, in short, an image of himself and another image of his reader; he makes his reader, as he makes his second self, and the most successful reading is one in which the created selves, author and reader, can find complete agreement.[36]

Such an agreement can, however, be reached along widely differing lines, for instance through disagreement—i.e., a subtly instituted opposition between reader and narrator—and this is what happens in *Vanity Fair*.

When the narrator pretends to be at one with the reader in evaluating a certain situation, the reverse is usually the case. For instance, he describes an old but rich spinster who is a member of the great Crawley family, into which Becky is going to marry, in fulfillment of her social aspirations:

> Miss Crawley was . . . an object of great respect when she came to Queen's Crawley, for she had a balance at her banker's which would have made her beloved anywhere. What a dignity it gives an old lady, that balance at the banker's! How tenderly we look at her faults if she is a relative (and may every reader have a score of such), what a kind good-natured old creature we find her! . . . How, when she comes to pay us a visit, we generally find an opportunity to let our friends know her station in the world! We say (and with perfect truth) I wish I had Miss MacWhirter's signature to a cheque for five thousand pounds. She wouldn't miss it, says your wife. She is my aunt, say you, in an easy careless way, when your friend asks if Miss MacWhirter is any relative. Your wife is perpetually sending her little testimonies of affection, your little girls work endless worsted baskets, cushions, and footstools for her. What a good fire there is in her room when she comes to pay you a visit, although your wife laces her stays without one! . . . Is it so, or is it not so?[37]

By using the first person plural, the narrator gives the impression that he is viewing through the reader's eyes the many attentions paid to the old lady with the large bank balance; for the reader such conduct is scarcely remarkable—indeed it is more the expression of a certain *savoir vivre*. By identifying himself with this view, the narrator seems to reinforce rather than to oppose this attitude, which is symptomatic of human nature. But in pretending merely to be describing 'natural' reactions, he is in fact seeking to trap the reader into agreeing with him—and as soon as this is accomplished, the reader realizes for himself the extent to which

---

[36] Booth, *The Rhetoric of Fiction*, pp. 137 f.
[37] Thackeray, *Vanity Fair*, I: 103 f.

consideration of personal gain shapes the natural impulses of human conduct.

In this way, the difference between the reader and the characters in the novel is eliminated. Instead of just seeing through them, he sees himself reflected in them, so that the superior position which the narrator has given him over the pretences and illusions of the characters now begins to fade. The reader realizes that he is similar to those who are supposed to be the objects of his criticism, and so the self-confrontations that permeate the novel compel him to become aware of his own position in evaluating that of the characters. In order to develop this awareness, the narrator creates situations in which the characters' actions correspond to what the reader is tricked into regarding as natural, subsequently feeling the irresistible urge to detach himself from the proceedings. And if the reader ignores the discreet summons to observe himself, then his critical attitude toward the characters becomes unintentionally hypocritical, for he forgets to include himself in the judgment. Thackeray did not want to edify his readers, but to leave them miserable,[38] though with the tacit invitation to find ways of changing this condition for themselves.

This predominantly intellectual appeal to the mind of the reader was not always the norm in the realistic novel. In Dickens, for example, emotions are aroused in order to create a premeditated relationship between the reader and the characters.[39] A typical illustration of this is the famous scene at the beginning of *Oliver Twist,* when the hungry child in the workhouse has the effrontery (as the narrator sees it) to ask for another plate of soup.[40] In the presentation of this daring exploit, Oliver's inner feelings are deliberately excluded, in order to give greater emphasis to the indignation of the authorities at such an unreasonable request.[41] The narrator comes down heavily on the side of authority, and can thus be quite sure that his hard-hearted attitude will arouse a flood of sympathy in his readers for the poor starving child. The reader is thus drawn so far into the action that he feels he must interfere. This effect, not unlike the tension at a Punch and Judy show, enables Dickens to convey contemporary reality to his readers. He follows traditional practice insofar as he brings about a total involvement of the reader in the action. In Thackeray things are different. He is concerned with preventing any

---

[38] Ibid., p. 225, and Thackeray, *The Letters and Private Papers,* II: 423.

[39] "Make 'em laugh; make 'em cry; make 'em wait" was the principle underlying Dickens's novels; see Kathleen Tillotson, *Novels of the Eighteen-Forties,* p. 21.

[40] See Charles Dickens, *The Adventures of Oliver Twist* (The New Oxford Illustrated Dickens) (London, 1959), pp. 12 f.

[41] Ibid., pp. 13 f.—especially p. 14, with the ironic comments of the author.

close liaison between reader and characters. The reader of *Vanity Fair* is in fact forced into a position outside the reality of the novel, though the judgment demanded of him is not without a tension of its own, as he is always in danger of sliding into the action of the novel, thereby suddenly being subjected to the standards of his own criticism.

The narrator does not aim exclusively at precipitating his reader into such situations of involuntary identification with the characters. In order to sharpen the critical gaze, he also offers other modes of approach, though these demand a certain effort at discrimination on the part of the reader—for instance, when he wishes to describe, at least indirectly, the various aspects of the important love affair between Amelia and Osborne:

> The observant reader, who has marked our young Lieutenant's previous behaviour, and has preserved our report of the brief conversation which he has just had with Captain Dobbin, has possibly come to certain conclusions regarding the character of Mr. Osborne. Some cynical Frenchman has said that there are two parties to a love-transaction: the one who loves and the other who condescends to be so treated. Perhaps the love is occasionally on the man's side; perhaps on the lady's. Perhaps some infatuated swain has ere this mistaken insensibility for modesty, dullness for maiden reserve, mere vacuity for sweet bashfulness, and a goose, in a word, for a swan. Perhaps some beloved female subscriber has arrayed an ass in the splendour and glory of her imagination; admired his dullness as manly simplicity; worshipped his selfishness as manly superiority; treated his stupidity as majestic gravity, and used him as the brilliant fairy Titania did a certain weaver at Athens. I think I have seen such comedies of errors going on in the world. But this is certain, that Amelia believed her lover to be one of the most gallant and brilliant men in the empire: and it is possible Lieutenant Osborne thought so too.[42]

Apparently simple situations are taken apart for the reader and split up into different facets. He is free to work his way through each one and to choose whichever he thinks most appropriate, but whether this decision favor the image of the cynical Frenchman or that of the infatuated swain, there will always remain an element of doubt over the relationship under discussion. Indeed the definite view that Amelia has of her

---

[42] Thackeray, *Vanity Fair*, I: 145. A key to such passages lies in the reflections conveyed to the reader near the beginning of the novel, as to whether what follows should be narrated in the "genteel . . . romantic, or in the facetious manner" (I: 59). Thus the author opens up a view of other modes of narration which would inevitably show the events in a different light. In this way, the author indicates to the reader what consequences are linked with a change in perspective.

relationship with Osborne acts as a warning to the reader, as such a final, unambiguous decision runs the risk of being wrong.

The reader is constantly forced to think in terms of alternatives, as the only way in which he can avoid the unambiguous and suspect position of the characters is to visualize the possibilities which they have not thought of. While he is working out these alternatives the scope of his own judgment expands, and he is constantly invited to test and weigh the insights he has arrived at as a result of the profusion of situations offered him. The esthetic appeal of such a technique consists in the fact that it allows a certain latitude for the individual character of the reader, but also compels specific reactions—often unobtrusively—without expressly formulating them. By refusing to draw the reader into the illusory reality of the novel, and keeping him at a variable distance from the events, the text gives him the illusion that he can judge the proceedings in accordance with his own point of view. To do this, he has only to be placed in a position that will provoke him to pass judgments, and the less loaded in advance these judgments are by the text, the greater will be the esthetic effect.

The "Manager of the Performance" opens up a whole panorama of views on the reality described, which can be seen from practically every social and human standpoint. The reader is offered a host of different perspectives, and so is almost continually confronted with the problem of how to make them consistent. This is all the more complicated as it is not just a matter of forming a view of the social world described, but of doing so in face of a rich variety of viewpoints offered by the commentator. There can be no doubt that the author wants to induce his reader to assume a critical attitude toward the reality portrayed, but at the same time he gives him the alternative of adopting one of the views offered him, or of developing one of his own. This choice is not without a certain amount of risk. If the reader adopts one of the attitudes suggested by the author, he must automatically exclude the others. If this happens, the impression arises, in this particular novel, that one is looking more at oneself than at the event described. There is an unmistakable narrowness in every standpoint, and in this respect the reflection the reader will see of himself will be anything but complimentary. But if the reader then changes his viewpoint, in order to avoid this narrowness, he will undergo the additional experience of finding that his behavior is very like that of the two girls who are constantly adapting themselves in order to ascend the social scale. All the same, his criticism of

118

the girls appears to be valid. Is it not a reasonable assumption then that the novel was constructed as a means of turning the reader's criticism of social opportunism back upon himself? This is not mentioned specifically in the text, but it happens all the time. Thus, instead of society, the reader finds himself to be the object of criticism.

V

Thackeray once mentioned casually: "I have said somewhere it is the unwritten part of books that would be the most interesting."[43] It is in the unwritten part of the book that the reader has his place—hovering between the world of the characters and the guiding sovereignty of the "Manager of the Performance." If he comes too close to the characters, he learns the truth of what the narrator told him at the beginning: "The world is a looking-glass, and gives back to every man the reflection of his own face."[44] If he stands back with the narrator to look at things from a distance, he sees through all the activities of the characters. Through the variableness of his own position, the reader experiences the meaning of *Vanity Fair.* Through the characters he undergoes a temporary entanglement in the web of his own illusions, and through the demand for judgment he is enabled to free himself from it and to get a better view of himself and of the world.

And so the story of the two girls and their social aspirations forms only one aspect of the novel, which is continually supplemented by views through different lenses, all of which are trained on the story with the intention of discovering its meaning. The necessity for these different perspectives indicates that the story itself does not reveal direct evidence as to its meaning, so that the factual reality depicted does not represent a total reality. It can only become total through the *manner* in which it is observed. Thus the narrator's commentary, with its often ingenious provocations of the reader, has the effect of an almost independent action running parallel to the story itself. Herein lies the difference between Thackeray and the naturalists of the nineteenth century, who set out to convince their readers that a relevant 'slice of life' was total reality, whereas in fact it only represented an ideological assumption which, for all the accuracy of its details, was a manipulated reality.

In *Vanity Fair* it is not the slice of life, but the means of observing it that constitute the reality, and as these means of observation remain as valid today as they were in the nineteenth century, the novel remains as

---

[43] Thackeray, *The Letters and Private Papers,* III: 391.
[44] Thackeray, *Vanity Fair,* I: 12.

'real' now as it was then, even though the social world depicted is only of historical interest. It is in the preoccupation with different perspectives and with the activation of the reader himself that *Vanity Fair* marks a stage of transition between the traditional and what we now call the 'modern' novel. The predominant aim is no longer to create the illusion of an objective outside reality, and the novelist is no longer concerned with projecting his own unambiguous view of the world onto his reader. Instead, his technique is to diversify his vision, in order to compel the reader to view things for himself and discover his own reality. The author has not yet withdrawn "to pare his fingernails," but he has already entered into the shadows and holds his scissors at the ready.

6

SELF-REDUCTION

The traditional hero of the novel is endowed with a quite specific function: he is the focal point of reference for virtually all events in the world he represents, and he gives the reader the opportunity to participate in these events. This even applies to the nineteenth-century novel, when the prominence of the hero can no longer be taken for granted, because the basic representative features still remain intact. Whatever historical changes the hero may have undergone, he retains an incontestable identity of his own; his self-awareness is unquestioned, and—for all the complications of human relationships—the undenied precondition for his actions is still his openness to "intersubjectivity."[1] "The modern consistency concept of reality implies that the self gains and fulfills its identity as a self-awareness through the potential accord between itself and the surrounding world; it implies also that it is the self's capacity for intersubjective reference which makes the given reality into an 'objective world.' In this sense subjectivity is taken for granted by the classical novel, for which it is the condition enabling out-

[1] I have taken up an idea expressed by Hans Blumenberg in his introduction to the discussion on this essay in *Die Nicht Mehr Schönen Künste* (Poetik und Hermeneutik, III), ed. H. R. Jauss (Munich, 1968), p. 669.

side reality to be conceivable as the sphere in which the characters undergo their experiences and perform their actions."[2] In the nineteenth century this structure was generally not called into question, because the heroes of the novel were meant to illuminate the naturalistic milieu, the destinies that sprang from it, and the actions that were connected with it in the form of variously motivated attempts to change it; but this structure was bound to undergo a transformation the moment it found itself taken as the actual theme of the novel. The self ceased merely to be a reflection of the world, and instead seemed to lose the world altogether on being reduced to the hitherto unquestioned factors that conditioned its function.

The extent to which this reduction has affected the subjective nucleus of literature can be gauged from the idea of the *Loss of the Self in Modern Literature*,[3] which is generally recognized as a characteristic both of modern fiction and of modern drama. From this point of view, taking the formal structure of subjectivity as the theme of the novel can only be regarded in terms of loss and destruction. Thus Charles I. Glicksberg begins his book *The Self in Modern Literature* (1963) with the sentence: "The modern writer is faced with the baffling problem of picturing a self that seems to have lost its reality."[4] Clearly the self needs a specific reality in order to take on a concrete form of its own, and when there is no such reality, its contours begin to blur. This would mean that the self could only be apprehended through the reality it represents, as Glicksberg shows in the individual analyses contained in his book.[5]

However, this problem can be viewed from another standpoint. If the self has "lost its reality" and yet still exists, then it cannot be totally identical with the reality it hypostatizes. And so all its manifestations can be regarded as merely pointing the way to the basic structure of subjectivity. When this structure is treated as the theme of the novel, subjectivity appears not as something lost but rather as the refutation of an

---

[2] Ibid., pp. 669 f.

[3] The title of W. Sypher's interesting book, *Loss of the Self in Modern Literature and Art* (Vintage Book) (New York, 1964).

[4] C. I. Glicksberg, *The Self in Modern Literature* (University Park, Pennsylvania, 1963), p. xi.

[5] In his book, Glicksberg gives a complete portrait gallery of such representative presentations of the self, e.g., "The Self without God," pp. 3 ff.; "The Animal Image of Self," pp. 39 ff.; "The Image of the Mechanical Self," pp. 48 ff.; "The Nihilistic Self," pp. 62 ff.; "The Relativity of the Self," pp. 71 ff.; "The Image of the Absurd Self," pp. 105 ff. The presuppositions underlying his judgment of the modern situation are somewhat debatable—e.g., "Without God, man must resign himself to living in the emptiness of space, the victim of sheer contingency. Twentieth-century literature reveals man with his lost self as the child of the finite and relative, not as a son of God" (p. 35). "When man is exiled from eternity, he becomes demoniacal. His empty self, without a spiritual center to which it can attach itself, seeks reassurance by allying itself with the chthonic, the primitivistic, the bestial" (p. 47).

122

historical concept of it that is no longer valid (taking subjectivity to mean the perfect mediation between self and world,[6] as was the view current in nineteenth-century thought and literature). It is essential to bear in mind the concepts of subjectivity developed in literature during the nineteenth century, for it is through them that one can best gain access to their modern descendants. The following analyses start from the assumption that subjectivity defines itself through the form of its self-communication, and we shall subsequently be examining those patterns of subjectivity in which such a definition has been outstripped.

I

The Self-Communication of Subjectivity in Autobiographical Fiction. W. M. Thackeray: *Henry Esmond*

English literature at the end of the nineteenth century is permeated by the demand for 'self-culture' stressed by Goethe and Hegel.[7] Walter Pater explained this demand in his essay on *Winckelmann:* "Certainly, for us of the modern world, with its conflicting claims, its entangled interests, distracted by so many sorrows, with many preoccupations, so bewildering an experience, the problem of unity with ourselves, in blitheness and repose, is far harder than it was for the Greek within the simple terms of antique life. Yet, not less than ever, the intellect demands completeness, centrality."[8] When this unity with oneself becomes the focal point, there arises "great art," which Pater distinguishes emphatically from merely "good art."[9] "Great art" for him means "such presentment of new or old truth about ourselves and our relation to the world as may ennoble and fortify us in our sojourn here."[10] As examples of great art Pater names The English Bible, Dante, Milton, Hugo's *Les Misérables,*

---

[6] See also D. Henrich, "Kunst und Kunstphilosophie der Gegenwart," in *Immanente Ästhetik— Ästhetische Reflexion* (Poetik und Hermeneutik, II), ed. W. Iser (Munich, 1966), pp. 18 ff.

[7] Its importance may be gauged from the fact that such totally different characters as Oscar Wilde and Cardinal Newman were equally preoccupied with it. Oscar Wilde, *Intentions and the Soul of Man* (London, 1908), p. 187, says: ". . . self-culture is the true ideal of man. Goethe saw it, and the immediate debt that we owe to Goethe is greater than the debt we owe to any man since the Greek days. . . . For the development of the race depends on the development of the individual, and where self-culture has ceased to be the ideal, the intellectual standard is instantly lowered, and, often, ultimately lost" (pp. 185 f.). See also John Henry Newman, *Apologia pro vita sua* (London, 1864), pp. 323 and 377; and Ch. F. Harrold, *John Henry Newman. An Expository and Critical Study of His Mind, Thought and Art* (London, New York, Toronto, 1945), pp. 138 f. Similar ideas are to be found in Matthew Arnold, *Culture and Anarchy* (London, 1889), p. viii.

[8] Walter Pater, *The Renaissance. Studies in Art and Poetry* (London, 1919), p. 227.

[9] Walter Pater, *Appreciations* (London, 1920), pp. 37 f.

[10] Ibid., p. 38.

and Thackeray's *Henry Esmond*.[11] This somewhat surprising collection is all the more remarkable in that Pater places Thackeray's fictional autobiography in a hallowed line of literature (The Bible, Dante, and Milton) which was still sacrosanct, even in the nineteenth century.[12] For Pater, *Henry Esmond*—published in the middle of the nineteenth century—was the last literary work to fulfill the presentational intention of great art. This judgment, delivered by one of the most influential critics of the late nineteenth century, bears out the choice of *Henry Esmond* as an illustration of a paradigmatic mediation between self and world.

Thackeray's *Henry Esmond* is an historical novel, though its subject matter entails what Lukács deplored as the reduction of history to the level of "private actions and reactions."[13] History is not interpreted here as the progressive fulfillment of an underlying purpose, but more as a reflection that gives the hero a greater chance of self-scrutiny. The grounds for this are in fact laid out in the introduction. Henry Esmond begins his autobiography with an attack on the concept of history as the actions of states and leaders, because the characters who act in history were neither better nor cleverer "than you and me . . . I would have History familiar rather than heroic."[14] This desire to regard history mainly as a record of personal experience is conditioned, as far as Esmond is concerned, by the peculiarities of human nature that he is aware of in looking back over his own life: "I look into my heart and think that I am as good as my Lord Mayor, and know I am as bad as Tyburn Jack. Give me a chain and red gown and a pudding before me, and I could play the part of Alderman very well, and sentence Jack after dinner. Starve me, keep me from books and honest people, educate me to love dice, gin, and pleasure, and put me on Hounslow Heath, with a purse before me, and I will take it."[15]

Potentially Esmond embodies the greatest possible contrasts, and precisely for this reason he needs a heightened degree of self-awareness in order to understand those conditions that have made him what ultimately he is. As he finds the alternative roles of judge and criminal equally

---

[11] Ibid.; see also Trollope's judgment, quoted in detail by Geoffrey Tillotson, *Thackeray the Novelist* (London, 1963), p. 127.

[12] See M. H. Abrams, *The Mirror and the Lamp. Romantic Theory and the Critical Tradition* (Norton Library) (New York, 1958), pp. 127, 176, and 295.

[13] See G. Lukács, *Der Historische Roman* (Berlin, 1955), pp. 213 f. and 219.

[14] William Makepeace Thackeray, *The History of Henry Esmond, The Works* (The Centenary Biographical Edition), ed. Lady Ritchie (London, 1911), X: 2.

[15] Ibid., p. 4.

conceivable for himself, his actual reactions to his own historically real world are of vital importance, since it is only through these reactions that he can find himself.

Even when he was young, Esmond asked himself the question: "Who was he, and what?"[16] And if the answers are sought in the context of history, they arise out of the effort to piece together a picture of the self from the subjective refractions of a reality that is regarded as objective. Historical processes and characters provoke Esmond to highly individual judgments, which illuminate his own personal attitudes insofar as his reactions represent only one among many possible evaluations of historical events. Thus it is history that first gives shape to Esmond's own individual profile. The concentration on a personal experience of history is what gave rise to Lukács's criticism of Thackeray's novel, because for him it means the abolition of "historical objectivity" and the devaluation "through subjectivism . . . of all those historical figures that occur in the novel."[17] And, indeed, if one sees *Henry Esmond* in the light of the Scott tradition, this judgment is valid. But with this novel, Thackeray was providing more of a reply to the Scott mode of writing than a continuation of it. The point has already been made by Loofbourow: "This creative synthesis of history and fiction—a sequence of expressive modes figuring cultural development, public events mirroring a private experience, a double perspective correlating past and present—was a significant break with the illustrative tradition."[18] Thackeray's deliberate reduction of the heroic and monumental side of history was what enabled him to present history as something that could be experienced, by means of which process he could depict the self-illumination of the hero. In this study we shall be concerned exclusively with this particular aspect of the novel and not with the changes of history presented through the medium of fiction.

The interaction between history and character is not to be taken merely as a one-sided determination of character through history, for otherwise Esmond's autobiography would only mirror purposes allegedly underlying history. This is why Esmond himself goes on to describe the na-

[16] Ibid., p. 68; see H. A. Talon's important article, "Time and Memory in Thackeray's Henry Esmond," *Two Essays on Thackeray* (Dijon, no date), pp. 33 f. The essay appeared originally in *Review of English Studies*, New Series 13 (1962).

[17] Lukács, *Der Historische Roman*, p. 217. On the meaning of 'subject' and 'subjective', see also R. Sühnel's epilogue to *Die Geschichte des Henry Esmond* (Exempla Classica, 77) (Frankfurt, 1963), p. 418.

[18] J. Loofbourow, *Thackeray and the Form of Fiction* (Princeton, 1964), p. 164. Kathleen Tillotson, *Novels of the Eighteen-Forties* (Oxford, 1961), p. 99, also stresses the duality of *Henry Esmond* as an 'historical novel' and a 'novel of memory'.

ture of the relation between history, self-scrutiny, and the record of that self-scrutiny: "But fortune, good or ill, as I take it, does not change men and women. It but develops their character. As there are a thousand thoughts lying within a man that he does not know till he takes up the pen to write, so the heart is a secret even to him (or her) who has it in his own breast. Who hath not found himself surprised into revenge, or action, or passion, for good or evil, whereof the seeds lay within him, latent and unsuspected, until the occasion called them forth?"[19]

Here the independent environment of man is regarded as having the sole function of actualizing the potential of the character, so that the individual can be confronted with his own individuality. But this potential is the concealed property of the self, and is subject to chance insofar as it needs a situation outside its own control to enable it to take on a concrete form.[20]

The autobiography thus becomes a process of self-observation, unfolding the potential of a character through those aspects that are given form by the historical environment. Every single reaction of Esmond is a limited expression which can never comprehend the whole of the self and yet, by accumulation, causes this whole gradually to emerge. Esmond is not motivated by any concrete or far-reaching aims, but his wishes tend to arise out of the various situations in which he finds himself. Now if his conduct were based on the desire to fulfill certain specific intentions, the life history he narrates could only have as its subject matter the success or failure of these plans, and then his autobiography would no longer describe his self but only the fate of one of his cherished ideals.

Esmond's self-revelation, then, is inseparable from empirical, historical situations. As a result of his Catholic upbringing, he is passionately in favor of the Stuart cause during his childhood.[21] This total identification with the opinions of his mentor—Father Holt—is shattered by political events;[22] Esmond has to adapt himself to the new masters of Castlewood House, and these want to turn him into a clergyman.[23] Solely out of devotion to Lady Castlewood, he declares himself willing to accept this—for him—disagreeable plan, but through force of circumstance it

---

[19] Thackeray, *Henry Esmond*, p. 182. J. A. Lester, Jr., "Thackeray's Narrative Technique," *PMLA* 69 (1954): 399, emphasizes Thackeray's basic concern throughout his work with the reactions of his characters: "Thackeray is more interested in his characters' reactions to events than he is in the events themselves." See also p. 402.

[20] Lukács, *Der Historische Roman*, p. 217, views this same situation negatively: ". . . the more closely he [Thackeray] pursues this private psychology, the more accidental everything appears from an historical perspective."

[21] See Thackeray, *Henry Esmond*, pp. 44 f., passim.

[22] Ibid., pp. 102 and 210 f.

[23] Ibid., pp. 103 f.

eventually comes to nothing.[24] These early experiences already reflect
the central feature of Esmond's life—a feature that remains constant at
every stage and indeed gives rise to the whole autobiographical record:
right from the beginning he finds himself involved in situations that
'turn sour' on him. But this very fact draws his attention to desires he
had hitherto been unaware of, so that a form of tension arises between
his knowledge of what he is supposed to do and his consciousness of
these new sentiments. In the course of time, he enters into new situations which run contrary to the now more concrete desires he has formed
and divert his intentions in unforeseen directions.[25] This clash between
the original desires and the new situations produces unexpected reactions,
and these turn Esmond's attention more and more to himself. He realizes
that the ideas he has been gradually developing all fall short when it
comes to the actual process of living,[26] and that he embodies untold possibilities of conduct that would never have come to light if his original
intentions had been fulfilled in reality.

The historical circumstances which Esmond describes should not be
regarded merely as the mechanical agents that release a preformed potential. This potential only *takes on* its form through the conditional nature
of the situation in which it is realized, and, indeed, it is the chance element of these many historical circumstances that brings the hidden features of the character out into the light, for if the situations were pre-
dictable or deliberately brought into being, the character's reactions
would already be part of the fulfilled potential. Esmond is always concerned with reducing the degree and range of the unknown. First of all,
he tries to find out who he actually is, and by the end of the first book,
he knows where he comes from. The fact that this explanation comes
one-third of the way through the book, and not right at the end, shows
that a person's identity is not synonymous with his origins. Once Esmond knows that he is the real heir to the title, he sees the world around
him in a completely new light, but now—out of love and consideration
for the Castlewood family—he must renounce making any use of this

[24] Ibid., pp. 161 f., 166, and 183 f.
[25] See especially the turning-point in Esmond's life after he has returned from an expedition
during the War of the Spanish Succession, and visits the Castlewood family again. He became a
soldier in order to impress Beatrix, but now relations have changed and Beatrix loves someone
else, while at the same time Esmond discovers his feelings for Lady Castlewood. It no longer fits
in with the new situation that he must return to the war. His original motive for becoming a
soldier has now become more or less invalid. His further participation in the war therefore takes
place under changed circumstances which naturally alter his whole attitude and so lead him to
see events in a completely different light. See ibid., pp. 228–56 and 345 f.
[26] Ibid., pp. 185 f. and 215.

knowledge.[27] Once again conditions in his immediate surroundings begin to get complicated, while the circumstances to which he has to react take on a far greater subtlety.

If reducing the unknown is a process of self-discovery, the question arises as to whether this process can ever have an end. The search for oneself forbids the setting of any one particular aim whose fulfillment would mean total knowledge—in other words, the process of self-discovery depends on there being unknown quantities that must be reduced. Esmond tries to work out the significance of those possibilities of his character that have been revealed to him, and in doing so he is bound to react to his own discoveries in a manner determined by his own memories. The function of this process is to establish his relations not only with his own past, but also with himself in the present, for his memories reveal what importance he attached and attaches to events during particular phases of his life.

The fictional autobiography assembles remembered reactions, which accumulate into a gestalt of subjectivity; Esmond filters them retrospectively through his mind in such a way that he realizes they have always conditioned his own conduct. A typical example is his judgment of Marlborough. As a soldier in the English army during the War of the Spanish Succession, Esmond sees the Duke at very close quarters. His observations are full of irony:

> Our Duke was as calm at the mouth of the cannon as at the door of a drawing-room. Perhaps he could not have been the great man he was, had he had a heart either for love or hatred, or pity or fear, or regret or remorse . . . for he used all men, great and small, that came near him, as his instruments alike, and took something of theirs, either some quality or some property . . . and having, as I have said, this of the godlike in him, that he could see a hero perish or a sparrow fall, with the same amount of sympathy for either. . . . He would cringe to a shoeblack, as he would flatter a minister or a monarch; be haughty, be humble, threaten, repent, weep, grasp your hand (or stab you whenever he saw occasion).—But yet those of the army, who knew him best and had suffered most from him, admired him most of all: and as he rode along the lines to battle or galloped up in the nick of time to a battalion reeling from before the enemy's charge or shot, the fainting men and officers got new courage as they saw the splendid calm of his face, and felt that his will made them irresistible.[28]

[27] Ibid., pp. 176 f. and 200 f.
[28] Ibid., pp. 260 f.

128

And after the Battle of Blenheim, Esmond writes: "Who could refuse his meed of admiration to such a victory and such a victor? Not he who writes: a man may profess to be ever so much a philosopher; but he who fought on that day must feel a thrill of pride as he recalls it."[29] This assessment of Marlborough indirectly reveals certain features of Esmond himself. Like the rest of the soldiers, he cannot altogether refrain from admiration for the victorious leader. But he sees through the superficial image of the Duke, distorted as it is by the glamorous aura of success, and attributes his reputation to sheer lack of conscience. Esmond destroys the image of the hero, thus laying bare the distasteful elements of character that have gone to make history, but at the same time he shows his own disapproval, which in turn reveals his own implicit scale of values. History remembered is history colored by Esmond's own judgment, but as well as shedding this individual light on history, Esmond is illuminating himself; furthermore, this self-illumination is also subject to Esmond's own scrutiny, for he asks himself why he is so critical of the Duke. One might suppose it is because he is morally offended by Marlborough's lack of scruples; but then, somewhat surprisingly, we learn that this dislike is based on Esmond's annoyance at having been ignored by the Duke during a levee: "A word of kindness or acknowledgment, or a single glance of approbation, might have changed Esmond's opinion of the great man; and instead of a satire, which his pen cannot help writing, who knows but that the humble historian might have taken the other side of panegyric?"[30] Although such a confession does not restore Marlborough's heroic image, it does show the extent to which Esmond's apparently moral criticism is based not on any sense of right and wrong, but on the chance wounding of his vanity.

In recalling the past, then, Esmond also clarifies the conditions that shaped his individual reactions. In this way, memory becomes a form of heightened self-awareness, as Esmond himself indicates toward the end of his memoirs: "We forget nothing. The memory sleeps, but wakens again; I often think how it shall be when, after the last sleep of death, the *réveillée* shall arouse us for ever, and the past in one flash of self-consciousness rush back, like the soul revivified."[31]

If one were to bring back the whole of the past into the present, human self-awareness would momentarily be complete and perfect. But as this is impossible in life, such an idea remains merely a metaphor to de-

[29] Ibid., pp. 261 f.
[30] Ibid., p. 269.
[31] Ibid., p. 435.

scribe the goal that memory is meant to achieve. Memory of the past is transformed here into the history of an increasing self-awareness of subjectivity. J. C. Powys, talking of the autobiographical process, remarks that only remembered truth is real truth, and he continues: "A person's life-illusion ought to be as sacred as his skin."[32] In the form of this "life-illusion," memory enables the self to achieve unity with itself and with the world around it.

We must not lose sight of the fact that *Henry Esmond* is the autobiography of a fictional character, and not of Thackeray himself. If it were the latter, the reader's main interest would lie in the concrete ideas Thackeray developed in the course of his confrontation with himself (which would presumably be the motive for his autobiography in the first place); but since this is a novel, one can only conclude that the intention is not to propagate Thackeray's views of life so much as to examine the whole process of autobiography as such, and to show in general the ways in which a man can enter into a relationship with himself. Esmond does not reflect merely on the events of his life but also on the contingencies which gave rise to the individuality of his experiences, and hence of his personality.

The narrative techniques of the novel not only convey but also mirror the relationship of the subject with himself. One would normally expect an autobiography to be told in the first person singular.[33] Esmond, however, uses mainly the third person, and his attitude toward his remembered experiences is just like that of an authorial narrator to the events he is presenting. Personal experiences are described as if they were someone else's. The resultant distance of self from self brings two things to the fore: first, the relative and temporary nature of the standpoints which conditioned earlier attitudes and events; second, the fact that in the meantime the faculty of conscious self-assessment must have developed considerably, since now it can view its own past with such detachment. The road to the self is a continual overcoming of the self, the success of which may be measured by the self's awareness that the manifestations of the past were limited and contingent.

This narrative detachment, however, only creates the framework for a

---

[32] J. C. Powys, *Autobiography* (London, ²1949), pp. 426 f. Toward the end of his account, Esmond writes: "Our great thoughts, our great affections, the Truths of our life, never leave us. Surely, they cannot separate from our consciousness; shall follow it whithersoever that shall go; and are of their nature divine and immortal." Thackeray, *Henry Esmond*, p. 423.

[33] For the distinction between autobiography, diary, and memoirs, see R. Pascal, *Design and Truth in Autobiography* (London, 1960), pp. 2 f., 5 f., 9, 10 f., 16 f., 45, 59, and 182.

whole variety of interacting attitudes that Esmond has toward himself. There are clear distinctions even within the third person singular form,[34] as Esmond looks back on his past through different perspectives: when he calls himself *Mr. Esmond* or *Colonel Esmond,* he is recalling a manifestation of himself that has long since become purely historical; when he refers to *Harry* or *Youth,* there is a continuing sympathy that links him with the person he was at that time; and when he recalls himself as *Esmond,* he is accepting himself, with varying degrees of approval, as the man he once was. And so there are subdivisions of perspective within the main perspective, and these themselves imply a judgment. Esmond also reverts frequently to the first person singular,[35] and at such moments he completely loses the detachment he has otherwise shown toward his own life. Here, too, there are various reasons for the change in perspective. Sometimes the first person narrative helps to substantiate what the writer feels to be an incontrovertible truth[36] with which he wishes to identify himself, despite the passage of time. At other times, situations are reproduced as if they were in the present, so that they retain an open-endedness which has not been properly closed by time.[37] Esmond often recalls particular conversations in order discreetly to reproduce other people's judgments of him, toning down the flatteries by linking them to the whim of the moment in which they were uttered.[38] And so the perspective of the first person also offers different possibilities of self-assessment which are sometimes more spontaneous than those arising out of the perspective of detachment. But what really gives the increasing self-awareness its true dimension is the interplay between these two conspectuses. The rounded self-judgment of the third person singular, which to a large extent determines the structure of the events narrated, is based on experiences that are still incomplete and often only partially relevant to such judgments—experiences from which the writer could not completely detach himself in order to gain a total view of them. The fact that the third person form is dominant throughout the novel shows the extent to which experience of life and the world is processed by the person describing it. Within these two basic perspectives—the first and third person views—there are certain clearly defined variations. In presenting his past, Esmond occasionally refers to his actual modes of writ-

[34] See Thackeray, *Henry Esmond,* pp. 112–14, 213–15, 393–95, passim.
[35] Central passages, such as the reflections on the individuality of Esmond's character and the connection between history and self-observation are in the first person singular; see ibid., pp. 4 and 182.
[36] E.g. ibid., pp. 92, 140, 210, 222, 327.
[37] E.g. ibid., pp. 315, 329, 343, 410–13, 460 f.
[38] E.g. ibid., pp. 396–400, 442.

ing. This necessity arises because of the special form of memory itself: Esmond has to endow his experiences with the same life they had originally in order to recreate the spontaneity of his reaction; but at the same time he cannot avoid viewing them from the standpoint of his later knowledge. What he has to do, then, is to capture the openness of the situations, side by side, as it were, with the now conscious evaluation of them, because only in this way can his previous involvement become the object of intellectual analysis. His judgment of his earlier self takes on a concrete form in proportion to his recognition of why he acted in one way and not in another, although in retrospect he could have reacted in apter ways than he did.[39] It is, then, essential that Esmond should not present his past exclusively with the benefits of hindsight, for if he did, he would obscure precisely the process he is trying to uncover—namely, how he came to an awareness of himself. And this is why he frequently talks about writing at those moments when his hindsight threatens to take over the account of the situation,[40] or the situation itself seems to him so complex that he feels obliged to interpolate his insight of the present.[41] In this presentation of memories, there is therefore a constant interplay between spontaneity and organization—the latter being understood as a form of interpretation that places the open situations of real life in a coherent context which, in turn, builds up the history of the self.

One variation of the first person technique is Esmond's occasional use of the first person plural. At such times he deals with collective experiences which could be shared by all men.[42] Even when this is not stated explicitly, he uses the first person plural to suggest to the reader that a particular insight has general validity for all human life—so that by drawing the reader into his judgment, he lures him into confirming the truth of his observation.[43] There are various reasons why Esmond needs this contact with the reader's experiences, the chief one being that these experiences can substantiate his claims to the truth of his self-observation through instances authenticated by themselves and not by him.

One last variation within the narrative perspectives consists of the numerous literary metaphors running through the book. The frequent recurrence of images borrowed mainly from the epic tradition may be regarded as a structural feature of the narrative, if only because they generally conclude events or reflections which Esmond himself has not yet

[39] E.g. ibid., p. 166.
[40] E.g. ibid., p. 142.
[41] E.g. ibid., pp. 75, 165 f., 269, 374.
[42] E.g. ibid., p. 104.
[43] E.g. ibid., pp. 185, 373, 423.

processed properly through memory. By means of literary allusions and quotations, Esmond inserts completely formulated ideas into his narrative when the situation invoked by memory seems complicated or inconsistent. These literary metaphors can fulfill various functions,[44] but they nearly always leave behind a trace of irony in the narrative; they might, for instance, offer a solution to the confusion which would be perfect, but would only be possible in literature;[45] or they might confirm the painfulness of an experience, without mitigating it;[46] or they can suggest individual perplexity without revealing its particularity, because even a retrospective view does not make it possible to capture the special nature of the past emotions.[47] This varied use of literary images adds an important dimension to the narrative perspectives already discussed, for they give a sort of provisional meaning to critical situations, taking on the function of hypothetical interpretations. Unlike the other perspectives, they delineate the border that divides certain knowledge of the self from the merely possible, and therefore hypothetical understanding of it. It is a mark of the extent to which self-awareness has been achieved here, that a hypothetical interpretation of the past can be shown for what it is and also be incorporated into memory.

These various perspectives, which we have separated from one another for the purposes of our discussion, are constantly interacting throughout Esmond's narrative. The interaction brings about an almost kaleidoscopic succession of mobile standpoints, from which there emerges the gradual self-illumination of subjectivity. The shifting of standpoints bears witness to an awareness that is the only way toward self-assessment, and that it is only the plurality of views which can give rise to an adequate picture of subjectivity. A single standpoint would merely transform the life recorded here into the representative illustration of one view formed almost independently of experience, whereas the multiplicity of standpoints shows that possibilities of judgment must arise first and foremost

---

[44] Loofbourow, *Thackeray*, p. 176 f., says: "Esmond's major insights are always related to a literal event . . . in each epic instance, the literal plot-progression momentarily ceases, and the crucial expressive sequence is developed in a context devoid of narrative action." "*Esmond's* classical parallels represent imaginative experience, and the quality of this experience is suggestively modified in the context of Thackeray's prose" (p. 116). On the function of images in Thackeray's style, see also Geoffrey Tillotson, *Thackeray the Novelist*, pp. 37 f. Re the ironic nature of literary metaphors or allusions, see especially Thackeray, *Henry Esmond*, p. 374. Re the ironic use of such metaphors, see, e.g., ibid., p. 403.

[45] See Thackeray, *Henry Esmond*, pp. 108 f., 269 f., and 385 f.; see also the conflict with Addison, who regards literature as transfiguration and therefore draws Esmond's sharp criticism upon himself (pp. 281 f.).

[46] Ibid., pp. 121, 243, 346, and 374 f.

[47] Ibid., p. 398.

out of experience of the self, which must come to terms with its own subjectivity. The self grasps historical reality through the perspectives it brings to bear, it enters into a relationship with itself through mobilizing its standpoints, and through this mobilization it also proves that it is constantly reflecting upon its own subjective judgments. Esmond is so conscious of this necessity that he actually gives voice to it: "We have but to change the point of view, and the greatest action looks mean; as we turn the perspective-glass, and a giant appears a pigmy. You may describe, but who can tell whether your sight is clear or not, or your means of information accurate?"[48]

This is why the ultimate aim of Esmond's self-scrutiny is to judge his life story from the viewpoint of the knowledge he has at the time of writing. The blind spots caused by lack of information can then be pinpointed in their contingency just as precisely as the consequences arising out of his hindsight. "For the autobiographer is not relating facts, but experiences—i.e. the inter-action of a man and facts or events. By experience we mean something with meaning, and there can be many varieties and shades of meaning."[49] And so from these shifting perspectives there grows a picture of Esmond, which presents itself, to use J. C. Powys's term, as the "life-illusion" of the identity now gained.

For the late nineteenth century, as shown by Pater, this unity of the self with the world was regarded as the intention of "great art." Like all definitive esthetic pronouncements, it proved to be fragile in the extreme; counteraction to it released other structures of subjectivity, and we shall examine some of these against the background of the Thackeray concept we have just outlined. *Henry Esmond* shows that if different experiences are to be coordinated, there must always be preconceptions at work, which in turn lead to the concretization of the self. As Roy Pascal has pointed out: "autobiography must always include, as a decisive element, the last type: the meaning an event acquires when viewed in the perspective of a whole life,"[50] for this is the only way in which one can create a relationship between self and world, and a consequent identity.

Now it is possible that the preconceptions necessary for self-communication may remain completely hidden, may tend to become arbitrary, or

[48] Ibid., p. 269.
[49] Pascal, *Design and Truth*, p. 16.
[50] Ibid., p. 17.

may sink to the level of a mere presupposition. In such cases, the extent and nature of subjectivity becomes more and more difficult to gauge, and the possibility of self-communication becomes Utopian. The reduction of subjectivity to be found in modern novels should not be seen as the loss of something that was once attainable; it serves rather to show up the various conditions of subjectivity that had remained concealed so long as they fulfilled specific functions in the novel, such as the communication of views of life. "Reduction" in this context means reversion to origin, and so does not have "a primarily negative sense."[51] As we are concerned here with a typological interpretation, we need not try to trace the development from Thackeray to the modern novel, especially as the term 'reduction' is not meant to signify an historical diminution of the Thackeray concept of subjectivity.

The works we shall now be examining are Faulkner's *The Sound and the Fury,* Ivy Compton-Burnett's *A Heritage and Its History,* and finally Beckett's trilogy *Molloy, Malone Dies,* and *The Unnamable.* It may well be claimed that historically these authors have virtually nothing in common, and that although they all wrote in English or—in Beckett's case—translated the text into English, each belongs to a different national literature; and indeed if one is concerned with influence, environment, historical context, or literary tradition, the choice will seem somewhat arbitrary. However, in matters of form and typology, there does exist a certain affinity between these writers, and this affinity is all the more significant precisely because they have nothing in common otherwise. Clearly, at the point of contact indicated, there must lie a problem that is central to the modern situation, since it arises simultaneously—though in various guises—from the works of writers whose intellectual backgrounds are so very diverse. These novels center on different modes of reduced subjectivity, and as our starting-point we shall examine narrative techniques.

Faulkner's novel is narrated mainly from three sharply opposed first-person viewpoints; Ivy Compton-Burnett's novel continually discloses the unpredictable reactions of the characters through an unbroken series of dialogues; and Beckett's trilogy is unfolded through the first-person account of a narrator who never ceases to suspect that his mode of narration, through the presuppositions inherent in it, is restricting his view of reality.

---

[51] M. Theunissen, *Der Andere* (Berlin, 1965), p. 27; see also the discussion on the meaning of the term 'reduction' (*Reduktion*), as understood in Husserl's phenomenology.

II

Perception, Temporality, and Action as Modes of Subjectivity.
W. Faulkner: *The Sound and the Fury*

With the exception of Joyce's *Ulysses,* Faulkner's *The Sound and the Fury* (first published in 1929) is probably the most important modern experiment in the use of narrative techniques to give form to individual structures of consciousness. The 'story,' presented from four different points of view, consists of events and impressions connected with the gradual decline of the Compson family in the Deep South. Through the first-person narratives of the Compson brothers, this single theme is split into a variety of fragments and facets, and even the final, authorial part does not bring these together in a clearly organized whole. Furthermore, the different accounts—all precisely dated—are not given in chronological order, so that the reader is forced to jump backward and forward in time, thus constantly supplying a background to each individually drawn picture. This even applies when events take on a degree of clarity that was lacking in the beginning—as in the third and fourth sections, which offer a partial untangling of the perplexities produced by Benjy and Quentin. Here we have the somewhat extraordinary effect that the un-expected explicitness, contained in Jason's account and that of the au-thor, seems somehow to impoverish the proceedings, for if the reader has taken the trouble to immerse himself in Benjy's erratic perceptions and in Quentin's consciousness, Jason's clearly defined attitude will appear decidedly banal—not least, *because* of its clarity.

As the individual narrative perspectives overshadow one another, there arises between them a sort of no-man's-land of unformulated connections, and it is these that involve the reader directly in the novel. The effect on him has been described by Richard Hughes as follows:

> It is here this curious method is finally justified: for one finds, in a flash, that one knows all about them, that one has understood more of Benjy's sound and fury than one had realized: the whole story be-comes actual to one at a single moment. It is impossible to describe the effect produced, because it is unparalleled; the thoughtful reader must find it for himself. It will be seen to be a natural corollary that one can read this book a second time at least. The essential quality of a book that can be read again and again, it seems to me, is that it

shall appear different at every reading—that it shall, in short, be a new book.[52]

These different appearances that confront the "thoughtful reader" are evoked by the structure of the text, which we are now going to examine in some detail.

The novel begins with a series of fluctuating impressions of April 7, 1928 which Benjy, an idiot, attempts to hold onto. Benjy differs from most other idiots in literature mainly because he is seen from inside and not from outside. The reader sees the world through his eyes and depends almost exclusively on him for orientation. As a result, the reader's attention is drawn to the peculiar nature of this perception, so that the subject matter seems to be the idiot's experience of life rather than his effect on the intersubjective world; indeed, this could only become the subject if he were seen in the context of normality. This, clearly, is why it is not until the fourth, authorial part of the novel that we are given the familiar picture of the idiot: ". . . the swing door opened and Luster entered, followed by a big man who appeared to have been shaped of some substance whose particles would not or did not cohere to one another or to the frame which supported it. His skin was dead-looking and hairless; dropsical too, he moved with a shambling gait like a trained bear. . . . His eyes were clear, of the pale sweet blue of cornflowers, his thick mouth hung open, drooling a little."[53] This description seizes on Benjy's external appearance, projecting it implicitly onto a normal human appearance in order to create the portrait of the idiot out of the differences. The contrast between normality and idiocy is an integral part of this section, which deals with the question of whether Benjy can continue to stay with the family or should be sent to a lunatic asylum.

The implicit criteria of normality are not available, however, when Benjy is viewed from the inside, unless one compares his monologue with psychiatric case histories, which even then will only yield meager results,

---

[52] R. Hughes, "Introduction," William Faulkner, *The Sound and the Fury* (Penguin Books) (Harmondsworth, 1964), p. 8. There is not space enough here for a discussion of the literature on Faulkner. A critical account of the important works is given in his introduction by M. Christadler, *Natur und Geschichte im Werk William Faulkners* (Beihefte zum Jahrbuch für Amerikastudien, 8) (Heidelberg, 1962). The main trends in Faulkner criticism are shown by H. Straumann in his essay "The Early Reputation of Faulkner's Work in Europe: A Tentative Appraisal," in *English Studies Today* (4th Series) (Rome, 1966), pp. 443-59.
[53] Faulkner, *The Sound and the Fury*, p. 244.

limited to establishing differences and similarities.[54] The fictional idiot viewed from the outside cannot be regarded merely as a symbol of human deformity, and, equally, the interior monologue cannot be simply a case history and nothing more:—everything depends on the function of the idiot in the context of what is to be presented.

First let us look at the signals the author gives the reader in Benjy's account. The various events, conversations, impressions, and ideas are expressed with precision and a quite undamaged syntax. What is missing, however, is a coherence between the individual sentences, which do not come together to form a larger unit of meaning.[55] The sentences seem to point in various directions without ever accomplishing the perception at which they are aimed. These undeveloped indications produce the impression that a 'plot' is in the process of being formed but is constantly being broken up. This impression is essentially the reader's own contribution, for Benjy himself offers up the fragments of his monologue as if they were part of a self-evident process. Indeed, it is his very passiveness in this respect that activates the reader, for the latter wants to understand why the thirty years of life that Benjy is surveying should dissolve in this way the moment he perceives them.

The author offers another aid by italicizing certain passages of the monologue in order to show differences in time which otherwise would probably not be apparent. But here, too, the clarification seems paradoxically to enhance the confusion. It has been calculated that in Benjy's monologue, 13 scenes from 13 different periods of time have been broken up into 106 fragments,[56] the arbitrary juxtaposition of which shows that for Benjy everything exists on a single time level. Just as the integral sentences serve to accentuate the lack of any integrated content, so do the time divisions show up the absence of any concept of time. Here again there is a definite effect on the reader. Benjy's past appears as a continuous but haphazard movement, brought about by a series of impressions that are specifically though erratically set in time. Some critics have called this movement a 'stream of consciousness',[57] but such a term is misleading, for it implies a direction—a stream flowing from the

[54] See, e.g., G. Irle, *Der psychiatrische Roman* (Stuttgart, 1965), pp. 114–24.

[55] See also O. W. Vickery's interesting essay "Language as Theme and Technique," in *Modern American Fiction. Essays in Criticism*, ed. A. W. Litz (New York, 1963), pp. 179 ff.

[56] See G. R. Stewart and J. M. Backus, " 'Each in its Ordered Place': Structure and Narrative in 'Benjy's Section' of *The Sound and the Fury*," *American Literature* 29 (1958): 440–56.

[57] See, e.g., R. Humphrey's view of Faulkner in *Stream of Consciousness in the Modern Novel* (Berkeley and Los Angeles, 1959). In his essay "The Form and Function of Stream of Consciousness in William Faulkner's *The Sound and the Fury*," *University of Kansas City Review* 19 (1952): 34–40, Humphrey discusses only the meaning of the symbols which determine the structure of the stream of consciousness.

past into the future. But this is not how events are presented in an interior monologue—on the contrary, one has to reverse the direction of the 'stream', as it is mainly present or future events that affect a character's retrospective perception and so mobilize memories afresh, endowing them with changing relevance.[58]

This is certainly what happens to Benjy,[59] when at the beginning of his monologue he sees some golfers through a hedge.[60] The present sets the past in motion and must inevitably give it a different appearance from before, because it has been aroused by something which did not exist at the time. This is why the interior monologue involves a continual changing of what is remembered. But with Benjy there is no time relation, so that his memories of thirty years and his impressions of April 7, 1928, are all flattened out on a single level. If the author had not indicated which was which, it would be almost impossible to gauge it from the monologue.

As Benjy's perception cannot distinguish between past and present, no one facet of his life is shaped or even influenced by any other. The lack of any such interaction, and the aimlessness with which events are lumped together, endows these events with an extraordinary self-sufficiency. It is as if we were confronted with the 'raw materials'[61] of reality waiting to be put together in a recognizable living form. Now these raw materials do in fact contain the outlines of a story which in the course of the novel is more and more clearly developed. But the result of this development is a gradual diminution of the richness of Benjy's monologue, so that the story as unfolded in the fourth part seems positively trivial.

Thanks to the signals inserted by the author, the reader will gain the impression from Benjy's monologue that he can only observe its reality (and so, at this stage, all reality) as a constant and elusive fragmentation. This effect is achieved in various ways. First and foremost is the fact that this is a form of perception devoid of any active consciousness. Benjy has a minimal, basically sensual ability to differentiate between things and people in his environment. If acts of perception lack coordination, the phenomena perceived will constantly disintegrate; there will be no dis-

---

[58] See the discussion on time perception in M. Merleau-Ponty, *Phenomenology of Perception*, transl. Colin Smith (New York, 1962), pp. 411 ff.

[59] Re the fascination that idiocy had for Faulkner, see Christadler, *Natur und Geschichte*, pp. 69 f.

[60] See Faulkner, *The Sound and the Fury*, pp. 11 ff. Re the form of the 'incidental' opening of novels, see R. M. Jordan, "The Limits of Illusion: Faulkner, Fielding, and Chaucer," *Criticism* 2 (1960): 284 f.

[61] See also J. Peper, *Bewusstseinslagen des Erzählens und erzählte Wirklichkeiten* (Studien zur amerikanischen Literatur und Geschichte, III) (Leiden, 1966), p. 129, and the literature he deals with. See also Jordan, "Limits of Illusion," pp. 286 f.

tance between the observer and the things observed, and this distance is essential if one is to be able to see in the first place. "Perception is precisely that kind of act in which there can be no question of setting the act itself apart from the end to which it is directed. Perception and the percept necessarily have the same existential modality, since perception is inseparable from the consciousness which it has, or rather is, of reaching the thing itself. . . . Vision can be reduced to the mere presumption of seeing only if it is represented as the contemplation of a shifting and anchorless *quale*."[62]

Merleau-Ponty's analysis can be directly applied to Benjy. He is restricted purely and simply to perception and registers only fleeting configurations of people whom he cannot differentiate into characters, despite the many details he gives about them. In fact, paradoxically, they seem undifferentiated precisely because of all these details, for they are given a definite reality which merges into an almost total blur through the welter of unrelated, fugitive information.[63] From this one can infer that Benjy experiences a good deal more than he realizes. But whatever he experiences flashes into and out of existence, because he is totally devoid of the consciousness that is the prerequisite for an overall field of perception which would guarantee a pattern for these experiences. This is why his perceptions merge into one another with such apparent arbitrariness.

This reduction to deintellectualized perception makes the reader feel that there is more in the fragmented figures and situations than Benjy's restricted vision can convey. There is a kind of compulsion for him to work out how things fit together—to gain the privileged overall view which he is normally granted in novels but of which he is deprived by Benjy's first-person narrative. In this way, he is forced to activate his own conscious mind, as it were to compensate for Benjy's lack of consciousness. The result for the reader is that he experiences Benjy's perspective not only from the inside—with Benjy—but also from the outside, as he tries to understand Benjy. It seems as if Benjy's life, as it constantly eludes his grasp through the fleetingness of its perceptions, takes on the unreality of a mirage, though Benjy himself never experi-

---

[62] Merleau-Ponty, *Phenomenology*, pp. 374 f.
[63] Only the relationship with Caddy, Benjy's sister, has any clear definition, as compared with relationships with the rest of the Compson household. Benjy continually speaks of the fact that Caddy smells of trees, but the monotonous repetition of this observation merely indicates his state of excitation and so conceals the individuality of Caddy, who obviously remains in a state of continual movement within Benjy's imagination. And so for Benjy, people seem to vary in importance. But as he cannot distinguish their individuality, the reader can get nothing but a blurred impression of them. See O. W. Vickery, *The Novels of William Faulkner: A Critical Interpretation* (Baton Rouge, [2] 1961), p. 31.

ences it as such, for it is the reader alone, who bears the burden of this experience, Benjy having a congenital immunity to such insights.

In actualizing situations of which Benjy himself is not aware, the reader is drawn into the narrative process and provoked into a wide variety of reactions. Whatever these may be (depending on the temperament of the individual reader), he finds himself forced into experiences which are quite unfamiliar to him, and the immediate impact of these experiences is to create tension. But tensions demand to be relieved, and this is what seems to be promised by the monologues of Benjy's brothers. As the idiot's perception was lacking in consciousness—the act which is "by definition, the violent transition from what I have to what I aim to have, from what I am to what I intend to be"[64]—one naturally assumes that an active consciousness will provide all the missing links.

And, indeed, the next monologue does present us with the one character in the novel who in fact has a highly developed, active consciousness. However, our expectations are not to be fulfilled—and if they were, we should probably say that *The Sound and the Fury* was a bad novel, for when tension is relaxed, and the reader's assumptions are confirmed, he will invariably lose interest. This would happen if the subjectivity reduced to mere perception were now to be shown as nothing more than a phantasma without a reality of its own, but instead we are confronted by an extremely conscious subjectivity which, in reflecting upon itself, still does not stabilize its own identity. As a result, the tension that grew out of the Benjy monologue is not resolved, but if anything enhanced.

Quentin's narrative begins with a reflection on time, which provides an indirect link with Benjy's disjointed, timeless world. Here the order of time does, at first sight, appear to offer the most basic guarantee that the rich variety of perceptions can be shaped into a coherent experience through which the self may observe itself. But the question arises as to whether the absence of such a time relation will necessarily prevent the self from, so to speak, objectifying itself. If it does, then time must possess a significance that is independent of subjectivity. Quentin's monologue is therefore concerned with the interdependence of time and subjectivity.

When he wakes up on the morning of June 2, 1910, and looks at his

---

[64] Merleau-Ponty, *Phenomenology*, p. 382. See also L. E. Bowling, "Faulkner: Technique of *The Sound and the Fury*," *Kenyon Review* 10 (1948): 558.

watch, he remembers what his father said to him when he gave him the watch:

It was Grandfather's and when Father gave it to me he said, Quentin, I give you the mausoleum of all hope and desire; it's rather excruci-ating-ly apt that you will use it to gain the reducto absurdum of all human experience which can fit your individual needs no better than it fitted his or his father's. I give it to you not that you may remem-ber time, but that you might forget it now and then for a moment and not spend all your breath trying to conquer it. Because no battle is ever won he said. They are not even fought. The field only reveals to man his own folly and despair, and victory is an illusion of philos-ophers and fools.[65]

Time here is seen from different points of view: as the mausoleum of hope it seems to nullify the fulfillment of all desires; as the *reductio ad absurdum* of all human experience it seems to uncover its own futility, which can only be temporarily overcome by pursuing pragmatic aims; as a chance to forget, it offers a brief respite from the need to conquer it; and as a battlefield, it reveals the outcome of all man's dreams and high ideals. If time can have so many meanings, the reason for the diversity must lie not in itself, but in the purposes which are projected onto it. Despite all the close relations between time and human intentions, for the Father it still has the character of an independent entity—a contin-ual provocation to arouse countless forms of reaction from man who suffers under it.

The ceaseless ticking of the watch seems like a living expression of this independence of time, which can only be measured in mechanical and not in human terms. The regularity of the ticking suggests the con-secutiveness through which past and present are linked together: "it can create in the mind unbroken the long diminishing parade of time."[66] If one can only go back far enough, says the Father, one will see Jesus and St. Francis "walking" again.[67] If time is regarded as the keeper of the unlosable, then interest lies not in time itself, but in the events it has contained—in other words, time is a purely external factor. Such con-clusions must have seemed dubious to the Father himself, for Quentin recalls two more statements pointing to the division between what time is and what occurs within time: "Father said that. That Christ was not

[65] Faulkner, *The Sound and the Fury*, p. 73.
[66] Ibid. J. Onimus, "L'Expression du temps dans le roman contemporain," *Revue de Littéra-ture Comparée* 28 (1954): 314, regards the impossibility of returning across time to the origin as a central problem in Faulkner.
[67] Faulkner, *The Sound and the Fury*, p. 73.

crucified: he was worn away by a minute clicking of little wheels."[68] If
time is an independent entity, measurable only as a mechanical process
and transcending everything that takes place inside it, this view of the
crucifixion is not altogether illogical, for time's independence of life can
only be shown by its indifference to life. Finally, Quentin recalls: "Father said that constant speculation regarding the position of mechanical
hands on an arbitrary dial which is a symptom of mind-function. Excre-
ment Father said like sweating. And I saying All right."[69] If the hands
gliding over the dial determine the activity of the mind, then man is constantly involved in concepts which are called forth by time itself. Time
is the force underlying a movement that is as inescapable as the functions
of one's own body. And yet it is present only as somebody's concept of
it. So much for the Father's views on time, recalled by Quentin as he
wakes up on the last morning of his life.

For Quentin the situation is somewhat different, in that the hands of
the watch have broken off and he feels uneasy at the ticking.[70] Sometimes he lays it face down, and eventually he decides to take the watch
to be repaired.[71] Against the background of the Father's ideas, this decision might be taken as an incipient allegory, but the desire to have the
watch repaired remains as transient as the Father's view that one must
attempt to overcome the vacuity of time through concrete, pragmatic
conceptions of it.

The trip to the watchmaker's is synchronized with an interior monologue of Quentin's, in which the division between time, as an independent, consecutive entity, and the concepts it provokes, is obliterated. As
in Benjy's monologue, the author has inserted a number of clear signals
that reveal three different, interlinking processes. Normal syntax, individual passages in italics, and in ordinary type without any punctuation
indicate different layers of consciousness in which is reflected Quentin's
actualization of his past and present. The passages in italics and those
without punctuation deal mainly with his memories of events that took
place within the family circle. The two different modes of presentation
are used in accordance with the type and the relevance of the events described: italics generally for unprocessed situations, and unpunctuated
monologue for external events. However, these passages—though clearly
distinguished through the print—often run together and so disrupt the

[68] Ibid., p. 74.
[69] Ibid.
[70] See ibid., pp. 76 f., 79, 80 f., 155, and 157. See also P. Lowrey, "Concepts of Time in
The Sound and the Fury," in *English Institute Essays* (1952), ed. A. S. Downer (New York,
1954), p. 70.
[71] See Faulkner, *The Sound and the Fury,* p. 79.

consecutiveness of past and present. Quentin's journey through the town acts as a random inducement to reinvoke past situations which, in their turn, release reflections which go far beyond his present situation. This interaction between different levels reveals a structural pattern of the interior monologue, the beginnings of which were already apparent in Benjy's section. The present actualizes particular impulses of the past, which appear strange and fragmentary because they are not remembered as they were, but as they are now under the influence and in the context of the present. This breaking up of the past is a sign of the inevitable change which it must undergo in the course of its reenactment, for now something is added which did not exist at the time, imposing an order which discounts the conditions and demolishes the context that originally prevailed.

In this process, time has a different gestalt from that which Quentin's Father had apparently given it. No longer is it a constant, independent force flowing from past to future and collecting en route all the answers to all the problems it has set; instead it can only take on a form through a self with a present that ceaselessly becomes a past and is replaced by a new, equally transient present. And so time as such is only conceivable in terms of the present working on the past; it is a process of continual, almost kaleidoscopic change, with an unending series of pasts taking shape through each individual present. Whenever something is remembered, it changes according to the circumstances under which it is remembered, but the resultant change in the past becomes a past itself which, in turn, can be remembered and changed again.

The close relations between time and subjectivity shape the structure of Quentin's monologue. The peculiar quality of time is that it constantly forms itself as the self experiences a present which passes but can be actualized anew. The connections between what is and what was are created by the self, which in fact only comes into being because of this very process. But as all experience is constantly exposed to a new present or future, it will constantly be in a state of flux, so that what has been experienced can never be fully understood, and what has been understood can never coincide totally with what constitutes the self.

This state of affairs is indicated by the general lack of coherence in Quentin's monologue. What is communicated first and foremost by the fragmented form is the fact that past and present can never be completely synthesized. Every incipient systematization is refuted by time, which as a new present exposes the ephemeral nature of any such synthesis. But it is only through subjectivity itself that time takes on its form of past, present, and future; the self is not the passive object of this process, but

144

actually conditions it. With which of its states, then, is the self to be identified? Is it that which existed in the circumstances of the past, is it that which it is at this moment in the present, or is it simply that force which constantly creates new connections and time relations but which, at the same time, constantly plunges every one of its visible manifestations into the maelstrom of change? The self is essentially incapable of completion, and this fact accounts both for its inadequacy and its richness. The knowledge that it can never be completely in possession of itself is the hallmark of its consciousness.[72]

Quentin repeatedly describes his attitudes and actions as shadows

---

[72] This problem is viewed somewhat differently by H. Meyerhoff, *Time in Literature* (Berkeley and Los Angeles, 1960), pp. 26–54. Although Meyerhoff's discussion "Of Time and the Self" does not refer specifically to Faulkner but draws its examples from Proust, Woolf, and Joyce, he holds fast to the old image of the flowing stream of time: "It is the 'stream of consciousness' which serves to clarify or render intelligible both the element of duration in time and the aspect of an enduring self. The technique is designed to give some kind of visible, sensible impression of how it is meaningful and intelligible to think of the self as a continuing unit despite the most perplexing and chaotic manifold of immediate experience. The continuity of the 'river' of time thus corresponds to the continuity of the 'stream' of consciousness within the self. In other words, the same symbol, 'riverrun,' expresses the same unity of interpenetration within time and the self. More specifically, this aspect of the self is conveyed by the effect of the associative technique, or the 'logic of images,' operating within the framework of the stream of consciousness. For what binds the chaotic pieces floating through the daydreams and fantasies of an individual into some kind of unity is that they make 'sense'—sense defined in terms of significant, associative images—only if they are referred to or seen within the perspective of the *same* self" (p. 37). The old image of the flowing river of time is offered as an analogy to the self, so that time can be envisaged as a duration and the self as the associative chain stretching out in this duration in order for its continuity to be conceivable. However, this category no longer applies to Faulkner's time consciousness (i.e., the temporality of the self), for the self cannot be actualized through the succession of its remembered forms. It is not surprising, then, that Proust provides the main evidence for Meyerhoff's conception of time and self. As we see in Faulkner, the self as a temporal phenomenon cannot ensure its own identity through memory, but for Meyerhoff it is memory that provides the basis for the ego's self-actualization in its imaginative form. "All psychological theories since have emphasized the integral relationship between memory and the self. The past, as we have seen, differs from the future, among other things in that it leaves records, whereas the future does not. And the mind is a recording instrument of peculiar sensitivity and complexity: I know who I am by virtue of the records and relations constituting the memory which I call my own, and which differs from the memory structure of others" (p. 43). One must see Faulkner's conception of time against this generally accepted background in order to realize the possibilities inherent in it. The temporality of the self cannot be properly grasped either through the image of the river of time or through the accumulating activities of memory. M. Le Breton, "Temps et Personne chez William Faulkner," *Journal de Psychologie Normale et Pathologique* 44 (1951): 344–54, imposes on Benjy and Quentin's behavior a normative concept of identity which is irrelevant to them (p. 346); but Le Breton rightly claims that time is Quentin's master—"un maître despotique" (see pp. 353 f.). We need not concern ourselves here with Sartre's critique of Faulkner's concept of time; see Peper, *Bewusstseinslagen des Erzählens,* pp. 135 ff. and H. Straumann, "Das Zeitproblem im englischen und amerikanischen Roman: Sterne, Joyce, Faulkner und Wilder," in *Das Zeitproblem im 20. Jahrhundert,* ed. R. W. Meyer (Berne, 1966), p. 156. Common ground between Faulkner and Sartre is pointed out by J. K. Simon, "Faulkner and Sartre: Metamorphosis and the Obscene," *Comparative Literature* 15 (1963): 216–25.

which he walks into or which hasten on ahead of him.[73] But these shadows are his reality. They incorporate the temporality of subjectivity, which is present in all the experiences of the self, as well as in the changing order which these experiences take on and cast off in the course of time. The self is never fixed, and so none of its manifestations can ever be complete; thus although it alone can constitute its past and its present, there is always a feeling that it is strangely unreal. In the last part of this monologue, Quentin reflects on this phenomenon:

> Sometimes I could put myself to sleep saying that over and over until after the honeysuckle got all mixed up in it the whole thing came to symbolize night and unrest I seemed to be lying neither asleep nor awake looking down a long corridor of grey half-light where all stable things had become shadowy paradoxical all I had done shadows all I had felt suffered taking visible form antic and perverse mocking without relevance inherent themselves with the denial of the significance they should have affirmed thinking I was I was not who was not was not who.[74]

As Quentin realizes that his own life dissolves into shadows and makes a fool of him because he imagined there was substance and meaning in it, the fact becomes apparent that the self cannot comprehend itself as the synthesis of its manifestations. There can be no such thing as a complete survey, and however eager the self might be to experience an apotheosis of its identity, its very consciousness refutes any such restriction. Quentin reflects on this, too: ". . . you are not lying now either but you are still blind to what is in yourself to that part of general truth the sequence of natural events and their causes which shadows every mans brow even benjys you are not thinking of finitude you are contemplating an apotheosis in which a temporary state of mind will become symmetrical above the flesh and aware both of itself and of the flesh."[75] Identity as an apotheosis of the self could only come into being if one of the possible states of that self could be hypostatized. Quentin also mentions the reason for this desire—to ward off finitude. But in Quentin's monologue, the self is reflected precisely in the consciousness of its own finitude. What, then, is this identity? According to what may be gauged from Quentin's monologue, it is the constant overlapping of temporal hori-

---

[73] See Faulkner, *The Sound and the Fury*, pp. 94, 104, 111, 122, and 154. Re 'shadow' as a key word in *The Sound and the Fury*, see K. G. Gibbons, "Quentin's Shadow," *Literature and Psychology* 12 (1962): 16–24, where the 'shadow' is given a completely psychological interpretation. A much more discerning interpretation of the shadow motif is offered by Vickery, *Novels of Faulkner*, p. 41.
[74] Faulkner, *The Sound and the Fury*, p. 154.
[75] Ibid., p. 160. See also P. Swiggart, *The Art of Faulkner's Novels* (Austin, 1962), p. 95.

zons opened up by the self, the intersection of attitudes and actions, and the potentiality of situations.

The effects of this condition are illustrated by two episodes which Quentin describes on the last day of his life. One records his reaction when an attempt is made to trace his conduct back to a particular motive; the other shows what happens when one acts in the present according to ideas that were only valid in the circumstances of the past.

When Quentin is walking through the suburbs of Boston, he is followed by a little girl.[76] He wants to get rid of her and decides to take her home, but the girl does not know where she lives, and so the two of them wander through the streets, aimlessly and yet with a specific aim in mind. The desire to get rid of the child awakens in Quentin the memory of how he once used to worry about his sister Caddy; at that time he wanted to win Caddy's love, and now he wants to be free of the child. These two contrasting desires change the direction of the past and shed new light on the present. The dumb persistence of the child and the painful relationship with the sister run into one another, creating a new situation, of which the past and present situations become mere shadows. Through the interplay of possibilities, what was real and what is real now takes on an element of unreality, and yet the thoughts now preoccupying Quentin come directly out of his past and his present. And so life can be marshalled into ever new orders—but at the cost of its own factualness, which becomes increasingly shadowy. When finally Quentin is found by the girl's brother, taken to the sheriff, and accused of wicked intentions, he reacts with wild laughter,[77] because he can only regard as absurd the reduction of his various thoughts to a single motive—especially of this nature; it is in fact his very lack of motivation that enables him to become involved in those processes of consciousness which show him his own constant movement between the possible future, present, and past.

But it is also absurd for Quentin to act in the present in a way that, at best, would have suited a past situation. This is what happens in the second episode. In a state of trance, Quentin gives a beating to his friend Gerald.[78] The fight starts because of a quite casual question, but one which weighs heavily on Quentin's personal existence: namely, having a sister.[79] This touches Quentin on a very sore spot, and suddenly Gerald

[76] See Faulkner, *The Sound and the Fury*, pp. 115 ff.
[77] Ibid., pp. 128 and 134. See also Vickery, *Novels of Faulkner*, p. 37.
[78] See Faulkner, *The Sound and the Fury*, pp. 136 ff.
[79] Ibid., p. 151.

appears to be his rival for Caddy's love, so that he takes a belated revenge on him. But by letting himself be taken over by motivations of the past, Quentin is behaving absurdly in the present. During the fight, his interior monologue increases in pace, while images of the past appear to him in such close-up proximity that they become blurred and distorted. Real events and mere imaginings become interchangeable, so that the total synchronization of past and present is possible only as a total unreality. Here again is confirmation of Quentin's basic experience: he cannot be contained in any of his own manifestations of himself, but at the same time his only point of reference is whatever of him has been actualized.

Each shadow-like gestalt of his life is the product of the unfathomable base, and shadow and base communicate themselves in time, which is both the producer and the product of the self. "It is true that I find, through time, later experiences interlocking with earlier ones and carrying them further, but nowhere do I enjoy absolute possession of myself by myself, since the hollow void of the future is for ever being refilled with a fresh present. There is no related object without relation and without subject, no unity without unification, but every synthesis is both exploded and rebuilt by time which, with one and the same process, calls it into question and confirms it because it produces a new present which retains the past."[80]

The Quentin monologue does not fulfill the expectation, arising out of the first part of the novel, that an active consciousness might bring about an integration between self and the world. Although the monologue *is* characterized by a higher level of consciousness, this only serves to divulge the ambiguity of the self, which is both the basis and the shadow of itself. This condition is made actual by the temporality of the self.

After the Quentin monologue, there remains little more than one's curiosity as to how the fragments of the story will be put together; and precisely at this moment, when total comprehension seems to be out of the question, the Jason monologue provides the reader with the privilege of overall vision that has been withheld from him till now. Typical of Jason is the decisiveness of his actions, which at first sight might be taken for the long awaited solution to the problems of the self. But the non-alignment of the first two monologues has already precluded the idea that they are in any way complementary, and so the apparent implica-

[80] Merleau-Ponty, *Phenomenology*, p. 240.

tion that the answer lies in action must clearly be treated with the utmost caution. Although the monologues both of Benjy and of Quentin eluded the reader's own everyday experience, they still influence his observation once he has regained a degree of detachment from the proceedings. Now that he is confronted by an apparently straightforward text, he will be concerned less with the 'solution' than with the conditions that give rise to such decisiveness. And so the potential experiences of the first two monologues serve to sharpen the reader's critical eye, creating a new background against which he will judge Jason's clear-cut actions.

The Jason monologue is simple enough to understand: the events he describes are coherent and the connections between them are clearly formulated. This clarity, however, is by no means identical with a greater insight or a more penetrating vision of the events—on the contrary: the very coherence of the Jason account strikingly diminishes the richness of the world contained in the Benjy and Quentin sections. For Jason things arrange themselves in accordance with his ideas; he has to provide for the Compson family, and for this reason alone he is pragmatic. But this fact is not enough to explain the attitude to the world which gives rise to the clarity of his monologue. Unlike Quentin, he lacks the capacity to reflect on things. This is particularly apparent when he tries to corroborate his own standpoint. Whenever he describes critical situations in which he has come across opposition to his views, he simply repeats the conversation that took place at the time, assuming that this will give weight to his opinion. A feature of primitive narration is the repetition of one's own words to indicate insistence on the rightness of what has been said. To find other means of corroboration, the speaker must look beyond himself, so that he can view moments of crisis from a different standpoint. But here the mode of narration is frequently that of the interior monologue, and even when it is a straightforward first-person singular account, Jason remains his own referee. His protestations of the rightness of his opinions suggest the underlying tensions between him and the world around him, but Jason is never conscious of the reasons for these tensions, although one would have expected him to be, in view of all the opposition he meets. For him, the world remains identical to his conceptions of it. This is the key to the decisiveness of his actions as well as to the ambiguity of that decisiveness. If, against the background of the Quentin monologue, one might be tempted to see action as the way out of the "pale cast of thought," Jason's monologue reveals the consequences that arise from the inevitable limitations of the person acting. In this connection, there is a revealing remark of Quentin's which deals precisely with the preconditions of action. On his way through Boston he comes across a group of boys who have spotted a trout in a pool and are already engaged in a lively discussion about what they will buy with the proceeds of their as yet uncaught catch. Quentin says: "They all talked at once, their voices insistent and contradictory and impatient, making of unreality a possibility, then a probability, then an incontrovertible fact, as people will when their desires become words."[81]

Now Jason's intention is to cheat his niece, who is a member of his household, of the money her mother is sending her.[82] This intention and the fulfillment of it are the focal point of his whole narrative. This is the main motive for his actions and accounts for the decisiveness of his conduct, which in turn accounts for the coherence of his narrative. As his wishes become "incontrovertible facts," the gap between himself and the world seems to have disappeared. But such "incontrovertible facts" contain a strong element of illusion, which is conveyed in two ways by Jason's monologue. First, he is blind to himself, because through his inability to achieve any critical detachment from himself he is unable to recognize himself in the mirror of his own judgments: he hates frauds, and is himself one; he cheats his niece because of her immoral conduct and behaves with equal immorality; the great schism between his judgment of others and his judgment of himself shows just how illusory his conduct is. Second, Jason finds that the world around him does not arrange itself according to his ideas after all. And so his attitude becomes all the more decisive, but only with the result that he proceeds more and more to lose control of his surroundings. In the course of his account, he becomes increasingly irritated, because he sees himself entangled through his own actions in situations where he is forced to depend on others. And the more firmly he acts, the more uncontrollable become these situations, which then, naturally, push him into further firm actions. It is precisely because Jason identifies himself with his ideas and his ideas with the world that he simply cannot bear opposition. But in trying to overcome opposition, he merely increases the scope of the uncontrollable. All this hot-headed action and increasing lust for power implies that mediation between self and world is Utopian, and this ele-

---

[81] Faulkner, *The Sound and the Fury*, p. 109.

[82] See ibid., pp. 187, 189, and esp. 194 ff. Re the view of Jason as the only 'healthy' Compson, and his ironic position in relation to his 'sick' brothers, see C. Brooks, *The Hidden God* (New Haven and London, 1963), p. 41. There is a somewhat far-fetched allegorical interpretation of Jason by C. Collins, "The Interior Monologues of *The Sound and the Fury*," in *English Institute Essays* (1952), ed. A. S. Downer (New York, 1954), p. 34: Collins sees him as the 'poor player' in that same speech of Macbeth's. The relations between the individual characters are viewed more cautiously by L. Thompson, "Mirror Analogues in *The Sound and the Fury*," in *William Faulkner, Three Decades of Criticism*, ed. F. J. Hoffman and O. W. Vickery (East Lansing, 1960), pp. 211-25.

ment emerges in proportion to the efforts made to produce such a mediation. Jason's attempts to bring his surroundings totally into line with himself compel him to try and control them; in doing so, he himself causes their uncontrollability.

Faulkner's novel ends with an authorial account of the day after the one described by Benjy and Jason. The Compson household is viewed from an external, neutral standpoint, focused principally on the negress Dilsey. In his appendix, Faulkner says of her: "DILSEY. They endured."[83] With these words, the author links the last section of his book with a central feature of his philosophy. "Endure" is an ambiguous word, with connotations both of suffering and of survival,[84] and it refers to that experience of the world that precedes all processes of reflection and can never be comprehensively grasped *by* reflection. Here we have in the last part of the novel a peculiar extension of the previous parts: against this background, the earlier, reduced forms of subjectivity are seen as processed modes of experiencing and comprehending the world. But at the same time they expose the unprocessed core on which they feed and which for them "constitutes . . . a kind of original past, a past which has never been a present."[85] This interaction between the processed and the unprocessed worlds is brought out in two ways. In the fourth part, there is the change in narrative perspective, which releases the world of the Compson brothers from the restrictions of the first-person view, and so endows it with an expansibility which none of the interior monologues can capture or even approach. But the interaction is also reflected within the monologues themselves, which take on a new dimension when viewed in this light. The images of reduced subjectivity which they provide do show certain basic features of subjectivity that are essential to an actualization of self and world; but in the course of this actualization, during which the self enters into a relationship with itself or with the world, the element of breakdown becomes apparent. Benjy is subjectivity reduced to the senses. It retains nothing but perception as a minimal distinction between itself and the world, and its unstable grasp lets slip whatever it tries to hold onto. The life of this self seems to be in a constant state of dynamic fragmentation. Quentin is subjectivity reduced to its conscious-

---

[83] William Faulkner, *The Sound and the Fury* (Vintage Book) (New York, no date), p. 22.
[84] See Peper, *Bewusstseinslagen des Erzählens,* pp. 160 ff.; see also A. Kazin, "Faulkner in His Fury," in *Modern American Fiction, Essays in Criticism,* ed. A. W. Litz (New York, 1963), p. 177, and Christadler, *Natur und Geschichte,* pp. 55 f., 62, and 177 f.
[85] Merleau-Ponty, *Phenomenology,* p. 242; see also the context in which this is discussed.

ness, which can only divulge the ambiguity of its temporality. As a potential of situations it is present in all its manifestations, but can only unfold itself as a spectrum of shadows because its existence in the here-and-now precludes its total existence in the there-and-then. And, finally, Jason is subjectivity reduced to action and dominance, which in its commitment to the pursuit of its aims brings about the dynamic uncontrollability of its surroundings.

By means of these different forms of reduction, the world of the Compson brothers is given different patterns, and these differences convey both the comprehension and the breakdown of the patterns. But it is the breakdown that divulges the unprocessed basis of experience—a basis that can only be communicated in this way because otherwise it could be misconstrued as an illustration of something else. And so out of the reduced forms of the self, and out of the breakdown of their respective patterns, there emerge—albeit obliquely—the unplumbed and unplumbable depths of the self, full of sound and fury, signifying . . . something.

III

The Unpredictability of Subjectivity.
I. Compton-Burnett: *A Heritage and Its History*

Historically, there is no connection between Ivy Compton-Burnett's work and Faulkner's. The form of presentation in fact is so different that at first sight it might seem difficult to bring the two novels under the same heading. Nathalie Sarraute regarded Ivy Compton-Burnett as a forerunner of the *nouveau roman;*[86] Faulkner, on the other hand, looked back to the technique of the interior monologue, as developed during the first two decades of the twentieth century, and perfected it for the self-presentation of subjectivity.

Ivy Compton-Burnett's novels consist of an almost continuous succession of dialogues, through which the spoken word loses the intimate, private character of the interior monologue. Through its constant adjustment to a partner, dialogue tends to exclude the introspection and self-reflection by which Faulkner's first-person narrators revealed themselves. The dialogue here discloses what the individual characters either conceal or cannot see, so that the process of self-discovery is no longer left to a person entangled in his own interior monologue, but is brought about by someone else. There are times when this revelation is quite

---

[86] See Nathalie Sarraute, *L'Ère du Soupçon. Essais sur le Roman* (Paris, 1956), pp. 119 ff.

brutal, but as the characters themselves seem to be virtually indifferent to the almost shocking confrontations with their real selves, the reader has to make what he can of the unexplained presentation of their blindness. Faulkner's characters talk to themselves, and in doing so they delve down internally into the unprocessed depths of the self; Ivy Compton-Burnett's characters talk to one another and so divulge externally those same unprocessed foundations of speech and action.

The constant use of the dialogue form has strong repercussions on the narrative, for it automatically sets all events in an immediate present and precludes the description of any external reality. Thus the social setting necessary for an alignment of past and present is shrunk to the barest minimum. The author has vanished behind the words of her characters, declining to comment or to explain, and so we are deprived of any background save the utterances of the characters themselves. And these are so devoid of context—and therefore so loaded with potential contexts— that they are endowed with a strange and disturbing inexhaustibility. This approach offers various possibilities for the actualization of the self, which we shall examine more closely with reference to *A Heritage and Its History* (first published in 1959).[87]

The dialogue form used in this novel is in many ways quite different from what we have come to expect of the drama. Ingarden has defined dramatic dialogue as follows:

> A conversation between two people is rarely a matter just of communication; it is concerned with something of much more vital importance—the influencing of the person to whom the words are addressed. In all "dramatic" conflicts, such as are developed in the world presented by the play, the speech addressed to a character is a form of action on the part of the speaker, and basically it only has any real importance for the events depicted in the play if it actually brings about a genuine advance in the action that is developing.[88]

However opposed may be the positions of the characters in the play, the dialogue in some way coordinates them. In *A Heritage and Its History*, this coordination, essential for dramatic dialogue, appears to lie in the common environment of the characters—that of the landed gentry at the turn of the century. Ivy Compton-Burnett herself said once: "I do not feel that I have any real or organic knowledge of life later than about

---

[87] This section is based on part of my essay "Dialogue of the Unspeakable" on pp. 242 ff. this volume; see also "Introduction," p. xiv.
[88] Roman Ingarden, *Das literarische Kunstwerk* (Tübingen, [2]1960), p. 408 f.

1910."[89] But the dialogue in her novel reflects a highly individual conception of this historically precise period. The form of conversation seems rather to diffuse than to bring out the situation of the characters in Victorian society. Even though the atmosphere of the Victorian family and home does pervade the whole novel, the words and actions of the individual members of that family continually exceed the limits of what was considered to be proper in that particular society. By going against the expectations arising out of the setting, the dialogue draws attention all the more intensively to the incalculable motives of human conduct that seem to be independent of that setting. And so the function of dialogue in the drama—communicating different positions and throwing emphasis on the common ground underlying the conversation— is here quite transformed. Now the dialogue makes the common ground —i.e., Victorian convention—dwindle to insignificance, blotting it out with the unfathomableness of human actions and reactions.

At first sight, these dialogues seem improbable to the reader, because they are unlike anything he has ever heard. But this impression arises mainly out of the author's refusal to link together the unexpected twists and turns of the conversation. In dramatic dialogue, statements are always linked together by the particular aim of the people talking, but in Ivy Compton-Burnett's novel, the aim—and therefore the link— has been left out. The dialogue at times seems almost like a sequence of effects without causes. And so the reader has to discover for himself the relevance of the different statements and replies. But obviously he will only be induced to do this if he is made witness to a conversation that is so different from the normal, familiar forms of conversation that he is provoked into attentive involvement. The provocation is achieved by depriving the reader of the distance that is necessary for him to understand the characters. He is placed so close to them that he cannot discern the motivation for what they are doing to each other, although he is fully aware that something is being done. In order to relieve his discomfort, he is forced to develop some sort of attitude toward the strange reactions of the people he is confronted with, and so, through his reactions to them, he comes to participate more and more in the unending dialogues.

This process might be easier to understand if we look at those passages which in fact come closest to fulfilling our normal expectations of dia-

---

[89] Quoted by Pamela Hansford Johnson, *Ivy Compton-Burnett* (London, 1951), p. 36. Until now the most comprehensive accounts of Ivy Compton-Burnett's novels are given by R. Liddell, *The Novels of I. Compton-Burnett* (London, 1955); and F. Baldanza, *Ivy Compton-Burnett* (Twayne's English Author Series) (New York, 1964).

logue. As J. L. Styan has put it, dialogue is directed toward a "predetermined end."[90] In *A Heritage and Its History*, this end is provided by the
following conflict: Simon Challoner himself shatters his own long-cherished dream of taking over the heritage from his uncle; the father does
die, but Sir Edwin marries, despite his advanced age, and Simon fathers
the child Sir Edwin's wife gives birth to. Thus the relations between the
characters become extremely involved, and in their life together they are
forced to conceal the wide range of consequences following on from this
critical turning point.[91] There is no lack of tense situations in which the
whole truth threatens to come out. At such moments, the most favored
technique is for the character to adjust himself to the person he is talking with, to lull his suspicions, and to head him off from the discovery
of the real situation.[92] The moment the dialogue is orientated toward
this end, it fulfills its dramatic function—namely, to maneuver the other
into a specific position. But here the agreement, based on a common
aim, is identical with suppression of the truth. Sir Edwin actually gives
voice to this fact:

> "It must not be," said his uncle. "We are to forget the truth. It
> must not lie below the surface, ready to escape."[93]

Forgetting the truth, then, is a precondition of the unanimity, and as
all the characters are implicated in this shady activity, there arises between them a bond which is dictated by social considerations and which
can best be summed up as convention. When the crisis over the real
origin of Sir Edwin's supposed son has reached its climax, Sir Edwin
says:

> "Civilised life exacts its toll. We live among the civilised."
> "The conventions are on the surface," said his wife. "We know the
> natural life is underneath."
> "We do; we have our reason. But we cannot live it. We know the
> consequences of doing so. If not, we learn."[94]

This distinction between convention and the natural life throws new
light on those features of the dialogue which we have been discussing up
to now; if the need for convention is uppermost, the characters will act

---

[90] J. L. Styan, *The Elements of Drama* (Cambridge, 1963), p. 12. Re the tendencies of Ivy
Compton-Burnett's language as opposed to those of dramatic dialogue, see Sarraute, *L'Ère du
Soupçon*, p. 122, and J. Preston's discussion of *A Heritage and Its History* in "The Matter in a
Word," *Essays in Criticism* 10 (1960): 348 ff.
[91] See Ivy Compton-Burnett, *A Heritage and Its History* (London, 1959), p. 103.
[92] Ibid., pp. 101 ff.
[93] Ibid., p. 115.
[94] Ibid., p. 160.

in relation to one another; but if their utterances are dictated by the natural life that lies below the surface of social convention, then their reactions tend to be incalculable.

This duality determines the structure of the dialogue in *A Heritage and Its History*. For the characters to be able to communicate at all, there has to be a certain amount of common ground established through convention. But just below the surface of this common ground seethes the natural life, which is liable to erupt at any moment. Whatever has been said can, merely by being communicated, appear different from what was meant, and the interplay of statements and replies merely accentuates the limitations of the views expressed—their motivation sometimes taking on a devastating transparency.[95] The form of this dialogue serves to bring out whatever has been concealed—consciously or unconsciously—by the speaker, so that the impartial observer will become increasingly aware of what has *not* been said. And so as the characters continue to supplement their statements by developing some unforeseen implication, the subject of the conversation constantly shifts onto new ground, leaving exposed and in disrepute the hitherto unquestioned presuppositions of convention and opinion. The dialogue shows the extent to which pragmatic requirements limit the scope of the natural life, thus bringing about a division between what is and what might have been. It draws attention to and exploits this division, proceeding as it does from conventional modes of conduct to a wide variety of unforeseen reactions, and these reactions in turn show the mode of conduct demanded by convention to be just one special case out of many possibilities.

The form of the dialogue is, of course, crucial for the drawing of the characters, for it is the only technique used to portray them. The author tells us nothing about them as individuals, and so we can only judge them by their own words. They all pursue very definite ends: Simon wants to succeed to his uncle's estate,[96] while his uncle seeks to exclude him from the heritage;[97] Hamish wants to marry his step-sister Naomi[98] and, when this proves impossible, to renounce the heritage.[99] Despite the firmness of these purposes, the characters act in such a way that most of their de-

---

[95] This is clear, for instance, in the opening dialogue between Simon and Walter Challoner. In the essay "Dialogue of the Unspeakable" I have tried to explain the special qualities of such conversations; see pp. 239 ff. of this volume.
[96] See Compton-Burnett, *A Heritage*, p. 7.
[97] Ibid., pp. 103 f.
[98] Ibid., pp. 145 f.
[99] Ibid., p. 167.

sires are frustrated, but as they seem relatively indifferent to their failure, it would appear that these all-important aims are in fact only random elements of their characters. When rational self-explanation and actual conduct are so patently inconsistent the characters inevitably lose the individuality we expect in a novel.

The originality of this form of characterization has called forth different responses from different critics—a number of them unfavorable. Pamela Hansford Johnson, for instance, writes: "The ease with which the persons of the novels may be confused in the memory is a genuine flaw, a flaw which above all, must make Miss Compton-Burnett always a writer for the 'few,' as only a few are able to make the concentrated intellectual effort she demands from them through both her virtues and her faults."[100] This criticism reflects expectations conditioned by the novel of the nineteenth century. Then the reader demanded an unmistakable identity for the character he was meeting—an identity that was formed not least by the individual environment and fate of that character. If Ivy Compton-Burnett's characters tend to lose their identity in the reader's memory, this is because the center of attention is not themselves, but their unpredictability. Their external appearance and their behavior dwindle into insignificance; they merely offer the starting-point for the dialogue, which then proceeds to leave its starting-point behind. Individual features are only necessary in order to get the conversation going, but the importance of this is to show the wealth of implications concealed in every utterance. The individual speaker may not even see, let alone be in control of these implications, and yet they all arise out of the opinion through which he is trying to express himself. Then, in his reply, the partner will seize on just one of the many implications of what has been said, ignoring the rest.

This process has two basic consequences. First, it can turn the original statement in a direction quite unintended by the speaker; second, the seizing on one implication in turn calls forth a host of new ones. And so we have a statement, extraction of a single implication leading to the reply, the reply in turn creating implications of which again only one will be selected as basis for the next statement etc. etc. Every utterance contains a wealth of possible implications, and every selection leads to a new store of implications.

This structure of the dialogue makes it impossible for any one theme to be consistently developed. But as each reply brings forth the precise formulation of one implication, there do arise at least the suggested out-

---

[100] Johnson, *Ivy Compton-Burnett*, p. 22.

lines of thoughts, ideas etc.—though these in turn are swiftly caught up in the whirl of changing and unforeseeable implications. Any starting-point can lead to such configurations, which then signalize the hitherto unplumbed depths of the human character, as they bring to light the un-expected and the unpremeditated. The characters themselves appear two-faced. What they say about themselves does not illuminate them as individuals so much as accentuate the unfathomableness of their inner recesses. The more steadfastly they pursue and identify with their goals, the more fictitious becomes the basis of their conduct. They fail to real-ize that their surface reactions are conditioned by pragmatic require-ments which can change from one situation to the next. The pragmatic-ally conditioned statement may be taken for the authentic expression of the person concerned, but the resultant concrete manifestation can in fact reflect nothing but the outer appearance of the character.

Time and again the dialogue exposes this situation, and indeed at the end of the novel it becomes the actual subject of conversation:

"Is Father a noble man?" said Ralph, as the door closed. "Or is he a deceiver of himself and others? Or what is he?"

"A mixture of them all, as we all are," said Naomi. "But exile ex-posed and stressed the parts. Suppose we had a similar love for our first home, and were affected by leaving it in the same way! He would hardly be able to complain. He may have been wise to darken our memories of it."

"I still fear a reaction from the new spirit. His position will become normal to him. It was indeed the other that was not. And he will have nothing besides."

"So that is what you think," said Graham.

"Well, thinking needs so much courage."

"I have enough," said Naomi. "The something besides will be there. And I am glad it will. It is not good to live without it."

"He is putting a memorial tablet to Hamish in the church," said Graham. "Hamish is to be described as Uncle Edwin's son. I daresay many people are not what they are thought to be."

"Most of them what they are known to be," said Naomi. "Secrets are not often kept. If they were, we should not know there were such things. And now we take more interest in them than in any others."[101]

If hidden implications are, so to speak, to be kept in play, the charac-ters' statements must have virtually no consequences for their relation-ships—otherwise a conflict would ensue which would fix on one particular situation and so exclude the possibility of unpredictable reactions. It is

---

[101] Compton-Burnett, *A Heritage*, pp. 239 f.

the "something besides" which has to be there, and so the dialogue, as the unfolding of innumerable implications, must be endless, in the sense of open-ended. The visible outline of the characters seems almost a matter of chance, depending on which implications are uppermost at one particular moment. And just as what we know appears to be a matter of chance, so the unforeseeable becomes a reality. The dialogue is "not a transcript of what he or she would have said in 'real life' but rather of what would have been said *plus* what would have been implied but not spoken *plus* what would have been understood though not implied."[102]

As the speakers are not aware of the welter of implications, only divulging them to a limited extent, and so never grasping them properly, there emerges a feature that is common to all of them: they are not confronted with an abstract unpredictability, but in fact produce it and reveal it themselves. For such a process to be made concrete, it is essential that it should not be diverted by moral considerations, for again a moral background would be fixed, and therefore would exclude implications instead of producing them. Pamela Hansford Johnson quite rightly called Ivy Compton-Burnett "the most amoral of living writers."[103] Morality could only impose limitations which would not be so very different in kind from those imposed by individual characterization. Any such qualification would involve a premature mapping of those regions of human reality that are only disclosed through the implications of what the characters say. This principle of composition can be seen even in the most ordinary situations—for instance, in the dialogue after Sir Edwin's long-awaited death, at the age of ninety-four:

"This day brings another back to me," said Julia. "The day when my husband was buried, Edwin's younger brother! All those years ago! Life is a strange thing. It will soon be my turn to follow."
"What ought we to say?" said Graham. "Silence means consent, and seems to mean it. And yet we can hardly disagree."
"Say nothing," said Simon.
"Father is in a sinister mood," said Ralph. "It can hardly be the loss of his uncle at ninety-four."[104]

Graham and Ralph, Julia's grandsons, have already stepped out of character in that they do not speak like children at all. But never in this nov-

---

[102] H. Corke, "New Novels," *The Listener* 58, no. 1483 (1957): 322, made this remark in discussing *A Father and His Fate*. However, it applies to the dialogue in all Ivy Compton-Burnett's novels, and Corke meant it in this sense.

[103] Johnson, *Ivy Compton-Burnett*, p. 11.

[104] Compton-Burnett, *A Heritage*, p. 188.

el is any consideration given as to whether characters seem what they are.[105]

The fact that the reply comes from a child is obviously quite irrelevant to the reaction depicted. One would have expected the usual mechanical remark to banish Julia's sentimental concern with her own death, but no such consolation is forthcoming. Graham realizes this, and in not giving her the conventional reply, he compels himself to ask how he ought to have reacted. The subject of his remark is the *possibilities* of reaction. However unnatural such a reply may seem, there is no denying the truth of its content. And if this truth seems hurtful, then we are bound to realize that consideration for others is a pragmatic precept based, precisely, on avoiding truth, as if truth itself were immoral.[106] Pragmatic precepts, however, will only be valid under certain conditions, so that a change in conditions will mean a change in conduct. This comes out clearly in what Simon and Ralph have to say. Simon advises his son Graham to keep quiet, but Ralph draws attention to the hidden motive behind his father's reply; for Simon is vexed at the fact that he himself destroyed his own chance of succeeding to the heritage.

Such an account of the implications behind the conversation should by no means be regarded as exhaustive. Any explanation will be as restricted as the characters' own unfolding of the implications, and even if it can illuminate some of the nuances, it can never encompass the full range of those implications. There may be quite different motives for Graham's statement and Simon's advice—but, in the absence of authorial explanation and definitive characterization, the reader is forced to make his own diagnosis. At the same time, however, by giving such an interpretation, he is automatically excluding other possibilities, and when other implications come to light, he must then modify his original interpretation.

The dialogue by its very nature defies any standardized interpretation, and yet the reader is always inclined to try and standardize,[107] comparing the fictitious characters with his own experience and attempting to bring them into line with his own familiar world. Here he finds himself prevented from applying these standards. The characters' lack of individuality prevents him from concentrating on their discernible features,

---

[105] See H. Spiel, *Der Park und die Wildnis. Zur Situation der neueren englischen Literatur* (Munich, 1953), pp. 128 f.

[106] Re the question of morality, see S. Hampshire, "The Art of a Moralist," *Encounter* 9 (1957): 80.

[107] See also Sarraute, *L'Ère du Soupçon*, p. 70.

and instead he finds himself confronted not by people but by conditions of human conduct. The normal contact between reader and characters is therefore broken, and so he must leave behind his own familiar world and plunge into the unknown. This participation is virtually forced on him by the composition of the characters, and—like the dialogue which both produces and is produced by them—they focus his attention not on what *is* there, but on what is not. They are blind to their own two-facedness, oblivious to the implications of what they say, or alternatively unmoved when confronted by them. The reader himself must strive to make sense of their inconsistencies, but instead of discovering the motives for their conduct, he will merely find that the concrete statements he has read are overshadowed by the statements that have not been written. The spoken word, as a manifestation of the pragmatic self, proves to be nothing but a particle of subjectivity, its incompleteness made abundantly clear by the fact that no sooner has it been uttered than it is swamped by its own unformulated implications. In this accentuation of the unwritten lies the dynamism of the dialogue, and if the characters seem strangely unaffected by a confrontation with these implications, the reader will be that much more aware not only of their blindness but also of the irrelevance of their actual conduct.

This process also underlies the plot of the novel. In an interview, Ivy Compton-Burnett once said the following about her characters and stories: "I think that actual life supplies a writer with characters less than is thought. . . . As regards plots, I find real life no help at all. Real life seems to have no plots. And as I think a plot desirable and almost necessary I have this extra grudge against life. But I do think there are signs that strange things happen, though they do not emerge. I believe it would go ill with many of us if we were faced by a strong temptation, and I suspect that with some of us it does go ill."[108] If "real life" only gives us a surface view of reality, because obviously it is shaped by existing conventions, only a fabricated plot will be able to lay bare the substrata of that reality. This fabrication becomes a sort of protest against the immediacy of the self-evident, which seems to exclude the need for any questioning. And so the plot sacrifices one of its most sacrosanct attributes: verisimilitude. But, paradoxically, this sacrifice is obviously made in the cause of truth. While the verisimilitude of the traditional

---

[108] Quoted by Johnson, *Ivy Compton-Burnett*, p. 36.

narrative served to produce the illusion of truth, the fabricated plot sets out to destroy any such illusory intentions. The consequences of this approach are to be seen in the plot of *A Heritage and Its History*.

Although the hopes and views of the characters are made apparent in the dialogue, their actions are often in striking contrast to the intentions they have expressed. This tendency is most evident in Simon Challoner. He fathers a child that removes all hope of his ever getting the long-cherished heritage. Just as unexpectedly, he marries Fanny, whose sister Rhoda is Sir Edwin's wife and mother of his (Simon's) child. Such a concatenation seems fabricated because the elements of the story arouse expectations typical of a Victorian social novel, but then take on a form which continually bursts open such a frame. Against the Victorian background, the actions of the characters sometimes seem quite absurd, but at the same time they show how very little control conventions really have over people's behavior. Obviously, the disastrous actions of the characters do not arise out of their personal wishes—and indeed they are often so completely contrary to their wishes that they seem like extraordinary quirks beyond the influence of any personal desires, let alone of convention. Perhaps it was anger at Sir Edwin's marriage that set Simon on the fatal path toward a relationship with Rhoda. Even for him, the motivation can only be a matter of conjecture, and in view of his aim in life it can never be properly understood. But if people's actions cannot be brought into line with their avowed intentions, then these intentions take on an ambiguity that no amount of analysis will ever fully remove.

The story brings this ambiguity out into the open. Through his impulsive behavior, Simon creates new realities, which impose unexpected conditions on the lives of the mother, the children, and also Sir Edwin himself. Simon continually tries to prepare his children for the possibility that they may have to spend the rest of their lives in the poorhouse. In this way he hopes to regain some sort of control over the unpremeditated consequences of his actions, but instead he merely alienates his children more and more, until finally they dismiss his scheme as simply a "figment of Father's brain."[109] But if openly pursued intentions are so obviously fictitious, then clearly there must be a wide gulf between what the character does and what the character is. Whatever the intention may be, it is only a partial motivating force, conditioned by the par-

[109] Compton-Burnett, *A Heritage*, p. 238.

ticular circumstances it is trying to cope with, but liable to lose its validity under different circumstances or when seen from a different standpoint. The moment we try to identify a character with one particular intention, we find his actions giving the lie to our identification. We are confronted with the fact that either the actions or the intentions are a sort of camouflage, and the reality lies in territory not hitherto exposed. The story lifts off the camouflage, but refrains from presenting us with the reality beneath. Indeed its most penetrating effects are achieved precisely by revealing the apparently inexplicable inconsistencies of the characters and leaving us floundering after the all-important but ungraspable motive.

Time and again in this story, we find that the actions of the characters are not calculated to help them fulfill their own wishes. The fact that at the end of the novel they do get what they wanted through no fault of their own relegates all their efforts in the course of the story to the level of irrelevance. This irrelevance accentuates two factors: first, the conditional nature of all the intentions pursued; second, the insignificance of any such intentions as regards the overall conduct of the character. When situations change, they do so mainly because of some unpremeditated action which cancels out all previous calculations, or because of the clarification of an implication which, similarly, cancels out the teleology of all that has been spoken. This confrontation between calculated and unpremeditated conduct would seem to contain all the elements essential for conflict. But in this story there is no conflict—Simon does not have to bear the consequences of his action—and this shows just how irrelevant the characters' intentions really are.

It is therefore only logical that by the end of the novel Simon cannot really identify himself with any of the selves that he has manifested and parted with. This is why he says: "I think being carried beyond ourselves carries ourselves further."[110] If this continual furtherance of the self is to be communicated to the reader, the 'story' must be based not on his expectations of everyday experience, but on the fundamental fluidity of human conduct, of which everyday experience is merely the tip of the iceberg. And so the construction of the novel, just like the characterization and the whole narrative technique, brings out the unpredictability of the self, at the same time unmasking convention as merely one restricted, pragmatically conditioned form of human reality.

[110] Ibid., p. 228.

IV

Subjectivity as the Autogenous Cancellation of Its Own Manifestations. S. Beckett: *Molloy, Malone Dies, The Unnamable*

The approach to the theme of subjectivity in Beckett's trilogy may be summed up by a remark of Nietzsche's, describing the workings of consciousness: "The interpretative character of all events. There is no such thing as an event in itself. What happens is a group of appearances, selected and brought together by an interpreting being. . . . There are no given facts. And it is the same with feelings and with ideas: in becoming conscious of them, I make a selection, a simplification, an attempt at forming a gestalt: that is what is meant by becoming conscious—a completely active re-formation."[111] Beckett's trilogy makes the reader conscious of this process itself, revealing not only the effects of such a "reformation" but also the conditions that bring it about.

The very titles of the three novels—*Molloy, Malone Dies,* and *The Unnamable*—draw attention to the first-person narrator's withdrawal into anonymity. While in the third novel he is the unnamable, in the first two his names seem like mere disguises which he has assumed. In retrospect, the masks of the unnamable appear to indicate certain references, limitations, and attitudes which have lost their validity in the final novel. But the unnamable is not completely free of the names which he has borne and which now prevent him from being at peace in his anonymity. The first two novels have prepared the way for the third, but they continue to exercise their influence upon it.

Perhaps the most durable of these influences is the extraordinary style, which in *Molloy* is fully formed. The sentence construction in this and in the subsequent novels is frequently composed of direct contradictions. A statement is followed by the immediate retraction of what has been stated. The degree of contradiction varies from modification or patent undermining right through to total negation, as for instance at the very end of *Molloy:* "I shall learn. Then I went back into the house and wrote, It is midnight. The rain is beating on the windows. It was not midnight. It was not raining."[112] This variable but ceaseless alternation between statement and negation remains the characteristic feature of the style in all three novels. The striking culmination of this trend at the close of *Molloy* is certainly not accidental, for it is a magnified echo of the cre-

---

[111] Friedrich Nietzsche, *Gesammelte Werke,* 16 (Musarionausgabe) (Munich, 1925), pp. 59 f. and 122.

[112] Samuel Beckett, *Molloy* (Grove Press) (New York, [7]no date), p. 241.

scendo and decrescendo of all the individual sentences. The technique results in a total devaluation of language by accentuating the arbitrariness with which it is applied to the objects it seeks to grasp.

The attentive reader will not be altogether unprepared for these closing sentences. Through the nature of his narrative, Molloy gives a number of indications, both direct and indirect, as to what conditions all these contradictory statements. He himself immediately questions a great number of his own findings—as, for instance, right at the beginning of the novel: "A and C I never saw again. But perhaps I shall see them again. But shall I be able to recognise them? And am I sure I never saw them again? And what do I mean by seeing and seeing again?"[113]

These are questions posed by a consciously reflecting mind which seeks to uncover the presuppositions that condition a statement, and thus to show that that statement is a barely tenable version of the facts it attempts to convey. However, the first-person narrator can only formulate his observations of himself and his surroundings by making such statements, for they are the only means by which he can build up the reality he wants to describe. And so whatever conditions his perception, becomes incorporated in the conclusions he draws from that perception. The world thus constituted is comprehensible and describable—but the question is whether this is the world the narrator is actually trying to capture in his narrative.

Molloy is fully aware of this question:

And when I say I said, etc., all I mean is that I knew confusedly things were so, without knowing exactly what it was all about. And every time I say, I said this, or, I said that, or speak of a voice saying, far away inside me, Molloy, and then a fine phrase more or less clear and simple, or find myself compelled to attribute to others intelligible words, or hear my own voice uttering to others more or less articulate sounds, I am merely complying with the convention that demands you either lie or hold your peace. For what really happened was quite different. And I did not say, Yet a little while, at the rate things are going, etc. . . . In reality I said nothing at all, but I heard a murmur, something gone wrong with the silence, and I pricked up my ears, like an animal I imagine, which gives a start and pretends to be dead. And then sometimes there arose within me, confusedly, a kind of consciousness, which I express by saying, I said, etc., or, Don't do it Molloy, ... Or which I express without sinking to the level of oratio recta, but by means of other figures quite as deceitful, as for example, It seemed to

[113] Ibid., pp. 18 f.

me that, etc., or, I had the impression that, etc., for it seemed to me nothing at all, and I had no impression of any kind.[114]

This reflection is embedded in a process which Molloy would like to narrate but which he has to falsify because the convention of narration has its own laws, that have little or no bearing upon actual reality. Narration sets out to convey something which cannot possibly be conveyed by it, and so any narrative representation must inevitably be a lie. Molloy is fully aware that both the presentation and the communication of any given reality can only result in the alteration of that reality, for the facts will be set in one context or another, and so it will be the context and not the facts that will be communicated. On the other hand, reality only takes shape for the observer in accordance with his own presuppositions. The first-person narrator can only bring this knowledge to bear by offering the reality he has observed as the mere product of his mode of presentation, which is unlikely to coincide with whatever may be the true nature of that reality.

This insight is conveyed by the alternation of statement and modification throughout the narrative, for every statement imposes a particular order on things, thus excluding much of what they might really be. The conscious mind that conducts the operation of stating and retracting is aware of the incongruence between object and meaning, and this is why the perceptions recorded in Molloy's monologue are constantly accompanied by reflections on how they took place and what conditioned the manner in which they took place. Thus a single act of perception often releases a chain reaction of self-observation, as the narrator seeks to find out what brought about the act and why it took the form it did take. This process is sometimes taken so far that the original perception and the self-questionings that spring from it become completely dissociated.

This dissociation is conveyed by the self-cancelling structure of the sentences, which indicate that a world perceived only in terms of phenomena is just as much a product of the conscious mind as one that is deliberately given a specific form. As both perception and interpretation of phenomena are qualified equally as offshoots of the conscious mind, the reality perceived must in itself clearly be totally devoid of any mean-

---

[114] Ibid., pp. 118 f. There is an important variation on this idea: "Not to want to say, not to know what you want to say, not to be able to say what you think you want to say, and never to stop saying, or hardly ever, that is the thing to keep in mind, even in the heat of composition" (p. 36); see also pp. 40 f. G. Zeltner-Neukomm, *Die eigenmächtige Sprache* (Olten and Freiburg, no date), p. 112, has observed that for Beckett words are "themselves a phenomenon of separation."

ing of its own. Thus the conscious mind turns its attention away from the interpretation of things and onto its own actual processes of interpretation.

The self-representation of Malone and of the unnamable takes place in the light of this knowledge. Malone lies in a room; he knows that he is soon going to die, only what concerns him is not death but the impossibility of getting to the end of himself.[115] As the world around him gradually disintegrates, so his conscious mind becomes increasingly active, filling the void with various forms. Molloy had still had an overall view of his own fragmented story, but for Malone this degree of self-detachment has shrunk considerably. Molloy had realized that all presentation is "re-formation"—summed up by his pithy epigram "Saying is inventing"[116] —and this realization is taken for granted during Malone's preoccupation with himself. Malone cannot therefore tell himself his own story before his death, because as a piece of self-representation this could only reflect its own conditional nature. And so he decides to tell himself stories which are quite obviously fictitious. Typically, he regards his intention of filling in the rest of his life with stories as "playing,"[117] diverting him from what would otherwise be the compulsion to write about himself— for whatever he were to maintain in writing about himself would only be how he appears to himself, but not what he actually is. He is therefore left with the choice of telling stories or, as sometimes happens, writing about writing.[118] In the first case he knows he is dealing with fictions; in the second he knows he is dealing with the mode of fiction itself. In telling stories, Malone knows he is telling lies, but this releases him from the terrible curse of describing his own situation and therefore telling lies about himself. He does not want to be the object of his own observations, even though he is really concerned with the question of who he

---

[115] See also M. Kesting, *Vermessungen des Labyrinths. Studien zur modernen Ästhetik* (Frankfurt, 1965), p. 68; also H. Kenner, *Samuel Beckett. A Critical Study* (Grove Press) (New York, 1961), pp. 65 f., and the literary parallels to which Kenner tries to relate the situation. For an illuminating introduction to the range of problems dealt with here, see R. Federman, *Journey to Chaos. Samuel Beckett's Early Fiction* (Berkeley and Los Angeles, 1965).

[116] Beckett, *Molloy*, p. 41. Molloy, however, reflects immediately on all the implications of this remark.

[117] Samuel Beckett, *Malone Dies* (Grove Press) (New York, [5]1956), pp. 2 f. and 4.

[118] See, e.g., ibid., p. 33: "I have just written, I fear I must have fallen, etc. I hope this is not too great a distortion of the truth." So long as Malone writes about what he has written, the danger of diverging from the truth is minimal, for writing is the vehicle of fiction; making writing itself the subject matter means moving within the mode of fiction and not using writing to translate other subjects into that mode.

is.[119] But in due course his fictitious stories begin to bore him, and he breaks off with the following:

What tedium. And I call that playing. I wonder if I am not talking yet again about myself. Shall I be incapable, to the end, of lying on any other subject? I feel the old dark gathering, the solitude preparing, by which I know myself, and the call of that ignorance which might be noble and is mere poltroonery. Already I forget what I have said. That is not how to play. . . . Perhaps I had better abandon this story and go on to the second, or even the third. . . . No, it would be the same thing. I must simply be on my guard, reflecting on what I have said before I go on and stopping, each time disaster threatens, to look at myself as I am. That is just what I wanted to avoid.[120]

He finds, then, that the stories are about himself after all, and the more stories he tries to tell, the clearer it becomes to him that the material is taken from his own life. "All the stories I've told myself, clinging to the putrid mucus, and swelling, swelling, saying, Got it at last, my legend."[121] And together with this insight goes the knowledge that such stories are only pretexts to avoid having to get to grips with the real self:

All is pretext, Sapo and the birds, Moll, the peasants, those who in the towns seek one another out and fly from one another, my doubts which do not interest me, my situation, my possessions, pretext for not coming to the point, the abandoning, the raising of the arms and going down, without further splash. . . . The horror-worn eyes linger abject on all they have beseeched so long, in a last prayer, the true prayer at last, the one that asks for nothing.[122]

In his stories he may see his legend, but at the same time he knows that this legend—even though it has sprung entirely from his own ideas—cannot be identical with his real self. After all, he has always been conscious of the fact that such stories are nothing but fabrications, and so clearly the legend arising from the stories can at best only be a distorted reflection of a distorted reflection of himself.

Subjectivity in *Malone Dies* is presented in the form of a ceaseless dialectic that is never synthesized. If the last, true prayer is for nothing, this desire is an answer to the need for self-understanding. In praying for nothing, the self seeks to release itself from this need. And yet the

[119] See, e.g., ibid., p. 17.
[120] Ibid., p. 12.
[121] Ibid., p. 51.
[122] Ibid., p. 107.

very facts of life, the desolation of tedium, the openness of the situation, and the void of approaching death drive Malone to counteract the void, tedium and openness with something specific. That is why he tells his stories, though he immediately retracts any meaning that threatens to become specific. This paradoxical behavior is symptomatic of his situation, the implications of which are made clear by the idea of playing—which is what Malone calls his story-telling. The stories are "play"[123] insofar as they are not devised for the sake of an ultimate meaning but only for meanings that will ward off the void. They provide a diversion and not a destination. In them, Malone continually goes beyond his known self in order to try and get to a last frontier of himself—a point which he is fully aware can never be reached.

Malone sees himself confronted by an unanswerable problem, which he formulates very early on in the book: "Live and invent. I have tried. I must have tried. Invent. It is not the word. Neither is live. No matter. I have tried."[124] Malone wants to know what it is to be alive. His bodily functions tell him nothing, and so he is forced to make statements about living. But these statements are all inventions, because they each assume that the edited version of life is identical with life itself. However, as there is no other means of grappling with the problem, he must go on inventing. Invention enables the self to confront itself with its own image. This image can only be an appearance, and any presentation of the appearance will endow it with a meaning, and the meaning will be that of the appearance, not of the self. Toward the end, Malone interrupts the stories of Macmann and Lemuel with the words: "I had forgotten myself, lost myself."[125] While life compels him to seek determinacy, he refutes any such determinacy in the stories, because he is fully aware of the purpose of the search. Thus the problem involved in "live and invent" remains insoluble, but it is through living and inventing that the self produces its own indeterminableness out of itself, by continually fictionalizing its various self-representations.

The fact that Malone regards this process as playing means that it can

---

[123] U. Schramm, *Fiktion und Reflexion. Überlegungen zu Musil und Beckett* (Frankfurt, 1967), pp. 205 f., regards the idea of the "endgame" as a model that can help explain the movement which takes place in Beckett's plays. This illuminating idea also applies to a certain extent to the novels, especially as Malone considers the game itself to be an esthetic possibility for 'playing' his situation. When he decides to tell stories and to make an inventory of his things, he says: "I have also decided to remind myself briefly of my present state before embarking on my stories. I think this is a mistake. It is a weakness. But I shall indulge in it. I shall play with all the more ardour afterwards. And it will be a pendant to the inventory. Aesthetics are therefore on my side, at least a certain kind of aesthetics" (p. 4).

[124] Beckett, *Malone Dies,* p. 18.

[125] Ibid., p. 97.

have no teleology that might endow the self with a final, determinate meaning. If it could, then the self would no longer be itself but the expression of something else. The only teleology there might be in the game is the rules of the game, which will condition the different possibilities of play. In the configurative meanings of the game, the self is present insofar as it is a possibility of meaning, and the more variations of play there are, the more prominently will the basic self emerge, increasingly overshadowing its individual manifestations. Malone is aware of this, too:

> My concern is not with me, but with another, far beneath me and whom I try to envy, of whose crass adventures I can now tell at last, I don't know how. Of myself I could never tell, any more than live or tell of others. How could I have, who never tried? To show myself now, on the point of vanishing, at the same time as the stranger, and by the same grace, that would be no ordinary last straw. Then live, long enough to feel, behind my closed eyes, other eyes close. What an end.[126]

This is the subject matter of the third novel, linked to the necessity of exceeding the degree of consciousness already reached in the process of self-representation. The nameless narrator refers to no normal, external objective reality at all. At least Malone had spoken of the room in which he was lying and of different gestures which his situation still allowed him to make. In *The Unnamable* such relics of an outside world have disappeared altogether. Malone could tell stories in order to relieve his boredom, though he knew that the material was drawn out of his own life, but for the unnamable this avoidance of the self is no longer possible through stories. His acute consciousness can see through the process even before it gets as far as story-telling. And yet the unnamable's record of his ceaseless monologue is permeated with recollections of Malone and other first-person narrators, and also with fragmentary references to other characters and voices. They act as spurs to his consciousness, so that the theme of this novel evolves out of the self-dissection of the first two. As far as the reader is concerned, the appearance of Malone, Molloy, and other characters offers a background of familiarity against which he can situate the searchings of the *The Unnamable*. *Malone Dies* showed that the attempt at self-observation through writing led inevitably to a process of fictionalization, and so this knowledge is already given to the unnamable. His writing therefore refers to the process of writing, and so

---

[126] Ibid., p. 19.

the range of writing itself is extended. But where can such an extension possibly lead?

The beginning and the end of the novel speak of the unavoidability of self-confrontation. The phrasing in each case is similar and shows the impenetrability of the self and its compulsion to self-observation. The beginning is as follows: "Where now? Who now? When now? Unquestioning. I, say I. Unbelieving. Questions, hypotheses, call them that. Keep going, going on, call that going, call that on."[127] The novel ends: ". . . perhaps they have carried me to the threshold of my story, before the door that opens on my story, that would surprise me, if it opens, it will be I, it will be the silence, where I am, I don't know, I'll never know, in the silence you don't know, you must go on, I can't go on, I'll go on."[128]

The "going-on" theme, which is echoed right through the novel, forms a kind of focal point for the highly conscious mind of the unnamable. Going on is an experience that defies integration and so acts as a constant stimulus for 'hypotheses' about himself. Every attempt at self-representation is thus transformed into a fleeting movement of 'hypotheses' that elude his grasp, so that he experiences himself under the inescapable compulsion of having to continue while knowing full well that whatever he writes down can be nothing but the record of an invented, or, to be more precise, a self-inventing character. Thus what cannot be integrated is shown to be the true reality, which defies the efforts of the conscious mind to grasp it. But if the conscious mind undergoes an experience which it is incapable of integrating, this very inability to integrate enables it to acknowledge its own unfathomableness.[129] This is the source of the tension to which the narrator is exposed and which comes to the fore in all the various phases of his account. The unnamable frequently points out that he has invented the other characters—from Murphy to Watt, and from Molloy to Malone—so that through these ramifications of his ego he can objectify and so render explicable certain conditions of himself: "Inexistent, invented to explain I forget what. Ah yes, all lies, God and man, nature and the light of day, the heart's outpourings and the means of understanding, all invented, basely, by me alone, with the help of no one, since there is no one, to put off the hour

---

[127] Samuel Beckett, *The Unnamable* (Grove Press) (New York, 1958), p. 3.
[128] Ibid., p. 179.
[129] For this observation I am indebted to Manfred Smuda; see also his book on *Becketts Prosa als Metasprache* (Theorie und Geschichte der Literatur und der schönen Künste, 10) (Munich, 1970).

171

THE IMPLIED READER

when I must speak of me."[130] But as the defensiveness of this passage shows, the self-inventions hit back at the unnamable: the "vice-exister(s),"[131] as he calls them elsewhere, begin to usurp him, and indeed even to tell him "what I am like."[132] And this means that he is now being invented by his own inventions; but he is aware of this process and so knows that all the insinuations of these characters which he records are themselves only a fiction. It is this knowledge alone which enables him to escape again from the state of being an invention.

The unnamable indicates this element of his knowledge by reproducing the statements his inventions make about him as quotations, so that he can accentuate the gap between what his characters want to make of him and what he really is. By writing, he cancels out the intention of what has been written, and so he frees himself from the conditional nature of his 'gestalten'. And as he cannot take up a 'metastandpoint' from which to write, he can only elucidate himself by inverting the written through writing. And so he never ceases to observe how his invented characters conceive him. But in order to be able to present this awareness, he confronts himself with himself as an invention of one of his own (invented) characters. And he can then go on to show that any statement about him must be inapposite, because it cannot capture his real self.

Such inappropriateness is necessary as the incomprehension of the self can only be brought out by the endless succession of fictitious concepts of it. "My inability to absorb, my genius for forgetting, are more than they reckoned with. Dear incomprehension, it's thanks to you I'll be myself, in the end. Nothing will remain of all the lies they have glutted me with."[133] Clearly, the basis of the self is that which cannot be integrated. Herein lies the teleology of the ceaseless process by which every view of the self is fictionalized. The unnamable is aware that the only chance of knowing the "incomprehension" of the self lies in seeing through his continual self-invention, which at the same time remains an indispensable process. In this way he discovers for himself his own inaccessibility, which he objectifies in his account by presenting every manifestation of himself in the state of its own obsolescence. Thus his account becomes more and more densely populated with indistinct 'gestalten', which on the one hand arise out of his urge to transcend his own constitution as mere "matter,"[134] but on the other are constantly

---

[130] Beckett, *Unnamable*, p. 22.
[131] Ibid., p. 37.
[132] Ibid., p. 38.
[133] Ibid., p. 51.
[134] He says of the 'gestalten' and voices: "Ah if they could only begin, and do what they

172

outstripped by the knowledge that they are only pictures of the unpicturable basis of the self.

At certain places in the narrative, this interaction becomes the actual subject matter—most strikingly when the conscious mind takes the invented characters to pieces: "Is there a single word of mine in all I say? No, I have no voice, in this matter I have none. That's one of the reasons why I confused myself with Worm. But I have no reasons either, no reason, I'm like Worm, without voice or reason, I'm Worm, no, if I were Worm I wouldn't know it, I wouldn't say it, I wouldn't say anything, I'd be Worm."[135] It is impossible for the narrator to conceive himself. But this very impossibility prevents him from finishing his writing. If he were to stop, he would have to face up to the motive that guided his action (writing) and so to the whole conditionality of the situation from which the motive derived. He would then be identical with a conditioned action, and this is what his knowledge prevents him from being. By going on, he documents the fact that he is aware of the inaccessibility of his basic unprocessed self, for in the course of his compulsive self-reproduction, he constantly transcends the limitations of his individual self-perceptions. As the act of presentation turns these into fictions, he regards them as consciousness without reality. Such a qualification presupposes that he is in possession of a reality which cannot be integrated through presentation. That reality is himself. But in order to remain himself, he must always remain conscious of the fictions that condition his self-representation.

This consciousness is apparent in his retraction of every gestalt of

---

want with me, and succeed at last, in doing what they want with me, I'm ready to be whatever they want, I'm tired of being matter, matter, pawed and pummelled endlessly in vain. . . . Ah if I could only find a voice of my own, in all this babble, it would be the end of their troubles, and of mine. That's why there are all these little silences, to try and make me break them" (pp. 84 f.). The fact that the unnamable is tired of being matter means that he cannot feel at ease in his purely factual state. Indeed it is this existing state that gives rise in the first place to the many voices, 'gestalten' and ideas which are invoked in order to make the material nature of the factual being comprehensible. At the same time, however, the unnamable knows that he is not identical with these 'gestalten'. That is why the voices also remain silent sometimes—though this is only in order to entice him once more into the inescapability of continual self-representation. But when the unnamable has the feeling, toward the end, that the voices have left him, he is near to a state of shock (p. 162). He had always felt that the problem in his situation was that he was forever being urged by the voices to go on inventing himself, but now his misery increases when they threaten to leave him, for in its pure, given state the self is incapable of finding any knowledge or peace. This was the fact that gave rise to the voices; now, after they have apparently faded away, they do not leave the unnamable in that pure, given state any longer, as they have equipped him with the knowledge that he cannot find peace in that situation. And this is why he must go on.

[135] Beckett, *Unnamable*, p. 83. In this context, see the critical discussion of Beckett by R. Baumgart, *Literatur für Zeitgenossen* (edition suhrkamp) (Frankfurt, 1966), pp. 165 ff., under the heading "Kein Nutzen aus Beckett."

himself the moment it has been formed. He thus deprives it of its representative character, but at the same time leaves it behind as one individual track of his life, which cannot be integrated into any overall order. It is this impossibility of integration that endows the track with its reality. And so by the continual retraction of his self-representations, he penetrates into the reality of his basic self. But as this base can never be formulated, he must go on. This is his one chance of becoming real—above all, because he has the consciousness necessary for the process: "I'm all these words, all these strangers, this dust of words, with no ground for their settling, no sky for their dispersing, coming together to say, fleeing one another to say, that I am they, all of them, those that merge, those that part, those that never meet, and nothing else, yes, something else, that I'm something quite different, a quite different thing, a worldless thing in an empty place."[136]

The Beckett trilogy is based on an extraordinary paradox. The novels show how it becomes increasingly impossible for their narrators to conceive themselves—i.e., to find their own identity; and yet at the same time it is precisely this impossibility that leads them actually to discover something of their own reality. This paradox is very hard to unravel. If one regards becoming conscious, in Nietzsche's terms, as "a completely active re-formation," it must be borne in mind that Beckett's characters are conscious of this process itself. Every activity of the conscious mind entails some sort of projection or assumption, insofar as this is the only way in which the given world can be made accessible for observation. In these novels, however, the conscious mind is not concerned with the outside world but with the activities of its own consciousness.

Once the conscious mind turns its attention to its own activities, it no longer functions as a means of translating outside data into comprehensible images; instead it focuses upon the projections and assumptions inherent in this process. But if these are shown up as preconditions for the

---

[136] Beckett, *Unnamable*, p. 139. A. Cronin, *A Question of Modernity* (London, 1966), p. 108, comments as follows on the unnamable's confrontations with himself: "The artist who is concerned only with the truth can arrive at it only by means of a fiction. The creations of The Unnamable—Molloy, Malone, Macmann and the rest—stand in Mr. Beckett's scheme, not only as surrogates of the Unnamable's non-existent personality, but as an illustration of this tortuous irony in the artist's search for himself. For there is a sense in which the voices are right, or at least appear to be right. It does seem that it is only by the adoption of a fictitious mechanism and the entry into a labyrinth that may never lead back to the self, that the self can be found." Re the contemporary context of the search for the self, see G. Zeltner-Neukomm, *Das Wagnis des französischen Gegenwartsromans* (rowohlts deutsche enzyklopädie, 109) (Reinbek, 1960), pp. 144 ff.

functioning of consciousness, then the resultant image of the self will in fact be only an image of a preconditioned and so restricted manifestation of the self. As the heightened consciousness reduces all its images of the self to their nonrepresentative individuality, the self can only experience its own reality through an unending sequence of unintegrated and unintegratable images. For it is the distinguishing mark of reality that it resists integration, and the conscious mind turned in upon itself is in a position to discover this truth. The discovery takes place in a process which, in the trilogy itself, is described as "finality without end."[137]

As regards the form of this process, we might turn once again to Merleau-Ponty:

> My absolute contact with myself, the identity of being and appearance cannot be posited, but only lived as anterior to any affirmation. In both cases, therefore, we have the same silence and the same void. The experience of absurdity and that of absolute self-evidence are mutually implicatory, and even indistinguishable. The world appears absurd, only if a demand for absolute consciousness ceaselessly dissociates from each other the meanings with which it swarms, and conversely this demand is motivated by the conflict between those meanings. Absolute self-evidence and the absurd are equivalent, not merely as philosophical affirmations, but also as experiences. . . . A truth seen against a background of absurdity, and an absurdity which the teleology of consciousness presumes to be able to convert into truth, such is the primary phenomenon."[138]

Absurdity and truth go hand in hand through Beckett's novels, and this brings us to the all-important question of how the reader can possibly respond to such texts—a question which we have avoided up to now, in order to bring out the fundamental nature of the problem confronting the reader. Unlike the Faulkner and Ivy Compton-Burnett novels, Beckett's trilogy deprives the reader not temporarily but totally of his usual privileged seat in the grandstand. These characters possess a degree of self-consciousness which the reader can scarcely, if at all, keep up with. Such texts act as irritants, for they refuse to give the reader any bearings by means of which he might move far enough away to judge them. The text forces him to find his own way around, provoking questions to which he must supply his own answers.

This technique can give rise to a wide range of reactions—the simplest

---

[137] Beckett, *Molloy*, p. 152.
[138] Merleau-Ponty, *Phenomenology*, pp. 295 f.

being to close the book because one considers the text to be nonsense. Such a decision, however, implies that the reader believes he has reliable criteria for judging what is sense and what is nonsense. Among readers who do not regard the text as nonsense, a common reaction is to search for an allegorical meaning. If the text could be brought completely into line with an underlying allegory, then one would have regained one's distance from it. But there are two sides to such a process. Does the allegorical meaning explain the text, or does the explanation serve to restore the distance one does not want to lose? We tend to be ill at ease when there is something which resists understanding, and so although the allegorical interpretation may be serving the text, it may well be serving nothing but our own peace of mind. The reader will find that such an interpretation will forever be chasing after the compulsive self-reproduction of the characters, without being able to catch up with it; this does not necessarily mean that the trail is false, but it will demand constant readjustment, and the more corrections one has to make, the more conscious one becomes that the projected 'allegory' cannot be equated with the intention of the text but is simply a 'heuristic fiction' to help one over the distressing loss of distance.

D. Wellershoff maintains that the reader cannot leave Beckett's trilogy "in any direction with the consciousness of being supported by the author. The paradoxical involvement can only be broken off through an experience of self-evidence which Beckett provokes by refusing to give it."[139] If each reader's own ideas fall short, because the personally conditioned meaning he ascribes to the text can only result in a limited comprehension of it, then those ideas themselves must stand in doubt. But which of us willingly allows his own basic concepts to become an object of scrutiny? For it must be realized that now comprehension means nothing less than evaluating the basis of the self that makes comprehension possible in the first place. In this way Beckett's text brings to the surface those presuppositions from which spring all operations of comprehension. And once the reader becomes conscious of these, he will find the very foundations of his knowledge beginning to shift beneath his feet. All those meanings which hitherto he had taken for granted, are now reduced to heuristic ideas, and these in turn can become the preconditions for new experiences of himself and of the outside world.

[139] D. Wellershoff, "Gescheiterte Entmythologisierung. Zu den Romanen Samuel Becketts," *Merkur* 17 (1963): 546. Cronin, *A Question of Modernity*, pp. 109 f., regards the transformation of experience as the vital function of the artist, as he says at the end of his Beckett interpretation: "If he is a great artist his vision is not only an addition to our already existing knowledge of experience, in the sense that he adds a segment to that yet uncompleted circle which is the total record of human experience, but it will underlie and colour the already existing segment."

Whenever this occurs, the reader approaches the level of consciousness of Beckett's characters, and he only leaves it again when he seeks confirmation of his own experience and so restricts their 'play' by imposing a meaning on it. If he enters into the movement of the text, he will find it difficult to get out again, for he will find himself increasingly drawn into the exposure of the conditions that underlie his own judgment. This conditionality as a subject for conscious reflection is all the more accentuated as the text precludes any standpoint from which it could be viewed as a whole.

In this process lies the esthetic dynamism of such texts: they resolutely resist all attempts at total comprehension, for this is the only way in which they can break down the barriers to the reader's contemplation of his own ideas. But if the reader refuses to allow the text to make its catalytic effect on his consciousness, this very decision brings about another effect: one can only release oneself from the text by trying to reduce the confusion of configurative meanings to a determinate, final meaning. In order to do this, the reader must stand at a distance from the text, but this distance, although it grants him a view, also ensures that his view will comprehend at most some of the possibilities of the text. And so in seeking a determinate meaning, the reader loses possibilities of meaning, and yet it is only through losing these possibilities that he can become aware of the freedom his faculty of understanding had enjoyed before he committed himself to passing judgments.

If Beckett's novels stimulate us into reconsidering our own preconceptions, then their intention can hardly be merely to represent the decadence of contemporary society. And yet they are often regarded as symptoms of decay, despair, and nihilism, even in cases where the reader's attitude shows that he would like to ascribe some lofty, if obscure significance to the texts. What prevents such readers from interpreting Beckett's characters and their world—in so far as they have a world—as purely and simply an expression of our agonized society, is the extraordinary activeness that typifies these characters. This is, at first sight, a surprising feature, as W. Sypher has pointed out: "We cannot speak of action in Beckett's novels, for the hero is fixed in what might be called a condition, which in some ways resembles the continuous texture in 'brutal' painting. The condition is not, however, inert; that is the puzzle. Inertia is to be expected."[140] This activeness cannot be counted among the

[140] Sypher, *Loss of the Self*, p. 150.

symptoms of decay. And so a vital component of the characters directly contradicts a theory that would have them as nothing but a reflection of the pathology of contemporary society. They are simply too productive to symbolize the decadence of a social order.

This compulsive creativity, together with a progressive deformation, makes the characters seem quite inaccessible to the reader. They are not representative figures, and they indicate nothing outside themselves to which the reader might latch on, in order to participate in their situation. In their unceasing self-reproduction, they are themselves the source of a creativity which may, momentarily, take on a configurative gestalt, but will at once have any such meaning taken away from it. This creative force does not build up a world one can make oneself at home in (and if it did, there would be no further need for that creative force). On the contrary, it reveals the conditional nature of everything it has produced, purely because the product takes on the character of a gestalt which it must lose again if the creative force is to go on creating. The process is never ending, because everything produced is also conditioned, and because it is known to be conditional, it has to be discarded. And if the self is the basis of this creative force, then it is only logical that it should confront itself with the shadows of possibilities that bring each other forth and then drive each other away.

If the decadence theory is inadequate because it has to ignore the creative force of the characters, the question arises as to whether any theory can incorporate this force. Here we have a peak of consciousness that does not destroy activity but instead actually produces it, and as the raw material it works on is an inexhaustible potential (the self), one's explanatory theory would need to be as comprehensive as the process itself is open-ended. What Beckett has achieved in these novels is to set the self free to pursue a course of endless self-discovery. It is a process which a nuclear physicist might identify immediately, in terms that fit perfectly into our literary context, as a supercritical chain reaction.

7

DOING THINGS IN STYLE:
An Interpretation of
"The Oxen of the Sun" in
James Joyce's *Ulysses*

I

Shortly after Joyce's *Ulysses* was published in 1922, T. S. Eliot saw in the multifarious allusions to the literature of the past the fabric indispensable to the literature of the future. "In using the myth, in manipulating a continuous parallel between contemporaneity and antiquity, Mr. Joyce is pursuing a method which others must pursue after him. They will not be imitators, any more than the scientist who uses the discoveries of an Einstein in pursuing his own, independent, further investigations. It is simply a way of controlling, of ordering, of giving a shape and a significance to the immense panorama of futility and anarchy which is contemporary history."[1] If the Homeric myth in *Ulysses* is to be regarded as a means of giving shape to a world of futility and anarchy, then clearly a link must be established between past and present that will enable the myth to exercise its 'ordering' function. The nature of this link is something that has caused many a headache to Joyce critics down through the years. Is the Homeric epic to be viewed as an "objective correlative"[2]—as defined by Eliot in his "Hamlet" essay—that

[1] T. S. Eliot, "Ulysses, Order and Myth," in *James Joyce: Two Decades of Criticism,* ed. Seon Givens (New York, 1948), p. 201. (The essay was published originally in 1923).
[2] T. S. Eliot, *Selected Essays* (London, [2]1951), p. 145. (The "Hamlet" essay was published originally in 1919.)

179

enables us to grasp the modern situation in the first place? Or does the literary parallel reveal a structural principle that moulds the modern world just as it did the ancient? These two lines of thought represent the two basic approaches to the function of the Homeric parallel. According to both, the apparent chaos of the "Welt-Alltag"[3] (World Weekday) of June 16, 1904, is related to the sequence of adventures in the *Odyssey*, and through this connection is to bring to life in the reader's mind the outlines of an order which is to be read into the events of that day. This view has gained currency through the fact that in the modern world we are denied direct insight into the meaning of events, so that the Homeric parallel appears to offer a way of projecting a hidden meaning onto the chaos of everyday life. But herein lies the inherent weakness of this approach, for it says nothing about the way in which myth and the present day can be brought together.[4]

If Homer's epic contains the meaning, and Joyce's novel contains only a confusing plethora of appearances interspersed with allusions to Homer, such a view must lead ultimately to a Platonizing interpretation of the modern novel. The *Odyssey* will then act as the ideal, while Bloom's wanderings are nothing but the copy of a homecoming which for Ulysses means completion, but for Bloom entails just one more grind in the

---

[3] A term used by H. Broch, *Dichten und Erkennen* (Zürich, 1955), p. 187, to describe June 16, 1904.

[4] See, among others, Stuart Gilbert, *James Joyce's Ulysses* (New York, 1955, [1]1930); Frank Budgen, *James Joyce and the Making of Ulysses* (Bloomington, 1960, [1]1934); W. Y. Tindall, *A Reader's Guide to James Joyce* (London, 1959), p. 128 ff.; Richard Ellmann, *James Joyce* (New York, 1959), pp. 541 f.; Wylie Sypher, *Rococo to Cubism in Art and Literature* (New York, 1960), p. 285; Richard Ellmann, "Ulysses and the Odyssey," *English Studies* 43 (1962): 423 ff. The idea of parallelism has also been extended beyond the *Odyssey*, for instance by Alan Dundes, "Re: Joyce—No in at the Womb," *Modern Fiction Studies* 8 (1962): 137 ff. There is a much more cautious but illuminating study of analogy and allusions by Robert Martin Adams, *Surface and Symbol: The Consistency of James Joyce's Ulysses* (New York, 1962). There is similar caution in some more recent studies of analogy. W. Y. Tindall, *James Joyce: His Way of Interpreting the Modern World* (New York, 1950), p. 102, rightly emphasizes that: "the Homeric pattern is only one level of the narrative Joyce composed." A. Walton Litz, *The Art of James Joyce* (London, 1961), p. 39, writes: "Similarly, there are many more Homeric references on the *Ulysses* note-sheets than ever made their way into the text, and we are forced to conclude that the parallel with the *Odyssey* was more useful to Joyce during the process of composition than it is to us while we read the book. Time and again he spoke of the comfort he derived from the narrative order of the *Odyssey:* it provided him—in his own words—with fixed 'ports of call.' The major parallels between the wanderings of Mr. Bloom and those of Ulysses are an important dimension of the novel, but in working out the trivial details of the Homeric correspondence Joyce was exploring his own materials, not preparing clues for future readers." Jackson I. Cope, "The Rhythmic Gesture: Image and Aesthetic in Joyce's *Ulysses*," *ELH* 29 (1962): 87, says the following about the parallelism: "If *Ulysses* is a novel of knowing, if its theme is the everpresence of recovered time in the creative form of the microcosm, we cannot forget that the most obvious mode of organization is the parallelism of mythic echo made living, like the sea in the shell, by being awakened in the protean rôles and memories of everyman."

ceaseless monotony of everyday life.[5] Whenever interpretation is dominated by the idea of an analogy, one is bound to be dogged by the consequences inherent in the old conception of the *analogia entis*.[6] There is, however, another possible interpretation of the Homeric parallel to *Ulysses,* and Joyce himself offered certain indications of this. He called the *Odyssey* "the most beautiful, all-embracing theme" in all world literature.[7] Going into details, he suggests that Ulysses embodies the most vivid conglomeration of all human activities, so that for him the Homeric hero becomes an archetype for humanity. Some Joyce scholars have tried to couple this statement with the idea that the modern novel is an attempt to renew Homeric archetypes.[8] And so the concept of literary permanence comes to the fore whenever the critic concerned makes a fetish of the 'unbroken tradition' of Western literature. But such a naive view of permanence demands a blind eye for all the differences between Joyce's novel and Homer's epic. Even though the permanence interpretation of *Ulysses* does not insist that Bloom is nothing but a return of Ulysses, it does insist that he *is* a Ulysses in modern dress.[9] Such a metaphor, however, obscures rather than illuminates the intention of Joyce's novel. Indeed both 'schools of thought'—that of analogy and that of permanence—even though they are backed up by some of Joyce's own statements, by existing parallels, and by the actual

[5] See Richard Ellmann, "Ulysses: The Divine Nobody," in *Twelve Original Essays on Great English Novels,* ed. Ch. Shapiro (Detroit, 1960), pp. 244 ff.; the degree of controversy surrounding such a parallelism can be seen, for instance, in such statements as Arland Ussher's *Three Great Irishmen* (London, 1952), p. 121: "The life of Mr. Bloom, however, could hardly be described as an Odyssey . . . any more than could that of the youthful Stephen Dedalus; though they had a good deal of an Athenian peripatos." Margaret Church, *Time and Reality: Studies in Contemporary Fiction* (Chapel Hill, 1962), p. 44, writes: "If Odysseus is representative of the heroic age and Bloom is representative of the human age, neither one acts as commentary on the other, for each is sufficient to his own age."

[6] This concept has been discussed anew by Gottlieb Söhngen, *Analogie und Metapher: Kleine Philosophie und Theologie der Sprache* (Freiburg, 1962). Wallace Stevens, *The Necessary Angel* (New York, 1951), p. 130, ends his essay on "Effects of Analogy" with the following observation: "It is a transcendence achieved by means of the minor effects of figurations and the major effects of the poet's sense of the world and of the motive music of his poems and it is the imaginative dynamism of all these analogies together. Thus poetry becomes and is a transcendent analogue composed of the particulars of reality, created by the poet's sense of the world, that is to say, his attitude, as he intervenes and interposes the appearances of that sense."

[7] See Ellmann, *Joyce,* p. 430.

[8] See W. B. Stanford, *The Ulysses Theme* (Oxford, [2]1963), who goes into the different nuances and variations in the continuity of the Homeric figure. Harry Levin, "What Was Modernism?," in *Varieties of Literary Experience,* ed. Stanley Burnshaw (New York, 1962), p. 322, writes: "It is the metamorphic impetus that provides this controlling device: the transmutation of Dublin citizens into mythical archetypes out of the *Odyssey.*" Rudolf Sühnel, "Die literarischen Voraussetzungen von Joyces *Ulysses,*" *GRM,* N.F. 12 (1962): 202 ff., rightly talks of this continuity as only a basis for studying the special qualities of *Ulysses.*

[9] See, for instance, Ellmann, "Ulysses: The Divine Nobody," pp. 246 ff., and Broch, *Dichten und Erkennen,* p. 193.

grouping of the episodes in the novel, shed light only on starting-points and not on intentions.

A hint as to the intention might be found in the oft quoted conclusion of Joyce's *A Portrait of the Artist as a Young Man:* "Welcome, O life! I go to encounter for the millionth time the reality of experience and to forge in the smithy of my soul the uncreated conscience of my race."[10] This corresponds to what we have come to expect in modern times of our novel-writers. Ernst Kreuder, in his treatise on the *Unanswerable,* has described it as follows: "We expect the novelist, by virtue of his imagination, his inventive energy, his story-telling art, and his creative vision, to take us out of an exhaustively explained world of facts and into the inexplicable. . . . The aim of the epic poet can be called a paradoxical one: the completion of the unbounded. The leading of the reader up to the indecipherableness of an existence that flows without end."[11] In the light of such an expectation, the Homeric parallel takes on a very precise function. If the novel is to uncover a new dimension of human existence, this can only present itself to the conscious mind of the reader against a background made recognizable by allusions and references which will thus provide a sufficient amount of familiarity. But the "uncreated conscience," which the novel is to formulate, cannot be the return of something already known—in other words, it must not coincide purely and simply with the Homeric parallel. Harry Levin has rightly pointed out that the links between Joyce and Homer are parallels "that never meet."[12] While the Homeric allusions incorporate into the text a familiar literary repertoire, the parallels alluded to seem rather to diverge than to converge. Here we have the conditions for a rich interplay that goes far beyond the lines of interpretation laid down by the analogy or permanence theories. Indeed there arises a certain tension out of the very fact that there is no clearly formulated connection between the archaic past and the everyday present, so that the reader himself is left to motivate the parallelism indicated as it were by filling in the gaps between the lines.

This process only comes to the fore if one in fact abandons the idea of the parallels and instead takes the modern world and the Homeric world as figure and ground—the background acting as a sort of fixed

[10] James Joyce, *A Portrait of the Artist as a Young Man* (London, 1952), p. 288. Irene Hendry, "Joyce's Epiphanies," in *James Joyce: Two Decades of Criticism,* ed. Seon Givens (New York, 1948), p. 39, calls this passage "the (final) epiphany in the *Portrait.*"

[11] Ernst Kreuder, *Das Unbeantwortbare: Die Aufgaben des modernen Romans* (Mainzer Akademie der Wissenschaften, Abhandlung der Klasse der Literatur, 1959, Nr. 2) (Wiesbaden, 1959), pp. 19, 25.

[12] Harry Levin, *James Joyce: A Critical Introduction* (New York, 1960, [1]1941), p. 71.

vantage point from which one can discern the chaotic movements of the present. By means of the allusions, Bloom's and Stephen's experiences are constantly set off against this background, which brings home to the reader the great gulf between Joyce's characters and those of Homer. If Bloom is, so to speak, viewed through Ulysses, and Stephen through Telemachus,[13] the reader who knows his Homer will realize what is missing in these two modern men. Thus greater emphasis is thrown on those features which do not coincide with Homer, and in this way the individuality is given its visible outline. Individuality is therefore constituted as the reverse side of what is suggested by the Homeric allusions; being conditioned by the very nonfulfillment of the expectations arising from these allusions. Joyce's characters begin to take on a life of their own the moment we, the readers, begin to react to them, and our reactions consist of an attempt to grasp and hold fast to their individuality—a process that would be quite unnecessary if they were immediately recognizable types representing an immediately recognizable frame of reference. Here the reader is compelled to try and find the frame of reference for himself, and the more intensively he searches, the more inescapably he becomes entangled in the modern situation, which is not explained for him but is offered to him as a personal experience.

The Homeric repertoire is not, however, only a background enabling us to grasp the theme of modern everyday life. The interaction can also be two-way, with Ulysses occasionally being viewed through the perspective of Bloom. This is significant in the light of the fact that for Joyce, Homer's hero epitomized humanity.[14] How, then, could he lack something which Bloom has simply by not being identical with Ulysses? Obviously because humanity never coincides completely with any of its historical manifestations—it is a potential which is realized differently at different times. Even if Ulysses is an ideal manifestation, this only becomes apparent through the Bloom perspective, which mirrors not just the ideality of Ulysses but also—and much more significantly—the fact that humanity, whatever its outward circumstances, can only be apprehended as individual manifestations arising out of reactions to historical situations. And so the Homeric myth itself takes on another dimension against the foreground-turned-background of the "Welt-Alltag"—a dimension aptly described by S. L. Goldberg as follows: "Once divorced from their origin in implicit, pious belief—and that is the only condition under

---

[13] It goes without saying that the Hamlet parallel also plays an important part for Stephen. But in principle the reference to Hamlet—or the elucidation of Stephen through Hamlet—serves to bring out his special situation, and so is very similar to the Homeric parallel.

[14] See the statement reproduced in Ellmann's *Joyce,* p. 430.

which we now know the myths of Greece and, for most of us, the myths of Christianity as well—their meanings are perpetually created in our experience, are the colouring they take on from the material into which we project them. The myth is like a potentiality of meaning awaiting actualization in the world we recognize as real, in a specific 'now and here'."[15]

II

The actualization of this potential is not left to the discretion of the individual reader. On the contrary, the manner in which he perceives and conceives events will be guided by the stylistic technique with which they are represented. In *Ulysses* the function of style is so important that a whole chapter is devoted to it. For Joyce, style as the technique of communication was of prime significance. When Stanislaus wanted to discuss fascism with his brother, Joyce remarked laconically: "Don't talk to me about politics. I'm only interested in style."[16] The chapter entitled "The Oxen of the Sun" sheds a good deal of light on this obsession, although Joyce critics generally have tended to look on it with a certain amount of embarrassment,[17] regarding the linguistic experiments as an obvious digression from the novel's apparent subject matter—everyday life in Dublin. The most acceptable explanation for this widespread unease is given by Goldberg, though he too has certain qualms about this chapter:

> The 'symbolic' scheme so violently obtruded into these chapters from 'Wandering Rocks' to 'Oxen of the Sun' attempts much the same effect as the Homeric parallel, but without its foundation and enactment in the characters' own lives and in the reader's belief in the abiding poetic truth of the original myth. The trouble with these chapters in short is that their order is not 'aesthetic' enough. Perhaps this is the necessary price for the attempt Joyce makes to shift our attention from the represented reality to the shaping activity of the artist. Given the strategic need to bring himself, as artist, into the action of his book, Joyce could hardly use the old tactic of direct authorial commentary. That would draw attention to him, but not as a dramatis

---

[15] S. L. Goldberg, *The Classical Temper: A Study of James Joyce's Ulysses* (London, 1961), p. 202.

[16] Quoted by Ellmann in his introduction to Stanislaus Joyce, *My Brother's Keeper* (London, 1958), p. 23.

[17] A typical negative judgment is given by Walter Allen, *Tradition and Dream* (London, 1964), p. 7. Less emphatic views are offered by, among others, Levin, *Joyce*, pp. 105 f.; Franz Stanzel, *Die typischen Erzählsituationen im Roman* (Wiener Beiträge zur Englischen Philologie, 63) (Vienna, 1955), p. 135; Litz, *The Art of James Joyce*, pp. 37 f. The stylistic experiments are very cautiously evaluated by M. Butor, *Repertoire* I, German transl. by Helmut Scheffel (Munich, no date), p. 108.

persona and certainly not as an unmoved mover suggested within yet
beyond the action. What he did, however, is in its way very like in-
truded authorial comment.[18]

If Joyce's 'failure' lies in the fact that here he discloses his technique
instead of continuing the dramatization of individual attitudes, by un-
raveling this technique we should be able to gain a good deal of insight
into its function within the novel's overall framework of presentation.
Here we might bear in mind Ezra Pound's pronouncement: "I believe in
technique as the test of a man's sincerity."[19]

The subject of this chapter is Bloom's visit to a maternity hospital.
There he and his friends wait for Mrs. Purefoy's confinement. The conversation is mainly about love, procreation, and birth.[20] The linguistic
presentation of these themes takes place on different, contrasting levels
of style. The chapter begins with an enigmatic invocation, and this is
followed by an equally cryptic succession of long and tortuous sentences,
which seem to lose their meaning as they progress. Immediately after
these comes the sequence of historical styles that takes up the whole of
the chapter. The subjects of love, procreation, and birth are dealt with
in all the characteristic styles of English literature, from alliterative prose
right through to pidgin English. "The Oxen of the Sun" starts with three
sentences, each of which is repeated three times. An impression of some
sort of magic arises out of these triads. The sentences are: "DESHIL
HOLLES EAMUS. Send us, bright one, light one, Horhorn, quickening
and wombfruit." And finally the Dada sounding "Hoopsa, boyaboy,
hoopsa."[21] These three sentences, deciphered, convey the following:
Bloom feels an urge to go to Holles Street, where Dr. Horne's maternity
hospital is situated. There is an invocation to the art of Dr. Horne to
help the fruit of the womb to come into the world. And finally we have
the threefold delight of the midwife as she holds the newborn babe in
her hands.[22] These banal contents leap to life through the use of Latin
words, Latin-sounding turns of phrase, a rhythmic beat, and an incanta-
tory evocativeness. But they also take on a peculiar sort of tension, for
the simplicity of the content and the complexity of the presentation
seem out of all proportion. Are linguistic montages and magic incanta-

[18] Goldberg, *The Classical Temper*, p. 288.
[19] Ezra Pound, *Literary Essays*, ed. T. S. Eliot (London, 1960), p. 9.
[20] For the purposes of this essay, the discussion is confined to the one central theme. Other
themes are brought in from time to time, and these, too, have their form imposed on them by
the style of the individual authors Joyce imitates.
[21] James Joyce, *Ulysses* (London: Bodley Head, 1958), p. 366.
[22] See also Gilbert, *James Joyce's Ulysses*, p. 296. For the purposes of this interpretation,
discussion of the other parallels has deliberately been avoided.

tions necessary to make us aware of ordinary, everyday events? This question, right at the beginning of the chapter, is symptomatic of the whole, and indeed here we have a technique which Joyce uses frequently in *Ulysses:* individual chapters begin with a sort of codified theme which is then orchestrated by the narrative process.[23] The invocation then gives way to a completely different style. With long-drawn-out, mainly unpunctuated sentences, an attempt is made to describe the nature and significance of a maternity hospital. But it is only after very careful study that the reader begins to discern this intention. The lack of punctuation excludes any logical linguistic pattern, and behind this there obviously lies the fear of making any concrete statement about the object to be described. Joyce himself gives voice to this fear: "For who is there who anything of some significance has apprehended but is conscious that that exterior splendour may be the surface of a downward-tending lutulent reality."[24] His awareness of the danger that he will capture only the surface view of things, makes him approach the object as it were from all linguistic sides, in order to avoid a perspective foreshortening of it. And so the long appositions are not set out as such, and dependent clauses are left unmarked, for divisions of this kind would involve premature definition of the object concerned. At the same time, however, the language makes wide use of specialized vocabulary and precise nuances of meaning, and this gives rise to the impression that the institution is to be described with the utmost exactitude, although in fact it tends to become more and more blurred. Through this effort to depict the object from as many sides as possible, the maternity hospital seems almost to become something living and moving. And this is a stylistic feature typical not only of the chapter in question, but also of important sections of the whole novel: language is used not to fix an object, but to summon it to the imagination. The multiplication of perspectives will blur the outline, but through it the object will begin to grow, and this growth would be stunted if one were to try and define, since definition involves restriction to a chosen viewpoint which, in turn, involves a stylization of the reality perceived. It is therefore scarcely surprising that practically every chapter of *Ulysses* is written in a different style,[25] in order—as Broch puts it—to transfer "the object from one stylistic illumina-

---

[23] See the interpretation given by E. R. Curtius, *Kritische Essays zur europäischen Literatur* (Berne, [2]1954), pp. 309 ff., and Stanzel, *Erzählsituationen im Roman,* pp. 130 ff.
[24] Joyce, *Ulysses,* p. 366.
[25] See also Philip Toynbee, "A Study of Ulysses," in *Modern British Fiction,* ed. Mark Schorer (New York, 1961), pp. 347 f., and Levin, *Joyce,* pp. 105 f. and 111 f.

tion to another," for only in this way is "the highest degree of reality"[26] to be achieved. The constant change of perspective modifies the definition inherent in each stylistic variant, and so reveals the object as something continually expanding. In this way, even the most commonplace things seem potentially illimitable.

From the invocation that opens this chapter, we may conclude that only a cryptic form of language can succeed in making statements about even the simplest of things. The relation between language and object becomes a mystery, and the tension arising from this is extended by the next stylistic form which, as it were, sets the object in motion through its changing nuances of observation. Thus the basis is laid for the subsequent array of styles emanating from the history of English literature. If one bears in mind the fact that the two different levels of style at the start of the chapter seek only to set us on the road to the maternity hospital and to evoke the nature of such institutions, whereas now we are to be confronted with the great themes of love, procreation, and birth, one might expect the gap between language and object to reach unbridgeable proportions. If the simple themes at the beginning were difficult to deal with linguistically, surely these much broader subjects will totally exceed the capacity of language. And yet, surprisingly, this is not so. Although he may be confused at first, the reader actually needs only a basic knowledge of English literature in order to understand completely all that is going on. Without doubt, Stuart Gilbert's commentary offers some very useful guidelines on this,[27] but critics have never really accepted the parallelism he suggests between the sequence of period styles and the development of the embryo, or the many other references and cross-symbols he worked out as a ground plan for *Ulysses.* Goldberg ends his critique of Gilbert's book with the question: "But if Mr. Gilbert's way of interpreting it [i.e., *Ulysses*] is generally felt to be wrong, what is the right way, and why?"[28] As far as "The Oxen of the Sun" is concerned, a provisional answer must be: because Gilbert's equation of the individual styles with embryonic development is too rigid—not unlike the analogy theory that always seeks to establish precise equivalents in *Ulysses* and the *Odyssey.* Gilbert overlooks the latent comedy that runs through the imitations and shows up the degree of deformation brought about by each individual style.

[26] Broch, *Dichten und Erkennen,* p. 191. However, he does not discuss the subject any further.
[27] See Gilbert, *James Joyce's Ulysses,* pp. 298 ff.
[28] Goldberg, *The Classical Temper,* p. 212.

We can gain a closer insight into the nature of the historical sequence of styles by having a look at a few examples: first, in imitation of old English poetry, we are given an alliterative prose impression of Dr. Horne's maternity hospital. A mainly substantival style captures the outside of things and sets them side by side *en bloc* and unconnected. It seems as if the articles of equipment described are simply there for their own sake, although the alliteration does hint at certain unformulated connections.[29] The function of the individual items remains hidden from perception, so that they take on an element of incomprehensibility which transforms their practical value into some secret sort of reference. The style itself brings about an effect of contrast, insofar as this austere, alliterative prose follows on directly from the attempt, through extreme nuances of language, to describe the nature and importance of a maternity hospital. The consequences of the next style are quite different: events in the maternity hospital are recounted in the form of a late medieval travel book. Everything seems somehow to be tinged with excitement. The surface description of things is conditioned by the need to understand the new in terms of the familiar. However, this technique gets into severe difficulties when the traveler is confronted by a tin of sardines in olive oil. The resultant comedy derives from the incongruity between a style rigidly seeking to define the object in its own gallant terms, and the mundane object itself. The determinant pressure exerted by this style is so great that the advertising agent Leopold Bloom suddenly becomes the medieval "traveller Leopold."[30] Then the language changes again: the characters waiting in the hall of the maternity hospital converse in the style of Sir Thomas Malory.[31] Once again the unifying tendency of the style affects the very identity of the characters. The medieval traveler Leopold of a moment ago now becomes "Sir Leopold." The highly stylized discussion concerns traditional moral problems connected with birth (e.g., whether a wife should be allowed to die for her baby), and then suddenly Stephen raises the subject of contraception. Now neologisms creep into the conversation[32] as signs of human independence, defining man's interference with the God-given order of things. Here it becomes evident that the style shaped by the ideal of Christian knight-

[29] Joyce, *Ulysses*, p. 368.
[30] Ibid., p. 369.
[31] Ibid., pp. 370 ff. For the key to the sequence of styles, see Gilbert, *James Joyce's Ulysses*, pp. 298 ff.; Budgen, *James Joyce*, pp. 215 ff., and Stanislaus Joyce, *My Brother's Keeper*, p. 104. No account has been taken here of the other parallels Gilbert mentions for this chapter. For an assessment of these, see especially Litz, *The Art of James Joyce*, pp. 34 f.
[32] See, for instance, Joyce, *Ulysses*, p. 372: "But, gramercy, what of those Godpossibled souls that we nightly impossibilise, which is the sin against the Holy Ghost, Very God, Lord and Giver of Life?"

hood is no longer capable of coping with the multifarious problems under discussion—namely, of love and procreation. Nevertheless, the attempt is made to use the system of references inherent in the ideal of the Christian knight in order to work out an idea of love that cannot be fitted into this system. This incongruity between style and object is apparent all through the series of imitations from one century to another. After a love passage in the language of the Arcadian shepherds, there arises an inner indignation against the trend of the conversation, and this is expressed in the form of a Bunyan allegory.[33] The spiritual conflict transforms the maternity hospital and its trappings into "the land of Phenomenon,"[34] with an unreal outer world giving way to the reality of the inner. The hidden thoughts and feelings of the people concerned are externalized as allegorical characters that enact the ensuing conflict. But here, too, the relation between object and style becomes absurdly unbalanced, as the lusts of the characters are suddenly allegorized, bringing about an extraordinary sort of psychomachia. In medieval literature, allegory personified the Christian moral code. The personification of sexual urges, carried to extremes by Joyce, destroys the whole principle of the form as it had been used up to and including Bunyan.

As a sort of relief from all this personified 'inwardness', there now follows a minute description of the external events of the evening, in the diction of Samuel Pepys.[35] The most insignificant trifles are so lovingly observed that they seem over life-size, and every detail becomes a whole world in itself. After this, the central subject of the chapter enters into the realm of Utopian projects, conveyed in the style of the moral weeklies.[36] In pseudoscientific detail the characters discuss various practical methods of controlling with mechanical perfection all the processes of intimacy. This latent Utopianism is conveyed through a number of tales which are intended to establish the illusion that these special cases actually happened in the lives of particular people. Through these stories, the reader is meant to accept as perfectly natural the life planned for him on a "national fertilising farm."[37] In order to bring about this acceptance, the style imitates the narrative form of the moral weeklies, which were designed to create intimate contact with the public. But here the style sets out projects which destroy all intimacy; again we have total incongruity.

[33] See Joyce, *Ulysses*, pp. 377 f.
[34] Ibid., p. 378.
[35] Ibid., p. 379.
[36] Ibid., pp. 384 ff.
[37] Ibid., p. 384.

The stylistic idiosyncrasies of the great eighteenth-century novelists offer plenty of variations on the love theme through the individualization of speech, while the nineteenth-century parodies nearly all hypostatize the moods and emotions associated with love. All these overblown treatments of the subject show an extremely one-sided view, for each style reveals a latent ideology, constantly reducing the reality to the scope of individual principles. In the language of Landor, the unseemly side of love is again glossed over, this time through the respectability of mythological characters.[38] There is a similar sweet innocence to be found in the homely Dickensian passage that follows a little later. Love is peace and domestic bliss.[39] But in between, there is a detailed section on sex determination and infant mortality that is couched in the scientific terminology of hygiene and biology, with the apparent claim of being able to define these phenomena within the theory of scientific positivism.[40] Again, the relation between subject and treatment is grotesque, and the overall parody is enhanced here by the actual sequence of the styles. Next we come to theological interpretations in the style of Ruskin, Carlyle, and Newman, setting the world of appearances against its metaphysical background—though here, too, we have different definitions of love and the world under perception. After this series of rich and varied styles, the language at the end of the chapter seems to explode into a chaos of possibilities, and in this confused linguistic hodgepodge meaning finally seems to go by the board; it fades away in the elusiveness of language.

III

From these briefly sketched examples we may draw certain conclusions which together will give us a degree of insight into the Joycean technique of style. Although the various consequences are very closely connected with one another, we shall gain a clearer understanding of them by first examining them separately. To begin with, this stylistic historical tour of English literature is designed to grasp a particular subject through language. Each individual style projects a clearly recognizable idea of love, procreation, or birth. Joyce's style imitations therefore fulfill the demands summarized by John Middleton Murry as follows: "Style is a quality of language which communicates precisely emotions or thoughts, or a

[38] Ibid., pp. 396 ff.
[39] Ibid., pp. 402 ff.
[40] Ibid., pp. 399 ff.

190

system of emotions or thoughts, peculiar to the author. . . . Style is
perfect when the communication of the thought or emotion is exactly accomplished; its position in the scale of absolute greatness, however, will
depend upon the comprehensiveness of the system of emotions and
thoughts to which the reference is perceptible."[41] The styles imitated
by Joyce are dominated by such thoughts or thought systems, and the
predetermined, predetermining nature of all style is demonstrated quite
unmistakably through the individual variations. The judgments inherent
in each style create a uniform picture of the subject presented, choosing
those elements of the given reality that correspond to the frame of reference essential to all observation.[42] The particular point of view, then, determines which individual phenomena out of all those present are, or are
not to be presented. And this, for Joyce, is the whole problem of style.
Presentability or nonpresentability is not a quality inherent to any observable reality, but has to be imposed on that reality by the observer.
This involves a latent deformation of the object perceived, which in extreme cases is degraded to the level of a mere illustration of some given
meaning. If now we go back to the beginning of the chapter, we notice
not only the counter-point that exists between the introduction and the
subsequent historical sequence of styles but also the richly contrasting
tensions between the different types of presentation. At the start it
seemed that banal objects could only be captured by a cryptic language,
while the next passage showed that as language approached, reality seemed
rather to withdraw than to come closer. The account was split up into a
bewildering number of facets, with language attempting to comprehend
the subject matter from every conceivable angle. To do this, it had to be
freed from the normative restrictions of grammar and syntax, for only
then could it sow all the nuances in the imagination of the reader. The
account could contain no judgment, because otherwise it would not be
presenting the object itself but the frame of reference in which the object was viewed. And it is such frames of references that are in fact presented by the ensuing series of imitations. Joyce's aim, however, was
not solely to show up the limitations of all styles through the systems
of thought underlying them but also to evoke those aspects of an object
that are kept concealed by the perspective mode of observation. Hence
the fact that virtually every chapter of *Ulysses* is written in a different

[41] John Middleton Murry, *The Problem of Style* (Oxford, 1960; [1]1922), p. 65; see also F. L.
Lucas, *Style* (London, [3]1956), pp. 14 ff. and Herbert Read, *English Prose Style* (Boston, 1961),
pp. 183 f.
[42] See Murry, *The Problem of Style*, p. 65.

style.[43] Herein lies a basic difference between Joyce and all other modern writers. Joyce wanted to bring out, if not actually to overcome, the inadequacy of style as regards the presentation of reality, by constant changes of style, for only by showing up the relativity of each form could he expose the intangibility and expansibility of observable reality. And so in "The Oxen of the Sun" we have the themes of love, procreation, and birth discussed in a series of historically sequent styles which each convey a single, one-sided viewpoint.

This leads us to the second conclusion to be drawn from the examples given. If style reproduces only aspects of reality and not—in contrast to its implicit claims—reality itself, then it must be failing in its intention. This idea is worked up through the element of parody in the stylistic impersonations. Joyce caricatures the formal restrictions of each style, so that Leopold Bloom, the main character in the novel, finds himself taking on a corresponding variety of identities. The resultant distortion is one that the reader can scarcely ignore, since he already knows a good deal about Bloom's character from the preceding chapters. We find the same distortion in the treatment of the main theme of the chapter, for it is not love itself that is presented, but only the way in which Malory, Bunyan, Addison, and the other writers understood it. Indeed one has the impression that the different views presented by the different styles exclude rather than supplement one another. With each author, the theme takes on a different shape, but each treatment seems to assume that it is offering *the* reality. And so there emerges a latent naïveté underlying every style. One might perhaps wonder which of the views comes closest to the truth, but it is patently obvious that every one of the authors has cut reality to the shape of a particular meaning not inherent in that reality. By parodying the styles, Joyce has exposed their essentially manipulative character. The reader gradually becomes conscious of the fact that style fails to achieve its ends, in that it does not capture reality but imposes upon it an historically preconditioned form.

---

[43] See Jacques Mercanton, "The Hours of James Joyce. Part I," *Kenyon Review* 24 (1962): 701 f., who reproduces the following statement by Joyce concerning the style of *Ulysses:* "The hallucinations in *Ulysses* are made up out of elements from the past, which the reader will recognize if he has read the book five, ten, or twenty times. Here is the unknown. There is no past, no future; everything flows in an eternal present. All the languages are present, for they have not yet been separated. It's a tower of Babel. Besides, in a dream, if someone speaks Norwegian to you, you are not surprised to understand it. The history of people is the history of language." Various observations on the problem of language are also to be found in Theodore Ziolkowski's essay "James Joyces Epiphanie und die Überwindung der empirischen Welt in der modernen deutschen Prosa," *Deutsche Vierteljahrsschrift für Literaturwissenschaft und Geistesgeschichte* 35 (1961): 594 ff.; see also Heinz Decker, "Der Innere Monolog," *Akzente* 8 (1961): 107. Re the function of the experiments in style, see "Patterns of Communication in Joyce's *Ulysses*," in this volume, pp. 225 ff.

The parody through which this process is set in motion contains a polemic element attacking this intrinsic tendency of style to edit observed realities. If now we think back to the invocation with which Joyce ended *A Portrait,* we must expect his meeting with reality to aim at an extension of experience beyond the frontiers of the already familiar. And for a presentation of this, there must, paradoxically, be total freedom from the restrictions of any one consistently sustained mode of presentation.

This brings us to our third conclusion. With his historical panoply of individual and period styles, Joyce exposes the characteristic quality of style—namely, that it imposes form on an essentially formless reality. Thus in the various views of love that are presented, the decisive influence is the historical conditions which shaped the understanding of the subject during the period concerned. Clearly, then, the theme itself is so multifarious that it can encompass every possible historical reflection of it, and the more clearly defined the judgment, the more historically conditioned is the style. Out of the series of parodies, then, emerges the fact that not only are the styles one-sided but they are also conditioned by sets of values that will change from period to period. In other words, the same subject (in this case, love) will take on a different form when viewed under different conditions or at different times. Which style can best capture the reality of the subject? The answer, clearly, is none, for all styles are relative to the historical conditions that shape them.

This brings us to a fourth and last conclusion: if the factors that shape a style are essentially historical, the resultant definition of the object to be described can only be a pragmatic one, since it depends on ever-changing historical conditions. But the pragmatic nature of style can only be exposed through some sort of comparative survey—in this case, the historical sequence—since none of the authors Joyce parodies would have regarded their own form of presentation as a merely pragmatic view of the subjects they were dealing with. Now if style can only accomplish a pragmatic definition, its function in illuminating observed reality must be figurative, or metaphorical, for the limited system of references that forms it is applied to the unlimited reality it is attempting to convey. This is the only way, of course, in which style can build up a uniform picture. But if style can only capture objects in a metaphorical manner, it must be counted simply as one of those rhetorical devices of which Lessing once said: "that they never stick strictly to the truth; that at one moment they say too much, and at another too little."[44] Joyce's

---

[44] G. E. Lessing, *Gesammelte Werke,* VII, ed. Paul Rilla (Berlin, 1956), p. 233; Lucas,

chronological exhibition of styles shows clearly that they are all metaphorical and can only offer a preconditioned, one-sided view of their
subject matter. The intrinsic aim of style is to capture a phenomenon as
accurately as possible, but being only a metaphor, it cannot help but
miss out a whole range of aspects of that phenomenon. Roman Ingarden,
in describing the views that come to light through the style of a work of
art, has said: "The views that we have during our experiences of one and
the same thing change in different ways, and much that in an earlier
view emerged only in the form of an unrealized quality will, in a later
view, be present and transformed into a realized quality. But present in
every view of an object are both realized and unrealized qualities, and it
is intrinsically impossible ever to make the unrealized qualities disappear."[45] Joyce's parodies seek to change "unrealized qualities" into
"realized," and with this process he shows us how the phenomenon itself
begins to expand—for every definition excludes aspects which must themselves then be defined.

If we take up Goldberg's view of "The Oxen of the Sun" as the author's commentary on his novel,[46] we may reasonably extend our findings to the use of style throughout the whole book. While the theme of
this one chapter is love, the theme of *Ulysses* itself is everyday human
life, and the stylistic presentation of this varies from chapter to chapter,
because it can never be grasped as a whole by any one individual style.
Only by constantly varying the angle of approach is it possible to convey
the potential range of the 'real-life' world, but in literature the 'approach'
is what gives rise to the style. By constantly changing the style, Joyce
not only conveys the preconditioned, one-sided nature of each approach
but also seems to set both object and observer in motion, thus accumulating an assembly of mobile views that show the essential expansiveness of
reality. In this sense, "The Oxen of the Sun" epitomizes the technique of
the whole novel. The sequence of styles brings out the one-sidedness of
each and the constant expansion of the subject. One aspect after another
appears within the mirror of style, but "hey, presto, the mirror is breathed
on" and that seemingly all-important facet "recedes, shrivels, to a tiny
speck within the mist."[47] What Joyce says in this chapter about sins or
evil memories is true also of these hidden aspects of reality, and in "The

Style, p. 15, asks: "What, in fact, is 'style?' A dead metaphor." See also Joyce's remark on literature, reproduced by Stanislaus Joyce, *My Brother's Keeper*, p. 105. On the pragmatic nature
of metaphor, see Hans Blumenberg, *Paradigmen zu einer Metaphorologie* (Bonn, 1960), pp. 19 ff.
[45] Roman Ingarden, *Das literarische Kunstwerk* (Tübingen, ²1960), p. 277.
[46] See Goldberg, *The Classical Temper*, p. 288.
[47] Joyce, *Ulysses*, p. 395.

Oxen of the Sun," as throughout the novel, this insight is constantly
developed: they are "hidden away by man in the darkest places of the
heart but they abide there and wait. He may suffer their memory to
grow dim, let them be as though they had not been and all but persuade
himself that they were not or at least were otherwise. Yet a chance
word will call them forth suddenly and they will rise up to confront him
in the most various circumstances."[48]

[48] Ibid., p. 403.

8

PATTERNS OF COMMUNICATION
IN JOYCE'S *ULYSSES*

I

Myth and Reality

J oyce called his novel *Ulysses* after Homer's hero, though the latter never appears in the book. Instead Joyce deals with eighteen
different aspects of a single day in Dublin, mainly following the
involvement of two characters—Leopold Bloom and Stephen Dedalus—
in events that take place between early morning and late at night. What,
then, is the connection between the *Odyssey* and June 16, 1904? Most
answers to this question try to join these two poles of the novel through
the 'tried and tested' ideas of the recurrence of archetypes, or the analogy between the ideal and the real.[1] In the first case, the explanation is
provided by the permanent nature of basic human conduct—and so *Ulysses* has its roots in things we already know; the second, Platonizing interpretation claims that the basic idea of the *Odyssey* is a homecoming,
while that of Bloom's wanderings is just a copy of a homecoming: for
Ulysses this means release from his sufferings, but for Bloom it is merely
a critical moment in the restless monotony of everyday life.

---

[1] For a detailed discussion of these two interpretations, see "Doing Things in Style," in this
volume, pp. 179 ff. For a critical assessment of the Homeric parallel, see also A. Esch, "James
Joyce und Homer, Zur Frage der Odyssee-Korrespondenzen im *Ulysses*," in *Lebende Antike*
(Symposion für Rudolf Sühnel), ed. H. Meller und H.-J. Zimmermann (Berlin, 1967), pp. 423 ff.

Although one is reluctant to dispute these lines of interpretation, they certainly suffer from the fact that not a single character from the *Odyssey* actually appears in *Ulysses*—in contrast to many modern texts, where the return of mythical figures is a fundamental theme—and Joyce's deliberate allusions to Homeric heroes and epic events show them in a different light from that with which we are familiar through the *Odyssey*. The permanence idea gets into difficulties here, as it is never clear what is to be equated with what, and who with whom. There are similar objections to the analogy thesis, which postulates a sort of declivity from Homer to the present. One simply does not have the impression that everyday life in Dublin has been conceived as the woeful decline of an ideality that existed in the past. And again there is no clear parallel between past and present. Nevertheless, one can understand why the permanence and analogy theories have proved so attractive to those trying to combine past and present in a single vision: they do, after all, offer a means of organizing the seemingly opaque chaos of everyday life by referring it back to meanings drawn from Homer. The solution is convincing by virtue of its simplicity—but from an esthetic point of view it is quite inadequate. Joyce himself once said, ironically, of his novel: "I've put in so many enigmas and puzzles that it will keep the professors busy for centuries arguing over what I meant, and that's the only way of insuring one's immortality."[2] If for a moment one examines this statement with a little more seriousness than was perhaps intended, one is faced with the question of what actually gives rise to this preoccupation with the enigmas. Is it the enigmas themselves, or is it perhaps the critical armory which the professors are constantly dipping into as they try to solve the riddles? Whichever it may be, the parallelism indicated by the title of the novel compels one to see Dublin and Homer in conjunction, principally because one is anxious to extract some kind of meaning from the apparent senselessness of everyday life. But, like all compulsions, this makes one blind to certain not insignificant facts: one of these is the peculiar nature of the two poles that constitute the novel.

No Homeric figures actually appear in *Ulysses,* and yet the novel cannot be described as a realistic depiction of ordinary life in Dublin, despite the vast number of verifiable details that run right through it. We have since learned that a great deal of this material was drawn from Dublin address books, topographical descriptions, and the daily press of that time, so that an astonishing wealth of names, addresses, local events, and

---

[2] Quoted by R. Ellmann, *James Joyce* (Oxford, 1966), p. 535.

even newspaper cuttings can actually be identified,[3] though in the text they frequently form a montage that is stripped of its context. Sometimes these details vanish away into the impenetrable private sphere of Joyce himself, and sometimes they seem to lead the reader into a veritable labyrinth when he attempts to collate them. In searching for and visualizing connections, he often loses the organizing principle of those connections he thought he had discovered. And frequently it seems as though the many details are simply there for their own sake and, through sheer weight of numbers, more or less deliberately blur the outline of events in the narrative.

The effect of all this is somewhat paradoxical, for it runs completely contrary to the expectations that the realistic novel had established in its readers. There, too, one was confronted with a wealth of details which the reader could see reflected in his own world of experience. Their appearance in the novel served mainly to authenticate the view of life offered.[4] But in *Ulysses* they are, to a great extent, deprived of this function. When details no longer serve to reinforce probability or to stabilize the illusion of reality, they must become a sort of end in themselves, such as one finds in the art-form of the collage. The unstructured material of *Ulysses* is taken directly *from* life itself, but since it no longer testifies to the author's preconception of reality, it cannot be taken *for* life itself. Thus the details illustrate nothing; they simply present themselves, and since they bear witness to nothing beyond themselves, they revoke the normal assumption that a novel represents a given reality. It is not surprising, then, that one is constantly returning to the title in order to try to create—through recourse to the *Odyssey*—some sort of frame of reference that will bring this chaos of detail under control and will endow everyday life with a pattern, with meaning, and with significance.

We now have a double frustration of our expectations: not only do the Homeric figures fail to appear in *Ulysses* but also the many details are deprived of their usual function. As a result, our attention is drawn to the evocative nature of the novel. We realize that all these details constitute a surplus that projects far beyond any organizational schema that the novel may offer us. And so each reading gives us a new chance to integrate the details in a different way—with the result, however, that

[3] It is the great merit of R. M. Adams's *Surface and Symbol. The Consistency of James Joyce's Ulysses* (New York, 1962) that he extracted this material from the novel and was able to identify it.
[4] See also H. R. Jauss, "Nachahmungsprinzip und Wirklichkeitsbegriff in der Theorie des Romans von Diderot bis Stendhal", in *Nachahmung und Illusion* (Poetik und Hermeneutik, I), ed. H. R. Jauss (Munich, 1964), pp. 161 f. and 241 f.

each form of integration brings about a sort of kaleidoscopic reshuffling of the material excluded.

By giving his novel this structure—whether consciously or unconsciously—Joyce was complying with a basic disposition of the reader, described by Northrop Frye as follows: "Whenever we read anything, we find our attention moving in two directions at once. One direction is outward or centrifugal, in which we keep going outside our reading, from the individual words to the things they mean, or, in practice, to our memory of the conventional association between them. The other direction is inward or centripetal, in which we try to develop from the words a sense of the larger verbal pattern they make."[5] These two tendencies seem to take the reader of *Ulysses* in completely different directions, which are divergent rather than convergent. As he reads, he finds that everyday life in Dublin is, so to speak, continually breaking its banks, and the resultant flood of detail induces the reader to try and build his own dams of meaning—though these in turn are inevitably broken down. Even the signal contained in the title seems to dispel rather than fulfill one's hopes of controlling the material, for the central frame of reference that one would so like to deduce from the *Odyssey* is never formulated anywhere in the text. According to whether one reads the novel from the Dublin viewpoint or from that of the *Odyssey,* one will get quite different 'images'. In the first case, the apparent lack of connection between the many details creates the impression of a thoroughly chaotic world; in the second, one wonders what the return of Ulysses in modern trappings is supposed to signify. Both approaches are, in themselves, relatively flabby, and the task of stiffening them up, and indeed bringing them together, is what the novel sets its reader.

Soon after the publication of *Ulysses,* Eliot and Pound both described the interaction of the two constituent poles of the novel, each using different metaphors. In his discussion of *Ulysses,* Eliot saw in the novel's references to tradition a demand that was to be made of all literature: "In using the myth, in manipulating a continuous parallel between contemporaneity and antiquity, Mr. Joyce is pursuing a method which others must pursue after him. They will not be imitators, any more than the scientist who uses the discoveries of an Einstein in pursuing his own, independent, further investigations. It is simply a way of controlling, of ordering, of giving a shape and a significance to the immense panorama

[5] N. Frye, *Anatomy of Criticism. Four Essays* (New York, [5]1967), p. 73.

of futility and anarchy which is contemporary history."[6] According to this, the mythic parallel is meant to give a constant outline to an order that is to be read into the events in Dublin. But this cannot mean—at least for Joyce—that the chaotic and enigmatic present is measured against the significance of Homeric archetypes. It would be closer to the truth to say that the mythic parallel offers patterns of perception, though what is perceived never conforms completely to these patterns. Indeed, the revelation of the irreducible differences is what constitutes the real function of the mythical patterns through which we are to look upon the modern world. The very fact that these cannot incorporate every-thing endows the nonintegrated material with the necessary degree of live tension to make us immediately aware of it. It is not by chance that Eliot refers back to Einstein in order to indicate how the 'discovery' of Joyce is to be evaluated and handled. The mythic parallel here is more in the nature of an explanatory hypothesis, and is scarcely to be interpret-ed as the return of the myth. It is simply a repertoire of patterns serving an overall strategy through which the present-day world is to be presented.

Ezra Pound, on the same subject, writes: "These correspondences are part of Joyce's mediaevalism and are chiefly his own affair, a scaffold, a means of construction, justified by the result, and justifiable by it only. The result is a triumph in form, in balance, a main schema, with contin-uous inweaving and arabesque."[7] Pound sees in the mythical correspond-ences nothing but preconditions for the construction of the novel—the scaffolding round the shell of the building to be erected. But the novel itself is more than the sum of its preconditions, and is in no way reduci-ble to this sum. Ultimately, the network of mythical correspondences forms nothing but a framework of presentation, which is so clearly de-lineated in the novel in order to draw attention to the limitations of all such organizational patterns. This applies in equal measure to the recog-nizable archetypes, but the question then arises as to what such limita-tions actually are meant to achieve.

II

Experiments in Style

The Homeric allusions in *Ulysses* open up an horizon which is certainly

---

[6] T. S. Eliot, "Ulysses, Order and Myth," in *James Joyce: Two Decades of Criticism*, ed. S. Givens (New York, 1948), p. 201. (The essay originally appeared in 1923.)

[7] E. Pound, *Literary Essays*, ed. T. S. Eliot (London, 1960), p. 406. (The essay on Ulysses originally appeared in 1922.)

not identical to that of the modern "World-Weekday,"[8] for between the present and the archetypes of the Homeric epic lies the whole of history, which could only be passed over if *Ulysses* were concerned with nothing but the return of archetypes. One should not forget, when considering the Homeric parallel, that Joyce permeated his novel with just as many Shakespearean allusions as Homeric. And even if one tries to equate Shakespeare's presence in *Ulysses* with the return of the archetypes, nevertheless there is no denying the fact that Joyce was obviously more interested in the various manifestations of such archetypes than in merely establishing their return. This certainly indicates that for him the archetype was, at most, a vehicle, but not a subject. The history of its manifestations takes precedence over its mythical nature. But what is this history, and in what form is it reflected in the novel?

Our answer to this question can, perhaps, best proceed from the experiments in style. These in themselves are an innovation, insofar as the eighteen chapters of the novel present the narrative through eighteen differently structured perspectives. Normally, when reading a novel, we are asked only once to adopt the author's chosen standpoint in order to fulfill his intentions—but here the same demand is made of us no less than seventeen extra times, for each chapter is written in a different style. Style, according to John Middleton Murry, "is a quality of language which communicates . . . . a system of emotions or thoughts, peculiar to the author."[9] We can talk of style when systematic viewpoints bring about a frame of reference that is to direct the reader's observations by selecting which facts are or are not to be presented.

This function of style is both its strength and its weakness, for inevitably it must restrict the field of observation. The meaning that it is to express can only take its shape through the process of selecting particular aspects of the phenomena to be presented, and so phenomena are reproduced mainly for the sake of what they will communicate to the reader. As style imposes a specific meaning and edits reality to coincide with this meaning, it reveals itself to be a "mythical analogue,"[10] which—as Clemens Lugowski has shown—not only implies a particular conception of reality but is also the agent that actually forms it. Although this " 'mythical artifice' . . . is the result of a deeply unconscious and indirect act of interpretation,"[11] for this very reason it will freeze the historical conditions under which such acts of interpretation came into being.

---

[8] "Welt-Alltag"—a term coined by H. Broch, *Dichten und Erkennen* (Zürich, 1955), p. 187, to designate June 16, 1904.

[9] J. M. Murry, *The Problem of Style* (London, [9]1960), p. 65.

[10] C. Lugowski, *Die Form der Individualität im Roman* (Berlin, 1932), p. 12.

[11] Ibid., p. 206.

In *Ulysses* Joyce shows up these limitations by thematizing the capacity of style itself. By constantly changing the perspective through the eighteen chapters, he draws attention to the normative pressure caused by the modes of observation inherent in any one style, thus revealing the extreme one-sidedness of each individual "act of interpretation." While the change of styles shows up these limitations, the process is underlined in the individual chapters by the surplus of nonintegrated, unstructured material. This, too, makes one aware of the limitations of the style in question, so that it often seems more real than the view of reality being presented at the time.

And so we have changes of style and nonintegrated material to show up the limitations of each style, and in addition to these two factors, there is even a kind of authorial commentary[12] which has these very limitations as its subject. This is the case in "The Oxen of the Sun," which Joyce critics have always approached with a kind of embarrassment.[13] T. S. Eliot had the impression that this chapter showed the "futility of all the English styles,"[14] and this must certainly have been at least one of the effects that Joyce was aiming at.

In this display of individual and period styles, we are made aware of the various assumptions that condition the different presentations of the theme. By parodying the styles, Joyce makes sure that we do not overlook the 'interpretative' nature of the forms of presentation. Leopold Bloom finds himself transformed into a variety of figures, in accordance with the particular style used: the medieval "traveller Leopold" changes into the Arthurian knight "Sir Leopold," who in turn leaps into a new context as "childe Leopold."[15] The reader cannot help being aware of the one-sidedness of all these characterizations, as he has already become familiar in the preceding chapters with the many-sidedness of Bloom's character. This same one-sidedness is equally evident in the central theme of the chapter. This does not deal with love, but only with the way in which Malory, Bunyan, Addison and the other writers conceived of love. The basically comic effect arises out of the impression one has that the views, expressed in such a variety of styles, exclude rather than supplement one another. With each author the main theme takes on a different shape, but as each style automatically and unquestioningly assumes that

---

[12] See also S. L. Goldberg, *The Classical Temper. A Study of James Joyce's Ulysses* (London, 1961), p. 288.

[13] For details and bibliography see "Doing Things in Style," in this volume, pp. 180 ff.

[14] Quoted by Ellmann, *James Joyce*, p. 490.

[15] Joyce, *Ulysses* (London: The Bodley Head, 1937), pp. 369 f.

it has captured the reality of the phenomenon, a latent naiveté comes to the surface. The question arises as to which of these individual views comes closest to the truth, but even then we realize that the individual authors, precisely through their selection of a particular means of presentation, have in fact edited the subject to form a single meaning and a single evaluation. The very fact that these meanings and evaluations seem to assume a normative validity makes us aware of the extent to which they depend on the historical situation from which they have sprung. If "The Oxen of the Sun" is taken, then, as the author's own 'commentary' on his work, one can scarcely expect him to organize his novel as yet another "act of interpretation." It is the *presentation* of everyday life that concerns him, and not the evaluation.

However, such a presentation also requires a form, and inevitably any form that Joyce chose would automatically foreshorten the phenomenon to be presented. And so one might assume that the chapters of the novel were organized, each as a sort of rebuttal to the others, with their respective *principium stilisationis*. The consequences of this principle of construction are very far-reaching. Joyce could parody the different styles in order to show the limitations of their capacity, but if he applied this technique to the whole novel, it would mean that in trying to present the events, etc., of June 16, 1904, he would have to parody himself continually. There are certainly traces of this in the text, but a constant self-parody would ultimately distract the reader from coming to grips with the events of June 16, 1904. And would this not in turn—like all parodies—lead primarily to a negative evaluation, as limited in its own way as the evaluations of the authors parodied? Such a form would itself constitute an "act of interpretation."

Is it possible for anything to be presented, and yet at the same time for the "act of interpretation" to be suspended without the object of presentation becoming incomprehensible? *Ulysses* is the answer to this question. In order to moderate, if not actually to neutralize, the interpretative nature of style, Joyce called upon virtually every stylistic mode that the novel had evolved during its comparatively short history. These he enriched with a whole armory of allusions and with the recall of archetypes. The multiplicity of these schemata, together with the complexity of their interrelationships, results in a form of presentation that in fact presents each incipient meaning simultaneously with its own diffusion. Thus the novel does not paint a picture of the "World-Weekday"—which means, ultimately, that it does not 'present' anything in the conventional sense—but, through the great variety of its perspectives, it offers possibilities for conceiving or imagining the "World-Weekday." These possibilities must be fulfilled by the reader himself, if he wants to make contact with the reality of the novel. One must therefore differentiate between 'presentation' (i.e., by the author) and 'imagination' (on the part of the reader). Of course, even if the 'interpretative acts' of the novel are obvious, the reader still has to imagine things for himself. But he will only conduct these 'interpretative acts' if the system of presentation leaves out the coordinating elements between observable phenomena and situations. In *Ulysses* this is brought about mainly through the overprecision of the system, which presents more conceivable material than the reader is capable of processing as he reads. And so it is not the style of the novel but the overtaxed reader himself that reduces the amount of observable material to manageable proportions. In doing so, he can scarcely avoid equating this reduced amount with the meaning. If one considers reactions to *Ulysses* over the last forty years—insofar as these can be gauged by the different interpretations offered—one can see how historically conditioned such meanings are. At the same time, it cannot be denied that the many possible permutations of meaning in *Ulysses* act as a constant inducement to the reader to formulate a meaning—and in doing so, he is forced to enter into the action of the novel.

The individual chapters of *Ulysses* act, to a greater or lesser degree, as signposts that point the way through the "World-Weekday," rather than guidebooks that impose on the reader a specific interpretation of the regions they represent. If we want to get a proper understanding of the function of the patterns of presentation, the allusions, and also the archetypes, it might be as well first to examine one or two concrete examples.

The novel begins with the parody of a church ritual. Mulligan, the medical student, holds his shaving-bowl aloft at the top of the Martello tower, and intones: *Introibo ad altare Dei.*[16] If this little curtain-raiser is a sign of what is to come, then we appear to be due for one long parody. At first this impression seems to be confirmed by the subsequent conversation between Mulligan and Stephen, for as he talks the former jumps abruptly from one stylistic level to another, everyday slang alternating with scholarly allusions to Greece, Irish mythology, and even Zarathustra.[17] Indeed individual allusions are sometimes broken up and even corrupted. Are we now to have a series of parodied stylistic levels?

[16] Ibid., p. 1.
[17] Ibid., pp. 5, 9, 20.

If so, there would be a danger of the tension soon flagging, for a parody of stylistic levels here might seem trivial after the initial 'exposing' of the mass. Moreover, it is scarcely possible to find a *tertium comparationis* for the various intersecting levels of Mulligan's speech.

It is also impossible to establish a purpose for such a parody, unless one wanted to conclude from the diffusion of stylistic levels that Joyce was advocating a purist use of language—an idea that is hardly worth considering. In fact, one gets the impression that what is stated is nothing but a stimulus to call forth its own reversal. Thus the profane distortions of the ritual of the mass take on a significance other than that of mere parody. Like the subsequent conversation, they point up the limitations of all clearly formulated statements and induce the reader to supply his own connections between the segmented stylistic levels. As the text offers no point of convergence for the phenomena it sets before him, the reader tends to load each detail with meaning, and since the meaning cannot be fully realized, there arises a latent tension between the unconnected phenomena. This basic pattern, with a few variations, runs right through the first chapter, which Joyce called "Telemachus."[18] The most important type of variation is the abrupt switch of narrator. In the middle of a third-person narrative we are suddenly confronted with statements in the first person,[19] which strike the reader so forcibly that he soon becomes more conscious of narrative patterns than of things narrated. And so here, as elsewhere in the novel, one gets the impression that one must constantly differentiate between the linguistic possibilities of style and the possible nature of the phenomena concerned.

The predominant pattern of reversal in this first chapter reduces all that is clear and concrete to a mere position in life, but life itself goes far beyond such positions. The next chapter, originally called "Nestor," reveals the implications of this fact, and naturally another collection of stylistic patterns is necessary to uncover these hidden consequences. Stephen's interior monologue is the dominant pattern in this chapter, but it is broken up by authorial passages, direct speech, and also quotations from Milton's *Lycidas*,[20] all set against and arising out of the back-

[18] These chapter headings are to be found in Joyce's 'note-sheets,' and he used them in grouping together his material. See A. W. Litz, *The Art of James Joyce. Method and Design in Ulysses and Finnegans Wake* (New York, 1964); for an assessment of their importance, see especially ibid., p. 39.

[19] See Joyce, *Ulysses*, pp. 7 f.
[20] Ibid., pp. 22 f.

ground of the morning lesson. They lead to reflections on history and man's possible place in history:

For them too history was a tale like any other too often heard, their land a pawnshop. Had Pyrrhus not fallen by a beldam's hand in Argos or Julius Caesar not been knifed to death? They are not to be thought away. Time has branded them and fettered they are lodged in the room of the infinite possibilities they have ousted. But can those have been possible seeing that they never were? Or was that only possible which came to pass? Weave, weaver of the wind. . . . It must be a movement then, an actuality of the possible as possible.[21]

It is not insignificant that this reflection on the possible is inspired specifically by historical processes in which everything appears to be so irrevocably fixed. Is this determinacy ultimately to be seen only as one possibility among many? What about the existences of historical individuals? If, through their deeds and sufferings, they stepped outside the jurisdiction of infinite possibilities, why should they now fall back into it? It seems almost like a sophism when Stephen asks whether Pyrrhus and Caesar even considered the possibility, when they were alive, that one day they would not be there, or that they would end as they did. Although he himself considers such thoughts to be mere speculations, they do not stop him from concluding that real life can only be understood as an actuality of one possibility among many. But if what happened did not happen inevitably, then the real is nothing but a chance track left by the possible. And if reality is nothing but one chance track, then it pales to insignificance beside the vast number of unseen and unfulfilled possibilities; it shrinks to the dimensions of a mere curiosity. The tendency apparent in these reflections of Stephen's runs parallel to that at the beginning of the novel, where whatever was said pointed the way to its own reversal, and whatever possibilities were excluded by each utterance were brought out by another.

The children are bored by the history lesson, and want Stephen to tell them a story: "Tell us a story, sir.—Oh, do, sir. A ghoststory."[22] Stephen himself has just had the impression that, when one thinks about it, history changes into a ghost story, albeit a different type from the one the children would like to hear. Bored by the factual, they are now asking for the fantastic, without realizing how much incomprehensibility lies in the factual. The text, of course, does not state this, but the manner in which the different perspectives are thrust against one another compels

[21] Ibid.
[22] Ibid., p. 22.

the reader to search for a link between them. The text offers him no guide as to how the different standpoints might be evaluated, and at best he can only orientate himself through the next perspective which, like that of the children, is inserted into Stephen's monologue. There is no ghost story; instead, the children begin to read verses from Milton's *Lycidas*—those lines where the mourning shepherd is consoled with the assurance that the dead do not perish. Evidently only poetry eternalizes; but poetry is fiction.

In this comparatively short section of text, there are three different intersecting patterns: interior monologue, direct speech, and literary quotations—all focused upon a relatively uniform theme which, however, takes on three different forms as it is presented to the reader. For Stephen reality is so overshadowed by the possible that it is deprived of its unique significance. The children are bored by what has been and want the titillation of the unreal. The literary quotation shows clearly that eternalization only exists in the medium of fiction. The text does not say how these three viewpoints are to be joined together, but simply offers three different possibilities for relating the real to the unreal. As the individual stylistic patterns intersect within the text, there is no hierarchic construction. The reflections of the inner monologue point inevitably to the private nature of the opinion expressed; the desires of the school children appear as something spontaneous and naive and the quotation as a kind of insurance without any reality. Although this need not be regarded as the only possible interpretation of the different patterns of the text, the conditions are certainly there for such an interpretation. Since these patterns are without a point of convergence, their meaning arises out of their interaction—a process which is set in motion by the reader himself and which will therefore involve him personally in the text.

Apart from the patterns we have mentioned, this process is encouraged above all by the end of the chapter, which deals with a conversation between Stephen and the headmaster, Mr. Deasy. The headmaster gives Stephen a letter which he wants published in the *Evening Telegraph,* because it contains his (Deasy's) solution to an important problem: foot-and-mouth disease. "I have put the matter into a nutshell, Mr Deasy said. It's about the foot and mouth disease. Just look through it. There can be no two opinions on the matter."[23]

For Mr. Deasy there can be no two opinions about this or about a number of other political problems in Ireland. But now the segmented

---

[23] Ibid., p. 30.

text pattern of Stephen's history lesson becomes the background to Mr. Deasy's unequivocal utterances, through which he seeks once and for all to set right existing realities. Again the text says nothing about any relationship between these two passages, but the reader will soon find a relatively straightforward way to bridge this gap. Viewed against the background of infinite possibilities, Mr. Deasy's self-confidence appears absurdly narrow-minded, and so the reader will most likely come to two conclusions: first, that Mr. Deasy is a pompous ass; second, and far more important, that any claim to knowledge is an automatic reduction of the infinite and discounts above all the changeability of phenomena. However, let it be emphasized once again—this interpretation will be the reader's, for there is no such statement in the text itself.

As regards the original chapter heading—"Nestor"—this offers yet another perspective, insofar as the reader will try to link the wisdom of Nestor with the pretension of Mr. Deasy. He will probably find that not only does Mr. Deasy suffer from the comparison, but so, too, does Nestor. For if, in Mr. Deasy's case, claims to knowledge presuppose unawareness of the changeability of phenomena, then the mythical wisdom of Nestor is open to re-evaluation by the reader.

The third chapter, originally called "Proteus," takes the experiment in yet another direction, at the same time bringing to a close the sections grouped under the heading "Telemachia," which deal with Stephen's inner situation before the appearance of Bloom. In comparison with the preceding chapters, one is struck by the relative uniformity of the stylistic pattern used here. Stephen's monologue forms the dominant *principium stilisationis,* though there are occasional traces of the authorial narrator. These latter, however, are of a special nature. Instead of relating the monologue to an overall situation, the author's voice here seems to be unable to keep up with Stephen's reflections and is virtually swamped by them. It no longer acts as a mediator between the context and the narrated situation; instead the monologue seems to abstract itself even from the authorial medium. With the authorial narrator thus deprived of his normal function, we are left with a gap between monologue and overall situation and, as always when such gaps arise, the reader is stimulated into forming his own connections. But in this case, his task is made doubly difficult by the fact that Stephen's monologue has no consistent pattern. At one moment it seems like a stream of consciousness, stirring up the past, the next it is a mere recording of observations on the beach at Sandymount, and then it is like a soliloquy or an introspective reflection which—unlike the conventional interior monologue—is not concerned with memory or observation, but with the conditions that initially give rise to memory and observation.

In the very first sentence of the monologue, we are made aware of the peculiar nature of Stephen's reflections:"Ineluctable modality of the visible: at least that if no more, thought through my eyes. Signatures of all things I am here to read, seaspawn and seawrack, the nearing tide, that rusty boot. Snotgreen, bluesilver, rust: coloured signs. Limits of the diaphane."[24]

Stephen tries to show the consequences that arise out of his inescapable restriction to his own perceptions. This is apparently only possible through concrete consideration of the actual mode of perception. If observation automatically involves so many preconceptions, then how is one to read the signatures of things? At best, seawrack and tide might be described as colors, but such a reduction not only impoverishes them—it also leads one swiftly to the borderline at which they resist perception and retreat into total opacity. It is perception itself that ultimately produces this opacity, which in turn appears to be a characteristic of the object which is to be perceived. Thus for Stephen, the subject under discussion is the frame of reference of perception itself. Perhaps this frame is such that in approaching objects, it changes them in order to make them accessible to one's comprehension.

Stephen tries to test this idea; he closes his eyes in order to 'see' if such a change really is produced by vision. He opens them again with the statement: "See now. There all the time without you: and ever shall be, world without end."[25] Obviously, things exist independently of one's comprehension and observation of them, and if this comprehension is, in turn, to be comprehended, it must be through the idea that the act of seeing is what produces the opacity of things. The monologue that follows is like an attempt to give form to this idea. Stephen's reflections on the limitations of observation culminate in a welter of fragmentary situations, images, characters, and contexts. The reader is perplexed, not least because this is not what he expects from analytical reflection in a novel. Normally, the aim of this sort of reflection should be progress toward clarity and truth—it should enlighten and not obscure.[26]

The perplexing effect of the monologue derives mainly from the fact

---

[24] Ibid., p. 33.

[25] Ibid., p. 34.

[26] Stephen is also conscious of this: "You find my words dark. Darkness is in our souls, do you not think? Flutier. Our souls, shamewounded by our sins, cling to us yet more, a woman to her lover clinging, the more the more." Ibid., p. 45.

that the individual sentences or passages, which all deal with recognizable but unrelated themes, are simply set side by side without any apparent connection. Thus the vacant spaces in the text increase dramatically in number. These may irritate the reader—but as far as the intention of the monologue is concerned, they are perfectly consistent. They prevent the reader from correlating what he observes, with the result that the facets of the external world—as evoked by Stephen's perception—are constantly made to merge into one another. However, the perplexity that this process causes in the reader cannot be the sole purpose of the text, if one considers Stephen's preceding train of thought. Here, as elsewhere, perplexity should be regarded rather as a stimulus and a provocation—though, of course, the reader is not obliged to take the bait and will, indeed, ignore it if he feels himself to be overtaxed. The point is that one *can* read something into this fragmentary text. Stephen's reflections on his acts of perception reveal a state of consciousness which has been described, in a different context, by Cassirer as follows: "The further consciousness progresses in its formation and division, and the more 'meaningful' its individual contents become—i.e., the more they take on the power to 'adumbrate' others—the greater is the freedom with which, through a change of 'viewpoint,' it can transform one gestalt into another."[27] It is this disposition of consciousness that is brought out through the ceaseless transformation of 'gestalten' in the monologue. But it should be added that the transformation is effected primarily by the way in which Stephen varies the distance between the observed reality and himself as the conscious observer. This variation ensures that the world which is open to perception cannot be confined to any one conscious frame of reference. A vital element of it is the continual retraction of each adopted attitude to everything that occurs on the beach at Sandymount, and the whole process functions through the gaps, interrupting the images formed by acts of perception, thus focusing the reader's attention on the interaction between perception and reality.

The text also offers indications of this process: "I throw this ended shadow from me, manshape ineluctable, call it back. Endless, would it be mine, form of my form? Who watches me here?"[28] This awareness of the necessity to separate modes of perception from the thing perceived, so that the observed world can take on its inherent multifariousness, is conveyed in the text through the gaps which prevent us from connecting the phenomena processed by observation. And so the mono-

---

[27] E. Cassirer, *Philosophie der symbolischen Formen* (Darmstadt, [4]1964), III: 185.
[28] Joyce, *Ulysses,* p. 45.

logue appears to release all the observed and recorded details from any overriding structure.

In the face of this impression, one might be tempted to regard this chapter as offering a focus for the whole manner of presentation of the "World-Weekday." Stephen's reflections on his own mode of observation, self-observation as a constant check on things observed, and the liberation of things perceived from the clutches of perception—these could easily be taken for the basic schema of the novel. But if this were so, Joyce would fall victim to his own trap. For then he would simply be replacing the styles he parodies with another of his own. For this very reason it is essential not to overlook the demarcation points through which he indicates the limitations of the mode of presentation in this chapter. First, we have nothing but the view of one character in the novel. The perspective is offered in the form of a monologue which sometimes seems to lose its way in the impenetrable individuality of the person delivering it. Second, even if one can follow these reflections, the very form of the monologue emphasizes the private nature of the ideas expressed, for the interior monologue is a private form of presentation, the ego addressing itself. And, finally, elsewhere in the novel Joyce gives certain indications as to how Stephen's cogitations are to be judged. Much later in the book—352 pages to be precise—in the chapter on the parody of styles (nota bene!), Stephen's introspective searchings are labeled "perverted transcendentalism."[29] Of course the Joyce reader needs a very good memory (and usually hasn't got one good enough) to recall all such indications, but even an average, if overburdened, memory will record enough to show that the mode of presentation in the "Proteus" chapter is to be seen only as a facet of and not as a paradigm for the presentation of everyday life.

We might add one more reflection on this chapter, and that concerns the Homeric parallel. Joyce called the chapter "Proteus," and we know from the *Odyssey* that Proteus keeps escaping from Menelaus and transforming himself into different shapes, because he does not want to yield the secret of how Menelaus can best get home. But Menelaus has been warned in advance not to be put off by these changes of form, because it is his courage that will compel Proteus to give away the vital secret. The transformations brought about by Stephen's thinking are somewhat different. Certainly it seems as though a secret is being kept from him, but, in contrast to the Homeric story, he is producing this secret himself. He knows he is inescapably restricted to observation, and he knows that

---

[29] Ibid., p. 399.

things change the moment one observes them. Every approach changes them into something different. And so the 'courage' of knowing just what it is that we can see and understand, actually blocks the way to the secret. The act of knowing itself produces the secret of things that change when they are observed. While the Homeric world order enabled Menelaus to learn the secret he coveted, the modern world uses its knowledge to reveal the fact that there *is* a secret—the indeterminate nature of all phenomena. As far as Menelaus is concerned, the knowledge wrested from Proteus leads directly to action; for Stephen, the knowledge that he is bound to his own forms of perception leads to an endless delving into the ultimate constitution of the world.

As it would be beyond the scope of this essay to deal with all the experiments of style in *Ulysses,* we shall confine ourselves to those that evince the most striking variations. One of these is undoubtedly the "Aeolus" chapter, which is especially relevant to our discussion, as in many respects it forms a contrast to the "Proteus" chapter. Bloom's visit to the newspaper office provides the framework for a curiously patterned form of narration. Analysis reveals two separate levels of the text, which one might call, for the sake of convenience, the micro- and the macrostructure of the chapter. The microstructural level consists of a large number of allusions which basically can be divided into three different groups: (1) those dealing with the immediate situation, Bloom's effort to place an advertisement at the newspaper office and the events connected with it; (2) those referring to completely different episodes outside the chapter itself, sometimes relating to incidents already described and sometimes anticipating things; (3) those passages which seem to slide into obscurity when one tries to work out exactly where they might be heading. However, as these allusions are not distinctly separated, but are in fact woven into an intricate pattern, each one of them tends to entice the reader to follow it. Thus the allusions themselves turn into microperspectives which, because of their very density, simply cannot be followed through to the end. They form abbreviated extracts from reality which inevitably compel the reader to a process of selection.

This is also true of the other stylistic pattern to be discerned within the microstructural stratum. Just as with the allusions, there is throughout an abrupt alternation between dialogue, direct and indirect speech, authorial report, first-person narrative, and interior monologue. Although such techniques do impose a certain order on the abundance of allusions, they also invest them with differing importance. An allusion by the author himself certainly has a function for the context different from one that is made in direct speech by one of the characters. Thus extracts from reality and individual events are not contracted merely into allusions, but, through the different patterns of style, emerge in forms that endow them with a varied range of relevance. At the same time, the unconnected allusions and the abrupt alternation of stylistic devices disclose a large number of gaps.

All this gives rise to the stimulating quality of the text. On the one hand, the density of allusions and the continual segmentation of style involve an incessant changing of perspectives, which seem to go out of control whenever the reader tries to pin them down; on the other hand, the gaps resulting from cuts and abbreviations tempt the reader to fill them in. He will try to group things, because this is the only way in which he can recognize situations or understand characters in the novel.

The macrostructure of the chapter lends itself to this need for 'grouping', though in a peculiar way. Heading and 'newspaper column' form the schema that incorporates the allusions and stylistic changes. The heading is an instruction as to what to expect. But the text which follows the caption reveals the composition described above, and so in most cases does not fulfill the expectation raised by the heading. As the newspaper headlines refer to various incidents in the city, the situation of Ireland, and so forth, they would seem to be concerned with everyday events, the reality of which is beyond question. But the column that follows frustrates this expectation, not only by leading commonplace realities off in unforeseeable directions, thus destroying the grouping effect of the headline, but also by fragmenting facts and occurrences in such a way that to comprehend the commonplace becomes a real effort. While the heading appears to gratify our basic need for grouping, this need is predominantly subverted by the text that follows.

In the "Aeolus" chapter, the reader not only learns something about events in Dublin on June 16, 1904 but he also experiences the difficulties inherent in the comprehension of the barest outline of events. It is precisely because the heading suggests a way of grouping from a particular viewpoint that the text itself seems so thoroughly to contradict our familiar notions of perception. The text appears to defy transcription of the circumstances indicated and instead offers the reader nothing but attitudes or possibilities of perception concerning these circumstances. In exploiting these possibilities, the reader is stimulated to a form of activity that B. Ritchie, in another context, has described as follows:

> The solution to this paradox is to find some ground for a distinction between "surprise" and "frustration." Roughly, the distinction can

be made in terms of the effects which the two kinds of experiences have upon us. Frustration blocks or checks activity. It necessitates new orientation for our activity, if we are to escape the *cul de sac.* Consequently, we abandon the frustrating object and return to blind impulsive activity. On the other hand, surprise merely causes a temporary cessation of the exploratory phase of the experience, and a recourse to intense contemplation and scrutiny. In the latter phase the surprising elements are seen in their connection with what has gone before, with the whole drift of the experience, and the enjoyment of these values is then extremely intense . . . any aesthetic experience tends to exhibit a continuous interplay between "deductive" and "inductive" operations.[30]

Now it does sometimes occur in this chapter that the expectations aroused by the headings are fulfilled. At such moments, the text seems banal,[31] for when the reader has adjusted himself to the nonfulfillment of his expectations, he will view things differently when they *are* fulfilled. The reason for this is easy to grasp. If the text of the column does not connect up with the heading, the reader must supply the missing links. His participation in the intention of the text is thus enhanced. If the text does fulfill the expectations aroused by the heading, no removing of gaps is required of the reader and he feels the 'let-down' of banality. In this way, the textual pattern in this chapter arouses continual conflicts with the reader's own modes of perception, and, as the author has completely withdrawn from this montage of possibilities, the reader is given no guidance as to how to resolve the conflicts. But it is through these very conflicts, and the confrontation with the array of different possibilities, that the reader of such a text is given the impression that something does happen to him.

It is perhaps not by chance that in this chapter the Homeric parallel has shrunk to the barest recollection, for the basic schema of composition is determined not by the scattering of news to all winds, but by the manner in which this scattered news is received. Joyce makes his theme out of that which did not concern Homer, and this also reveals something of the strategy of literary allusions that Joyce used in *Ulysses.*

A highlight of the experiments in style is the chapter Joyce originally called "Circe"—often designated as "Walpurgis Night." This presents

---

[30] B. Ritchie, "The Formal Structure of the Aesthetic Object," in *The Problems of Aesthetics,* ed. E. Vivas and M. Krieger (New York, 1965), pp. 230 f.

[31] See Joyce, *Ulysses,* p. 118.

scenes of 'nighttown' Dublin in a series of dialogues in dramatic form. The very use of this form automatically precludes any long stretches of narrative. If one regards the grouping together of events as a basic element of narrative, it would seem as though here the novel is in fact trying to free itself from this basic condition. Even where there is some narration, it is in the form of stage directions, which deprives it of its real narrative character. However, despite its lay-out the chapter can scarcely be called a play at all. The monologues, dialogues, stage directions, exits and entrances it consists of have almost completely lost their dramatic function. The conflicts between the characters end as abruptly as they began, and the cast of characters grows bigger and bigger, for it is not only the characters in the novel that take part in the play—we are also suddenly confronted with Lord Tennyson[32] and Edward VII,[33] the gas-jet whistles,[34] the retriever barks,[35] the voices of all the damned and those of all the blessed ring out,[36] and the end of the world—a two-headed octopus—speaks with a Scottish accent.[37]

The unremitting expansion of the cast is combined with the most extraordinary dialogues. In dramatic dialogue characters generally aim at influencing one another, but here this basic function is carried to extremes. When, at the beginning, Bloom is surrounded by different partners and is confronted with events of the past and present he assumes the form that is being alluded to.[38] Sometimes this tendency is taken to absurd lengths—as in the scene with Bella Cohen, the whore-mistress, when he changes into a woman and creeps timidly under the sofa in order to play a subservient role opposite Bella, who meanwhile has swollen up into a masculine monster.[39] The effect of dramatic dialogue here is so exaggerated that Bloom simply falls into the role assigned to him by his partner. This speedy compliance is not without its problems for the partners either, for Bloom's change of form does not exactly increase their security as regards the process of acting and reacting.

Such scenes show clearly that the dramatic elements are no longer part of any dramatic structure, so that the 'play' rapidly divorces itself from its own 'genre.' While the narrative residue is confined to mere setting of the scene, the dramatic text loses all dramatic teleology. The

---

[32] Ibid., p. 555.
[33] Ibid., pp. 557 and 560.
[34] Ibid., pp. 485 and 550.
[35] Ibid., p. 567.
[36] Ibid., p. 565.
[37] Ibid., p. 481.
[38] See, for instance, ibid., pp. 423 f., 433 f.
[39] Ibid., pp. 500 f.

reader is simply confronted with what is said 'on stage,' and in view of the erosion both of narrative and dramatic forms here, he will feel that the effects of these dialogues get more and more out of control. Consequently, he will be inclined to regard the whole thing as a ridiculous fantasy.

The question is, though, what constitutes the fantasy? While the ramifications of the 'action' become ever more unpredictable, the figure of Bloom becomes ever more dominant. And this figure is shown from a variety of quite astonishing angles. At the very beginning there is a significant, if somewhat indirect allusion to this process, for the stage direction describes Bloom walking through Dublin in the darkness, and looking in convex and concave mirrors which continually change his appearance.[40] This is the theme that is developed throughout the chapter. What Bloom is seems to depend on the perspective from which he is viewed, and his mirror image depends on his environment at the time. It is not surprising then that in the course of the night Bloom becomes Lord Mayor of Dublin[41] and, indeed, the illustrious hero of the whole nation.[42] The beautiful women of Dublin's upper crust go into ecstasies over him[43] and, in the passion of their hero-worship, many commit suicide.[44] However, these same women also take part in a court scene, accusing Bloom of perverse conduct.[45] The question remains open as to whether Bloom is projecting his own feelings onto the accusers, or is trying to rid himself of these feelings by ascribing them to others. In such indeterminate situations, all statements are potential revelations of character. There are innumerable examples of this kind, and if we wanted to list them all, we should virtually have to retell the whole chapter.

The basis of this expansion of Bloom appears to consist of two factors, the one rather more obvious than the other. To deal with the more obvious factor first: in nighttown, everything becomes real for Bloom that is omitted, concealed, or repressed in his daily life. If these aspects of himself are given the same degree of reality as the others, then his life up to now will appear in a somewhat different light. Everyday life, it would seem, has made him into a fragmented character, and only now, in nighttown, can this character once more take on its full potentiality. An obvious case, one might assume, for psychoanalysis. But to preclude any

---

[40] Ibid., p. 414.
[41] Ibid., pp. 455 f.
[42] Ibid., pp. 460 f.
[43] Ibid., pp. 458 f.
[44] Ibid., pp. 467 f.
[45] Ibid., pp. 443 f.

premature analysis, Joyce has already parodied this type of interpretation through the medical student Buck Mulligan, in one of the earlier scenes of the chapter.[46] It seems, then, that the emergence of Bloom's hidden selves is not to be viewed as a symptom of repression, or as a way around the censorship imposed by the superego, but rather as an attempt to realize the potential of a character which in everyday life can never be anything more than partially realized.

This potential becomes richer and richer with the great variety of forms that the hitherto familiar character of Bloom adopts. And, conversely, if one wished to identify the Bloom of everyday life, one would be obliged more and more to pare down this rich virtual character. The everyday Bloom is merely a collection of individual moments in the course of his life—a collection which is infinitely smaller than that of the unlimited possibilities of the Bloom that might be. In the "Circe" chapter, it seems as though each Bloom character is simply a starting-point for a new character, and he himself is present only as the dynamic force producing, linking, and invalidating manifestations of his own potential.

We must now consider how this indeterminate force is translated into all these determinate, if limited forms, and the answer lies in the second, less obvious, factor characterizing the "Circe" chapter. Whatever Bloom reveals of himself is revealed because he is in a particular situation; the forms of his character arise out of changing contexts of life, and so each form is bound to a particular perspective—indeed, this is the only way in which the potential can be realized. With each situation, the character is displayed under specific circumstances, and the faster these change and the more impenetrable the sequence of the individual situations, the more abundant will be the array of possibilities through which the character can reveal itself.

We can now see clearly the function of the extraordinary mode of presentation in this chapter. The drastic reduction of narrative and the abandonment of dramatic coherence intensify the isolation of the individual situations. The disconnectedness virtually makes each one an end in itself, and the reality of the chapter consists in the change from one situation, and hence one manifestation of character, to another. This process is supported by the stage directions—the narrative residue—which relegate the reality of the town of Dublin to a mere theatrical setting. When the obtrusive reality of environment has been cancelled out, the character is inevitably abstracted from all outside restrictions and left free to de-

---

[46] Ibid., pp. 468 f.

velop its vast array of possibilities.[47] However, if the unreality of a changing character is to be presented as the reality of this chapter, then it is essential that the reader should constantly be prevented from joining up the patterns of the text. And precisely because there are so many patterns in this text, coupled with the particular expectations which each produces, the omission of connecting links gives rise to a greater degree of reader-provocation than is normal even in this highly provocative book. Here we have dramatic forms with no dramatic intention; we have narrative traces of an author, but he has concealed himself almost completely behind stage directions that serve no stage and head in no direction. The whole chapter seems to drift on unpredictable tides, and if it is to be brought to anchor, then the only weight heavy and steady enough is that of Bloom's potential character. This, however, seems like some sort of fantastic hallucination, for such a reversal of the possible and the factual simply does not correspond to our own experiences, but ". . . we should never talk about anything if we were limited to talking about those experiences with which we coincide, since speech is already a separation."[48] If one considers the multifarious potential of Bloom as a fantasy, one is already entering into a kind of trap. For such an impression—bordering on a judgment—implies that one knows all about the difference between reality and possibility. Here such differences are extremely blurred—though whether the ultimate effect of this blurring is to perplex or to illuminate must depend on the reactions of the individual reader. What can be said, though, is that an hallucination arising out of pure nonsense would certainly lack any sort of tension, whereas this chapter can scarcely be described as lacking in tension. The high degree of indeterminacy ensures a variety of tensions which, in their turn, will lead the reader to recall to mind—and possibly to see in a different light —all that he had previously learned about Bloom.

This collection of memories is almost certain to be conjured up as a background to the "Circe" chapter. In them the reader will seek the connecting principle denied him, but whatever he may find there, every manifestation of Bloom's character prior to the "Circe" chapter is bound now to seem like the faintest shadow of the vast potential. Who, then, is the real Bloom? Is he what is manifested, or is he the possible? At

---

[47] F. Kermode, *The Sense of an Ending. Studies in the Theory of Fiction* (New York, 1967), p. 141, says with reference to a remark of Sartre's concerning characters in a novel: "The characters . . . ought surely to be 'centres of indeterminacy' and not the slaves of some fake omniscience." In the "Circe" chapter, Bloom's character is revealed most emphatically as a "centre of indeterminacy."

[48] M. Merleau-Ponty, *Phenomenology of Perception,* transl. Colin Smith (New York, 1962), p. 337.

one point Stephen remarks: ". . . the fundamental and the dominant are separated by the greatest possible interval."[49] If we take the fundamental as the potential and the dominant as the manifestations we have in a nutshell the 'argument' of "Circe." Bloom, unlike the traditional character in a novel, has no identity but only a "constitutive instability"[50] which enables him to change character as often as he changes situation. The only enduring feature of Bloom is his changeability. Against this background, the conventional assumption that man can be defined in terms of actions, reactions, urges, fantasies, and embodiments of consciousness appears as pure myth.

There remains the question of the Homeric allusion. Harry Levin's observation that the *Odyssey* and *Ulysses* are parallels "that never meet,"[51] applies to this chapter even more than to most others. While Ulysses's friends were turned into swine by Circe, he himself was able to resist the sorcery thanks to the magic plant Moly given to him by Hermes. Ulysses remained himself because he was able to resist Circe's witchcraft. Bloom becomes himself by being transformed into the possibilities of his own character. Transformation means reduction in the *Odyssey*, and expansion in *Ulysses*.

Of a quite different sort is the stylistic experiment in the chapter originally called "Ithaca," which is of particular interest since it deals with the theme of homecoming. This archetypal situation is presented here as an uninterrupted sequence of questions and answers involving the main characters. To all appearances this interrogation is conducted by an anonymous narrator, who more or less asks himself what Bloom and Stephen think, do, feel, intend, communicate, mean etc., and then proceeds, himself, to give answers that are as wide-ranging as they are detailed. But what exactly is the purpose of this inquiry, and why should the narrator be asking all the questions, since he appears to know all the answers anyway?

The effect of the mode of presentation in this chapter is that it seems constantly to place a barrier between the reader and the events of Bloom's nocturnal homecoming that are to be narrated; instead of describing these events, it appears to be continually interrupting them. In this way, the characters in the novel seem to fade into the distance—espe-

---

[49] Joyce, *Ulysses,* p. 479.
[50] This is the translation of a term used by Ortega y Gasset to describe the given nature of man. See details in Kermode, *Sense of an Ending,* pp. 140 f., footnote.
[51] H. Levin, *James Joyce. A Critical Introduction* (New York, [2]1960), p. 71.

cially since each question is assigned an answer which is so loaded with precise detail that the reader's comprehension is in danger of being utterly swamped. This tends to divert the reader's attention away from the events and onto the curious nature of this question-and-answer process. For, obviously, the intention of the chapter must lie in this and not in the details of the nocturnal events. But if the mode of presentation sets aside rather than describes the events, and obtrudes on the reader instead of orientating him, then the only justification for this 'going against the grain' must be that it exposes something which generally would be obscured by the mode of presentation.

Let us consider an example. When Bloom comes home, he puts some water on the stove because he wants to have a shave. The question-and-answer process now concerns the boiling of the water:

> What concomitant phenomenon took place in the vessel of liquid by the agency of fire?
> The phenomenon of ebullition. Fanned by a constant updraught of ventilation between the kitchen and the chimneyflue, ignition was communicated from the faggots of precombustible fuel to polyhedral masses of bituminous coal, containing in compressed mineral form the foliated fossilised decidua of primeval forests which had in turn derived their vegetative existence from the sun, primal source of heat (radiant), transmitted through omnipresent luminiferous diathermanous ether. Heat (convected), a mode of motion developed by such combustion, was constantly and increasingly conveyed from the source of calorification to the liquid contained in the vessel, being radiated through the uneven unpolished dark surface of the metal iron, in part reflected, in part absorbed, in part transmitted, gradually raising the temperature of the water from normal to boiling point, a rise in temperature expressible as the result of an expenditure of 72 thermal units needed to raise 1 pound of water from 50° to 212° Fahrenheit.[52]

The amount of scientific data—in this chapter a typical feature which becomes even more complicated elsewhere—shows how difficult it is to give the required reason for the phenomenon in question.

An impression akin to fantasy is evoked by the chain of cause and effect which, instead of going straight back to the primal cause, seems only to bring out more and more dependent factors. The more precise the description of these factors, the further into the distance recedes the primal cause and the more aware we become of the unexplainability of

---

[52] Joyce, *Ulysses,* p. 634.

what is to be explained. As the narrator asks more and more questions, the answers demonstrate not his knowledge so much as the unobtainability of the right answers—and this is emphasized by the very preciseness of what *is* known. Thus the tendency underlying this question-and-answer process is one that aims at showing the degree of indeterminability inherent in all phenomena. It is scarcely surprising then that new quèstions are constantly thrown up which are meant to limit the amount of indeterminacy, but instead—thanks to their very precision—in fact increase it.

One's immediate reaction to the mass of scientific detail offered in answer to often quite banal questions is bewilderment. And this is so because a simple process is given a precise description. Obviously, then, our normal conception of such processes must be less precise and consequently seems to be straightforward. Why should it be made complicated? Perhaps in order to show the extent to which our knowledge and our decisions are based primarily on pragmatic considerations? However, it is only in this way that we can in fact form conceptions of everyday phenomena. The question-and-answer process makes us aware that the degree of indeterminacy is irreducible, thus indicating that all the semiconsistent conceptions we have of everyday phenomena can only become conceptions because they ignore the unexplainability of reality. They are, in this sense, a fiction.

Now if indeterminacy is only to be removed by means of fiction, the reader finds the ground cut away from beneath his feet whenever he realizes this. The "Ithaca" chapter keeps maneuvering him into a position from which he can escape only by taking up a definite attitude. He might decide that the chain of ironic answers forms a parody of scientific pedantry. But, as Northrop Frye states in another context, the ironic solution is: "the negative pole of the allegorical one. Irony presents a human conflict which . . . is unsatisfactory and incomplete unless we see in it a significance beyond itself. . . . What that significance is, irony does not say: it leaves that question up to the reader or audience."[53] This is the sort of irony we find in the "Ithaca" chapter, which uses its ironic elements to give the reader responsibility for finding his own solution. This, of course, involves interpreting, and in order to ensure that interpretation be kept in its proper perspective, certain warning signals are built into the text. To the question: "What qualifying considerations allayed his [i.e., Bloom's] perturbations?" comes the answer: "The dif-

---

[53] N. Frye, "The Road of Excess," in *Myth and Symbol. Critical Approaches and Applications,* ed. B. Slote (Lincoln, [2]1964), p. 14.

ficulties of interpretation since the significance of any event followed its occurrence as variably as the acoustic report followed the electrical discharge and of counterestimating against an actual loss by failure to interpret the total sum of possible losses proceeding originally from a successful interpretation."[54]

The main problem of interpretation, then, lies in the fact that the meaning of any one event is incalculably variable. The image of the electrical discharge, which disperses its sound waves in all directions, shows that every event, as soon as it happens, sets up a whole spectrum of meanings. If we try to extract one of these meanings and pass it off as *the* meaning of the event, then automatically we are shutting out all the other meanings.

Normally we understand by a successful interpretation one that conveys a specific meaning. But according to the answer given here, an interpretation can only be successful if it takes into account the "possible losses" caused by interpretation—in other words, if it succeeds in returning to the phenomenon interpreted its whole spectrum of possible meanings. And this, as the answer makes clear, is difficult.

Meanings have a heuristic character which, particularly in these scientifically couched answers, bring out the many-sidedness of the phenomena described. In such a description, the phenomena will appear all the richer in meaning if no one meaning dominates. In the "Ithaca" chapter, aspects are not static but seem to be moving, offering an infinitely wider range of perspectives than could be offered if the author were merely to present the reader with his own classified interpretation of the phenomenon. And however confused the reader may feel through this bewildering multiplicity, at least he now has the chance of experiencing for himself something of the essential character of the phenomena. The heightened indeterminacy enables him to view so many different aspects from so many different standpoints, and from the interaction of these aspects and perspectives he himself continually and dynamically formulates the meaning. In this way it is possible for the reader to experience the phenomenon more as itself than as the expression of something else.

Joyce called this chapter "Ithaca." But what sort of homecoming is this? For Ulysses it meant the end of his adventurous journey, with all its attendant dangers and sufferings, and also his reckoning with the suitors; but for Bloom the homecoming passes with innumerable trivial acts and a fantastic, if impotent, condemnation of all Molly's lovers. No one is excepted from this universal anathema; it applies ultimately to

[54] Joyce, *Ulysses*, p. 637.

marriage as an institution and even to Bloom himself. "What then remains after this holocaust? Only himself with his desires—not as husband or householder but as Leopold Bloom, an Einziger with no Eigentum."[55] Yet again, then, we have in the Homeric allusion a parallel which, if anything, runs in the opposite direction from the original, showing up the individuality of Bloom against the background of what the reader might expect from the archetypal homecoming.

The stylistic experiments of *Ulysses* end with Molly Bloom's much discussed interior monologue, which has the difficult task of bringing to an end an action which essentially cannot be ended. Here the old familiar problem of how a novel is to end appears in its most radical form. The end cannot be presented as a completion, for whose completion should it denote? The conventional rounding-off is clearly impossible here, and so too is its companion piece, the slow fade-out: for after what the experiments have revealed, this would be nothing but a sign of resignation and, in the long run, a meaning grafted on. Joyce had resolved that he would finish the novel with the word "Yes,"[56] and whatever feelings one may have about this intention, the tenor of the whole is one of affirmation. Thus the end had to incorporate the movement of the novel as a whole, enabling the reader to forget that it was the end.

Molly Bloom as the Penelope of *Ulysses*, closes an action that began with Telemachus. It is not only in this external sense that we have a movement doubling back on itself; the interior monologue also shows how a return to memory becomes a new present. The total lack of punctuation suggests a continuum. The ego is united with itself, addressing to itself its own remembered past, and from this world of private reference, the reader is to a large extent excluded. To him, this ego appears less as a continuum than as a kaleidoscopic juggling of fragmentary facets. The framework of the monologue is given by a number of external details. Molly notes that Bloom has come home, has obviously brought someone with him, and finally goes to bed. The alarm clock tells her the time, and in the pale light of early morning she sees the flowers on the wallpaper, which remind her of stars.[57] The external impulses keep losing themselves in the memories they evoke, and these in turn broaden out into events that have not taken place. The present of this nocturnal

---

[55] F. Budgen, *James Joyce and the Making of Ulysses* (Bloomington, 1960), p. 261.

[56] See S. Gilbert, *James Joyce's Ulysses* (New York, [7]1960), p. 403, and also a statement of Joyce's quoted by A. W. Litz, *The Art of James Joyce,* p. 46.

[57] See Joyce, *Ulysses,* p. 740.

hour is also overshadowed by a different present, and yet remembered past and existing present are not confronted one with the other; instead, what is remembered actually becomes the present simply because it has been freed from the conditions that originally called it into being. It takes on an existence of its own. But in contrast to its original state, the past now is liberated from all restrictions of time and space, and so situations flow into one another elliptically, regaining the openness of outcome which they had been deprived of long ago in the past.

Here, then, we have the first characteristic of the monologue. Not only does it bring back past life but it also frees it from its past determinacy. Individual situations which had formed links in the chain of the course of life now become open again, once more assuming their inherent richness of potential. The monologue eradicates the teleology of this course of life. It does not convey past and present in the style of an autobiography that is to deliver the meaning of the life concerned, but it shows that the life concerned is like a chain of coincidences if one bears in mind all the possibilities that were inherent in the situations before they became linked together. Once they are released from their specific life-order, situations can be seen through the perspectives of other situations which, through limitations of time and space in 'real' life, had not even the remotest connection. Thus the past remembered suggests completely new combinations, and Molly's own life comes back to her with a surplus of possibilities which can at least give the illusion of a different life-order.

Just like the other stylistic patterns in *Ulysses,* the interior monologue here breaks situations up into fragments and withholds from the reader any principle that might bind them together. In view of this disconnectedness, all events of the past, all future wishes, all lost opportunities are placed on the same level, so that Molly's life, as she recalls it, appears to be in a constant state of transformation. But what is transformed into what? Normally in a novel we are able to define the changes and to hold onto the similarities as our connecting-points, but here there seems only to be perplexity. If the remembered past were brought back as a sort of compensation for frustrated desires, then one could orientate Molly's memories through her particular situation at this particular hour of the night. And if it is a matter of returning to that stage in the past where it was still an unresolved present, then we should have a constant unwinding of retrospective possibilities—like a film being run backward. But neither of these standpoints is clearly discernible in Molly's monologue. She does not seem to be looking back at the past from the standpoint of the present, or to be returning to the past in order to gaze at her situation at five o'clock this morning. As a person, in fact, she seems to disappear behind the richness of her own life. The more indeterminate her character threatens to become, the more dynamic is the impression we have of her life: dynamic, because the reader is confronted with more and more viewpoints to which the individual facets are to be related, or into which they can be transformed. As the monologue does not accentuate any one organizing principle behind all the transformations, these convey an impression of continual expansion—and indeed suggest the inexhaustibility of the past—precisely because there is no point of convergence. The reader finds himself constantly driven by the urge to group things together, to unravel the tangle, but any attempt to do so will tend to reflect his own personal preferences rather than any supposed 'objective' meaning. But perhaps the meaning is the reflection of these preferences.

There remains the question of the Homeric parallel. With the past returning into the present and the present releasing the past from its determinacy there arises the idea of the recurrent cycle. Molly would then be even more than Penelope—she would be Mother Earth herself. But her monologue by no means fulfills the conditions of the mythic cycle. It lacks that essential element—the fact that when things have passed through all the different stages and forms of their realization, they return once more to themselves. It is true that at the end Molly returns to the point where she began—she recalls the first love scene with Bloom—but even the recollected love scenes in this monologue are far more like serial variations than a cyclic return. Molly cannot be reduced to any of her aspects, or even to her love-memories. Nowhere does her whole being come to light, but it is this very emerging of aspects that brings out the driving force which constitutes the inner being. And it is only fitting that the interior monologue should end the novel in a form which sets a life free from all the restrictions of—precisely—its form.

III

The Function of the Experiments in Style

The implication of a novel written in several different styles is that the view expressed by each style is to be taken only as one possible facet of everyday reality. The accumulation of facets has the effect of making these seem like a mere suggestion to the reader as to how he might observe reality. The perspectives provided by the various chapters of the novel abruptly join up, overlap, are segmented, even clash, and through their very density they begin to overtax the reader's vision. The density of the presentational screen, the confusing montage and its interplay of perspectives, the invitation to the reader to look at identical incidents from many conflicting points of view—all this makes it extremely difficult for the reader to find his way. The novel refuses to divulge any way of connecting up this interplay of perspectives, and so the reader is forced to provide his own liaison. This has the inevitable consequence that reading becomes a process of selection, with the reader's own imagination providing the criteria for the selection. For the text of *Ulysses* only offers the conditions that make it possible to conceive of this everyday world—conditions which each reader will exploit in his own way.

What does the achievement of the various modes of presentation consist of? First, one can say that they bring to bear a form of observation which underlies the very structure of perception. For we "have the experience of a world, not understood as a system of relations which wholly determine each event, but as an open totality the synthesis of which is inexhaustible. . . . From the moment that experience—that is, the opening on to our *de facto* world—is recognized as the beginning of knowledge, there is no longer any way of distinguishing a level of *a priori* truths and one of factual ones, what the world must necessarily be and what it actually is."[58] Through their countless offshoots, the different styles of *Ulysses* preclude any meaning directed toward integration, but they also fall into a pattern of observation that contains within itself the possibility of a continual extension. It is the very abundance of perspectives that conveys the abundance of the world under observation.

The effect of this continual change is dynamic, unbounded as it is by any recognizable teleology. From one chapter to the next the 'horizon' of everyday life is altered and constantly shifted from one area to another through the links which the reader tries to establish between the chapter styles. Each chapter prepares the 'horizon' for the next, and it is the process of reading that provides the continual overlapping and interweaving of the views presented by each of the chapters. The reader is stimulated into filling the 'empty spaces' between the chapters in order to group them into a coherent whole. This process, however, has the following results: The conceptions of everyday life which the reader forms undergo constant modifications in the reading process. Each chapter provides a certain amount of expectation concerning the next chapter. However, the gaps of indeterminacy which open up between the chapters tend to diminish the importance of these expectations as a means of orientat-

[58] Merleau-Ponty, *Phenomenology*, pp. 219 and 221.

ing the reader. As the process continues, a 'feedback' effect is bound to develop, arising from the new chapter and reacting back upon the preceding, which under this new and somewhat unexpected impression is subjected to modifications in the reader's mind. The more frequently the reader experiences this effect, the more cautious and the more differentiated will be his expectations, as they arise through his realization of the text. Thus what has just been read modifies what had been read before, so that the reader himself operates the 'fusion of the horizons', with the result that he produces an experience of reality which is real precisely because it happens, without being subjected to any representational function. Reality, then, is a process of realization necessitating the reader's involvement, because only the reader can bring it about. This is why the chapters are not arranged in any sequence of situations that might be complementary to one another; in fact, the unforeseen difference of style rather seems to make each chapter into a turning-point as opposed to a continuation. And as the whole novel consists of such turning-points the process of reading unfolds itself as a continual modification of all previous conceptions, thus inverting the traditional teleological structure of the novel.

IV

The Archetypes

What part do the Homeric allusions play in the overall effect of the work? Do they, or do the archetypes recognizable in *Ulysses,* offer a means of comprehending the novel and ultimately giving it a representative meaning after all? It must be said that the intention underlying the stylistic experiments does not seem to point in that direction. The Homeric allusions vary in density and directness. It is worth noting that they always take on an ironic note when they are clear and direct; Bloom's cigar as Ulysses's spear is a typical example.[59] Such ironic traits draw attention to differences, and however these may be interpreted they are bound to prevent us from equating *Ulysses* with the Homeric parallel. At the same time, the allusions—assuming we take note of them in the first place—draw the archaic world into the everyday life of the novel, though the outline of the ancient story cannot be regarded as encompassing this life.

We might say that the main function of the allusions is to draw attention to the virtual features of the two worlds. At times the Homeric

---

[59] For such parallels, see R. Ellmann, "The Divine Nobody," in *Twelve Original Essays on Great English Novelists,* ed. Ch. Shapiro (Detroit, 1960), pp. 244 f., esp. 247.

myth is even inverted, with the episodes from the *Odyssey* to be understood as pointers to specific empirical or everyday aspects of life. Everyday appearances are not to be referred back to some underlying meaning; we proceed from the myth and its meaning and see the variety of
appearances into which it can be broken up. Things which remain implicit or even totally concealed in the *Odyssey* are revealed in *Ulysses,*
and the change of perspective—from Homer to the present, and from the
present back to the archaic world—enables both past and present to illuminate one another.

Through the allusions is projected a background that embraces the
whole of European literature from Homer to Shakespeare. The reader
is provoked into a process of recognition, for recognition, like grouping,
is part of his natural disposition and is an elementary activity in reading.
As he recognizes the implications of the allusions, he tries to equate them
with the events now being set before him, but he finds that they do not
actually coincide. There is just enough common ground to make him
aware of the differences, and the process of equating and differentiating
is one that will be both disturbing and stimulating.

If *Ulysses* does not hark back to the *Odyssey,* and Joyce does not—so
to speak—rise out of Homer, then the various transformations which the
reader feels constantly forced to experience will not cease with the establishment of a common pattern. As we have already seen, the whole structure and stylistic texture of the novel is geared to such transformations,
and a common pattern, of whatever type, would run counter to its basic
intentions. The allusions offer a background which, in its own way, remains as fluid as the foreground it sets off, and this very fluidity is the
fundamental prerequisite for the effect of the novel.

What of the archetypes themselves? To what extent can they be described as elements of a recurrent myth? The homecoming, the city, and
the quest[60]—these are three archetypes which constitute an important
structural pattern in the novel and which make *Ulysses* into a sort of
glorified epic (the city being a considerably rarer archetypal ingredient of
epic literature). In fact, the closest link between *Ulysses* and the *Odyssey*
is the homecoming, although Bloom's homecoming does, of course, take
place within the city. The quest already shows external differences, insofar as Telemachus searched for his father, while Bloom searches for his
son. In the *Odyssey* there is no equivalent to the city as "new Bloomusa-

[60] See N. Frye, *Anatomy of Criticism,* pp. 118 f. and 141.

lem."[61] If we consider the closest link—the homecoming—we will find, just as we did with the direct Homeric allusions, that the similarities serve in fact to point up the differences. For Ulysses the homecoming means the end of his sufferings, whereas for Bloom—the "conscious re-actor against the void incertitude,"[62] as he is called in the "Ithaca" chapter—it brings nothing but a heightened sensitivity to the unforesee-able; even more significantly, there is no recognizable parallel anywhere in the novel between characters or archetypal situations. But since the title indicates a connection, we automatically become aware of the dif-ferences.

If one looks at Bloom against the background of Ulysses, one is im-mediately struck by two things: the difference in stature between the humble citizen of Dublin and the Homeric hero, and the many features of Bloom's conduct that either go beyond or fall short of what we know of Ulysses's character. Bearing in mind that Joyce considered Ulysses himself to be the most comprehensive specimen of human conduct,[63] one must also say that Bloom adds a few variants of his own to this 'per-fection'—though of course without ever becoming more 'perfect' than Ulysses. Clearly, Bloom lacks most of Ulysses's characteristics, and vice versa, but however far Bloom may fall below the exalted standards of the Homeric hero, the very allusion of the title makes us think of Bloom as a Ulysses, and so offsets those elements of the character which pre-vailing conventions prevented Homer from dealing with. Human con-duct in Homer appears rigidly stylized against that of the everyday Dub-liner, while Bloom's conduct (and that of the other characters, too) is as fluid as the other is rigid. And so it would seem that the Homeric paral-lel is drawn, not to demonstrate the hopeless decline of the modern world compared with its former state, but to communicate the enormous variety of possibilities of human conduct. By evoking and simultaneous-ly deforming archetypal patterns, Joyce succeeds in conveying and throw-ing into relief the uniqueness of Bloom as a citizen of the modern world. The Homeric archetype provides a starting-point for this individualiza-tion of Joyce's Ulysses [i.e., Bloom]. Just as a cartoonist takes an exist-ing face and then distorts its features in order to bring out its unique-ness, so too does Joyce (though obviously in a far less obtrusive man-ner) take an existing form and manipulate it this way and that in order to convey its singularity. Indeed, it is the very fact that Bloom can be pulled and pushed in this way that sets him apart from the ideality of

---

[61] Joyce, *Ulysses,* p. 461.
[62] Ibid., p. 694.
[63] See R. Ellmann, *Joyce,* p. 430.

Ulysses and makes him recognizable as an individual human being, with all the complications and uncertainties thereby involved. The archetype is the general mould; the form Joyce extracts from that mould is the unique character of Bloom.

There is, then, a form of interaction between the Homeric archetype and its modern counterpart. As Joyce evolves constantly changing patterns from the former, so Ulysses's reactions assume a paradigmatic character, and the homecoming, for instance, is transformed into an 'ideal' homecoming. However, one must bear in mind the fact that the 'archetype'[64] does not exist in itself, but must be brought into existence by a realization. It is, so to speak, an empty frame that requires the concrete powers of style and language to provide the picture. The archetype, then, can take on as many forms as there are forms of presentation, so that we cannot really say even that the homecoming in the *Odyssey* is *the* archetype. It is only one rendering among many possible renderings, and, in the light of all the variations apparent in the novel, it becomes retrospectively as restricted as they are. The archetype as such remains a structured blank that bears all potential realizations within itself and provides the basis for all its own subsequent variations.

Clearly, if archetypal situations are potentially subject to so many different presentations, then no one presentation can claim representative significance. For this insight, again we are indebted to the Homeric parallel: by reducing the *Odyssey* homecoming to the level of one idealized realization, *Ulysses* shows all its limitations—and the same applies to the other archetypes of city and quest. Dublin is no heavenly Jerusalem, but as "Bloomusalem"[65] it is the place of exile of one of the unredeemed; the quest is characterized by the uncertainty of what is found, for although Bloom and Stephen finish under one roof, Molly's thoughts are already on relations with the young 'intellectual,'[66] Bloom's son. In each case, the recurrent archetypal situation lacks the expected archetypal fulfillment—it is left open-ended.

The function of the archetype in relation to the presentational strategy of the novel is, then, to offer a kind of framework. Homecoming, city, and quest are the frames within which the picture of everyday life can be

---

[64] N. Frye has a very different conception of the archetype. The most succinct definition I could find in his writings is in the essay "The Archetypes of Literature," which is reprinted in his collection of essays: *Fables of Identity. Studies in Poetic Mythology* (New York, 1963). "The myth is the central informing power that gives archetypal significance to the ritual and archetypal narrative to the oracle. Hence the myth *is* the archetype, though it might be convenient to say myth only when referring to narrative, and archetype when speaking of significance" (p. 15).

[65] See Joyce, *Ulysses*, p. 461.

[66] See also Gilbert, *James Joyce's Ulysses*, pp. 386 and 394.

put together. This, of course, does not mean that the composition is determined by the frame. The mode of presentation ensures that the countless literary and historical allusions will not be marshalled into a single cut-and-dried meaning—not for the sake of making the allusions appear meaningless, but purely in order to preserve the infinite potential of their meaning.

V

The Reader's Quest and the Formation of Illusion

If the archetypes provide the action with a frame, the different styles and allusions to literature, both ancient and modern, give the reader more than enough scope to piece together his own picture. David Daiches has observed that: "If Joyce could coin one kaleidoscopic word with an infinite series of meanings, a word saying everything in one instant yet leaving its infinity of meanings reverberating and mingling in the mind, he would have reached his ideal." [67] Certainly this is the direction in which Joyce was striving, and as the limitations of each separate meaning are uncovered, giving rise to new meanings, so the reader is made to feel the overall inaccessibility of the events and characters in question. Any presentation implies selection, and any selection implies omission. Here the omissions lead to new selections in the form of new styles, but as the styles and selections increase, so does the range of implication and omission. The more determinate the presentation, the more 'reality' there is to catch up on, but in his very efforts to catch up, the reader produces in himself the awareness that the world he is trying to comprehend transcends the acts of comprehension of which he is capable.

The composition of *Ulysses* mirrors this impression. Edmund Wilson has summed up both the reader's impression and the structure of the novel as follows: "I doubt whether any human memory is capable, on a first reading, of meeting the demands of 'Ulysses.' And when we reread it, we start in at any point, as if it were indeed something solid like a city which actually existed in space and which could be entered from any direction." [68] The reader is virtually free to choose his own direction, but he will not be able to work his way through every possible perspective, for the number of these is far beyond the capacity of any one man's naturally selective perception. If the novel sometimes gives the impression of unreality, this is not because it presents unreality, but simply because it swamps us with aspects of reality that overburden our limited

---

[67] D. Daiches, *The Novel and the Modern World* (Chicago, [4]1965), p. 129.

[68] E. Wilson, *Axel's Castle. A Study in the Imaginative Literature of 1870–1930* (London: The Fontana Library, 1961), p. 169.

powers of absorption. We are forced to make our own selections from the perspectives offered and, consequently, in accordance with our own personal disposition, to formulate ideas that have their roots in *some* of the signs and situations confronting us.

This form of reading is predetermined by the novel itself, with its network of superimposed patterns that evoke constantly changing 'pictures' of everyday life. Each reading is a starting-point for the composition of such 'pictures', and indeed the whole process of reading *Ulysses* is a kind of composition. (The same, it is true, can be said of all reading, but in the case of this novel the demands made on the reader's creativity are far greater than normal.) No one picture is representative, and one cannot even say that any one pattern is in itself determinate or determinant, for the different sections of the text only go so far as to offer signs that can be grouped together to form a context. The patterns are, as it were, transitory units which are necessary if everyday life is to be experienced, but are in no way binding as to the nature of the experience.

Each 'picture' composed out of each pattern represents one possible meaning of the text concerned, but the reader will not be content to accept each 'picture' as an end in itself. He will search for a 'complete picture' of everyday life, and this is precisely what the novel withholds from him. The patterns offer him nothing but the conditions for and variations of the presentability of everyday life. There is no overriding tendency, and the mass of details presents itself to the reader to organize in accordance with his own acts of comprehension. This, in turn, demands a heightened degree of participation on the reader's part. The novel thus places itself in the category of "cool media,"[69] as McLuhan called those texts and other media which, through their indeterminacy, allow and even demand a high degree of participation.

Herein lies the main difference between *Ulysses* and the tradition of the novel. Instead of providing an illusory coherence of the reality it presents, this novel offers only a potential presentation, the working out of which has to be done actively by the reader. He is not led into a ready-made world of meaning, but is made to search for this world. Thus reading itself has an archetypal structure which, just like the archetypes in the text, is unable to lead to any defined goal. It is a quest which brings to the surface the possibility of any number of findings. Thus it is possible to discover many different 'pictures' of the everyday world, but they will never converge into a defined picture—and it is this very fact that compels the reader to continue his search. Even though he will never find the object of his search, on his way he will meet with a vast array of possible conceptions, through which the reality of every-

[69] See M. McLuhan, *Understanding Media. The Extensions of Man* (New York, ³1966), pp. 22 f.

day life will come alive in a corresponding number of ways. As these conceptions are not joined together, every picture remains representative of no more than one aspect of reality. The reading process unfolds as a "categorical aspection,"[70] in the sense that the aspects of reality that group together into a 'picture' are continually merging and diverging, so that the reader can experience that reality as he goes along, but being thus entangled in it he can never hope to encompass it all.

The reader, however, will still be continually tempted to try to establish some consistency in all the signs, patterns, fragments, etc. But whenever we establish consistency, "illusion takes over."[71] "Illusion is whatever is fixed or definable, and reality is best understood as its negation: whatever reality is, it's not *that*."[72] The truth of this statement becomes apparent as one reads *Ulysses*. At first the inconsistency of the stylistic patterns and structures impels the reader to formulate illusions, because only by joining things together can he comprehend an unfamiliar experience. But even while he is in the process of linking things up, he is bringing into being all the other possibilities of the text that defy integration; and these in turn proceed to overshadow the consistency he had begun to establish, so that in the process of illusion-forming the reader also creates the latent destruction of those very illusions. He will begin to distrust the convenient patterns he has been building and will eventually himself perceive that they are nothing but the instruments he uses to grasp and pare down the mass of detail. Now the very fact that it is he who produces and destroys the illusions makes it impossible for him to stand aside and view 'reality' from a distance—the only reality for him to view is the one he is creating. He is involved in it, in precisely the same way that he gets involved in 'real life' situations. Thus for many Joyce readers, 'interpretation' is a form of refuge-seeking—an effort to reclaim the ground which has been cut from under their feet. Perhaps Bloom's attempts to instruct his wife contain the most succinct summary of Joyce's whole method:

> With what success had he attempted direct instruction? She followed not all, a part of the whole, gave attention with interest, comprehended with surprise, with care repeated, with greater difficulty remembered, forgot with ease, with misgiving remembered, rerepeated with error.
>
> What system had proved more effective?
>
> Indirect suggestion implicating self-interest.[73]

---

[70] For the use of this term in describing esthetic objects, see V. C. Aldrich, *Philosophy of Art* (Englewood Cliffs, 1963), pp. 21–24.

[71] E. H. Gombrich, *Art and Illusion* (London, ²1962), p. 278.

[72] Frye, *Anatomy of Criticism*, pp. 169 f.

[73] Joyce, *Ulysses*, pp. 647 f.

9

DIALOGUE OF THE UNSPEAKABLE:
Ivy Compton-Burnett:
A Heritage and Its History

I

In her essay "Conversation et sous-conversation" (1956), Nathalie Sarraute wrote: ". . . pour la plupart d'entre nous, les oeuvres de Joyce et de Proust se dressent déjà dans le lointain comme les témoins d'une époque révolue. Le temps n'est pas éloigné où l'on ne visitera plus que sous la conduite d'un guide, parmi les groupes d'enfants des écoles, dans un silence respectueux et avec une admiration un peu morne, ces monuments historiques."[1] The revolutionary experiments in form conducted by 'modern' writers have already taken on the distant luster of classical works of art, with an exemplariness sufficiently historical for it to be recognized even by schoolchildren (and perhaps only by them and their mentors!). In the same context, Nathalie Sarraute comments on Virginia Woolf's theory of the novel, developed during the nineteen-twenties, that it was permeated by a naive confidence which reminded one of the "innocence d'un autre âge."[2]

[1] Nathalie Sarraute, *L'Ere du Soupçon: Essais sur le Roman* (Paris, 1956), p. 82.
[2] Ibid., p. 81. Ivy Compton-Burnett once said the following in an interview:
Interviewer: What about Virginia Woolf?
Miss C.-B.: Well, is she really a novelist?
Interviewer: It's an open question, perhaps.
Miss C.-B.: I admire her use of words, I enjoy most of her work, but I wouldn't actually call her a good novelist.

Nathalie Sarraute's detachment from novels which can still be regarded as modern, arises from the conviction that new forms must be found, if hitherto uncharted territories of human reality are to be communicated. In this she has touched on a question that has long preoccupied literary critics—namely, whether the modern novel after Joyce and Proust can possibly find any new variations on the theme of probing and presenting reality. As evidence of such a variation, she quotes Ivy Compton-Burnett,[3] who in a long series of similar novels since the middle 'twenties has been using certain techniques which are beginning to change the conception of the modern novel handed down to us by Joyce and Virginia Woolf. Any consideration of Ivy Compton-Burnett's novels must therefore keep in view the whole panoply of modern narrative patterns in order to gauge the extent of her achievement. The choice of *A Heritage and Its History* (1959)[4] as a subject for discussion arose out of the question whether the relative uniformity of her novels would not rob them of their effectiveness after a number of years. If a novel written in 1959 can have virtually the same impact as one written in the 'twenties, then clearly she must have found an inexhaustible form to illuminate the social conditions that constitute her field of exploration.

II

Ivy Compton-Burnett's novels consist of a continuous succession of dialogues, and her constant use of this form has strong repercussions on the narrative itself: the direct speech automatically sets the events of the novel in the immediate present. While we normally expect a narrative to offer us a vantage point from which we can judge events in their totality, here the dialogue thwarts our expectations by ensuring that events remain firmly embedded in the present, deprived of the usual perspective of hindsight. In the "Vorsatz" to the *Magic Mountain,* Thomas Mann wrote: "stories must be in the past, and the more in the past they are, one might say, the better it is for them, in their capacity as stories, and for the narrator, the whispering wizard of the imperfect tense."[5] Dropping the imperfect tense means abandoning the privileged position that has always been virtually a component part of narrative.[6] Of course real-

"Interview with Miss Compton-Burnett," *A Review of English Literature* 3 (1962): 103.
[3] See Sarraute, *L'Ère du Soupçon,* pp. 119 ff.
[4] Ivy Compton-Burnett, *A Heritage and Its History* (London, 1959).
[5] Thomas Mann, *Der Zauberberg* (Berlin, 1956), p. 5.
[6] Concerning the importance of the imperfect for narrative, there is already a great deal of controversial literature. See Käte Hamburger, "Das epische Präteritum," *Deutsche Vierteljahrsschrift für Literaturwissenschaft und Geistesgeschichte* 27 (1953): 329 ff.; Käte Hamburger, *Die Logik der Dichtung* (Stuttgart, 1957); H. R. Jauss, *Zeit und Erinnerung in Marcel Prousts*

istic novels written in the past tense usually have some passages of dialogue which lessen the distance between the reader and the events and characters, bringing them out of the narrative background and into the immediate present; but such conversations are usually closely interwoven with circumstances and situations already 'completed' and serve simply to dramatize them in order to make them more vivid. The change to the present tense brings about a direct confrontation between reader and characters, whereas the past tense has no such immediacy. "When we . . . narrate, we leave direct speech and go into another world that is past or fictitious."[7] The past indicates completeness, the present leaves the outcome open. So long as the dialogue serves only to animate the narrated world, its function is to vary the emphasis given to different aspects of the situation and characters—it is a way of throwing them into relief. But if the situation and characters are presented almost exclusively through their dialogue, the presentation must inevitably remain on a single level—and this is the case with *A Heritage and Its History*. There is no indication as to what is and is not of prime significance; we must decide that for ourselves. Nor is there an integrated, self-contained world such as was offered by the nineteenth-century realistic novel, for integration and self-containment of this sort are essentially a fiction, not to be found in the open-ended world of reality. In this respect, the dialogue in *A Heritage and Its History* is a stylistic device used for no less a purpose than to produce a 'real-life' situation such as no narrative could ever produce, because it is barred from reality by its fictitious completeness.

The panorama of social and historical events, which even in Joyce and Virginia Woolf still forms a differentiated background to the novel, is shut out by the dialogue technique. All that remains of a shrunken outside reality is an old house, but even this is not actually described; it is simply alluded to in the course of the various conversations held by characters that are quite devoid of any environmental setting. This insulation of the characters endows their endless conversations with a strange sort of incalculability, insofar as they can never be fixed to any consistent set of circumstances.

This impression is reinforced by the author's almost total withdrawal

---

'*A la recherche du temps perdu*' (Heidelberg, 1955), pp. 19 ff.; Franz Stanzel, "Episches Präteritum, erlebte Rede, historisches Präsens," *Deutsche Vierteljahrsschrift für Literaturwissenschaft und Geistesgeschichte* 33 (1959): 1 ff.; K. A. Ott, "Über eine 'logische' Interpretation der Dichtung," *Germanisch-Romanische Monatsschrift*, N.F. 11 (1961): 214 ff.; Roy Pascal, "Tense and the Novel," *Modern Language Review* 57 (1962): 1 ff.; Harald Weinrich, *Tempus. Besprochene und erzählte Welt* (Stuttgart, 1964), pp. 44 ff. and others. For the purpose of this essay, the imperfect is regarded only as the means of presentation of a completed fictional narrative.
[7] Weinrich, *Tempus,* p. 91.

from the proceedings. Those traces of the author's[8] presence that are there consist only of the occasional, neutral observation: "said Sir Edwin," "said Graham to Ralph"[9] etc. But by no means all the speakers are identified in this way; very often there is no indication at all as to who is speaking. And so the author's sporadic *inquit* interpolations seem to be there in order to help the reader, but the very sparseness and neutrality of the 'help' are liable to cause more bewilderment than enlightenment: we know the author is there, but if she is there, why doesn't she tell us more—for instance, about the motives that give rise to the conversations? The implication is either that she does not know them herself, or that she wants to withhold them from us. Either way, we are made more conscious of what she does *not* tell us, and as a result the characters in the novel take on a degree of independence from the author that is not dissimilar to the gap between the characters and the reader. And the more independent they are, the less we know of them,[10] for we have nothing but their own words to understand them by, and—just as in real life—a person's statements void of any background are liable as much to obscure as to enlighten. At most, the author's occasional interpolations indicate to the reader that she was simply the witness of a conversation that he, the reader, will be more directly involved in, having to identify the speakers himself. The independent existence of the characters means that the reader cannot be prepared for what he is about to 'overhear'— he can only be a witness like the author, left to draw his own conclusions.

This observation is borne out by the fact that the author does not show a preference for any one character in the novel. Thus there is no central perspective such as the novel since Henry James has usually offered its readers as a means of orientation.[11] The main character in *A Heritage and Its History* offers only one viewpoint, and this is rapidly cancelled out by those of the other characters. There simply is no hierarchy of perspectives, and this impression is reinforced at the end of the

---

[8] Here I have deliberately used the term 'author.' This refers to the *author's voice in fiction*, which is not to be confused with the author who has written the novel. For this important distinction, see Wayne C. Booth, *The Rhetoric of Fiction* (Chicago, 1961); see especially Part II, "The Author's Voice in Fiction," pp. 169 ff.; and Part III, "Impersonal Narration," pp. 271 ff. Concerning the distance between author and characters in Ivy Compton-Burnett's novels, see also Paul West, *The Modern Novel* (London, 1963), p. 68.

[9] Compton-Burnett, *A Heritage*, pp. 148 f.

[10] E. M. Forster, *Aspects of the Novel* (London, 1958), p. 61, still regarded it as an essential quality of characters in a novel, that they should be completely knowable. This is the difference between them and characters in real life. Of Moll Flanders he says: ". . . she cannot be here because she belongs to a world where the secret life is visible, to a world that is not and cannot be ours."

[11] See, among others, Booth, *The Rhetoric of Fiction*, pp. 271 ff.

novel, when the events have been disentangled, and suddenly the question is raised as to who actually is the hero of the story:

"And who is the hero?" said Naomi.
"Hamish?" said her brother, in question.
"Uncle Walter might turn out to have been so all the time. But he is inclined to suggest it himself, and that is against it."
"Father," said Ralph. "It can be no one else. And if we think, it is no one else. Unless my saying it makes me the hero myself."[12]

The characters themselves realize how difficult it is to gauge the individual importance of themselves and the others. If the 'hero' is the man with a particularly high degree of self-awareness, it must be pointed out that, in this regard, there are plenty of characters better qualified than the father, Simon Challoner. His focal position is brought about simply by the fact that he is the prospective heir to the title and estate and is therefore the pivot round whom the whole action turns. But despite his central position, neither he nor any of the other characters offers a central perspective, so that we have a continual plurality of viewpoints, which in turn bring about certain specific effects. The vision of each individual is shown to be strictly limited and the dialogue brings out these limitations as each partner undermines the opinion just presented. What may seem simple in a single statement, suddenly appears disturbingly ambivalent.

The reader is liable to be unsettled by this loss of central perspective. Without the "ficelles"[13] which Henry James gave as guidelines to the action, the reader finds himself face to face with the unprocessed 'reality' of the characters. The undefined and undefinable nature of the action is an esthetic provocation, causing him to develop for himself the possibilities of understanding that arise out of the world offered to him. To do this, he has to rally all his faculties of perception, and the author's occasional comments in the text serve to highlight this need. Instead of explaining what she has reported, as the reader will naturally expect her to do, she merely describes the appearance of some of the characters,[14] or makes observations which add virtually nothing to what we have already deduced from the dialogue—as when she informs us[15] that Mrs. Challoner is worried about her husband's health, although we have already had a dialogue between the two sons about this very situation.[16]

---

[12] Compton-Burnett, *A Heritage*, p. 240.
[13] See Henry James, *The Art of the Novel*, ed. R. P. Blackmur (New York, 1937), pp. 322 ff.
[14] See Compton-Burnett, *A Heritage*, pp. 6, 13, 15.
[15] Ibid., p. 13.
[16] Ibid., pp. 10 ff.

The author seems to see her characters only from the outside, reproducing the dialogue, and occasionally their gestures,[17] and generally giving
the impression that in fact she knows very little, if anything, about them.
She pretends only to be an extremely attentive observer, and this is the
position the reader, too, must adopt if he wants to understand what is
going on.

As we have seen, then, the dialogue technique and the extreme sparsity and neutrality of the author's interpolations reduce narrative to a bare
minimum. In this way, we are confronted directly by the actual 'reality'
of the characters, instead of by an edited version of that reality, so that
both author and reader appear to stand at an almost identical distance
from the people they are observing. By her explanations of trivialities
and her silence on matters of importance the author signalizes her presence in order to highlight her self-effacement. And the greater her re-
serve, the more acute will be our attention. Thus the very passiveness of
the author's presentation acts as a stimulus to activate the reader.

III

We must now take a closer look at the dialogue, which forms the main
bulk of the text. The novel begins with a conversation between the
brothers Walter and Simon Challoner, who live with their parents on the
country estate of their uncle Sir Edwin Challoner:

> "It is a pity you have not my charm, Simon," said Walter Challoner.
> "Well, we hardly want a double share in a family."
> "I am glad you are all without it. It is untrue that we cannot have
> too much of a good thing. I could not bear to be one amongst many.
> It would not suit the something there is about me."
> "I don't see anything to mind in it."
> "But is there anything about you, Simon?"
> "It would not help me, if there was. One amongst many is what I
> am. The number of us is my trouble. My uncle has his dealings with
> my father, and my father passes them on to me. I have no personal
> scope. My youth is escaping without giving me anything it owes me.
> I see it shortening before my eyes. And Uncle must leave everything
> to Father, before I even become the heir. It throws my life into an
> indefinite future. I never put it into words, but I carry a burden about
> with me."
> "It is praiseworthy not to put it into words. I wonder how it would
> be, if you did."
> "Words do not hasten things," said Simon.

[17] Ibid., p. 9.

"No, or yours would have done so. Can it be that you have death in your heart? What a different thing from charm! To think of the gulf between us! I wonder if there is any outward sign of it."[18]

Here, then, at the beginning of the conversation, our expectations as regards the function of the dialogue are fulfilled, insofar as the characters communicate with each other and thereby disclose something of themselves. The individuality of the two brothers, apparent in their own judgments of themselves, leads to the revelation of certain hidden driving forces. As the prospective heir, Simon talks of his increasing frustrations; Walter's reply lays bare the appalling desire underlying Simon's discontent. This probing shapes the whole conversation. Simon does not seem expressly to want the death of those who are standing in his way, and yet Walter leads him all the more remorselessly toward confessing precisely this desire:

"I am held back in everything. Look at this room and its dinginess! It gets darker with every day. It is that creeper smothering the house. And I can do nothing. When the place is mine, I shall have it cut away."

"I did not mean you to be led as far onward as that. Uncle Edwin and Father would both have to die."

"Well, people must die in the end."

"Of course they must not. People are immortal. You must have noticed it. Indeed you betray that you have."

"I wish I could think I was. My time will be too short to serve any purpose. And there are things I want to do so much."[19]

No sooner has Simon let out his hidden feelings than Walter abruptly leads the conversation off in another direction. Instead of the moral indignation we might expect from him, he counters Simon's brutal statement with the puzzling, paradoxical claim that people are immortal. Through the immediate shock effect of "of course . . . not," the whole subject matter of the conversation shifts onto a new plane. Simon takes up Walter's extraordinary statement as if it were perfectly natural. The very fact that he does not seem to regard Walter's remark as senseless or impossible—as he himself would like to be immortal—gives away his frustrated attitude toward the 'immortals', and hence the intensity of his preoccupation with the heritage.

This twist in the conversation endows the dialogue with an unusual

[18] Ibid., pp. 5 f.
[19] Ibid., p. 7.

form, which may be easier to comprehend if we turn to another section
dealing with the same subject matter. Simon asks Walter:

"Do you really think that Father will live to eternity?"
"Of course I do not. I should be as ashamed of it, as you would. I
meant an eternity of nothingness, which was a good thing to mean. It
almost seems you might mean something else. I admire Father for
quietly facing extinction. I see nothing in facing eternity, when we
should all like to so much."
"What does Father think himself?" said Simon.
"He thinks what we do, and knows we think it. It makes it hard to
know how to behave with him."
"He said we were to forget it. I suppose he meant what he said."
"Simon, how can you suppose that?"
"If he heard us talking, what would he think?"
"That we were covering our feelings. Or I hope he would. And in
my case there would be truth in it. In yours there is the knowledge
that there will be a person less in your path."
"I do not really consider that. If I did, I should not talk of it. And
it will not be so much of a change for me. I have seen Uncle's life as a
better one than Father's. And a feeling is not less strong, that another
can exist with it."
"I think the strife between them weakens it, when it is not strong
enough to kill the other."
"You need not be so sure you are nobler than I am."
"I am sure," said Walter.[20]

The thought running through the conversation between the brothers
now takes on an even more complicated form than before. Simon is dis-
turbed by the possibility that his father might live forever. But the conversation has led to a change in circumstances, and this obviously affects
Walter's attitude toward immortality: he no longer refers to it as something clear and unambiguous, but instead draws attention to the very diversity of meaning surrounding the term. Now he says that the possibility of eternal life does not mean the same for their father as it does for
Simon, the prospective heir. This view seems to be a relief for Simon,
but at the same time it adds unexpected complications to his relationship with his father. What would the latter think if he knew their secret
feelings about him? The supposition that he already knows tends to increase rather than reduce the discomfort. And so Simon tries to represent his utterances about his father's death as hypothetical reflections,
but these are obviously two-edged: the apparently humanitarian motive

[20] Ibid., pp. 27 f.

is suppressed by Simon himself when he thinks about his uncle's health, which will make his father's death irrelevant as far as his position as prospective heir is concerned. He defends his double standards, and Walter attacks them, whereupon Simon casts aspersions upon Walter's integrity—though apparently making little impression.

If we think back to the starting-point of this particular dialogue, we will see that the subject matter has splintered off in several different directions, with the implication that there may be many more aspects of the subject not yet touched upon by the selection of thoughts present in the dialogue itself. The angle of approach is continually changing, as the brothers expose hidden elements of each other's statements. The scope of the conversation is thus continually expanding to embrace more and more of the themes arising out of the one central topic—Father's death. It is a kind of pebble-in-the-pond technique, though the ripples tend to be highly unpredictable.

This technique is in many ways quite different from the dialogue form we have come to expect of the drama.[21] "A conversation between two people is rarely a matter just of communication; it is concerned with something of much more vital importance—the influencing of the person to whom the words are addressed. In all 'dramatic' conflicts, such as are developed in the world presented by the play, the speech addressed to a character is a form of action on the part of the speaker, and basically it only has any real importance for the events depicted in the play if it actually brings about a genuine advance in the action that is developing."[22] However opposed may be the positions of the characters in the play, the dialogue in some way coordinates them. In *A Heritage and Its History,* this coordination, essential for dramatic dialogue, appears to lie in the common environment of the characters—that of the landed gentry at the turn of the century. Ivy Compton-Burnett herself said once: "I do not

---

[21] See Edwin Muir, *The Structure of the Novel* (London, 1957), pp. 41 ff., where there is a discussion of the relation between dialogue and plot in the novel. On this subject, Ivy Compton-Burnett said the following:

> *Interviewer:* Your dialogue has been compared with that of dramatists like Congreve and Oscar Wilde. Quite apart from this question of likeness and influence, it is impossible not to wonder about the source of the theatrical quality in your novels, which comes out particularly well when they are broadcast. . . . But you have never actually tried to write a play?
>
> *Miss C.-B.:* No, I never have. I think a novel gives you more scope. I think I should call my books something between a novel and a play, and I feel the form suits me better than the pure play. It gives more range and a little more length, and it doesn't subject me to the mechanical restrictions of a play ("An Interview," p. 101).

[22] Roman Ingarden, *Das literarische Kunstwerk* (Tübingen, [2]1960). pp. 408 f.

feel that I have any real or organic knowledge of life later than about 1910."[23] But the dialogue in her novel reflects a highly individual conception of this historically precise period. The form of conversation seems rather to diffuse than to bring out the situation of the characters in Victorian society. Even though the atmosphere of the Victorian family and home does pervade the whole novel, the words and actions of the individual members of that family continually exceed the limits of what was considered to be proper in that particular society. By going against the expectations arising out of the setting, the dialogue draws attention all the more intensively to the incalculable motives of human conduct that seem to be independent of that setting. And so the function of dialogue in the drama—communicating different positions and throwing emphasis on the common ground underlying the conversation—is here quite transformed. Now the dialogue makes the common ground—i.e., Victorian convention—dwindle to insignificance, blotting it out with the unfathomableness of human actions and reactions.

This process might be easier to understand if we look at those passages which in fact come closest to fulfilling our normal expectations of dialogue. As J. L. Styan has put it, dialogue is directed toward a "predetermined end."[24] In *A Heritage and Its History,* this end is provided by the following conflict: Simon Challoner himself shatters his own long-cherished dream of taking over the heritage from his uncle; the father does die, but Sir Edwin marries, despite his advanced age, and Simon fathers the child Sir Edwin's wife gives birth to. Thus the relations between the characters become extremely involved, and in their life together they are forced to conceal the wide range of consequences following on from this critical turning-point.[25] There is no lack of tense situations in which the whole truth threatens to come out. At such moments, the most favored technique is for the character to adjust himself to the person he is talking with, to lull his suspicions, and to head him off from the discovery of the real situation.[26] The moment the dialogue is orientated toward this end, it fulfills its dramatic function—namely, to maneuver the other into a specific position. After Simon has, with resignation, married the sister of Sir Edwin's wife, his daughter Naomi one day confronts him with her desire to marry Hamish, who as Sir Edwin's

---

[23] Quoted by Pamela Hansford Johnson, *Ivy Compton-Burnett* (London, 1951), p. 36.

[24] J. L. Styan, *The Elements of Drama* (Cambridge, 1963), p. 12. Concerning the different directions taken by Ivy Compton-Burnett's dramatic dialogue, see Sarraute, *L'Ère du Soupçon,* p. 122, and John Preston's discussion of *A Heritage and Its History* in "The Matter in a Word," *Essays in Criticism* 10 (1960): 348 ff.

[25] See Compton-Burnett, *A Heritage,* p. 103.

[26] Ibid., pp. 101 ff.

supposed son is the official heir. The family is naturally horrified at this threatened union between half-brother and half-sister, and the latter can only interpret the violent and unanimous opposition as evidence of a conspiracy. Naomi asks: "What is there behind it all? There seems to be a sort of conspiracy. Did you foresee the question, and agree on a common line?"[27]

Up until this moment, relations between the grown-ups had always been far from harmonious, so that their unanimity must now naturally seem suspicious. In such a situation, the interchange between characters once more fulfills the function of dramatic dialogue: one partner seeks to influence the other into accepting or fulfilling a premeditated plan. For this purpose, there has to be a close interlocking of statement and reply. But here the agreement, based on a common aim, is identical with suppression of the truth. Sir Edwin actually gives voice to this fact: "It must not be," said his uncle. "We are to forget the truth. It must not lie below the surface, ready to escape."[28]

Forgetting the truth, then, is a precondition of the unanimity, and as all the characters are implicated in this shady activity, there arises between them a bond which is dictated by social considerations and which can best be summed up as convention. When the crisis over the real origins of Sir Edwin's supposed son has reached its climax, Sir Edwin says:

"Civilised life exacts its toll. We live among the civilised."
"The conventions are on the surface," said his wife. "We know the natural life is underneath."
"We do; we have our reason. But we cannot live it. We know the consequences of doing so. If not, we learn."[29]

This distinction between convention and the natural life throws new light on those features of the dialogue which we have been discussing up to now: if the need for convention is uppermost, the characters will act in relation to one another; but if their utterances are dictated by the natural life that lies below the surface of social convention, then their reactions tend to be incalculable.

This duality forms the structure of the dialogue in *A Heritage and Its History*. For the characters to be able to communicate at all, there has to be a certain amount of convention; but if they were to move only

[27] Ibid., p. 150.
[28] Ibid., p. 115.
[29] Ibid., p. 160.

along the paths laid down for them by their social life together, their contact could only be bought at the price of the truth. If convention is based on a lie, then the implication is that reality is concealed by pragmatic purposes which, for the time being at any rate, are equated with life itself. However, there is no denying the fact that convention has a vital part to play; if there were not a certain amount of such common ground, otherwise incomprehensible views could not be communicated at all. But the moment views are expressed, a host of unexpressed implications are bound to be formed, and these in turn tend to obliterate the common ground and lead to *terra incognita*. From the presence of these two distinct elements, the dialogue takes on a striking tension; there is a constant interplay between calculated, pragmatic statements and the sudden glimpse below the surface into the underlying reality.

The conventionally orientated statement is necessary, then, as a springboard for the hidden truths. Pragmatic requirements limit the scope of the natural life, thus bringing about a division between what is and what might have been. The dialogue draws attention to and exploits this division, proceeding as it does from conventional modes of conduct to a wide variety of unforeseen reactions; at the same time, these reactions show the mode of conduct demanded by convention to be one special case out of many possibilities. This gives rise to the strange atmosphere of the novel: it contradicts one's usual expectations, for it does not offer us the normal, representative extract from reality. Instead the reader finds himself confronted by a fluctuating sequence of reactions, the teleology of which becomes more and more obscure; and since this whole process is presented through the medium of direct speech, the continual ramification of the events takes on an almost overwhelming immediacy.

IV

The form of the dialogue is, of course, crucial for the drawing of the characters, as all other techniques of verbal portraiture, such as are basic even to most novels of the twentieth century, are dispensed with here. By eliminating narrative the author has cut off her characters from the detailed environment which normally helps us to understand people's actions and individuality. Indeed, it is often the narrative actions which bring out the individuality, while dialogue and interior monologue serve only to illuminate or animate those features not brought out by the narrative. Ivy Compton-Burnett has abandoned this traditional, authorial method of characterization, and indeed she goes even further than most dramatists (let alone novelists) in her self-effacement, for even playwrights usually allow themselves a few explanatory stage directions and descriptions.

Through the almost total absence of a narrated setting, the dialogue seems strangely devoid of context, and this unrelatedness is all the more puzzling and provocative by virtue of the preciseness of what is said. The dialogue arouses the impression that it springs from some premeditated course of action, and yet at the same time it keeps the motivation well hidden. As the narrator herself has nothing to say about the individual qualities of the characters, we have to try and orientate ourselves by the opinions they themselves express. They all pursue very definite ends: Simon wants to succeed to his uncle's estate,[30] while his uncle seeks to exclude him from the heritage;[31] Hamish wants to marry Naomi[32] and, when this proves impossible, to renounce the heritage.[33] Despite the firmness of these purposes, the characters act in such a way that most of their desires are frustrated, but as they seem relatively indifferent to this failure their individuality becomes harder and harder for the reader to gauge. Of course a certain degree of individuality is essential, for otherwise there could be no conversation and no expression of individual viewpoints. But what is far more striking than the characterization is the fact that every statement contains a wealth of implications which the individual can neither see nor control. Indeed, the characters are not even concerned with viewing all the implications, but in their reply to a statement will simply seize on one of its implications, ignoring the rest. This process has two basic consequences. First, it can turn the original statement in a direction quite unintended by the speaker; second, the seizing on one implication in turn calls forth a host of new ones. And so we have a statement, extraction of a single implication leading to the reply, the reply in turn creating implications of which again only one will be selected for the next statement, etc., etc. Every utterance contains a wealth of possible implications, and every selection leads to a new store of implications. This structure of the dialogue makes it impossible for any one theme to be consistently developed. But as each reply brings forth the precise formulation of one implication, there do arise at least the suggested outlines of thoughts, ideas, etc.—though these in turn are

[30] Ibid., p. 7.
[31] Ibid., pp. 103 f.
[32] Ibid., pp. 145 f.
[33] Ibid., pp. 167 f.

swiftly caught up in the whirl of changing and unforeseeable implications. Any starting-point can lead to such configurations, which then signalize the hitherto unplumbed depths of the human character, as they bring to light the unexpected and the unpremeditated. The characters themselves appear two-faced. What they say about themselves does not illuminate them as individuals so much as accentuate the unfathomableness of their inner recesses. The more steadfastly they pursue and identify with their goals, the more fictitious becomes the basis of their conduct. They fail to realize that their surface reactions are conditioned by pragmatic requirements which can change from one situation to the next. The pragmatically conditioned statement may be taken for the authentic expression of the person concerned, but the resultant concrete manifestation can in fact reflect nothing but the outer appearance of the character. Time and again the dialogue exposes this situation. But if the hidden forces of the human potential are to be brought to light, it is essential that relationships remain unaffected by the interchanges, for otherwise a conflict would be formed which would inevitably lead to a fixing of positions, and this would end the flow of unforeseeable reactions.

The configurations formed by the dialogue therefore have a strangely indeterminate nature, though this does not mean they are any the less real. They convey the individual outline of the character, together with the hitherto untapped potential of his reactions—and this potential could not possibly be conveyed if his individuality were defined once and for all. What we have then is a temporary 'gestalt' of the real man and the potential man, but this 'gestalt' must in turn be broken up in order that the potential continue to be unfolded. Through its very structure, the dialogue is capable of an endless succession of implications, and as a result the visible outline of the characters seems almost a matter of chance, depending on which implications are uppermost at one particular moment. And just as what we know appears to be a matter of chance, so the unforeseeable becomes a reality. The dialogue, then, is "not a transcript of what he or she would have said in 'real life' but rather of what would have been said *plus* what would have been implied but not spoken *plus* what would have been understood though not implied."[34]

---

[34] Hilary Corke, "New Novels," *The Listener* 58, no. 1483 (1957): 322. This remark actually concerned *A Father and His Fate,* but it is equally valid for all of Ivy Compton-Burnett's novels and was meant in this sense by Corke.

If we bear in mind the fact that the speakers are not aware of the welter of the implications they bring about and can themselves only reveal
these implications to a limited extent, then we shall gain a clearer understanding of the principle of composition underlying the characters in this
novel. They are not confronted with the unknown, but actually produce
it out of themselves. The originality of this form of characterization
has called forth different responses from different critics—a number of
them unfavorable. Pamela Hansford Johnson, for instance, writes: "The
ease with which the persons of the novels may be confused in the memory is a genuine flaw, a flaw which, above all, must make Miss Compton-
Burnett always a writer for the 'few,' as only a few are able to make the
concentrated intellectual effort she demands from them through both
her virtues and her faults."[35] This criticism reflects expectations conditioned by the novel of the nineteenth century. Then the reader demanded an unmistakable identity for the character he was meeting—an identity that was formed not least by the individual environment and fate of
that character. If Ivy Compton-Burnett's characters tend to lose their
identity in the reader's memory, this is because the center of attention
is not themselves, but their unpredictability.

For this reason, the conduct of the persons in this novel must remain
independent of preconceived values of good and evil. Pamela Hansford
Johnson quite rightly called Ivy Compton-Burnett "the most amoral of
living writers."[36] Morality could only impose limitations which would
not be so very different in kind from those imposed by individual characterization. Any such qualification would involve a premature mapping
of those regions of human reality that are only disclosed through the
implications of what the characters say. This principle of composition
can be seen even in the most ordinary situations—for instance, in the dialogue after Sir Edwin's long-awaited death, at the age of ninety-four:

> "This day brings another back to me," said Julia. "The day when
> my husband was buried, Edwin's younger brother! All those years ago!
> Life is a strange thing. It will soon be my turn to follow."
> "What ought we to say?" said Graham. "Silence means consent,
> and seems to mean it. And yet we can hardly disagree."
> "Say nothing," said Simon.
> "Father is in a sinister mood," said Ralph. "It can hardly be the
> loss of his uncle at ninety-four."[37]

[35] Johnson, *Ivy Compton-Burnett*, p. 22.
[36] Ibid., p. 11.
[37] Compton-Burnett, *A Heritage*, p. 188.

Graham and Ralph, Julia's grandsons, have already stepped out of character in that they do not speak like children at all. But never in this novel is any consideration given as to whether characters seem what they are. The fact that the reply comes from a child is obviously quite irrelevant to the reaction depicted. One would have expected the usual mechanical remark to banish Julia's sentimental concern with her own death, but no such consolation is forthcoming. Graham realizes this and, in not giving her the conventional reply, he compels himself to ask how he ought to have reacted. The subject of his remark is the *possibilities* of reaction. However unnatural such a reply may seem, there is no denying the truth of its content. And if this truth seems hurtful, then we are bound to realize that consideration for others is a pragmatic precept based, precisely, on avoiding truth, as if truth itself were immoral.[38] Pragmatic precepts, however, will only be valid under certain conditions, so that a change in conditions will mean a change in conduct. This comes out clearly in what Simon and Ralph have to say. Simon advises his son Graham to keep quiet, but Ralph draws attention to the hidden motive behind his father's reply; for Simon is vexed at the fact that he himself destroyed his own chances of succeeding to the heritage.

Such an account of the implications behind the conversation should by no means be regarded as exhaustive. Any explanation will be as restricted as the characters' own unfolding of the implications, and even if it can illuminate some of the nuances, it can never encompass the full range of those implications. There may be quite different motives for Graham's statement and Simon's advice—but in the absence of authorial explanation and definitive characterization, the reader is forced to make his own diagnosis. At the same time, however, by giving such an interpretation, he is automatically excluding other possibilities, and when other implications come to light, he must then modify his original interpretation. The dialogue by its very nature defies any standardized interpre-

---

[38] On the question of morality, Stuart Hampshire, "The Art of a Moralist," *Encounter* 9, no. 5 (1957): 80, says: "First, Miss Compton-Burnett is a moralist, in a sense of the word that allows that there have been many great French moralists and very few English. The pleasure of the moralist is to probe through the decent conventions to the natural laws of conduct and feeling in which we have all really believed and to find apt words for them: if possible, a few words, the maxim that puts the smothered general truth shortly and only once. This is the pleasure of discussion, of intellectual surprise, of the contrast of what is ordinarily said with what is really believed, of the ambiguity of a situation condensed in plain words, of having every side expressed, nothing smothered. The art of the moralist must be difficult in English, because there is no tradition of it, outside a healthy intellectual horseplay, as in Shaw: more difficult still, if the story is to be carried forward to a climax for which the reader waits, as in a detective story, to know who loses and who wins, and—not usually the same—who is guilty and who is innocent."

tation, and the author's deliberate renunciation of detailed characterization serves to keep the reader from becoming involved with the characters as such, and to involve him instead in the whole process of discovery. The moment he has been deluded into 'interpreting' a statement, he finds himself compelled to ask why an implication has been revealed that he himself had not thought of before. It is only then that he begins to penetrate below the surface into those nether regions which the real characters inhabit. And so if these characters seem to us more like patterns than people, this impression will testify to the fact that an apparently indispensable principle underlying the conception of novel characterization has in this novel been given up altogether: namely, the individual self as the focal point of reference.

This highly significant change can be more easily understood if we have a brief look at what still rank as modern forms of presentation in the novels of Virginia Woolf and James Joyce. The characters of these two authors are structured mainly by the stream of consciousness conveyed by the interior monologue. ". . . the novels that are said to use the stream-of-consciousness *technique* to a considerable degree prove, upon analysis, to be novels which have as their essential subject matter the consciousness of one or more characters; that is, the depicted consciousness serves as a screen on which the material in these novels is presented. . . . Interior monologue is, then, the technique used in fiction for representing the psychic content and processes of character, partly or entirely unuttered, just as these processes exist at various levels of conscious control before they are formulated for deliberate speech."[39] The interior monologue reveals the consciousness of the characters, as it is formed out of impressions and memories. Individual consciousness is necessary for the variety of experiences to be brought into relation with one another. While the world of the interior monologue is a tangled confusion of associations, the effort to coordinate its elements points to the unmistakable, individual identity of the character concerned. The world experienced in the interior monologue creates the illusion that contingent reality, captured as it were right at the beginning of articulation, is capable of being comprehended. In this way there arises a 'picture' of the contingent nature of reality, which depends for its authenticity on a common

---

[39] Robert Humphrey, *Stream of Consciousness in the Modern Novel* (Berkeley and Los Angeles, 1959), pp. 2 and 24.

point of reference for all the details that appear in the consciousness: this point of reference is the self. But reality looks different from the standpoint of each observer, for the self determines the perspective as well as the actual possibility of perceiving such a disconnected reality. For this reason, the interior monologue does not produce anything like the effect of alienation caused by Ivy Compton-Burnett's dialogue technique. Even though the contents of the stream of consciousness will vary in each individual case, the reader can still keep track of the incoherent memories and impressions by referring to the individual self that produces them. Once the self as the point of reference has gone, characters become characterless: they are deprived of the individuality we still find for instance in Mrs. Ramsay (*To the Lighthouse*) and Leopold Bloom (*Ulysses*). Seen from the standpoint of Ivy Compton-Burnett, such characters seem almost like 'normal people', for the fluctuations of their conscious minds denote an unmistakable individuality. We are also confronted with an extensive account of the world outside, which contributes a good deal to the shaping of this individuality. The more reality is refracted in the conscious minds of Mrs. Ramsay and Leopold Bloom, the clearer become their personal characteristics. Ivy Compton-Burnett's characters, on the other hand, seem almost faceless, and even the direst catastrophes scarcely affect them. Ultimately they are there primarily to unfold implications which, in their turn, bring about a never-ending series of unforeseeable reactions.

This technique, with its effect of alienation, has its roots in a problem that is basic in the novel and in most other art forms. Within a limited space the author has to try and portray an illimitable reality.[40] This paradox can only be resolved from case to case by a process of selection—offering a particular conception of reality as if that were identical with reality itself. The realistic novel has always used this form of illusion, presenting 'a slice of life' as the whole of reality.[41] In the modern novel, however, there is a deliberate attempt to make the reader aware of the distinction between techniques of presentation and the reality thereby presented. The more 'unnatural' the reader finds the techniques, the less the danger that he will take the selection for reality, as the realistic novel

---

[40] See Hans Blumenberg, "Wirklichkeitsbegriff und Möglichkeiten des Romans," in *Nachahmung und Illusion* (Poetik und Hermeneutik, I), ed. H. R. Jauss (Munich, 1964), pp. 21 ff.
[41] See "Doing Things in Style. An Interpretation of 'The Oxen of the Sun' in James Joyce's *Ulysses*," in this volume, pp. 190 ff.

sought to make him do. The modern novel, then, breaks down traditional criteria of judgment in an attempt to reduce to a minimum the preconceptions necessary for the presentation of reality. One such minimal
value is the self of the interior monologue in the novels of Virginia Woolf
and James Joyce. For Ivy Compton-Burnett, however, the self is either
a myth or simply a stylistic device to present not reality but the *disconnectedness* of reality. She herself once said: "My writing does not seem
to me 'stylised'."[42] At first sight this remark might seem astonishing,
for her endless series of dialogues have a quite 'unnatural' and so "stylised" effect, because we are not used to this sort of thing in 'real life'.
However, if one defines stylization in terms of those preconceptions necessary in the novel for a presentation of reality, then it must be said,
paradoxically, that Ivy Compton-Burnett's novels contain an absolute
minimum of such preconceptions. There is no confusion or identification of means of presentation and thing presented. The reader is made
constantly aware of the distinction, for the author does not stylize the
reactions of her characters, as she renounces any form of coordination
that might join the dialogue into a coherent whole.

V

This principle also underlies the plot of the novel. In the interview we
have already quoted several times, Ivy Compton-Burnett said the following about her characters and stories: "I think that actual life supplies a
writer with characters less than is thought. . . . As regards plots, I find
real life no help at all. Real life seems to have no plots. And as I think a
plot desirable and almost necessary I have this extra grudge against life.
But I do think there are signs that strange things happen, though they do
not emerge. I believe it would go ill with many of us, if we were faced
by a strong temptation, and I suspect that with some of us it does go
ill."[43] If "real life" only gives us a surface view of reality, because obviously it is shaped by existing conventions, only a fabricated plot will
be able to lay bare the substrata of that reality. This fabrication becomes
a sort of protest against the immediacy of the self-evident, which seems
to exclude the need for any questioning. And so the plot sacrifices one
of its most sacrosanct attributes: verisimilitude. But, paradoxically, this

---

[42] Quoted by Johnson, *Ivy Compton-Burnett*, p. 36.

[43] Ibid., p. 36. Unfortunately I did not have access to the interview with Ivy Compton-Burnett published by Margaret Jourdain in *Orion*. The following observation is worth noting:

> *Interviewer:* Perhaps if we had had experiences like those in your books we would keep
> quiet about them.
> *Miss C.-B.:* Well, perhaps that is so—perhaps that is what it is ("An Interview," p. 107).

sacrifice is obviously made in the cause of truth. While the verisimilitude of the traditional narrative served to produce the illusion of truth, the fabricated plot sets out to destroy any such illusory intentions. The consequences of this approach are to be seen in the plot of *A Heritage and Its History*.

Although the hopes and views of the characters are made apparent in the dialogue, their actions are often in striking contrast to the intentions they have expressed. This tendency is most evident in Simon Challoner. He fathers a child that removes all hope of his ever getting the long-cherished heritage. Just as unexpectedly, he marries Fanny, whose sister Rhoda is Sir Edwin's wife and mother of his (Simon's) child. Such a concatenation seems fabricated because the elements of the story arouse expectations typical of a Victorian social novel, but then take on a form which continually bursts open such a frame. Against the Victorian background, the actions of the characters sometimes seem quite absurd, but at the same time they show how very little control conventions really have over people's behavior. Obviously the disastrous actions of the characters do not arise out of their personal wishes—and indeed they are often so completely contrary to their wishes that they seem like extraordinary quirks beyond the influence of any personal desires, let alone of convention. Perhaps it was anger at Sir Edwin's marriage that set Simon on the fatal path toward a relationship with Rhoda. Even for him, the motivation can only be a matter of conjecture, and in view of his aim in life it can never be properly understood. But if people's actions cannot be brought into line with their avowed intentions, then these intentions take on an ambiguity that no amount of analysis will ever fully remove.

The story brings this ambiguity out into the open. Through his impulsive behavior, Simon creates new realities, which impose unexpected conditions on the lives of the mother, the children, and also Sir Edwin himself. Simon continually tries to prepare his children for the possibility that they may have to spend the rest of their lives in the poorhouse. In this way he hopes to regain some sort of control over the unpremeditated consequences of his actions, but instead he merely alienates his children more and more, until finally they dismiss his scheme as simply a "figment of Father's brain."[44] But if openly pursued intentions are so obviously fictitious, then clearly there must be a wide gulf between what the character does and what the character is. Whatever the intention may be, it is only a partial motivating force, conditioned by the particular cir-

[44] Compton-Burnett, *A Heritage*, p. 238.

cumstances with which it is trying to cope, but liable to lose its validity under different circumstances or when seen from a different standpoint. The moment we try to identify a character with one particular intention, we find his actions giving the lie to our identification. We are confronted with the fact that either the actions or the intentions are a sort of camouflage, and the reality lies in territory not hitherto exposed. The story lifts off the camouflage, but refrains from presenting us with the reality beneath. Indeed, its most penetrating effects are achieved precisely by revealing the apparently inexplicable inconsistencies of the characters and leaving us floundering after the all-important but ungraspable motive.

Time and again in this story, we find that the actions of the characters are not calculated to help them fulfill their own wishes. The fact that at the end of the novel they do get what they wanted through no fault of their own relegates all their efforts in the course of the story to the level of irrelevance. This irrelevance accentuates two factors: first, the conditional nature of all the intentions pursued; second, the insignificance of such intentions as regards the overall conduct of the character. When situations change, they do so mainly because of some unpremeditated action which cancels out all previous calculations, or because of the clarification of an implication which, similarly, cancels out the teleology of all that has been spoken. This confrontation between calculated and unpremeditated conduct would seem to contain all the elements essential for conflict. But in this story there is no conflict—Simon does not have to bear the consequences of his action—and this shows just how irrelevant the characters' intentions really are.

In the dialogue, too, one is constantly made aware of the incongruence between utterance and situation—and indeed this is its basic theme. The characters make every effort to grasp their situation through words, without ever being able to do so properly, and so the whole perspective governing their vision is shown to be something completely provisional. And taking the provisional for the final is what constitutes the character of convention as it is constantly laid bare by the artificial construction of the plot. The construction shows clearly how, in view of the opaqueness of their own situations, the characters are forced to act as if they knew what they were doing, but they—like convention—depend on the circumstances of the moment, and when these change (even if the change is through their own unpremeditated actions) they must change, too. And so we pass from one catastrophe to another, with each disaster showing up the fictitious nature of convention, which, of course, lives by the claim that it controls everything through its rational definitiveness. This exposure of the fraudulence of convention serves to throw full emphasis on the unfathomable depths of the human character. Simon says at one point: "I think being carried beyond ourselves carries ourselves further."[45] In this process of self-discovery and self-extension, convention has an important part to play, for it is only when we have become aware of the provisional nature of apparently self-evident truths that we can progress beyond them. This is why the dialogue offers not only what is said but also the implications of what is said, for it is in the implications that the deeper realities lie. They tell us—or rather suggest to us—what remained unthought in the process of a particular action or self-revelation. And the more firmly the characters appear to fix themselves, the greater is the range of implications, so that the unpredictable basis of their behavior begins more and more to overshadow the actions themselves, and the external view—pictured in accordance with those actions—is seen to be nothing but convention. The fact that this process can never be brought to any conclusion shows that the human character can never be definitively fixed. Whenever it appears to become definitive, the aspect involved is promptly unmasked as merely provisional, but this very provisionalness draws attention to the protean potential of the individual.

As we have seen, this process could only be shown through a fabricated plot that was not concerned with everyday experience but with the hidden variations of human conduct, of which everyday experience is merely the solid cream that has risen to the surface. The story brings out the unforeseen and unpremeditated elements of human behavior and unmasks convention as a form of human reality that is weighed down on all sides by a multitude of restrictive, yet only temporary, conditions.

The fact that the novel is dressed up in the trappings of Victorian convention serves mainly to arouse certain expectations in the reader, which can then, of course, be productively destroyed. The customs of Victorian society seem to offer him a cosily familiar background, but such monstrous things occur against this background that the reader will soon find himself thoroughly disoriented. It is only then that he can begin to be aware of the elusiveness of reality—an awareness forced upon him by the sheer unexpectedness of the characters' actions and reactions. Only when convention has been destroyed can we see what convention has been hiding from us.

VI

In its construction, the twists and turns of its dialogue, its blurred char-

45 Ibid., p. 228.

acterization, and the artificiality of its plot, *A Heritage and Its History* is clearly not concerned with establishing any illusion of 'real life'. Instead it concentrates on making the reader conscious of the gap between techniques of presentation and realities to be presented, so that he will not confuse the one with the other. The more artificial the techniques, the less likelihood there is of such confusion—and in this respect the work is in direct contrast to the tradition of the realistic novel, which concentrated almost exclusively on building up the illusion that presentation and reality were one and the same thing. In *A Heritage and Its History*, the dialogue—which is virtually the sole form of presentation— is deliberately made to appear unnatural, precisely in order to prevent this illusion from coming into being. Thus technique and reality are kept separate, and this fact alone acts as an irritant to a reader who is accustomed to novels that give him a consistent, 'realistic' picture of the world. "What 'comes out' of a conversation no-one can know in advance."[46] The dialogue in Ivy Compton-Burnett's novel develops this idea on a massive scale, so that reality appears as something surprising, unexpected, and unpredictable. This effect is only possible because of the fact that we are accustomed to seeing reality through just one pair of eyes (our own, or—for instance—the novelist's), whereas now we become aware that the consistency imposed by any perspective vision is bound to be illusory. And so being made, as we are here, to experience the impermeable potential of human reality, we are forced ultimately into questioning our own conceptions of this reality.

The paradox of Ivy Compton-Burnett's novel is that her unrealistic dialogue presents a reality that could not be presented by any realistic technique. By refusing to select particular aspects of a particular world and pass them off as a truth complete in itself, she has laid bare an inexhaustible fund of new possibilities, and the more artificial her technique of presentation, the more possibilities she unfolds. The clearly defined heritage may be the starting-point of the novel, but it is the undefinable history that constitutes its reality.

[46] H. G. Gadamer, *Wahrheit und Methode* (Tübingen, 1960), p. 361; see also on pp. 361 ff. the remarks on the hermeneutic character of conversation.

10

WHEN IS THE END NOT THE END?
The Idea of Fiction in Beckett

I

Although I am not of the opinion that in this dark age it is only negativism that is fit for literature, nevertheless the affirmative view, even though it may from time to time criticize the 'by-products' of the age, does smack of hypocrisy."[1] This striking statement by Ernst Fischer is to be found in an article on Beckett which presents Fischer's ideas on modern Marxist esthetics. In fact, Beckett's work offers nothing affirmative, and for this reason it has often been regarded as simply the image of an existence characterized—in the words of Georg Lukács—by the "most fundamental pathological debasement of man."[2] Such judgments are by no means confined specifically to Marxist literary criticism; they also arise when attempts are made to expound Beckett against the background of metaphysics or literary history, and they are often made with the same emphasis. Though one may suppose that even Beckett's critics do not always expect from literature an affirmative statement on the modern condition, nevertheless their judgments would seem to depend on a traditional criterion of literature; namely, that it should give a representative view of life.

---

[1] Ernst Fischer, *Kunst und Koexistenz. Beitrag zu einer modernen marxistischen Ästhetik* (Hamburg, 1966), p. 21.
[2] Georg Lukács, *Wider den missverstandenen Realismus* (Hamburg, 1958), p. 31.

Beckett's texts, however, cannot simply be reduced to the representation of a given reality; their negativeness consists precisely in the fact that they resolutely refuse to comply with this traditional criterion. If one looks for affirmation in Beckett, all one will find is the deformation of man—and even this is only half the story, for his characters frequently behave as if they were no longer concerned in their own misery; like so much else, this is already behind them, and whenever they speak of it one has the impression that the situations they mention already belong to the past. One cannot even say with certainty that Beckett's texts confirm the misery of modern society, although they appear to do so. The moment one tries to restrict them to a specific meaning, they slide away in a new direction. Their meaning cannot be pinned down (unless one takes them to be a revelation of the limitation of 'meaning' in general). However, this gives rise to objections against Beckett, as put forward by Reinhard Baumgart, who compares Beckett's works to the science of fundamentals. But the "science of fundamentals can be put into practice only indirectly and with difficulty; the practical basis for life that used to emerge from literature is thus very hard to extract from the works of Beckett. The very radicalism of the questions he raises makes his writings inapplicable to everyday life."[3] What is this radicalism of Beckett's that precludes his offering any guidelines for his reader? Beckett's works are a continual (though never completed) 'exit', and each stage of the exit is only a starting-point for more 'exiting'. The frequency of the end in Beckett seems to imply 'salvation', but we could only understand 'end' as 'salvation', in the normal sense of the word, if we knew what goal was in view when the 'end' came. In Beckett, though, there is no mention of this goal, and if there were, then the fascination of the 'end' would disappear. "The end is terrific!"[4] says Clov in *Endgame*. Beckett's characters go round and round the end with such unswerving devotion that their activity simply destroys any idea that the end is only to be seen as the desire to finish off, as the great weariness, or even as the great satiety. If these were the motives, the characters would be more likely to do and say nothing. The variations on the 'end theme' are simply too numerous for them all to be regarded as merely a symptom of the longing for relief.

The recurrent indifference and apathy and the lack of concern for what actually lies beyond the end give one the impression that the end, however indefinite it may be, is a goal in itself. But when something

[3] Reinhard Baumgart, *Literatur für Zeitgenossen* (edition suhrkamp) (Frankfurt, 1966), p. 166.
[4] Samuel Beckett, *Endgame* (London, 1958), p. 34.

becomes a goal in itself, it is automatically released from those standards of judgment that have previously applied. Here, analogous to 'art for art's sake', we have 'end for end's sake', and it is in this sense that the end appears to have a function similar to that of 'salvation' without actually meaning salvation.

The end has a long history, and the fact of man's preoccupation with it would seem to indicate that the 'end' does not merely mean coming to a stop, but rather that it contains other elements that can never be fully grasped, so that one tries continually to define its precise nature. A dominant feature of this history is the Apocalypse. Perhaps this is even the starting-point. In any case, the Apocalypse provides a vital precondition for men's visions and descriptions of the end: we know what happens when the end comes. This forms a constant feature in the history of man's expectations in regard to the end, and such knowledge was always regarded as unassailable, even if it was contradicted by time and circumstances. If expectations were not fulfilled, (e.g., if the prophesied end of the world did not take place), there was no question of abandoning one's conceptions of the end—they merely had to be adapted to the new situation. In his book *The Sense of an Ending,* Frank Kermode suggested the following interpretation for this curious phenomenon: "Men . . . make considerable imaginative investments in coherent patterns which, by the provision of an end, make possible a satisfying consonance with the origins and with the middle. That is why the image of the end can never be *permanently* falsified. But they also, when awake and sane, feel the need to show a marked respect for things as they are; so that there is a recurring need for adjustments in the interest of reality as well as of control."[5] But if the image of the end can never be permanently falsified, then the connection between origin, middle, and end has to be constantly reestablished. In order for knowledge of the end to remain permanent, life must continually be given a new interpretation—and in such a way that the interpretation coincides with life itself. In Beckett's texts, this identification between life and interpretation is constantly broken up.

The adaptability that characterizes the images of the end cannot obscure, let alone cast any doubt on, their truth content. This is also true when the meaning of the end depends on unmistakable historical circumstances, which this meaning promises to transcend. But if the meaning of the end can be adjusted to suit the requirements of different historical situations, then each time the meaning is bound to be characterized by distinct historical features. One would think, then, that history

[5] Frank Kermode, *The Sense of an Ending* (New York, 1967), p. 17.

itself should show all these expectations up for what in reality they are: images of human hopes and human fears. But despite the changing contents of these images, there is never ever any suggestion, even by the latter day eschatologists, that this is all a matter of human projections. On the contrary, the urge to construct images is so marked that even the discrediting of definite prophecies has no repercussions on this activity. But if the end can only be brought into current life by means of images, then these images, in comparison with the reality of life, must be regarded as a fiction. This lack of reality, however, does not reduce their effect but, in the light of historical experience, seems rather to heighten it. "Fictions are for finding things out, and they change as the needs of sense-making change."[6] Kermode has therefore aptly described them as "concord-fictions,"[7] for they close that very gap in human affairs that is actually caused by the end. Bacon had already pointed a finger in this direction when he said of fictions that they "give some show of satisfaction to the mind, wherein the nature of things doth seem to deny it."[8]

The fiction of the end is both a necessity and a paradox, for the end is an event that one cannot avoid and yet that one cannot hope to understand in its true nature. It is an event that must inevitably exclude any insight into itself, has to be tolerated, and yet in itself is intolerable. It is this paradox that gives rise to the creation of the fiction, for fictions alone can fill in the gaps apparent in man's knowledge. This explains the high degree of certainty about the character of the end, as evinced by all these fictions, and also explains the often radical revisions in men's expectations as new situations arise. The usefulness of these fictions can be gauged merely from the fact that the question of their truthfulness is never even considered. Indeed, the power of the fiction lies in the fact that its origin remains concealed. Thus, none of the many conceptions of the end has ever contained the suggestion that its images are designed simply to satisfy a human need—even though this is their real origin. Perhaps such a claim, if it had ever been voiced, would have been regarded as cynical, for uncovering the truth behind fictions means destroying the very thing that fiction is attempting to provide—i.e., the satisfaction of a human need. Beckett's texts aim deep down at the anthropological roots of fiction, and so they take their place within the history of 'the end', not so much in the sense of another manifestation of these expectations, as in an unveiling of our own need for fictions. The violent reactions and

[6] Ibid., p. 39.
[7] Ibid., p. 62.
[8] Quoted by Kermode, *Sense of an Ending*, p. 63.

also the nagging discomfort aroused by Beckett's texts suggest that he has hit his mark.

The negativeness of these texts would seem to consist in the fact that they refuse to satisfy our elementary needs, and that whenever we think we have found something definite to satisfy our needs, we are made to realize that what we have found is only a fiction. Furthermore, we see that we are constantly fabricating fictions in order to create reliable guidelines or even realities for ourselves, though in the end they turn out to be no such thing. These texts also show clearly that in spite of the knowledge revealed to us concerning our needs, we still cannot do without our fictions, so that these needs become the basis of our own entanglement with ourselves. And from this, no fiction can release us.

II

Beckett already touched on this subject in the *Proust* essay he published in 1931 at the age of twenty-five, when qualifying for a teaching post in romance philology at Trinity College Dublin. Although the essay was conceived as a Proust interpretation, long passages of it are more in the nature of a manifesto, for which *Remembrance of Things Passed* provided the starting-point. Beckett is concerned primarily with uncovering the illusions that gave rise to Proust's central intentions, above all the identity of the 'ego', as rediscovered in memory.

"The aspirations of yesterday were valid for yesterday's ego, not for to-day's. We are disappointed at the nullity of what we are pleased to call attainment. But what is attainment? The identification of the subject with the object of his desire. The subject has died—and perhaps many times—on the way."[9] To believe that memory is in a position to establish a connection—denied by life itself—between the many manifestations of the ego, means for Beckett a final capitulation to habit: "The laws of memory are subject to the more general laws of habit. . . . Habit is the ballast that chains the dog to his vomit."[10] If habit could connect up the different phases of our lives, then we should have to go through life looking constantly behind us; but life itself does not run backward, so that if we allow habit to orient us, we are deceiving ourselves with fictions. The function of habit is to remove the strangeness from life; this is why we constantly have recourse to our memories. What memory retains has already passed through the filter of habit and has lost

[9] Samuel Beckett, *Proust* (Evergreen) (New York, 1958), p. 3.
[10] Ibid., pp. 7 f.

those painful sharp edges associated with first observation; thus Beckett calls memory an "agent of security."[11] If this need for security gives rise to our projecting a meaning onto the objects before us, then we automatically cut ourselves off from those experiences that can only arise if we allow the objects to work their effect on us without sheltering behind our preconceptions of their meaning. "But when the object is perceived as particular and unique and not merely the member of a family, when it appears independent of any general notion and detached from the sanity of a cause, isolated and inexplicable in the light of ignorance, then and then only may it be a source of enchantment. Unfortunately Habit has laid its veto on this form of perception."[12]

Here we see the outline of a problem that runs through Beckett's text in something like a series of variations. The haphazardness of objects activates our need for tidy arrangements, which drives us to establish connections and link the objects together. It is this process that destroys the "enchantment of reality." For observation conditioned by habit cannot permit the experience of contingency. One might conclude that this makes literature necessary, since literature can confront us directly with something strange, and if we cannot absorb the experience of this strange object, then the possibility exists that we shall discover how our own 'habit' of acquiring experience functions. We can only talk of experiences if our preconceptions have been modified or transformed by them. This is the background against which we must view the works of Beckett.

Like the *Proust* essay, Beckett's first novel, *Murphy*, published in 1937, is dominated by the attempt to expose the truth behind the commonplace. There, literary conventions are unmasked as mere devices dependent on specific situations. But unlike the *Proust* essay, the novel is a piece of fiction, which means that Beckett's anatomy of fiction is itself conducted through a fictional medium. The attempt to reveal the basis of fiction through fiction itself means that the process of revelation can never end.

For this reason, *Murphy*, too, is nothing but the beginning of this process. The first sentence reads: "The sun shone, having no alternative, on the nothing new."[13] The indication that the sun shone and so had no alternative, deflates the beginning of the novel to the level of triviality. But

---

[11] Ibid., p. 10.
[12] Ibid., p. 11.
[13] Samuel Beckett, *Murphy* (Evergreen) (New York, 1957, 1965, 1967), p. 1.

usually the beginning is important, because it denotes the direction in which the events and their significance are to move. Beckett begins by wiping out any such significance. What is left is a form of words devoid of content and of function. *Murphy* is full of such verbal 'sockets', and the reader may sometimes feel tempted to put in his own interpretative 'plug' in order to supply the meaning which the author has removed. If this does happen, then the whole thing becomes abstruse—but only so long as one insists on regarding the novel as a representative portrayal of reality.[14]

But what is supposed to be representative about the wish of the 'hero' to go into a lunatic asylum and finally to go mad himself? At best, perhaps a withdrawal from his social environment or, less convincing, the withdrawal from body into spirit and, quite inconceivably, the withdrawal from the recognizable forms of spiritual activity into a movement that is only recognizable so long as it destroys everything it has produced. As Murphy tries to bring himself back to the point that can be identified as that which 'makes him tick', so he seems to himself to be getting farther and farther away from what he really is. In the depths of his spirit, we learn: "Here there was nothing but commotion and the pure forms of commotion. Here he was not free, but a mote in the dark of absolute freedom. He did not move, he was a point in the ceaseless unconditioned generation and passing away of line. Matrix of surds."[15] What happens here has been made explicit in a different context by Maurice Merleau-Ponty in his *Phenomenology of Perception:*

My absolute contact with myself, the identity of being and appearance cannot be posited, but only lived as anterior to any affirmation. In both cases, therefore, we have the same silence and the same void. The experience of absurdity and that of absolute self-evidence are mutually implicatory, and even indistinguishable. The world appears absurd, only if a demand for absolute consciousness ceaselessly dissociates from each other the meanings with which it swarms, and conversely this demand is motivated by the conflict between those meanings. Absolute self-evidence and the absurd are equivalent, not merely as philosophical affirmations, but also as experiences.[16]

There are experiences that we can only have, but into which we cannot gain any insight. One of these is the absolute contact of the ego with itself, which is why Murphy releases himself from all worldly ties, in or-

[14] Cf. Manfred Smuda, *Becketts Prosa als Metasprache* (Munich, 1970), pp. 31 f.
[15] Beckett, *Murphy,* p. 112.
[16] Maurice Merleau-Ponty, *Phenomenology of Perception,* transl. Colin Smith (New York, 1962), pp. 295 f.

der to get to the point at which in his attitude toward himself he can finally coincide with himself.

This gives rise to a reality that cannot be penetrated by human knowledge. Such a situation can only be presented in the manner of absurdity, which indicates that self-evidence and knowledge exclude one another—or, in other words, that knowledge of self-evidence does not lend itself to be questioned. It is characteristic of Beckett's texts that from the very beginning they are concerned with those experiences of which we can never know anything. In *Murphy*, this is the synchronization of the ego with itself; in the trilogy, it is the experience of the end. And so in Beckett's novels, from fiction itself the impression is drawn that no statement—not even a hypothetical one—can be made about a reality that is detached from human perception. This is the reason why the novels have an absurd effect, for inherent in the process of presentation is the awareness that what is to be presented lies far beyond the capabilities of fiction. But what is it that enables such excessive demands on the capabilities of fiction to concern us anyway? The answer may be found in the following passage in Kermode's *The Sense of an Ending:*

> . . . the need we continue to feel is a need of concord, and we supply it by increasingly varied concord-fictions. They change as the reality from which we, in the middest, seek a show of satisfaction, changes. . . . They do this, for some of us, perhaps better than history, perhaps better than theology, largely because they are consciously false.[17]

And so fiction is able to give us such comforting answers to our human problems because it is unreal. Our compensation for what cannot be perceived is the knowledge pretended by fiction, which is "consciously false." For this very reason, the truth behind the fiction must not be revealed, and fiction itself must not be 'falsified'.

III

This, however, is the very thing that happens in Beckett's trilogy of novels *Molloy, Malone Dies,* and *The Unnamable,* which appeared originally in French between 1951 and 1953 and were translated into English for the most part by Beckett himself. Here, the theme of *Murphy* returns again, but on a vastly different scale. The titles of the individual sections of the trilogy draw attention to the withdrawal of the first-person narrator into ultimate anonymity. While the first-person narrator of the third novel is the unnamable, the names in the first two novels act as masks that the narrator has assumed. Hindsight reveals that the masks of the

---

[17] Kermode, *Sense of an Ending,* pp. 63 f.

unnamable refer to particular relationships, limitations, and attitudes which, in the last novel, have lost all substance. But the unnamable is not completely free from the names which he once bore and which now stop him from relaxing in his anonymity.[18] Clearly, one cannot get rid of fictions quite so easily.

The first-person narrators in the trilogy have an unsurpassable awareness of what is happening while they are narrating, or of what happens when they try to pin down what they want to write about. It is this awareness that determines the order of sentences in the first novel. This consists of a continual alternation of statement and qualification of what has been stated. The tendency, however, is not toward a consolidation of meaning, as one might normally expect from the development of a text, so much as toward a more or less complete contradiction of whatever has been stated. The first-person narrator avoids any kind of arrangement of the things he has observed. He does not want to confine them within the limits of his perception and impose an arbitrary uniformity on them; he wants, rather, to expose the deformities that occur to them through the very act of perception.[19] But even this insight becomes an object of reflection for Molloy: "I could therefore puzzle over it endlessly without the least risk. For to know nothing is nothing, not to want to know anything likewise, but to be beyond knowing anything, to know you are beyond knowing anything, that is when peace enters in, to the soul of the incurious seeker."[20] But the words he uses also give him away.

Molloy wants peace—that is what he is searching for. This peace, however, cannot be obtained through what one knows, but only through the knowledge that whatever is knowable is nothing. This knowledge in turn is directly relevant to those experiences which we know exist, but about which we also know that insight into their very nature is denied us. One of these is, of course, the end. The question arises as to whether it can be enough for us to say about a certain situation that we know nothing. Is it not here, in fact, that we need our fictions, which, however "consciously false" they may be, at least pretend to a knowledge of the unknowable? In spite of his awareness and cool reasoning, Molloy is not completely free from the desire to imagine the end, and he falls into the very temptation to which his insight should prevent him from succumbing. "For what possible end to these wastes where true light never was, nor any upright thing, nor any true foundation, but only these leaning things, for ever lapsing and crumbling away, beneath a sky without mem-

---

[18] For a detailed discussion see "Self-Reduction," in this volume, pp. 171 ff.
[19] For details see ibid., pp. 165 ff.
[20] Samuel Beckett, *Molloy* (Grove Press) (New York, 1955), p. 86.

ory of morning or hope of night. These things, what things, come from where, made of what? And it says that here nothing stirs, has never stirred, will never stir, except myself, who do not stir either, when I am there, but see and am seen. Yes, a world at an end, in spite of appearances, its end brought it forth, ending it began, is it clear enough?"[21] Here the end is still visualized in detailed images, and obviously an end without such images is not conceivable. But at the same time, Molloy asks if the images are apt—and this at the very moment when the end is beginning to assume the almost familiar eschatological features of a revelation. Is the peace Molloy is searching for perhaps impossible without images? If so, then the images would be the obstacles to peace, for one only creates images in terms of one's own human reality, and it is exactly this reality of which one seeks to be free. The end is therefore inconceivable without images and irrelevant with images. These are the problems developed in the remaining novels of the trilogy.

In *Malone Dies,* the first-person narrator no longer reports on different phases of his life, as Molloy had done, but simply reports on what happens when one reports. Molloy had already been aware of the fact that all representation is but an 'arrangement'—tersely summed up as "Saying is inventing"[22]—and this is also assumed by Malone as he waits for his end. Right up till his death he passes time by writing, but his writing concerns writing itself. He would like to get to the point where he is only writing about the fact that he is writing. It is impossible to make the actual act of writing the object of the writing, because you cannot write unless you have something to write about, but the act of writing automatically prevents you from capturing the complete reality of the object with which you seem to be concerned. Malone is aware of this. And so he describes what results from writing as being lies. With this as a basic premise, it follows that the moment you are conscious of what happens in writing, writing itself can only be understood as a continual moving away from the false images that arise from writing. Thus the never-ending discovery of fictions created by writing remains the only possibility of writing one's way toward the truth about writing.

The truth about writing consists in the discovery of its fictional character. But why does this discovery have to be made over and over again, without end? The answer lies in the alternative course that has enmeshed Malone: "Live and invent. I have tried. I must have tried. Invent. It is not the word. Neither is live."[23] Malone's alternative is a bas-

[21] Ibid., p. 53.
[22] Ibid., p. 41.
[23] Samuel Beckett, *Malone Dies* (Grove Press) (New York, [5]1965), p. 18.

ic dilemma of life itself. Though we are alive, we do not know what it means to be alive. If we try to find out what it means to be alive, we are forced to seek the meaning of something we cannot possibly know. And so the continual invention of images and, at the same time, the rejection of their claims to truth, provide the only means of coping with this dilemma. In this way, we do not fall victim to our own inventions, but to a certain extent we do satisfy the urge to know something about that which cannot be known. Thus we cannot abandon our fictions, but nevertheless ought to realize that they are fictions, as this is the only certain knowledge we can hope to obtain.

If we feel inclined to regard this fact as absurd, this inclination is only another expression of the fact that we are still searching for certainty where we know there can be none and that in spite of this knowledge we still take the image for the truth. In *Malone Dies,* our need for fiction is constantly frustrated. What happens here, should not occur, if fiction is not to be robbed of its effect. Malone reveals the nature of this fiction, which is that fictions are "consciously false." But falsifying fictions is more than just adapting them to changing needs.

An anatomy of the fiction contained in Beckett's trilogy discloses the "complementarities" that are constantly supplied by the fictions and serve to complement and give form to that which remains inconclusive or open in each particular situation in life. The scale on which such gaps are closed can vary considerably. Every historical period will have different gaps for which "complementarities" have to be supplied. There are gaps in human affairs, too, which require to be filled in. This applies not only to the uncertainty of the end but also to the nonstop fabrication of fictions that is necessary in everyday empirical life. This is where fictions are most likely to be confused with realities, simply because they are so useful. Beckett bursts open the character of fiction as "concord-fiction" not for the sake of being destructive, but because the very composition of his texts aims at running contrary to the continual closing of gaps inherent in "concord-fiction." By betraying the fictions, he reestablishes the openness of the situations he deals with. This is the dominant trend in the third novel of the trilogy, *The Unnamable.*

This anonymous being has cast off all the fictional figures through whom he had named himself. Names had always cropped up when he had attempted to get a grip on himself in given situations. But it is difficult for him to get rid of these "vice-exister(s)."[24] Not only do they pursue him, but they also keep usurping him by telling him who he is.[25] And

[24] Samuel Beckett, *The Unnamable* (Grove Press) (New York, 1958), p. 37.
[25] Cf. ibid., p. 38.

because this is what he wants to know, he feels that the old fictions are continually seeking to reinvent him in order to fulfill his wish. At the same time, however, he is also aware that every suggestion he writes down from these figures can only be a fiction. This knowledge enables him to avoid being continually reinvented. With something like happiness, he states: "Dear incomprehension, it's thanks to you I'll be myself, in the end. Nothing will remain of all the lies they have glutted me with."[26] This utterance is highly ambivalent. First, it means that only by accepting incomprehensibility is it possible to see through the fictions that pretend to know the unknowable; that is the situation of the unnamable at the moment in which he makes this statement. But in addition to this, it is the incomprehensibility of reality, and indeed of the ego itself, that gives rise to the creation of fiction. To pursue both lines of thought at virtually the same time seems highly problematical, but it is this very problem that the unnamable is trying to settle. With his insight, he destroys what is promised by the fictions. And this rejection of fiction, its unmasking as a lie, then becomes the condition for establishing an open situation as regards life in general. Without the production and subsequent negation of fictions, this open situation could not possibly be established. But this, in turn, means that even in cases such as the unnamable is concerned with, the usefulness of fiction cannot be dispensed with. That is to say, even the unmasked fiction cannot destroy itself. A great comfort for literature and a great nuisance for ideology!

From this state of affairs there arise two consequences. These can be described as two basic structures that are common to Beckett's prose and drama. Each individual work itself creates a certain starting-point. The mere fact that something is written means that a start has been made or, alternatively, that writing has given rise to a start. If one writes, it must always be about something. This leads to the first structural feature of these texts: they consume their own starting-points. But as this starting-point is itself the subject of the writing, however drastically it may be reduced it can never completely disappear. Hence the second structural feature of Beckett's texts: if the content of the writing is the consumption of its own starting-point, then, in accordance with its structure, it can never come to an end. Fictions, according to Kermode, are for finding things out. The fiction which Beckett is constantly questioning shows that, in fact, we are alive because we cannot settle anything

[26] Ibid., p. 51.

final, and this absence of finality is what drives us continually to go on being active.

IV

This line of thought is also apparent in the curious piece of prose written in 1965 and entitled *Imagination Dead Imagine*. By imagining that the power of imagination itself is dead, we are invited to loosen our grip on the world to that extent that we should curb or annihilate our urge to interpret our surroundings.

The text begins with the sentence: "No trace anywhere of life, you say, pah, no difficulty there, imagination not dead yet, yes, dead, good, imagination dead imagine."[27] Do all traces of life disappear if we imagine that the power of imagination is extinguished? On the contrary, the text shows how, once the power of imagination has been separated from the world, its very unfixedness gives rise to a dynamism that produces continuous configurations and then swallows them up again. It is only the imagined death of imagination that brings out its inextinguishability. But whenever the power of imagination is fixed to a worldly context in which it is used to fill in the gaps there arises fiction. Beckett's novels are therefore fictional texts which do not deal with fictions, but continually strive to nullify fiction. The act of "decomposition" forms the creative impetus of these texts.

The problem that Beckett attempts to solve is: how can you picture something in words and forms that is the source from which words and forms emanate, but whose inherent nature prohibits its expression in words and forms? So he tries in *Imagination Dead Imagine* to eliminate the expectation (expectation being the impetus toward meaning) in words. Beckett allows the words of *Imagination Dead Imagine* to be experienced but not to be known (in terms of meaning). The impetus toward meaning destroys the experience of the word and for this reason Beckett cancels out all contextual references. The following passage from the middle of the text provides a good starting-point for a specific, if brief, textual study: "Rediscovered miraculously after what absence in perfect voids it is no longer quite the same, from this point of view, but there is no other. Externally all is as before and the sighting of the little fabric quite as much a matter of chance, its whiteness merging in the surrounding whiteness."[28] This passage clearly illustrates Beckett's process

<hr>

[27] Samuel Beckett, *Imagination Dead Imagine* (London, 1965), p. 7.
[28] Ibid., p. 11.

of creation.[29] Pure chance makes this expression possible, and whether or not a specifie content is generated out of the void is never firmly stated, since the whiteness of the content merges with the whiteness around it. There is no context for this specific event, and when it is placed within a context it disappears. All potential points of reference within the texts are blatantly arbitrary and contribute no unique context or meaning to the text. Yet the text is full of commands: "Go back out, move back . . . ascend . . . descend, go back in,"[30] that invite the reader to a participation in the experience of the text itself. The author, at one point, exclaims that this "may seem strange."[31] By saying this he is trying to demonstrate his sympathy as a guide who recognizes the difficulty of experiencing a void of meaning. This text is not a sterile monologue, it is an invitation to participation. The words themselves seem almost to beg to be embraced on their own terms. The phrase logically negates itself, destroying its own meaning, and it is this destruction of meaning that lends the phrase its potential to be experienced by the reader.

What is 'gained' by this can perhaps be summed up by a quotation from John Cage, who states in his book *Silence:* "Our intention is to affirm this life, not to bring order out of chaos nor to suggest improvements in creation, but simply to wake up to the very life we're living, which is so excellent once one gets one's mind and one's desires out of its way and lets it act of its own accord."[32]

V

Opposed to such an awakening, however, are certain difficulties caused by human behavior. Beckett's plays draw attention to these difficulties and show perhaps even more clearly than his novels the conditions that give rise to them. In a letter to his New York producer Alan Schneider, Beckett speaks of his drama as the "power of the text to claw."[33] There is no doubt that his plays do claw at one, but we feel this effect above all because they lead us to an increased amount of activity. This is certainly true of Beckett's first great dramatic success *Waiting for Godot,* which was published in 1952 and had its premiere the following year. When asked who Godot was and what he stood for, Beckett replied, "If I knew,

[29] For these remarks on *Imagination Dead Imagine* I am indebted to a paper by Jan R. Reber which he submitted in my Beckett-Seminar at Wesleyan University in the fall term 1970/71.
[30] Beckett, *Imagination Dead Imagine,* p. 8.
[31] Ibid.
[32] John Cage, *Silence* (Cambridge, Mass., 1961), p. 95.
[33] Quoted by Hugh Kenner, *Samuel Beckett. A Critical Study* (New York, 1961), p. 165.

I would have said so in the play."[34] What, then, can the audience know, and what experience will they gain from a play that refuses to divulge its meaning? In *Waiting for Godot,* as in many other of Beckett's plays, nothing is decided. Even the apparently decisive waiting of Vladimir and Estragon for Godot gradually becomes more and more aimless as the 'action' proceeds. This increasing indeterminacy acts as a provocation to the audience. Waiting that loses sight of its purpose begins like a mystery, but develops into mere mystification. If the waiting is an end in itself, then there arises the situation that the actions, words, and gestures of the characters become increasingly indefinite. Then not only does the waiting become aimless but also the language of the characters no longer corresponds to what the intention of language ought to be. This expanding indeterminacy stimulates the audience into the act of 'determining'. The more we try to project meaning onto the aimless 'action', the further we get from the characters and the nearer to our own ideas, to which we then begin to cling to an ever increasing degree, as shown by the great *Godot* debate in the *London Times.* As the largely indeterminate situations in the text refuse to divulge who Godot is and what is the meaning of the waiting, it seems as if this play is seeking to shut out its audience. But this is something quite intolerable for us, and so the spectator who has been locked out struggles with increasing intensity to break into the play again, bringing with him all the meanings and decisions that have been withheld from him. If the play won't tell him what it means, then he will decide for himself what it ought to mean. The result is, that the spectator is, so to speak, dragged along in the wake of the play, trying increasingly hard to catch up by means of interpretation. And the harder he tries, the further behind he falls, and the play which he had tried to break into with his specific interpretations, simply goes ahead regardless of him. This gives rise to a strange experience: as the meaning projections of the spectator are incapable of removing the indeterminacy of the situations, so the two main characters seem more and more free and unconcerned. They seem to be quite indifferent to the earnestness assumed by the spectator.

Vladimir and Estragon do not possess this freedom right from the outset; it is brought to life, if not exactly created, by the resolution of the spectator to impose a definite meaning on the indeterminate situations in the play. The more the spectator feels compelled to do this, the greater the freedom of Vladimir and Estragon. The spectator's interest in Godot is disproportionately larger than that of the two protagonists.

[34] Quoted by Martin Esslin, *The Theater of the Absurd* (New York, 1961), p. 12.

And if the spectator moves toward Godot, the protagonists move away from the spectator. If the spectator wants to know whether Godot is really God, the two men waiting seem like clowns because they do not appear to grasp the earnestness of the situation. But these situations are created, in the first place, by the spectator himself, for the determination of his attitude always brings forth a contrary reaction from the drama itself. Indeed, the text is so designed that it constantly calls forth a desire for determinacy which the spectator cannot escape but which inevitably drives him further and further into the trap of his own limitations.

Here, the problem of fiction arises again in a different, and existentially intensified manner. The spectator at a Beckett play feels for himself the need for and the consequence of "concord-fiction," which forms a basis for his act of meaning projection. The highly indeterminate actions of the characters, precisely because of the lack of consequence in these (simulated) actions, draw the spectator into the play because he wants to impose consistency, purpose, and meaning on it. But in doing so, the spectator becomes the only real person in the play. The fictional text, by its extreme indeterminacy, has led him to make the decisions he thought necessary and meaningful, but then, the moment he has made them, the characters stand round the baffled spectator and—metaphorically speaking—'experience him' in his frustration. For he is worried about something they have left behind: the closing of open situations by means of fictions. At this point we get the special and inimitable effect unique to Beckett theater, tersely summed up by Hugh Kenner: ". . . for art has suddenly refused to be art and brought forward living pain."[35] A precondition for such reactions is an intensive participation in the action on the part of the spectator. And the more intensive this participation, the more fluid become the boundaries between literature and reality— and this in a play whose supposedly absurd character would seem to indicate that it had nothing to do with reality anyway. Finally, we are forced to revise, and indeed to transform, our ideas as to what is reality.

This is the tendency underlying one of Beckett's most provocative plays, *Endgame*. The title is a pointer to what is to come: the end is not to be shown, it is to be played: "Me—(*he yawns*)—to play,"[36] are Hamm's first words in this play, as he replies to Clov's statement: "Finished, it's finished, nearly finished, it must be nearly finished."[37] The degree to which Clov and Hamm are dominated by the idea of playing can be seen not only from the fact that they frequently refer to their activities as a game[38] but also from the fact that all their activities are without conse-

[35] Kenner, *Samuel Beckett*, p. 174.
[36] Beckett, *Endgame*, p. 12.
[37] Ibid.
[38] Cf. ibid., pp. 44 and 51.

quence. When Clov smashes the toy dog down on Hamm's head, the reaction is the contrary of what we expect: Hamm wants Clov to hit him
with an axe. It is little wonder, then, that in all such actions both of
them are careful to remove all meaning from their game:

> HAMM: We're not beginning to . . . to . . . mean something?
> CLOV: Mean something! You and I, mean something! [*Brief laugh*]
> Ah that's a good one!
> HAMM: I wonder. [*Pause*] Imagine if a rational being came back to
> earth, wouldn't he be liable to get ideas into his head if he observed
> us long enough.[39]

These are the very ideas that go whirling through the spectator's mind;
he may tend to regard all the weird goings-on as part of a game, but he
finds that the rules of this game are not divulged. He cannot help searching for them, and in so doing he discovers that the game could be said to
run according to various codes, but these originate not in the form of
the game itself so much as in the meaning projections of the spectator.
If the rules of the *Endgame* have to be projected onto it by the spectat-
or, then clearly the text itself cannot establish that any one of the possibilities is the correct one. And if one does draw up a consistent code to
apply to the whole game, it can only be at the expense of all other levels
of the text; and when the spectator turns his attention to those levels
excluded by the 'code' he seems to be fixed on, he has no alternative
but to reject his own meaning projections. Thus *Endgame* compels its
spectator to reject the 'meanings' it stimulates, and in this way conveys
something of the 'unendingness' of the end and the nature of the fictions
which we are continually fabricating in order to finish off the end or to
close the gaps in our own experiences. By compelling the spectator to
reject the meaning he himself has suggested, *Endgame* offers a new experience, unique to the world of literature, in which one is enabled to penetrate below the surface of one's own meaning projections and to gain insight into those factors that guide the individual in his personal mode of
interpretation. In this way, too, there lies a chance that the individual is
able to free himself from the restrictions of his own outlook. The negativeness of Beckett's texts, then, consists in the technique he uses in order to involve us in the complex process of manufacturing fictions and
to open our eyes to the nature of fiction itself. If this awareness is inapplicable to everyday life, one might as well question the standards of
everyday life when they cannot tolerate this awareness, or—even worse—
when they attempt to suppress it.

[39] Ibid., p. 27.

11

THE READING PROCESS:
A Phenomenological Approach

I

The phenomenological theory of art lays full stress on the idea that, in considering a literary work, one must take into account not only the actual text but also, and in equal measure, the actions involved in responding to that text. Thus Roman Ingarden confronts the structure of the literary text with the ways in which it can be *konkretisiert* (realized).[1] The text as such offers different "schematised views"[2] through which the subject matter of the work can come to light, but the actual bringing to light is an action of *Konkretisation*. If this is so, then the literary work has two poles, which we might call the artistic and the esthetic: the artistic refers to the text created by the author, and the esthetic to the realization accomplished by the reader. From this polarity it follows that the literary work cannot be completely identical with the text, or with the realization of the text, but in fact must lie halfway between the two. The work is more than the text, for the text only takes on life when it is realized, and furthermore the realization is by no means independent of the individual disposition of the reader—though

[1] Cf. Roman Ingarden, *Vom Erkennen des literarischen Kunstwerks* (Tübingen, 1968), pp. 49 ff.
[2] For a detailed discussion of this term see Roman Ingarden, *Das literarische Kunstwerk* (Tübingen, ²1960), pp. 270 ff.

this in turn is acted upon by the different patterns of the text. The convergence of text and reader brings the literary work into existence, and this convergence can never be precisely pinpointed, but must always remain virtual, as it is not to be identified either with the reality of the text or with the individual disposition of the reader.

It is the virtuality of the work that gives rise to its dynamic nature, and this in turn is the precondition for the effects that the work calls forth. As the reader uses the various perspectives offered him by the text in order to relate the patterns and the "schematised views" to one another, he sets the work in motion, and this very process results ultimately in the awakening of responses within himself. Thus, reading causes the literary work to unfold its inherently dynamic character. That this is no new discovery is apparent from references made even in the early days of the novel. Laurence Sterne remarks in *Tristram Shandy:* ". . . no author, who understands the just boundaries of decorum and good-breeding, would presume to think all: The truest respect which you can pay to the reader's understanding, is to halve this matter amicably, and leave him something to imagine, in his turn, as well as yourself. For my own part, I am eternally paying him compliments of this kind, and do all that lies in my power to keep his imagination as busy as my own."[3] Sterne's conception of a literary text is that it is something like an arena in which reader and author participate in a game of the imagination. If the reader were given the whole story, and there were nothing left for him to do, then his imagination would never enter the field, the result would be the boredom which inevitably arises when everything is laid out cut and dried before us. A literary text must therefore be conceived in such a way that it will engage the reader's imagination in the task of working things out for himself, for reading is only a pleasure when it is active and creative. In this process of creativity, the text may either not go far enough, or may go too far, so we may say that boredom and overstrain form the boundaries beyond which the reader will leave the field of play.

The extent to which the 'unwritten' part of a text stimulates the reader's creative participation is brought out by an observation of Virginia Woolf's in her study of *Jane Austen:*

> Jane Austen is thus a mistress of much deeper emotion than appears upon the surface. She stimulates us to supply what is not there. What she offers is, apparently, a trifle, yet is composed of something that expands in the reader's mind and endows with the most enduring form

---

[3] Laurence Sterne, *Tristram Shandy* (London, 1956), II, 11: 79.

of life scenes which are outwardly trivial. Always the stress is laid upon character. . . . The turns and twists of the dialogue keep us on the tenterhooks of suspense. Our attention is half upon the present moment, half upon the future. . . . Here, indeed, in this unfinished and in the main inferior story, are all the elements of Jane Austen's greatness.[4]

The unwritten aspects of apparently trivial scenes and the unspoken dialogue within the "turns and twists" not only draw the reader into the action but also lead him to shade in the many outlines suggested by the given situations, so that these take on a reality of their own. But as the reader's imagination animates these 'outlines,' they in turn will influence the effect of the written part of the text. Thus begins a whole dynamic process: the written text imposes certain limits on its unwritten implications in order to prevent these from becoming too blurred and hazy, but at the same time these implications, worked out by the reader's imagination, set the given situation against a background which endows it with far greater significance than it might have seemed to possess on its own. In this way, trivial scenes suddenly take on the shape of an "enduring form of life." What constitutes this form is never named, let alone explained in the text, although in fact it is the end product of the interaction between text and reader.

II

The question now arises as to how far such a process can be adequately described. For this purpose a phenomenological analysis recommends itself, especially since the somewhat sparse observations hitherto made of the psychology of reading tend mainly to be psychoanalytical, and so are restricted to the illustration of predetermined ideas concerning the unconscious. We shall, however, take a closer look later at some worthwhile psychological observations.

As a starting point for a phenomenological analysis we might examine the way in which sequent sentences act upon one another. This is of especial importance in literary texts in view of the fact that they do not correspond to any objective reality outside themselves. The world presented by literary texts is constructed out of what Ingarden has called *intentionale Satzkorrelate* (intentional sentence correlatives):

Sentences link up in different ways to form more complex units of meaning that reveal a very varied structure giving rise to such entities

[4] Virginia Woolf, *The Common Reader*, First Series (London, 1957), p. 174.

276

as a short story, a novel, a dialogue, a drama, a scientific theory. . . . In the final analysis, there arises a particular world, with component parts determined in this way or that, and with all the variations that may occur within these parts—all this as a purely intentional correlative of a complex of sentences. If this complex finally forms a literary work, I call the whole sum of sequent intentional sentence correlatives the 'world presented' in the work.[5]

This world, however, does not pass before the reader's eyes like a film. The sentences are "component parts" insofar as they make statements, claims, or observations, or convey information, and so establish various perspectives in the text. But they remain only "component parts"—they are not the sum total of the text itself. For the intentional correlatives disclose subtle connections which individually are less concrete than the statements, claims, and observations, even though these only take on their real meaningfulness through the interaction of their correlatives.

How is one to conceive the connection between the correlatives? It marks those points at which the reader is able to 'climb aboard' the text. He has to accept certain given perspectives, but in doing so he inevitably causes them to interact. When Ingarden speaks of intentional sentence correlatives in literature, the statements made or information conveyed in the sentence are already in a certain sense qualified: the sentence does not consist solely of a statement—which, after all, would be absurd, as one can only make statements about things that exist—but aims at something beyond what it actually says. This is true of all sentences in literary works, and it is through the interaction of these sentences that their common aim is fulfilled. This is what gives them their own special quality in literary texts. In their capacity as statements, observations, purveyors of information, etc., they are always indications of something that is to come, the structure of which is foreshadowed by their specific content.

They set in motion a process out of which emerges the actual content of the text itself. In describing man's inner consciousness of time, Husserl once remarked: "Every originally constructive process is inspired by pre-intentions, which construct and collect the seed of what is to come, as such, and bring it to fruition."[6] For this bringing to fruition, the literary text needs the reader's imagination, which gives shape to the interaction of correlatives foreshadowed in structure by the sequence of the sentences. Husserl's observation draws our attention to a point that

---

[5] Ingarden, *Vom Erkennen des literarischen Kunstwerks*, p. 29.

[6] Edmund Husserl, *Zur Phänomenologie des inneren Zeitbewusstseins, Gesammelte Werke* (The Hague, 1966), 10:52.

plays a not insignificant part in the process of reading. The individual sentences not only work together to shade in what is to come; they also form an expectation in this regard. Husserl calls this expectation "pre-intentions." As this structure is characteristic of *all* sentence correlatives, the interaction of these correlatives will not be a fulfillment of the expectation so much as a continual modification of it.

For this reason, expectations are scarcely ever fulfilled in truly literary texts. If they were, then such texts would be confined to the individualization of a given expectation, and one would inevitably ask what such an intention was supposed to achieve. Strangely enough, we feel that any confirmative effect—such as we implicitly demand of expository texts, as we refer to the objects they are meant to present—is a defect in a literary text. For the more a text individualizes or confirms an expectation it has initially aroused, the more aware we become of its didactic purpose, so that at best we can only accept or reject the thesis forced upon us. More often than not, the very clarity of such texts will make us want to free ourselves from their clutches. But generally the sentence correlatives of literary texts do not develop in this rigid way, for the expectations they evoke tend to encroach on one another in such a manner that they are continually modified as one reads. One might simplify by saying that each intentional sentence correlative opens up a particular horizon, which is modified, if not completely changed, by succeeding sentences. While these expectations arouse interest in what is to come, the subsequent modification of them will also have a retrospective effect on what has already been read. This may now take on a different significance from that which it had at the moment of reading.

Whatever we have read sinks into our memory and is foreshortened. It may later be evoked again and set against a different background with the result that the reader is enabled to develop hitherto unforeseeable connections. The memory evoked, however, can never reassume its original shape, for this would mean that memory and perception were identical, which is manifestly not so. The new background brings to light new aspects of what we had committed to memory; conversely these, in turn, shed their light on the new background, thus arousing more complex anticipations. Thus, the reader, in establishing these interrelations between past, present and future, actually causes the text to reveal its potential multiplicity of connections. These connections are the product of the reader's mind working on the raw material of the text, though they are not the text itself—for this consists just of sentences, statements, information, etc.

This is why the reader often feels involved in events which, at the time of reading, seem real to him, even though in fact they are very far from his own reality. The fact that completely different readers can be differently affected by the 'reality' of a particular text is ample evidence of the degree to which literary texts transform reading into a creative process that is far above mere perception of what is written. The literary text activates our own faculties, enabling us to recreate the world it presents. The product of this creative activity is what we might call the virtual dimension of the text, which endows it with its reality. This virtual dimension is not the text itself, nor is it the imagination of the reader: it is the coming together of text and imagination.

As we have seen, the activity of reading can be characterized as a sort of kaleidoscope of perspectives, preintentions, recollections. Every sentence contains a preview of the next and forms a kind of viewfinder for what is to come; and this in turn changes the 'preview' and so becomes a 'viewfinder' for what has been read. This whole process represents the fulfillment of the potential, unexpressed reality of the text, but it is to be seen only as a framework for a great variety of means by which the virtual dimension may be brought into being. The process of anticipation and retrospection itself does not by any means develop in a smooth flow. Ingarden has already drawn attention to this fact and ascribes a quite remarkable significance to it:

> Once we are immersed in the flow of *Satzdenken* (sentence-thought), we are ready, after completing the thought of one sentence, to think out the 'continuation,' also in the form of a sentence—and that is, in the form of a sentence that connects up with the sentence we have just thought through. In this way the process of reading goes effortlessly forward. But if by chance the following sentence has no tangible connection whatever with the sentence we have just thought through, there then comes a blockage in the stream of thought. This hiatus is linked with a more or less active surprise, or with indignation. This blockage must be overcome if the reading is to flow once more.[7]

The hiatus that blocks the flow of sentences is, in Ingarden's eyes, the product of chance, and is to be regarded as a flaw; this is typical of his adherence to the classical idea of art. If one regards the sentence sequence as a continual flow, this implies that the anticipation aroused by one sentence will generally be realized by the next, and the frustration of one's expectations will arouse feelings of exasperation. And yet literary texts are full of unexpected twists and turns, and frustration of expectations. Even in the simplest story there is bound to be some kind of

[7] Ingarden, *Vom Erkennen des literarischen Kunstwerks,* p. 32.

279

blockage, if only because no tale can ever be told in its entirety. Indeed, it is only through inevitable omissions that a story gains its dynamism. Thus whenever the flow is interrupted and we are led off in unexpected directions, the opportunity is given to us to bring into play our own faculty for establishing connections—for filling in the gaps left by the text itself.[8]

These gaps have a different effect on the process of anticipation and retrospection, and thus on the 'gestalt' of the virtual dimension, for they may be filled in different ways. For this reason, one text is potentially capable of several different realizations, and no reading can ever exhaust the full potential, for each individual reader will fill in the gaps in his own way, thereby excluding the various other possibilities; as he reads, he will make his own decision as to how the gap is to be filled. In this very act the dynamics of reading are revealed. By making his decision he implicitly acknowledges the inexhaustibility of the text; at the same time it is this very inexhaustibility that forces him to make his decision. With 'traditional' texts this process was more or less unconscious, but modern texts frequently exploit it quite deliberately. They are often so fragmentary that one's attention is almost exclusively occupied with the search for connections between the fragments; the object of this is not to complicate the 'spectrum' of connections, so much as to make us aware of the nature of our own capacity for providing links. In such cases, the text refers back directly to our own preconceptions—which are revealed by the act of interpretation that is a basic element of the reading process. With all literary texts, then, we may say that the reading process is selective, and the potential text is infinitely richer than any of its individual realizations. This is borne out by the fact that a second reading of a piece of literature often produces a different impression from the first. The reasons for this may lie in the reader's own change of circumstances, still, the text must be such as to allow this variation. On a second reading familiar occurrences now tend to appear in a new light and seem to be at times corrected, at times enriched.

In every text there is a potential time sequence which the reader must inevitably realize, as it is impossible to absorb even a short text in a single moment. Thus the reading process always involves viewing the text through a perspective that is continually on the move, linking up the different phases, and so constructing what we have called the virtual dimension. This dimension, of course, varies all the time we are reading.

[8] For a more detailed discussion of the function of "gaps" in literary texts see Wolfgang Iser, "Indeterminacy and the Reader's Response in Prose Fiction," *Aspects of Narrative* (English Institute Essays), ed. J. Hillis Miller (New York, 1971), pp. 1–45.

However, when we have finished the text, and read it again, clearly our extra knowledge will result in a different time sequence; we shall tend to establish connections by referring to our awareness of what is to come, and so certain aspects of the text will assume a significance we did not attach to them on a first reading, while others will recede into the background. It is a common enough experience for a person to say that on a second reading he noticed things he had missed when he read the book for the first time, but this is scarcely surprising in view of the fact that the second time he is looking at the text from a different perspective. The time sequence that he realized on his first reading cannot possibly be repeated on a second reading, and this unrepeatability is bound to result in modifications of his reading experience. This is not to say that the second reading is 'truer' than the first—they are, quite simply, different: the reader establishes the virtual dimension of the text by realizing a new time sequence. Thus even on repeated viewings a text allows and, indeed, induces innovative reading.

In whatever way, and under whatever circumstances the reader may link the different phases of the text together, it will always be the process of anticipation and retrospection that leads to the formation of the virtual dimension, which in turn transforms the text into an experience for the reader. The way in which this experience comes about through a process of continual modification is closely akin to the way in which we gather experience in life. And thus the 'reality' of the reading experience can illuminate basic patterns of real experience:

> We have the experience of a world, not understood as a system of relations which wholly determine each event, but as an open totality the synthesis of which is inexhaustible. . . . From the moment that experience—that is, the opening on to our *de facto* world—is recognized as the beginning of knowledge, there is no longer any way of distinguishing a level of *a priori* truths and one of factual ones, what the world must necessarily be and what it actually is.[9]

The manner in which the reader experiences the text will reflect his own disposition, and in this respect the literary text acts as a kind of mirror; but at the same time, the reality which this process helps to create is one that will be *different* from his own (since, normally, we tend to be bored by texts that present us with things we already know perfectly well ourselves). Thus we have the apparently paradoxical situation in which the reader is forced to reveal aspects of himself in order to experience a reality

---

[9] M. Merleau-Ponty, *Phenomenology of Perception*, transl. Colin Smith (New York, 1962), pp. 219, 221.

which is different from his own. The impact this reality makes on him
will depend largely on the extent to which he himself actively provides
the unwritten part of the text, and yet in supplying all the missing links,
he must think in terms of experiences different from his own; indeed, it
is only by leaving behind the familiar world of his own experience that
the reader can truly participate in the adventure the literary text offers
him.

III

We have seen that, during the process of reading, there is an active interweaving of anticipation and retrospection, which on a second reading
may turn into a kind of advance retrospection. The impressions that
arise as a result of this process will vary from individual to individual,
but only within the limits imposed by the written as opposed to the unwritten text. In the same way, two people gazing at the night sky may
both be looking at the same collection of stars, but one will see the
image of a plough, and the other will make out a dipper. The 'stars' in a
literary text are fixed; the lines that join them are variable. The author
of the text may, of course, exert plenty of influence on the reader's
imagination—he has the whole panoply of narrative techniques at his disposal—but no author worth his salt will ever attempt to set the *whole*
picture before his reader's eyes. If he does, he will very quickly lose
his reader, for it is only by activating the reader's imagination that the
author can hope to involve him and so realize the intentions of his text.

Gilbert Ryle, in his analysis of imagination, asks: "How can a person
fancy that he sees something, without realizing that he is not seeing it?"
He answers as follows:

Seeing Helvellyn [the name of a mountain] in one's mind's eye does
not entail, what seeing Helvellyn and seeing snapshots of Helvellyn entail, the having of visual sensations. It does involve the thought of having a view of Helvellyn and it is therefore a more sophisticated operation than that of having a view of Helvellyn. It is one utilization
among others of the knowledge of how Helvellyn should look, or, in
one sense of the verb, it is thinking how it should look. The expectations which are fulfilled in the recognition at sight of Helvellyn are
not indeed fulfilled in picturing it, but the picturing of it is something
like a rehearsal of getting them fulfilled. So far from picturing involving the having of faint sensations, or wraiths of sensations, it involves
missing just what one would be due to get, if one were seeing the mountain.[10]

[10] Gilbert Ryle, *The Concept of Mind* (Harmondsworth, 1968), p. 255.

If one sees the mountain, then of course one can no longer imagine it, and so the act of picturing the mountain presupposes its absence. Similarly, with a literary text we can only picture things which are not there; the written part of the text gives us the knowledge, but it is the unwritten part that gives us the opportunity to picture things; indeed without the elements of indeterminacy, the gaps in the text, we should not be able to use our imagination.[11]

The truth of this observation is borne out by the experience many people have on seeing, for instance, the film of a novel. While reading *Tom Jones*, they may never have had a clear conception of what the hero actually looks like, but on seeing the film, some may say, "That's not how I imagined him." The point here is that the reader of *Tom Jones* is able to visualize the hero virtually for himself, and so his imagination senses the vast number of possibilities; the moment these possibilities are narrowed down to one complete and immutable picture, the imagination is put out of action, and we feel we have somehow been cheated. This may perhaps be an oversimplification of the process, but it does illustrate plainly the vital richness of potential that arises out of the fact that the hero in the novel must be pictured and cannot be seen. With the novel the reader must use his imagination to synthesize the information given him, and so his perception is simultaneously richer and more private; with the film he is confined merely to physical perception, and so whatever he remembers of the world he had pictured is brutally cancelled out.

IV

The 'picturing' that is done by our imagination is only one of the activities through which we form the 'gestalt' of a literary text. We have already discussed the process of anticipation and retrospection, and to this we must add the process of grouping together all the different aspects of a text to form the consistency that the reader will always be in search of. While expectations may be continually modified, and images continually expanded, the reader will still strive, even if unconsciously, to fit everything together in a consistent pattern. "In the reading of images, as in the hearing of speech, it is always hard to distinguish what is given to us from what we supplement in the process of projection which is triggered off by recognition . . . it is the guess of the beholder that tests the medley of forms and colours for coherent meaning, crystallizing it into shape

[11] Cf. Iser, "Indeterminacy," pp. 11 ff., 42 ff.

when a consistent interpretation has been found."[12] By grouping together the written parts of the text, we enable them to interact, we observe the direction in which they are leading us, and we project onto them the consistency which we, as readers, require. This 'gestalt' must inevitably be colored by our own characteristic selection process. For it is not given by the text itself; it arises from the meeting between the written text and the individual mind of the reader with its own particular history of experience, its own consciousness, its own outlook. The 'gestalt' is not the true meaning of the text; at best it is a configurative meaning; ". . . comprehension is an individual act of seeing-things-together, and only that."[13] With a literary text such comprehension is inseparable from the reader's expectations, and where we have expectations, there too we have one of the most potent weapons in the writer's armory—illusion.

Whenever "consistent reading suggests itself . . . illusion takes over."[14] Illusion, says Northrop Frye, is "fixed or definable, and reality is best understood as its negation."[15] The 'gestalt' of a text normally takes on (or, rather, is given) this fixed or definable outline, as this is essential to our own understanding, but on the other hand, if reading were to consist of nothing but an uninterrupted building up of illusions, it would be a suspect, if not downright dangerous, process: instead of bringing us into contact with reality, it would wean us away from realities. Of course, there is an element of 'escapism' in all literature, resulting from this very creation of illusion, but there are some texts which offer nothing but a harmonious world, purified of all contradiction and deliberately excluding anything that might disturb the illusion once established, and these are the texts that we generally do not like to classify as literary. Women's magazines and the brasher forms of the detective story might be cited as examples.

However, even if an overdose of illusion may lead to triviality, this does not mean that the process of illusion-building should ideally be dispensed with altogether. On the contrary, even in texts that appear to resist the formation of illusion, thus drawing our attention to the cause of this resistance, we still need the abiding illusion that the resistance itself is the consistent pattern underlying the text. This is especially true of modern texts, in which it is the very precision of the written details

---

[12] E. H. Gombrich, *Art and Illusion* (London, 1962), p. 204.
[13] Louis O. Mink, "History and Fiction as Modes of Comprehension," *New Literary History* I (1970): 553.
[14] Gombrich, *Art and Illusion*, p. 278.
[15] Northrop Frye, *Anatomy of Criticism* (New York, 1967), pp. 169 f.

which increases the proportion of indeterminacy; one detail appears to contradict another, and so simultaneously stimulates and frustrates our desire to 'picture,' thus continually causing our imposed 'gestalt' of the text to disintegrate. Without the formation of illusions, the unfamiliar world of the text would remain unfamiliar; through the illusions, the experience offered by the text becomes accessible to us, for it is only the illusion, on its different levels of consistency, that makes the experience 'readable.' If we cannot find (or impose) this consistency, sooner or later we will put the text down. The process is virtually hermeneutic. The text provokes certain expectations which in turn we project onto the text in such a way that we reduce the polysemantic possibilities to a single interpretation in keeping with the expectations aroused, thus extracting an individual, configurative meaning. The polysemantic nature of the text and the illusion-making of the reader are opposed factors. If the illusion were complete, the polysemantic nature would vanish; if the polysemantic nature were all-powerful, the illusion would be totally destroyed. Both extremes are conceivable, but in the individual literary text we always find some form of balance between the two conflicting tendencies. The formation of illusions, therefore, can never be total, but it is this very incompleteness that in fact gives it its productive value.

With regard to the experience of reading, Walter Pater once observed: "For to the grave reader words too are grave; and the ornamental word, the figure, the accessory form or colour or reference, is rarely content to die to thought precisely at the right moment, but will inevitably linger awhile, stirring a long 'brainwave' behind it of perhaps quite alien associations."[16] Even while the reader is seeking a consistent pattern in the text, he is also uncovering other impulses which cannot be immediately integrated or will even resist final integration. Thus the semantic possibilities of the text will always remain far richer than any configurative meaning formed while reading. But this impression is, of course, only to be gained through reading the text. Thus the configurative meaning can be nothing but a *pars pro toto* fulfillment of the text, and yet this fulfillment gives rise to the very richness which it seeks to restrict, and indeed in some modern texts, our awareness of this richness takes precedence over any configurative meaning.

This fact has several consequences which, for the purpose of analysis, may be dealt with separately, though in the reading process they will all

[16] Walter Pater, *Appreciations* (London, 1920), p. 18.

be working together. As we have seen, a consistent, configurative meaning is essential for the apprehension of an unfamiliar experience, which through the process of illusion-building we can incorporate in our own imaginative world. At the same time, this consistency conflicts with the many other possibilities of fulfillment it seeks to exclude, with the result that the configurative meaning is always accompanied by "alien associations" that do not fit in with the illusions formed. The first consequence, then, is the fact that in forming our illusions, we also produce at the same time a latent disturbance of these illusions. Strangely enough, this also applies to texts in which our expectations are actually fulfilled —though one would have thought that the fulfillment of expectations would help to complete the illusion. "Illusion wears off once the expectation is stepped up; we take it for granted and want more."[17]

The experiments in gestalt psychology referred to by Gombrich in *Art and Illusion* make one thing clear: ". . . though we may be intellectually aware of the fact that any given experience *must* be an illusion, we cannot, strictly speaking, watch ourselves having an illusion."[18] Now, if illusion were not a transitory state, this would mean that we could be, as it were, permanently caught up in it. And if reading were exclusively a matter of producing illusion—necessary though this is for the understanding of an unfamiliar experience—we should run the risk of falling victim to a gross deception. But it is precisely during our reading that the transitory nature of the illusion is revealed to the full.

As the formation of illusions is constantly accompanied by "alien associations" which cannot be made consistent with the illusions, the reader constantly has to lift the restrictions he places on the 'meaning' of the text. Since it is he who builds the illusions, he oscillates between involvement in and observation of those illusions; he opens himself to the unfamiliar world without being imprisoned in it. Through this process the reader moves into the presence of the fictional world and so experiences the realities of the text as they happen.

In the oscillation between consistency and "alien associations," between involvement in and observation of the illusion, the reader is bound to conduct his own balancing operation, and it is this that forms the esthetic experience offered by the literary text. However, if the reader were to achieve a balance, obviously he would then no longer be engaged in the process of establishing and disrupting consistency. And since it is this very process that gives rise to the balancing operation, we may say

[17] Gombrich, *Art and Illusion*, p. 54.
[18] Ibid., p. 5.

that the inherent nonachievement of balance is a prerequisite for the very dynamism of the operation. In seeking the balance we inevitably have to start out with certain expectations, the shattering of which is integral to the esthetic experience.

Furthermore, to say merely that "our expectations are satisfied" is to be guilty of another serious ambiguity. At first sight such a statement seems to deny the obvious fact that much of our enjoyment is derived from surprises, from betrayals of our expectations. The solution to this paradox is to find some ground for a distinction between "surprise" and "frustration." Roughly, the distinction can be made in terms of the effects which the two kinds of experiences have upon us. Frustration blocks or checks activity. It necessitates new orientation for our activity, if we are to escape the *cul de sac*. Consequently, we abandon the frustrating object and return to blind impulse activity. On the other hand, surprise merely causes a temporary cessation of the exploratory phase of the experience, and a recourse to intense contemplation and scrutiny. In the latter phase the surprising elements are seen in their connection with what has gone before, with the whole drift of the experience, and the enjoyment of these values is then extremely intense. Finally, it appears that there must always be some degree of novelty or surprise in all these values if there is to be a progressive specification of the direction of the total act . . . and any aesthetic experience tends to exhibit a continuous interplay between "deductive" and "inductive" operations.[19]

It is this interplay between 'deduction' and 'induction' that gives rise to the configurative meaning of the text, and not the individual expectations, surprises, or frustrations arising from the different perspectives. Since this interplay obviously does not take place in the text itself, but can only come into being through the process of reading, we may conclude that this process formulates something that is unformulated in the text and yet represents its 'intention.' Thus, by reading we uncover the unformulated part of the text, and this very indeterminacy is the force that drives us to work out a configurative meaning while at the same time giving us the necessary degree of freedom to do so.

As we work out a consistent pattern in the text, we will find our 'interpretation' threatened, as it were, by the presence of other possibilities of 'interpretation,' and so there arise new areas of indeterminacy (though we may only be dimly aware of them, if at all, as we are continually making 'decisions' which will exclude them). In the course of a novel, for in-

[19] B. Ritchie, "The Formal Structure of the Aesthetic Object," in *The Problems of Aesthetics,* ed. Eliseo Vivas and Murray Krieger (New York, 1965), pp. 230 f.

stance, we sometimes find that characters, events, and backgrounds seem to change their significance; what really happens is that the other 'possibilities' begin to emerge more strongly, so that we become more directly aware of them. Indeed, it is this very shifting of perspectives that makes us feel that a novel is much more 'true-to-life.' Since it is we ourselves who establish the levels of interpretation and switch from one to another as we conduct our balancing operation, we ourselves impart to the text the dynamic lifelikeness which, in turn, enables us to absorb an unfamiliar experience into our personal world.

As we read, we oscillate to a greater or lesser degree between the building and the breaking of illusions. In a process of trial and error, we organize and reorganize the various data offered us by the text. These are the given factors, the fixed points on which we base our 'interpretation,' trying to fit them together in the way we think the author meant them to be fitted. "For to perceive, a beholder must *create* his own experience. And his creation must include relations comparable to those which the original producer underwent. They are not the same in any literal sense. But with the perceiver, as with the artist, there must be an ordering of the elements of the whole that is in form, although not in details, the same as the process of organization the creator of the work consciously experienced. Without an act of recreation the object is not perceived as a work of art."[20]

The act of recreation is not a smooth or continuous process, but one which, in its essence, relies on *interruptions* of the flow to render it efficacious. We look forward, we look back, we decide, we change our decisions, we form expectations, we are shocked by their nonfulfillment, we question, we muse, we accept, we reject; this is the dynamic process of recreation. This process is steered by two main structural components within the text: first, a repertoire of familiar literary patterns and recurrent literary themes, together with allusions to familiar social and historical contexts; second, techniques or strategies used to set the familiar against the unfamiliar. Elements of the repertoire are continually backgrounded or foregrounded with a resultant strategic overmagnification, trivialization, or even annihilation of the allusion. This defamiliarization of what the reader thought he recognized is bound to create a tension that will intensify his expectations as well as his distrust of those expectations. Similarly, we may be confronted by narrative techniques that establish links between things we find difficult to connect, so that we are forced to reconsider data we at first held to be perfectly

[20] John Dewey, *Art as Experience* (New York, 1958), p. 54.

straightforward. One need only mention the very simple trick, so often employed by novelists, whereby the author himself takes part in the narrative, thus establishing perspectives which would not have arisen out of the mere narration of the events described. Wayne Booth once called this the technique of the "unreliable narrator,"[21] to show the extent to which a literary device can counter expectations arising out of the literary text. The figure of the narrator may act in permanent opposition to the impressions we might otherwise form. The question then arises as to whether this strategy, opposing the formation of illusions, may be integrated into a consistent pattern, lying, as it were, a level deeper than our original impressions. We may find that our narrator, by opposing us, in fact turns us against him and thereby strengthens the illusion he appears to be out to destroy; alternatively, we may be so much in doubt that we begin to question all the processes that lead us to make interpretative decisions. Whatever the cause may be, we will find ourselves subjected to this same interplay of illusion-forming and illusion-breaking that makes reading essentially a recreative process.

We might take, as a simple illustration of this complex process, the incident in Joyce's *Ulysses* in which Bloom's cigar alludes to Ulysses's spear. The context (Bloom's cigar) summons up a particular element of the repertoire (Ulysses's spear); the narrative technique relates them to one another as if they were identical. How are we to 'organize' these divergent elements, which, through the very fact that they are put together, separate one element so clearly from the other? What are the prospects here for a consistent pattern? We might say that it is ironic—at least that is how many renowned Joyce readers have understood it.[22] In this case, irony would be the form of organization that integrates the material. But if this is so, what is the object of the irony? Ulysses's spear, or Bloom's cigar? The uncertainty surrounding this simple question already puts a strain on the consistency we have established and, indeed, begins to puncture it, especially when other problems make themselves felt as regards the remarkable conjunction of spear and cigar. Various alternatives come to mind, but the variety alone is sufficient to leave one with the impression that the consistent pattern has been shattered. And even if, after all, one can still believe that irony holds the key to the mystery, this irony must be of a very strange nature; for the formulated text does not merely mean the opposite of what has been formulated. It may even

---

[21] Cf. Wayne C. Booth, *The Rhetoric of Fiction* (Chicago, 1963), pp. 211 ff., 339 ff.

[22] Richard Ellmann, "Ulysses. The Divine Nobody," in *Twelve Original Essays on Great English Novels,* ed. Charles Shapiro (Detroit, 1960), p. 247, classified this particular allusion as "mock-heroic."

mean something that cannot be formulated at all. The moment we try
— to impose a consistent pattern on the text, discrepancies are bound to
arise. These are, as it were, the reverse side of the interpretative coin, an
involuntary product of the process that creates discrepancies by trying
to avoid them. And it is their very presence that draws us into the text,
compelling us to conduct a creative examination not only of the text but
also of ourselves.

This entanglement of the reader is, of course, vital to any kind of text,
but in the literary text we have the strange situation that the reader cannot know what his participation actually entails. We know that we share
in certain experiences, but we do not know what happens to us in the
course of this process. This is why, when we have been particularly impressed by a book, we feel the need to talk about it; we do not want to
get away from it by talking about it—we simply want to understand more
clearly what it is in which we have been entangled. We have undergone
an experience, and now we want to know consciously *what* we have experienced. Perhaps this is the prime usefulness of literary criticism—it
helps to make conscious those aspects of the text which would otherwise
remain concealed in the subconscious; it satisfies (or helps to satisfy) our
desire to talk about what we have read.

The efficacy of a literary text is brought about by the apparent evocation and subsequent negation of the familiar. What at first seemed to be
an affirmation of our assumptions leads to our own rejection of them,
thus tending to prepare us for a re-orientation. And it is only when we
have outstripped our preconceptions and left the shelter of the familiar
that we are in a position to gather new experiences. As the literary text
involves the reader in the formation of illusion and the simultaneous
formation of the means whereby the illusion is punctured, reading reflects the process by which we gain experience. Once the reader is entangled, his own preconceptions are continually overtaken, so that the
text becomes his 'present' while his own ideas fade into the 'past;' as
soon as this happens he is open to the immediate experience of the text,
which was impossible so long as his preconceptions were his 'present.'

V

In our analysis of the reading process so far, we have observed three important aspects that form the basis of the relationship between reader
and text:[1] the process of anticipation and retrospection,[2] the consequent
unfolding of the text as a living event,[3] and the resultant impression of
life-likeness.

Any 'living event' must, to a greater or lesser degree, remain open. In

reading, this obliges the reader to seek continually for consistency, because only then can he close up situations and comprehend the unfamiliar. But consistency-building is itself a living process in which one is constantly forced to make selective decisions—and these decisions in their
turn give a reality to the possibilities which they exclude, insofar as they
may take effect as a latent disturbance of the consistency established.
This is what causes the reader to be entangled in the text-'gestalt' that he
himself has produced.

Through this entanglement the reader is bound to open himself up to
the workings of the text and so leave behind his own preconceptions.
This gives him the chance to have an experience in the way George Bernard Shaw once described it: "You have learnt something. That always
feels at first as if you had lost something."[23] Reading reflects the structure of experience to the extent that we must suspend the ideas and attitudes that shape our own personality before we can experience the unfamiliar world of the literary text. But during this process, something
happens to us.

This 'something' needs to be looked at in detail, especially as the in-
corporation of the unfamiliar into our own range of experience has been
to a certain extent obscured by an idea very common in literary discussion: namely, that the process of absorbing the unfamiliar is labeled as
the *identification* of the reader with what he reads. Often the term 'identification' is used as if it were an explanation, whereas in actual fact it is
nothing more than a description. What is normally meant by 'identification' is the establishment of affinities between oneself and someone outside oneself—a familiar ground on which we are able to experience the
unfamiliar. The author's aim, though, is to convey the experience and,
above all, an attitude toward that experience. Consequently, 'identification' is not an end in itself, but a stratagem by means of which the author stimulates attitudes in the reader.

This of course is not to deny that there does arise a form of participation as one reads; one is certainly drawn into the text in such a way that
one has the feeling that there is no distance between oneself and the
events described. This involvement is well summed up by the reaction of
a critic to reading Charlotte Brontë's *Jane Eyre:* "We took up *Jane Eyre*
one winter's evening, somewhat piqued at the extravagant commendations we had heard, and sternly resolved to be as critical as Croker. But

[23] G. B. Shaw, *Major Barbara* (London, 1964), p. 316.

as we read on we forgot both commendations and criticism, identified ourselves with Jane in all her troubles, and finally married Mr. Rochester about four in the morning."[24] The question is how and why did the critic identify himself with Jane?

In order to understand this 'experience,' it is well worth considering Georges Poulet's observations on the reading process. He says that books only take on their full existence in the reader.[25] It is true that they consist of ideas thought out by someone else, but in reading the reader becomes the subject that does the thinking. Thus there disappears the subject-object division that otherwise is a prerequisite for all knowledge and all observation, and the removal of this division puts reading in an apparently unique position as regards the possible absorption of new experiences. This may well be the reason why relations with the world of the literary text have so often been misinterpreted as identification. From the idea that in reading we must think the thoughts of someone else, Poulet draws the following conclusion: "Whatever I think is a part of *my* mental world. And yet here I am thinking a thought which manifestly belongs to another mental world, which is being thought in me just as though I did not exist. Already the notion is inconceivable and seems even more so if I reflect that, since every thought must have a subject to think it, this *thought* which is alien to me and yet in me, must also have in me a *subject* which is alien to me. . . . Whenever I read, I mentally pronounce an *I*, and yet the *I* which I pronounce is not myself."[26]

But for Poulet this idea is only part of the story. The strange subject that thinks the strange thought in the reader indicates the potential presence of the author, whose ideas can be 'internalized' by the reader: "Such is the characteristic condition of every work which I summon back into existence by placing my consciousness at its disposal. I give it not only existence, but awareness of existence."[27] This would mean that consciousness forms the point at which author and reader converge, and at the same time it would result in the cessation of the temporary self-alienation that occurs to the reader when his consciousness brings to life the ideas formulated by the author. This process gives rise to a form of communication which, however, according to Poulet, is dependent on two conditions: the life-story of the author must be shut out of the work and the individual disposition of the reader must be shut out of the act

---

[24] William George Clark, *Fraser's* (December, 1849): 692, quoted by Kathleen Tillotson, *Novels of the Eighteen-Forties* (Oxford, 1961), pp. 19 f.
[25] Cf. Georges Poulet, "Phenomenology of Reading," *New Literary History* I (1969): 54.
[26] Ibid., p. 56.
[27] Ibid., p. 59.

of reading. Only then can the thoughts of the author take place subjectively in the reader, who thinks what he is not. It follows that the work itself must be thought of as a consciousness, because only in this way is there an adequate basis for the author-reader relationship—a relationship that can only come about through the negation of the author's own life-story and the reader's own disposition. This conclusion is actually drawn by Poulet when he describes the work as the self-presentation or materialization of consciousness: "And so I ought not to hesitate to recognize that so long as it is animated by this vital inbreathing inspired by the act of reading, a work of literature becomes (at the expense of the reader whose own life it suspends) a sort of human being, that it is a mind conscious of itself and constituting itself in me as the subject of its own objects."[28] Even though it is difficult to follow such a substantialist conception of the consciousness that constitutes itself in the literary work, there are, nevertheless, certain points in Poulet's argument that are worth holding onto. But they should be developed along somewhat different lines.

If reading removes the subject-object division that constitutes all perception, it follows that the reader will be 'occupied' by the thoughts of the author, and these in their turn will cause the drawing of new 'boundaries.' Text and reader no longer confront each other as object and subject, but instead the 'division' takes place within the reader himself. In thinking the thoughts of another, his own individuality temporarily recedes into the background, since it is supplanted by these alien thoughts, which now become the theme on which his attention is focussed. As we read, there occurs an artificial division of our personality, because we take as a theme for ourselves something that we are not. Consequently when reading we operate on different levels. For although we may be thinking the thoughts of someone else, what we are will not disappear completely—it will merely remain a more or less powerful virtual force. Thus, in reading there are these two levels—the alien 'me' and the real, virtual 'me'—which are never completely cut off from each other. Indeed, we can only make someone else's thoughts into an absorbing theme for ourselves, provided the virtual background of our own personality can adapt to it. Every text we read draws a different boundary within our personality, so that the virtual background (the real 'me') will take on a different form, according to the theme of the text concerned. This is inevitable,

[28] Ibid.

if only for the fact that the relationship between alien theme and virtual background is what makes it possible for the unfamiliar to be understood.

In this context there is a revealing remark made by D. W. Harding, arguing against the idea of identification with what is read: "What is sometimes called wish-fulfilment in novels and plays can . . . more plausibly be described as wish-formulation or the definition of desires. The cultural levels at which it works may vary widely; the process is the same. . . . It seems nearer the truth . . . to say that fictions contribute to defining the reader's or spectator's values, and perhaps stimulating his desires, rather than to suppose that they gratify desire by some mechanism of vicarious experience."[29] In the act of reading, having to think something that we have not yet experienced does not mean only being in a position to conceive or even understand it; it also means that such acts of conception are possible and successful to the degree that they lead to something being formulated in us. For someone else's thoughts can only take a form in our consciousness if, in the process, our unformulated faculty for deciphering those thoughts is brought into play—a faculty which, in the act of deciphering, also formulates itself. Now since this formulation is carried out on terms set by someone else, whose thoughts are the theme of our reading, it follows that the formulation of our faculty for deciphering cannot be along our own lines of orientation.

Herein lies the dialectical structure of reading. The need to decipher gives us the chance to formulate our own deciphering capacity—i.e., we bring to the fore an element of our being of which we are not directly conscious. The production of the meaning of literary texts—which we discussed in connection with forming the 'gestalt' of the text—does not merely entail the discovery of the unformulated, which can then be taken over by the active imagination of the reader; it also entails the possibility that we may formulate ourselves and so discover what had previously seemed to elude our consciousness. These are the ways in which reading literature gives us the chance to formulate the unformulated.

<hr />

[29] D. W. Harding, "Psychological Processes in the Reading of Fiction," in *Aesthetics in the Modern World*, ed. Harold Osborne (London, 1968), pp. 313 f.

NAME INDEX

Italic page numbers denote discussion, and page numbers in roman type denote simple citation. Compiled by Sibylle Kisro.

295

296

NAME INDEX

Levin, Harry, 181-82, 184, 186, 219
Lewis, C. S., 4, 18-19
Liddell, R., 154
Litz, A. Walton, 138 (ed.), 151 (ed.), 180, 184, 188, 205, 223
Loofbourow, John, 106, 125, 133
Lowrey, P., 143
Lucas, F. L., 191, 193
Lugowski, Clemens, 9, 12, 23, 201
Lukács, Georg, 5, 10, 27, 86, 124-26, 257
Lydgate, John, 4

McKillop, A. D., 66
McLuhan, Marshall, 232
Malory, Sir Thomas, 188, 192, 202
Mann, Thomas, 235
Martz, Louis L., 61, 64-65, 67
Marx, Karl, 257
Maynadier, H. G., 60-61
Mercanton, Jacques, 192
Merleau-Ponty, Maurice, 139-41, 148, 151, 175, 218, 226, 263, 281
Meyerhoff, H., 145
Miller, James E., Jr., 58
Miller, J. Hillis, (ed.) 48, 59, 280
Milton, John, 123-24, 205, 207
Mink, Louis O., 284
Morris, Corbyn, 73
Muir, Edwin, 242
Mukařovský, Jan, 34
Murry, John Middleton, 190-91, 201

Newman, John Henry (Cardinal), 123, 190
Nietzsche, Friedrich, 164, 174
Nieuhoff, 64

Onimus, J., 142
Ortega y Gasset, J., 219
Ott, K. A., 236
Otto, Walter F., 15

Pascal, Roy, 130, 134, 236
Pater, Walter, 123-24, 134, 285
Paulson, Ronald, 46
Peper, J., 139, 145, 151
Pepys, Samuel, 189
Piper, W. B., 73
Poulet, Georges, 292-93
Pound, Ezra, 185, 199-200
Powys, J. C., 130, 134
Preston, John, 29-30, 47, 56, 155, 243
Proust, Marcel, 145, 234-35, 261
Prudentius, 14-15

Raleigh, John Henry, 99
Ray, Gordon N., 104
Read, Herbert, 73, 191
Reber, Jan R., 270
Reeve, Clara, 82
Richards, I. A., 45
Richardson, Samuel, 30-31, 33, 40, 45-46, 59, 61-64, 69-70, 72, 87, 101; *Clarissa Harlowe*, 30, 60-62, 64, 71, 101; *Pamela*, 33, 46, 62-63; *Sir Charles Grandison*, 62
Rickert, Heinrich, 96
Ritchie, B., 213-14, 287
Rogers, Woodes, 64
Romberg, Bertil, 62
Ronte, Heinz, 55
Ruskin, John, 190
Ryle, Gilbert, 282

Sarraute, Nathalie, 152, 155, 160, 234-35, 243
Sartre, Jean-Paul, 145, 218
Scheffel, Helmut, (transl.) 108, 184
Schirmer, W. F., 22, 25-26
Schneider, Alan, 270
Schöffler, Herbert, 1-3
Schramm, U., 169
Scott, Sir Walter, 72, 76, *81-100*, 125; *Essay on the Drama*, 95; *General Preface*, 81, 84; *Heart of Midlothian*, 88; *Ivanhoe*, 83, 95; *Waverley*, *81-99*
Secord, A. W., 64
Shakespeare, William, 201, 228
Sharrock, R., 7, 19, 25
Shaw, George Bernard, 249, 291
Simon, J. K., 145
Sitwell, Osbert, 61
Smith, Colin, (transl.) 139, 218, 263, 281
Smollett, Tobias, *57-80*; *Compendium of Voyages*, 64-65; *Humphry Clinker*, *57-80*; *Roderick Random*, 67-68; *Travels through France and Italy*, 61, 66
Smuda, Manfred, 171, 263
Söhngen, Gottlieb, 181
Spiel, H., 160
Spilka, Mark, 45-46
Stanford, W. B., 181
Stanzel, Franz, 184, 186, 236
Stendhal, 87, 99
Sterne, Laurence, 30-31, 73, 78, 275
Stevens, Wallace, 181
Stewart, Dugald, 78-79
Stewart, G. R., 138
Straumann, H., 137, 145
Striedter, Jurij, 68
Strutt, Joseph, 83-84, 90, 93
Styan, J. L., 155, 243
Sühnel, Rudolf, 125, 181, 196 (Symp. für)
Swiggart, P., 146
Sypher, Wylie, 122, 177, 180

Talon, H. A., 3, 18, 24, 26, 110, 112, 125
Tave, Stuart M., 73-74
Tawney, R. H., 5
Thackeray, William Makepeace, *101-20*, *123-35*; *Henry Esmond*, *123-34*; *Vanity Fair*, *101-20*
Theunissen, M., 135
Thiel, G., 5

297

SUBJECT INDEX

Actualization, xii, 151, 153, 184
Adumbration, 42, 210
Affirmation, xiii, 43, 45
Allegory, 3-4, 7, 12, 14-18, 23, 27-28, 176, 189; allegorical actions, 8; allegorical figures, 13, 16-17, 19, 21, 111; allegorical function, 18; allegorical interaction, 17; allegorical mode, 14-15; allegorical name, 53; allegorical pattern, 16; allegorical presentation, 15; allegorical road, 10; allegorical *significatio,* 18; allegorical structure, 18; court allegory, 15
Anticipation, 278-83, 290
Archetype, 181, 181 n, 196, 200-01, 203-04, 227-32, 230 n; archetypal homecoming, 223; archetypal patterns, 229; archetypal situation, 219, 229; archetypal structure, 232
Assumptions, 174, 198, 202, 219
Author-reader dialogue, 46, 55
Author-reader relationship, 102-03, 293
Awareness, 33, 35-36, 43

Blanks, xiii, 113. *See also* Gap

Caricature, 41
Certitudo salutis, xiii, 4-5, 7, 14, 20-21, 23
Combination, 70-71, 76, 78-80, 224
Communication, 153, 219-20, 240, 242, 244; between author and reader, 30, 76; means of, 57; patterns of, 80, 84, 98-99,

196, 292; of shadow and base, 148; of something by the text to the reader, 33, 58, 64-65, 88, 90, 96-97, 100, 135, 144, 152, 154, 156, 163, 166, 191, 201, 229, 235, 243, 245
Composition, xii, 78-79, 79 n, 108, 159, 166 n, 180 n, 214, 232, 248
Concord-fiction, 2
Conduct, 21, 156-57; of characters, 19, 36, 88, 126, 128, 150, 158, 247, 254; modes of human, 7, 14, 82-83, 87, 106, 163, 196, 229, 255; motives of human, 154, 161, 243; norms of human, xiii, 9, 35-36, 45, 245, 249 n
Configurative meaning, 42, 44, 46
Consciousness, 110, 130 n, 136, 138 n, 139-41, 143, 145-47, 145 n, 151, 165, 170, 173-78, 208, 210, 219, 250-51, 263, 277, 292-94
Consistency, 42, 74, 93, 96, 99, 121, 233, 256, 272, 283-86, 289, 291; consistency-building, 291; consistent pattern, 284-85, 287, 289-90
Contingency, 73-74, 93, 98, 122 n, 130, 134, 250, 262
Contrast: of positions in the text, 42, 49, 52-53; the principle of, 47-48; techniques of, used by Fielding, 48-50
Convergence, 42, 52
Correspondence, 60, 71
Court allegories, 15

299